A Language for the World

NEW AFRICAN HISTORIES

SERIES EDITORS: JEAN ALLMAN, ALLEN ISAACMAN, DEREK R. PETERSON, AND CARINA RAY

David William Cohen and E. S. Atieno Odhiambo, *The Risks of Knowledge*

Belinda Bozzoli, *Theatres of Struggle and the End of Apartheid*

Gary Kynoch, *We Are Fighting the World*

Stephanie Newell, *The Forger's Tale*

Jacob A. Tropp, *Natures of Colonial Change*

Jan Bender Shetler, *Imagining Serengeti*

Cheikh Anta Babou, *Fighting the Greater Jihad*

Marc Epprecht, *Heterosexual Africa?*

Marissa J. Moorman, *Intonations*

Karen E. Flint, *Healing Traditions*

Derek R. Peterson and Giacomo Macola, editors, *Recasting the Past*

Moses E. Ochonu, *Colonial Meltdown*

Emily S. Burrill, Richard L. Roberts, and Elizabeth Thornberry, editors, *Domestic Violence and the Law in Colonial and Postcolonial Africa*

Daniel R. Magaziner, *The Law and the Prophets*

Emily Lynn Osborn, *Our New Husbands Are Here*

Robert Trent Vinson, *The Americans Are Coming!*

James R. Brennan, *Taifa*

Benjamin N. Lawrance and Richard L. Roberts, editors, *Trafficking in Slavery's Wake*

David M. Gordon, *Invisible Agents*

Allen F. Isaacman and Barbara S. Isaacman, *Dams, Displacement, and the Delusion of Development*

Stephanie Newell, *The Power to Name*

Gibril R. Cole, *The Krio of West Africa*

Matthew M. Heaton, *Black Skin, White Coats*

Meredith Terretta, *Nation of Outlaws, State of Violence*

Paolo Israel, *In Step with the Times*

Michelle R. Moyd, *Violent Intermediaries*

Abosede A. George, *Making Modern Girls*

Alicia C. Decker, *In Idi Amin's Shadow*

Rachel Jean-Baptiste, *Conjugal Rights*

Shobana Shankar, *Who Shall Enter Paradise?*

Emily S. Burrill, *States of Marriage*

Todd Cleveland, *Diamonds in the Rough*

Carina E. Ray, *Crossing the Color Line*

Sarah Van Beurden, *Authentically African*

Giacomo Macola, *The Gun in Central Africa*

Lynn Schler, *Nation on Board*

Julie MacArthur, *Cartography and the Political Imagination*

Abou B. Bamba, *African Miracle, African Mirage*

Daniel Magaziner, *The Art of Life in South Africa*

Paul Ocobock, *An Uncertain Age*

Keren Weitzberg, *We Do Not Have Borders*

Nuno Domingos, *Football and Colonialism*

Jeffrey S. Ahlman, *Living with Nkrumahism*

Bianca Murillo, *Market Encounters*

Laura Fair, *Reel Pleasures*

Thomas F. McDow, *Buying Time*

Jon Soske, *Internal Frontiers*

Elizabeth W. Giorgis, *Modernist Art in Ethiopia*

Matthew V. Bender, *Water Brings No Harm*

David Morton, *Age of Concrete*

Marissa J. Moorman, *Powerful Frequencies*

Ndubueze L. Mbah, *Emergent Masculinities*

Judith A. Byfield, *The Great Upheaval*

Patricia Hayes and Gary Minkley, editors, *Ambivalent*

Mari K. Webel, *The Politics of Disease Control*

Kara Moskowitz, *Seeing Like a Citizen*

Jacob Dlamini, *Safari Nation*

Alice Wiemers, *Village Work*

Cheikh Anta Babou, *The Muridiyya on the Move*

Laura Ann Twagira, *Embodied Engineering*

Marissa Mika, *Africanizing Oncology*

Holly Hanson, *To Speak and Be Heard*

Paul S. Landau, *Spear*

Saheed Aderinto, *Animality and Colonial Subjecthood in Africa*

Katherine Bruce-Lockhart, *Carceral Afterlives*

Natasha Erlank, *Convening Black Intimacy in Early Twentieth-Century South Africa*

Morgan J. Robinson, *A Language for the World*

A Language for the World

The Standardization of Swahili

Morgan J. Robinson

OHIO UNIVERSITY PRESS

ATHENS, OHIO

Ohio University Press, Athens, Ohio 45701
ohioswallow.com
© 2022 by Ohio University Press
All rights reserved

Printed in the United States of America
Ohio University Press books are printed on acid-free paper ∞ ™

Library of Congress Cataloging-in-Publication Data
Names: Robinson, Morgan J., 1986– author.
Title: A language for the world : the standardization of Swahili / Morgan J. Robinson.
Other titles: New African histories series.
Description: Athens : Ohio University Press, 2022. | Series: New African histories |
    Includes bibliographical references and index.
Identifiers: LCCN 2022028000 (print) | LCCN 2022028001 (ebook) | ISBN 9780821424957
    (paperback) | ISBN 9780821424940 (hardcover) | ISBN 9780821447819 (pdf)
Subjects: LCSH: Swahili language—Standardization. | Swahili language—History. |
    Swahili language—Social aspects. | Sociolinguistics—Africa, East.
Classification: LCC PL8701 .R63 2022 (print) | LCC PL8701 (ebook) | DDC 496/.392—
    dc23/eng/20220721
LC record available at https://lccn.loc.gov/2022028000
LC ebook record available at https://lccn.loc.gov/2022028001

Contents

Illustrations

Preface

What follows is a history of Standard Swahili—a dialect of the Swahili language, written in the Latin script, that was codified over the course of a century. Today, Swahili is a national or official language in Tanzania, Kenya, the Democratic Republic of the Congo, Rwanda, and Uganda, as well as a working language of the African Union, the East African Community, and the Southern African Development Community. The language, with varieties spoken by over two hundred million people, is taught at universities not only across the continent, but around the world.

In all its forms, Swahili has long been imbricated in local and regional identity construction in eastern Africa: at times associated with an ethnicity ("the Swahili" people of the coast), a social status ("Swahili" as shorthand for slave traders, for Muslim soldiers, or for enslaved ancestry), and with a nation-state (Tanzania in particular). For its part, Standard Swahili has inspired proponents and critics of equal vehemence, some celebrating its power to unify, others denouncing it as a stifling linguistic imposition.

This book leaves aside any such dichotomous characterizations of the language, focusing on the intellectual history of its standardization by diverse participants from East Africa and Europe. The book is organized around periods of conversation, translation, and codification that took place between 1864 and 1964. Zanzibar in the mid-nineteenth century serves as the opening context, home of missionaries, formerly enslaved students, and a printing press; the story concludes on the mainland in the mid-twentieth century, as nationalist movements added Standard Swahili to their anticolonial and nation-building toolkits.

Acknowledgments

Archival research is often described as lonely work, and sometimes it can feel that way, but the years spent writing this book have been filled with wonderful people and places. There is nothing quite like the quiet society of a reading room or library as the world whirls by outside the window. I will begin with those spaces, the archives on which this work is based. Enormous thanks go first to the staff at the Zanzibar National Archives, including Salum Suleiman. My work at the Tanzania National Archives would not have been possible without the sponsorship of Professor Josephat Rugemalira and the approval of COSTECH. I cannot sing the praises of Martias Joseph Selestin, my research assistant and friend of nearly fifteen years, highly enough. Thanks, too, to the staff of the Commonwealth and African Collections at the Bodleian in Oxford, including Lucy McCann; the Special Collections at SOAS University of London and John Langdon, who endured my pestering questions; and the United Kingdom National Archives at Kew. Catherine Wakeling of the USPG Archive helped me secure images, for which I am very grateful.

This project has received financial support from the Department of History at Princeton University, the Princeton Institute for International and Regional Studies, the Princeton Center for the Study of Religion, the Department of History and the Office of Research and Economic Development at Mississippi State University, and the Bernadotte E. Schmitt Grant for Research from the American Historical Association. A Humboldt Research Fellowship from the Alexander von Humboldt Foundation has given me the space to finish the book in a beautiful setting while diving into the next project, and I thank the foundation as well as Andreas Eckert for their support.

This book was shaped by the Department of History at Princeton University and the people it brought into my life. Emmanuel Kreike's advising style was exactly what I needed: a high tolerance for bad ideas, gentle pushes in the right direction, and an ever-open door. I have also accumulated lifelong debts to Mariana Candido, Jacob Dlamini, Michael Laffan, and Michael Gordin for their support. Marcia Schenck, Elisa Prosperetti, Kristen Windmuller-Luna, Fabian Krautwald, Zack Kagan-Guthrie, Alden Young, and Kim Worthington provided close-knit community and invaluable feedback. I am also incredibly grateful for the friendships and intellectual connections of graduate school, including those of Paris Spies-Gans, Emily Prifogle, Emily Kern, Katlyn Carter, Nikhil Menon, Richard Anderson, Sean and Sara Vanatta, Patrick De Oliveira, Dan Barish, Olivier Burtin, Diana Andrade Melgarejo, Randall Pippenger, Fidel Tavárez, Veronica Valentin, Joel Suarez, and Andrew Edwards. Outside of the Department of History, the hours spent in Firestone Library were formative, and a special thanks to Carol Houghton for helping me to hunt down images.

At Mississippi State I found the support and intellectual community that brought this book to fruition, and I have my colleagues to thank for that—in particular Alan Marcus for always making it happen, and Alexandra Hui, Julia Osman, and Courtney Thompson, who fed my brain and my stomach from the moment I landed in Starkville. The Interlibrary Loan Staff at Mitchell Memorial Library have tolerated my left-field requests with professionalism and helped me get my hands on much that I needed.

Among the broader community of historians of Africa, my enduring gratitude goes to Elisabeth McMahon for her excellent company, good advice, and boundless generosity. Thanks as well to Corrie Decker, Stephen Pierce, Thomas McDow, Erik Gilbert, Emma Hunter, Coleman Donaldson, Michael Panzer, Matthew Hopper, and Wendy Belcher for always letting me tag along and sharing ideas. To my Swahili teachers Ann Biersteker and John Kiarie Wa'Njogu I owe all that I know of the language, though they are not to be blamed for my linguistic shortcomings! Meg Arenberg offered help with translations, for which I cannot thank her enough. Iain Walker hosted the History and Politics of Belonging in Indian Ocean Societies conference in Halle at a crucial moment in my thinking about the project, and I thank him and the other workshop participants including Franziska Fay, Felicitas Becker, and the sorely missed Pier Larson.

Thank you to Derek Peterson and all the New African Histories series editors at Ohio University Press, to Rick Huard for his support during this process, and to Theresa Winchell and Tyler Balli for their editing prowess.

My grandparents Jean and James Holigan and Rosemary and Edward Robinson are the family's original scholars, and Jean continues to shape my outlook on life. No matter where we are in the world, Caitlin Well and Sara Schiller connect me to home, and without their friendship I would feel perpetually adrift. My family—Nancy, Peter, Liz, and Gabriella Robinson—have shown me that one can work hard *and* find pleasure in the little things, can be at once fiercely independent *and* value community. They are the foundation without which nothing would be possible, including this book. And finally, Christian Flow—my *Lieblingsmensch* and faithful travel companion—has simply filled my life with more joy than I ever could have dared imagine, and his curiosity and keen eye are reflected in much of this work.

Hakuna marefu yasiyo na ncha, so let's get to it.

Abbreviations

BDL	Commonwealth and African Collections, Bodleian Libraries
CMS	Church Missionary Society
CO	Colonial Office, UK National Archives
EALB	East African Literature Bureau
EASC	East African Swahili Committee
ILC	Inter-Territorial Language Committee
OUP	Oxford University Press
SOAS	Special Collections, SOAS University of London
TANU	Tanganyika African National Union
TNA	Tanzania National Archives
UMCA	Universities' Mission to Central Africa
ZNA	Zanzibar National Archives

Introduction

OWEN MAKANYASSA could hold a word in the palm of his hand. It was a power he shared with printers the world over, one that assured that his own horizons extended far beyond the old handpress that he knew so well. As a young man, Makanyassa had been enslaved and transported from the east coast of Africa.[1] But at some point before reaching its intended destination, the vessel that carried him was intercepted by the forces of the Sultan of Zanzibar, likely for failing to pay a customs duty or some other infringement. After disembarking, Makanyassa and a handful of other captives from the ship were sent to the station of the Universities' Mission to Central Africa (UMCA), an Anglican missionary society that had recently come to the island and was situated at a rented house in Stone Town.[2] A few years later, Makanyassa was among the first students to enter the mission school at Kiungani, an institution built on land purchased outside of the town and that opened in 1871 as a high school for formerly enslaved students, eventually becoming a renowned teacher-training and theological college.[3] Though his teachers reported with some disappointment that Makanyassa did not show "any capacity for the work of a Missionary," his contributions to the organization exceeded what they ever would have been as a teacher or a priest.[4] Owen Makanyassa spent the next twenty-five years (at least) working in the UMCA printing office, beginning as a student and eventually managing operations between the tenures of European printers.

In the course of his long career, Makanyassa printed a host of materials, including Swahili translations of several hymns, parts of the Gospels, and parables.[5] He also produced parts of a Swahili school primer and spelling book and several English-language reports, as well as various small jobs that the mission press took on as a source of revenue.[6] In 1874, accompanying a priest going on leave, Makanyassa and a fellow printer traveled to England, where they apprenticed at a press "so as to see English work."[7] Speaking and reading both English and Swahili, neither of which was his mother tongue, working the handpress until the mission purchased a new machine in the 1890s, Makanyassa was often praised for the accuracy of his work.[8] He married another mission student, Barbara Luise Rikwa—on which occasion the mission's annual report remarked that they "were the oldest and of most weight at Kiungani and Mbweni, so it was a very great occasion"—and he helped to organize a Kiungani reunion in 1893, printing and distributing invitations to his former schoolmates.[9] Makanyassa's world was undoubtedly centered on Zanzibar and the printing office there. However, besides his physical travels between continents, Makanyassa was also connected to a broader community through the words printed at his press, words which reached from Zanzibar to readers across east-central Africa and on to England, words that he helped to call into being and that in turn helped to create his community. For as we shall see, language standardization and community-construction were concomitant processes that spanned decades and geographic boundaries, unfolding in often unpredictable ways.

How, for instance, should we locate someone like Owen Makanyassa? He is a figure who confounds some of our more familiar historiographic instincts. It will not do merely to emphasize the "top-down," hegemonic constraints of colonialism. Nor does the "bottom-up," subversive agency of the colonial subject adequately describe the man whom we meet at the UMCA press. Owen Makanyassa was not in control of the words that he held in his hand; he was never asked to compose a piece of writing for the press (though some of his fellow mission adherents were and did). And yet the printed appearance of these words would not have happened without Makanyassa and his colleagues at the press. Likewise, the language of the pieces that Makanyassa printed, the Zanzibar dialect of Swahili, was not his own; nor, clearly, was it the language of the UMCA's European missionaries. And yet it became their shared medium of communication; and as they worked toward a standardized version of Swahili, it became a shared medium of communication for a broader and broader collection of interlocutors.

FIGURE 0.1. Owen Makanyassa (back row, fourth from left, with hand to mouth) and his fellow printers. Bodleian Libraries, University of Oxford, UMCA Box List A–F, A1(IV)B, Mallender Scrapbook. Reprinted with permission of the United Society Partners in the Gospel.

So, is this a story of top-down constraint, or bottom-up agency? It is obviously both, and therefore, truly, neither. This book is built around such examples of neither-hither-nor-thither phenomena: people, objects, and ideas whose literal and figurative movement were intrinsically multidirectional. This is not simply a desire to have it both ways, to point to the gray area and throw up one's hands. I prefer instead to see it as looking for the duck-rabbit: a gestalt shift image that first appears to some observers as a duck and others a rabbit, made famous by philosophers and historians of science.[10]

Welche Thiere gleichen einander am meisten?

Kaninchen und Ente.

FIGURE 0.2. An early "duck-rabbit" image, which appeared in the German magazine *Fliegende Blätter,* October 23, 1892.

My intent is to confront the ambiguous image and, accepting the presence of both forms, to examine each in kind rather than foreclosing interpretation by refusing to see one for the other. My aim is also to demonstrate the openness of either state: one may see the rabbit first, but once the duck is pointed out, its obviousness can be startling. And, sometimes, we might just find a lion thrown into the mix, for to insist on directionality or dichotomy is to impose a frame that belies the actual dynamism of most situations. The history recounted here—a history of Standard Swahili, which is entwined with countless other histories—underlines the fact that states such as top-down and bottom-up, oppressive and empowering, indigenous and foreign, are not binary and in fact are rarely amenable to interpretation as merely the one or the other. Events, people, and ideas move rapidly and sometimes surprisingly back and forth between categories like these, from duck to rabbit to something else altogether, all at once and back again.

In 1873, Rev. Edward Steere wrote an update-cum-fundraising piece for the home supporters of the Universities' Mission. On the back cover of the short pamphlet were printed the words "ZANZIBAR. PRINTED BY OWEN MAKANYASSA. SEPTR. 1873."[11] This is the only imprint of Makanyassa's name (that I have found) on a product of his press, and it presents us with a productive puzzle. Why did Makanyassa emblazon this particular piece with his name—a name that was at once his and not his, an adoption following the ruptures of enslavement and entry into the mission context? Was Makanyassa proud of his work on the pamphlet? Was he proud of the work of the mission as described within it? Did Steere ask him to include it, to show supporters the kind of work being done by mission students? Was the imprint of his name an expression of individuality, or of belonging? Once again, the only possible answer seems to be yes, and no, and therefore all and also none of these—a duck-rabbit moment caught in printed form.

THE TEMPORAL DUCK-RABBIT

This book is anchored by two species, if you will, of the duck-rabbit that are inherent to projects of standardization: temporal and directional. Let us begin with the former. Wilfred Whiteley, one-time director of the East African Swahili Committee, once argued, "As a national language Swahili has an extremely short history, dating back only to the attainment of independence in December, 1961; as a standard language its history reaches back only to the 1930s; and as the second language of large populations its popularity goes back no further than the middle of the nineteenth century."[12] Whiteley is not the only scholar to offer such an abbreviated history of the language, and particularly of Standard Swahili. As the conventional narrative would have it, Swahili first grew powerful as a trading lingua franca, carried from coast to interior via the caravan routes that supplied the early nineteenth-century world with ivory and slaves. Then European missionaries entered the picture, using the language as an evangelical tool, setting the stage for the appropriation of Swahili by the German and British colonial regimes. Finally, in an ironic and triumphant twist, the Tanganyika African National Union—that country's anticolonial nationalist party—embraced the language during its push for independence and utilized it as a powerful force of postcolonial nation-building. In this teleological telling, time moves unhesitatingly forward, with standardization (and standardizers) seemingly focused from the beginning on the long-term endpoint of the nation-state; consequently, Standard Swahili's role as a "double-edged sword" utilized by anticolonial nationalists has been celebrated just as resoundingly as the language has been denigrated for its links to the colonial project—and both conclusions contain a great deal of truth.[13]

Yet my central concern is not to assess which edge of that sword was the duller, nor to trace origins in order to classify "the standard" in linguistic terms; it is rather the *process* of standardization that frames the action and influences the winding change over time described here. As Derek Peterson, writing about the Gikuyu language of central Kenya, argues, "Standard Gikuyu was never 'standard.'"[14] The language's dictionaries, grammars, orthographies, and other written traces were constantly changing, and Peterson demonstrates that linguistic innovation is "never done" because languages and linguistic communities are constantly being "tested against other models of human society."[15] At times these models were located in the past, at times in the present, and sometimes in an anticipated or wished-for future. The same holds for Swahili. In the 1930s, for instance, the organization tasked with standardizing the language for the British colonial administrations of East Africa (the Inter-Territorial Language Committee), printed three Swahili dictionaries. In the eyes of some outside observers (particularly those providing financial support for the outfit), the appearance of the dictionaries meant that the standardization of Swahili had been completed. But for the members of the committee, the standardizers themselves, the assumption was altogether different: their office copies of the dictionaries were printed in interleaved style so that they could make additions and revisions just as soon as they were published. That is, for those most deeply involved in the process, standardization as an end-state, an accomplishment, was never achieved. Clearly, if a language is to go on being used and useful, a perfectly uniform, unchanging version can never and will never exist. Standardization, however, was and is an *ideal* that drives action; it is a set of processes and projects that, over time, allows for a shared linguistic baseline and mutual comprehensibility among speakers and writers. Yet the usefulness of the Standard Swahili dictionaries in the short-term, to meet the needs of the 1930s and 1940s, as well as their purported rootedness in linguistic precedent and the "expertise" of the past, did not mean that their creators were not also thinking about the long-term implications of their creation and their revision. The appearance of the rabbit, as it were, does not mean that the duck was not also there.

The history of Standard Swahili is a particularly useful way to explore time and temporality because its standardization spanned many decades and generations and incorporated multiple processes. Here it might be helpful to take a quick-fire tour of language standardization in other contexts: What are some of the potential forms that codification could take? We have, on one hand, the examples of English or French, for which historians have uncovered the work of slow, largely undirected, centripetal forces of political, economic, and cultural power that, in retrospect, made these languages seem the inevitable victors in the linguistic arena.[16] Benedict Anderson referred to these as "unselfconscious" processes of codification, and though I might quibble with his dismissal of any potential forethought, there is no doubt that language standardization in Western Europe prior to the eighteenth century was "haphazard," particularly in contrast to the concerted, often nationalistic projects that began in that century and ran straight through to the mid-twentieth century.[17] Starting in the 1700s, Anderson characterized these later projects as either "popular nationalist movements" or "official nationalisms." The latter, rising in response to the potentially disruptive enthusiasms of the former, often featured the production of dictionaries and grammars of specifically chosen versions of languages, from Russian to Ukrainian to Norwegian—henceforth the "national" language—often by state-sponsored scholars.[18] In some cases, the impulse was to graft a national identity onto a crumbling dynastic one; at other times it was to differentiate one's realm from that of a powerful neighbor or interloper. Madagascar offers a compelling example of such state-sponsored linguistic work: the kings and queens of that East African island were very conscious of the power of language, a power that, when unified, could pull subjects closer to the royal court and, when divided, could pull them away from it. In the early nineteenth century, Madagascar's Queen Ranavalona I—building upon the interest in unifying the Malagasy language demonstrated by her predecessor King Radama—sponsored an extensive dictionary-making project that included not just British missionaries but also "hundreds of literate native speakers" who participated under orders of the crown.[19] And while Ranavalona's project usefully blurs the precolonial/colonial, indigenous/foreign historiographic divide, the involvement of clergymen alongside Malagasy speakers was typical of the kind of codification that took place on the cusp of formal colonization. Missionaries were often among the first Europeans interested in projects of language standardization in the extra-European world, and only later was their work—and their linguistic data—picked up by colonial states as part of the imperial toolkit. There were also, in the early twentieth century, similarly top-down, concerted, and relatively rapid standardization projects that took place outside or beside the European colonial sphere, such as those of modern Turkish, Mandarin, or Hebrew—enterprises which sought to buttress "modernization," nation-building, or religious revival.[20] However, even the most concertedly top-down processes required the linguistic knowledge of indigenous speakers. Take, for instance, the work of Benaiah Ohanga, a schoolteacher from Kenya. Ohanga, a Dholuo speaker, envisioned that language's future as one of standardized, cross-border use; he enlisted the resources of the Luo Union (a welfare association) and the colonial state's Luo Language Committee, to encourage writing in the language, and even produced his own contribution to its codification: a school primer titled *How to Spell Luo*.[21]

The standardization of Swahili incorporated several of these types of processes, emerging from such divergent projects as biblical translations, grammar studies, newsletter contributions, dictionary creation, and novel writing. Moving between the telescopic, long-term view of its codification and the microscopic stories of its standardizers, one can see the overlapping, sometimes contradictory impulses that caused different projects of community-construction to converge on the same object. With Swahili, standardization becomes quite clearly not just one story but many, all operating on different timescales, from short-term exigency to planned, durable finality.[22] Conceptions of time were in fact central to codification. The notion that the creation of a uniform standard language would be in the interest of colonial subjects, for example, was based on the assumption that colonial rule would persist indefinitely. Language itself was broadly perceived as "timeless," "traditional," or "organic," something that evolved slowly and in predictable ways, and even the most constructed of languages had to borrow from existing linguistic repertoires.[23] But standard languages also had to be useful in addressing present concerns, while the hope, of course, was that the standard would remain useful for all future needs, that it would grow with speakers and writers and adapt to internal and external changes. Thus, "the standard" of any language was constantly under revision, toggling between backward-facing fixity and forward-looking fluidity. Keeping these temporal tensions in mind, each chapter of this book addresses a period in the process of Swahili's standardization, uncovering the assumptions about time made by the various participants.

THE DIRECTIONAL DUCK-RABBIT

The second category of duck-rabbit that I hope to bring into focus is a directional one. By this I refer not to cardinal directions but rather to the directions in which power and action flowed. No individual, institution, colony, or nation-state can control a language—only groups of speakers and writers can do that. And yet, powerful individuals, institutions, colonies, and nation-states can imbue certain forms of language with particular kinds of power; they can penalize or reward based on linguistic standards, and they can increase or decrease the political marginality of one linguistic group in comparison to another. These statements are as true for Standard Swahili as for any other dialect or language. Recognizing only the top-down, oppressive direction of linguistic power, or only the bottom-up, empowering direction, is to deny the rabbit in the duck and the duck in the rabbit. Even a work as beautifully written and carefully considered as John Mugane's *The Story of Swahili,* whose author is clearly an admirer of Swahili in its many different forms, is at moments startlingly disparaging toward its standardized version. Mugane is entirely correct in his assertion that "the might of Swahili is not maintained by those in power from their palaces and ivory towers but by ordinary people in the highways and byways of everyday life."[24] These "ordinary people" were involved, too, in the process of standardization, though reduced in Mugane's narrative to "colonial creators and their African pupils."[25] Less critical takes on standardization have similarly overemphasized particular flows of power; take, for instance, Rocha Chimerah's assertion that "the [Universities'] Mission to Central Africa headed by [Bishop Steere] was wholly responsible for the standardisation of this language. . . . East Africans today owe their standard form of the language to Dr. Edward Steere and his mission in Zanzibar."[26] As I hope to demonstrate throughout the book, standardization was not the task of any single person, entity, or class of people; in fact, East African schoolchildren, clerks, translators, instructors, scholars, and servants were among the most important teachers of the "official" linguists, whether those were missionaries, government officials, or academics. Schoolchildren and clerks were also, no doubt, placed in positions that were subordinate to European missionaries and colonial officials, who often denied the former's expertise even as they put it to use. Quoting Michael Halliday's work on applied linguistics, Mugane stresses that "the history of language is part of human history, it is not some mysterious surrogate process that goes bubbling along on its own."[27] This is surely the case, and it demands that the history of Standard Swahili be peopled by the speakers and writers who were making choices, teaching, and learning about the language across many decades.

Let us take a brief look, for example, at the story of Samuel (Samwil) Chiponde. Chiponde was born on mainland east-central Africa and entered the Kiungani school on Zanzibar in 1886. Whether he was formerly enslaved or was born free and sent to Zanzibar for higher education, I do not know; the mission priest Godfrey Dale once described him as "a Yao by birth, a Mission boy by education who has worked for years in the Bondei country and is now in daily touch with educated and literary Swahilis."[28] Regardless of his exact background, Chiponde was a linguistic intermediary. He rose quickly through the ranks of the mission and became a deacon in March of 1898; five years later, in 1903, he was ordained as a priest.

In late 1892, while teaching and preaching on Zanzibar, Chiponde took over the role of chief editor of the UMCA's Swahili-language periodical,

Msimulizi ("The Narrator" or "The Reporter")—compiling the very words that Owen Makanyassa put into print. *Msimulizi* was a magazine written and produced by the African students of the mission, and, as we shall see, it had a crucial role in the dissemination of the UMCA's standard of Swahili. And through it, Chiponde, Makanyassa, and countless contributors participated in a process of linguistic knowledge production, though they did not refer to their work as "standardization." In the first half of the book, in fact, I use the term purely analytically, as shorthand for the processes by which diverse people sought linguistic commensurability. It was not until the 1920s when "standardization" began to be frequently and explicitly invoked in East Africa, with the launching of official, institutionalized projects of codification. Such distinctions are, however, never perfect, for the linguistic knowledge production of the nineteenth century had systematic qualities and shared with the later, official projects of standardization a similar goal: a common version of Swahili that could be used for relatively frictionless communication.

Returning to Samuel Chiponde: from the mid-nineteenth through the turn of the twentieth century, the members of the UMCA, both African and European, had been compiling their varied knowledge of Swahili as the mission solicited input from formerly enslaved students, Muslim Zanzibaris, and mainlanders from any number of linguistic communities, printing Swahili handbooks, dictionaries, and other publications. Then, in the 1890s, Chiponde joined the newly formed Translation Committee of the Universities' Mission (sometimes referred to as the Revision Committee), thereby transferring his influence to a process of "official" knowledge production that approximated later standardization committees. Codification became a specialized task under the concerted control of a small group of experts (a group which, nevertheless, relied on a relatively wide range of interlocutors to do its work). Three decades and one colonial regime later, Chiponde appears again in the historical record, attending a conference convened by the British colonial administration in Dar es Salaam. The 1925 meeting laid the foundation for a new project of official knowledge production, that of the Inter-Territorial Language Committee—the institution that would attempt to control the definition of "Standard Swahili." At the conference, Chiponde reflected on his personal history as a Swahili standardizer: "I had the honour of being, a Member of the Swahili Revision Committee of the U.M.C.A. in Zanzibar. I have sat on several occasions revising books of every description, Holy Bible and other books."[29] Chiponde lamented the persistent disagreements between missionary linguists, noting "I hope that this Committee will not have the same effect. I do not know who is responsible for seeing that this work is carried out, I believe all of us are responsible . . . all of us must bear in mind that the fruits of this Conference are more for the future of Africa than for the present."[30]

I have mentioned that Chiponde was ordained as a priest in 1903; what I failed to point out was that, sometime between 1913 and 1925, he had been defrocked, left the Universities' Mission, and taken a job as interpreter in the British High Court in Dar es Salaam.[31] And his views in 1925 were, if not pro-British, then decidedly not anticolonial. "I should only like to add a few words," he declared at the meeting, "and that is, it is of no use for me to teach the British Empire how to rule. It will be of no use to fight against the wave of civilisation."[32] He concluded by calling upon the colonial administration of Tanganyika "to try and educate an African in a way that he should know his duty as a true citizen, and teach him in a way so that he himself will be able to choose right from wrong."[33] To refer to Tanganyikans as citizens rather than subjects, while simultaneously welcoming European trusteeship, Chiponde's recorded statements make it very difficult to classify him as either a collaborator *or* a challenger. Four years before the Dar es Salaam conference, he had been among a group of African civil servants who demanded that their salaries and benefits be brought level, or closer to level, with civil servants classified under the "Asian" racial category.[34] Agitation like this "pioneered African politics in Tanganyika," though the calls may have initially been for reform within the colonial system rather than an exit from that system altogether.[35]

Taking in the entirety of the figure of Samuel Chiponde, one might ask, Do we have a top-down or bottom-up driver of action? Chiponde was a defrocked priest, he was a colonial subject who worked for the colonial administration, and he was a political organizer. Chiponde was also an individual who, for nearly all his life, was involved in the standardization of Swahili, both officially and unofficially. "A teacher may begin to teach Swahili," he declared in 1925, "but the boys will finish learning by themselves: the language is already on his lips even when he is born."[36] This was not, of course, really the case, because Swahili was the mother tongue of relatively few East Africans. Yet in his role as court interpreter, or as editor of *Msimulizi*, Swahili was the language that connected Chiponde to his fellow East Africans, and to projects as seemingly antithetical as colonial rule and anticolonial agitation, precolonial community-construction, and postcolonial nation-building. Samuel Chiponde was intrinsically, simultaneously, perpetually both inside and outside the fold. And Chiponde's role in various stages of Swahili's standardization, from the nineteenth to the twentieth centuries, offers another one of those productive puzzles on which this study is built.

Throughout the history of Standard Swahili, knowledge production shifted back and forth between official and unofficial realms, relying on distinct sources of authority, projecting different confidences and insecurities—but always with the object of communication front of mind.

COMMENSURABILITY AND PORTABILITY

While this book focuses on the interplay between short- and long-term planning, official and unofficial knowledge production, and oppression and empowerment, I also hope to demonstrate that no matter the motivations driving one group of standardizers or another, the outcome by the mid-twentieth century was a version of Swahili that was commensurable and, thus, highly portable. Regarding the former: commensurability requires the elements in question to be not the same, but comparable. The person who first sees the duck will easily see the rabbit when it is pointed out, though their default view may always be the duck. In her study of climate science in nineteenth-century Austria-Hungary, Deborah Coen notes that "commensurate" as a verb has long been out of use, leaving English with no word "to denote the process of negotiation that produces a measurement standard." She deploys instead the term "scaling" to describe "the work that goes into mediating between different ways of measuring the world."[37] Scale is just as much a part of the history of Standard Swahili as it is of climate science: the multiscalar nature of language, from official textbooks and exams to daily conversations, is apparent. I use "standardization" rather than "scaling" to describe the process of making Swahili widely commensurable because it is the term most often applied to linguistic projects. Scaling can, according to Coen, be a subconscious process that humans do every day.[38] At other times, however, making things commensurable requires concerted effort, and scaling "depends on an agreed-upon definition of a standard unit and its instantiation in an exemplary object," behind which, Coen admits, "lurk hidden histories of contention."[39] Coen's research focuses on the possibilities of scaling, expressing optimism that humans have been and are able to make things commensurable, and giving us historical examples of scientists doing just that.

There can be, however, as Coen notes, a compulsory side to commensurability, and it is this aspect that On Barak explores in his study of time, technology, and "modernity" in Egypt. Making things commensurable, Barak reminds readers, usually requires that one party, generally the less powerful one, change to *become*, to *make itself* or to *be made*, comparable to a standard. "Because it was calendrically synchronized with the global economy," he writes, "Egypt was already behind—on its payments, among other things.

Commensurability revealed itself again to be a protocol of differentiation."[40] In fact, Barak insists that comparison and a desire for commensurability has often proliferated difference, not least because a standard can explicitly be rejected for personal, political, artistic, or other reasons. Barak's work uncovers the variety of Egyptian nationalisms that were built upon "countertempos" that "fed off a standard they could not meet."[41] And he focuses his historical examination on these different scales—the countertempos and alternative timelines—not because they represent an alternative modernity that was "outside the abstract logic of historicism, and thus free from notions of progress or linear chronology."[42] Rather, Barak follows "chronological historicist lines" because, as he stresses, he wishes to "[convey] a commitment to the emancipatory potential of this countertemporality *within* the contours of a single hierarchical modernity."[43] For an East African example of countertemporality, one could point, for instance, to the stubborn persistence of commercial, "premodern" dhow traffic in colonial Zanzibar and Pemba alongside the self-consciously "modern" and supposedly overwhelming presence of steamships, or to the "temporizing" agency of debtors, creditors, sultans, and confectioners moving between nineteenth-century Oman and East Africa.[44] Standard Swahili likewise inhabited, and facilitated, all sorts of countertempos: on one hand, by existing as the standard and thereby inheriting a certain amount of political power, it offered the constraint against which some could protest. These countertempos included coastal speakers who continued to use their own dialects or to write using the Arabic script, or, more recently, Sheng-speaking Kenyans who deliberately deploy non-Standard Swahili forms of language. For others, meanwhile, Standard Swahili offered the medium through which to convey their political or creative messages—for as we shall see, one can be subversive in Standard Swahili, too. These are all among the "overlapping swahiliphone publics" that make up the "Swahiliphone world," which stretches from the coast of East Africa into the interior, across the Indian Ocean and beyond, collecting countertempos as it goes.[45]

This attention to multiplicity within standardization is not an implicit argument that the process was wholly inclusive and empowering, for it was not. Building on the work of those who take seriously the intellectual history of African languages, this book pivots precisely on the ambiguity surrounding the question of whether standardized versions of African languages have been emancipatory or oppressive, forward- or backward-looking.[46] Inevitably, the choice and promotion of one version of a language as *standard* negatively affects those whose language has, suddenly, been deemed *nonstandard.*[47] For Swahili, this is a political issue that continues to have consequences for speakers of dialects or other, more localized languages.[48] Creative and personal composition in all of Swahili's dialects has a long, storied history, and it has continued right alongside the standardization process.[49] But I argue that before we can even begin to reconcile the (salutary or constraining) consequences of codification, we must seek to understand the process itself.

An argument about the inclusivity or otherwise of standardization, moreover, would be impossible to sustain because standardization, as I use the term, encompasses multiple projects, official and unofficial, collective and personal, that sometimes tugged in different directions, moving at different speeds, but that were driven by a shared ideal—a commensurable mode of written communication. And this is where commensurability lends itself to portability. While Swahili has been a "language on the road" for centuries, the linguistic and material outcomes of standardization—schoolbooks, dictionaries, grammars, legal translations, novels, et cetera—have allowed it to move faster and further, starting with the far-flung mission stations of the UMCA, through pan-Africanist institutions such as the African Union, to university campuses around the world.[50] And while some advocates of the language worry that this portability has required a flattening of the multifarious landscape of Swahili, the flourishing of nonstandard forms (old and new) alongside the standard suggests not only that deviations from it have never been "impermissible," but also that codification has opened just as many avenues of exchange, encouraged just as many countertempos, as it has foreclosed.[51]

Pier Larson described the "contradictory possibilities of vernacular literacy and official language" among the Malagasy diaspora in the Indian Ocean, showing how standardization pulled some communities together while tearing others apart, regardless of the intentions of the standardizers. "These were not inevitable consequences of the linguistic programs of king and foreigner. They were the result of the ways in which Malagasy speakers in different parts of the Big Island's ocean of letters took up the challenges of reading and writing in their varying circumstances."[52] Because writers used and use Swahili, too, in a multitude of ways, it has also at once united and divided; and because standardization, too, describes not one project but multiple processes, it could never be entirely inclusionary nor entirely exclusionary. Projects of standardization were at times more or less inclusive, more or less exclusive, more or less open to acknowledging "vernacular" knowledge as central to the endeavor.[53] It is the historian's job to interrogate all such mirages, whether of open collaboration, objective scientific observation, settled linguistic fact, or hegemonic linguistic imposition. Standard Swahili, and the processes which brought such a concept into being, embraced all and therefore, again, none of these.

Encompassing the years between roughly 1864 and 1964, the work that follows begins in the middle of some timelines and ends before the conclusion of others. Swahili "as a language definably different from its closest relatives" has existed since about 800 CE.[54] The oldest extant written documents date to about 1700, and its "oral literary tradition" (and likely its written tradition as well) long before that.[55] The history of Swahili written in the Arabic script, or in a modified form referred to as 'Ajamī, is much longer than its written tradition in the Latin script; so while the first uses of the Latin script to write Swahili mark a useful starting point for the story to be told here, it must be understood within the long history, as well as the contemporary life, of Arabic-script Swahili.[56] Likewise, the standardization of Latin-script Swahili took place over the course of many decades; even once the decision was made to use the Latin script and a particular dialectical form in the arena of colonial officialdom, this only stuffed the debates, disagreements, and incomplete understandings inside the pages of printed translations, dictionaries, and grammars, and behind the connotation of completeness embedded within the very term "Standard."[57]

Geographically, much of the narrative takes place within the borders of modern-day Tanzania (including Zanzibar), though interterritorial efforts at standardization do take center stage at various moments. Does this limitation not reinforce the kind of teleologies I am trying to dissolve? Perhaps. But the historical actors engaged in standardization were not themselves thinking about the borders of a nation-state—nor even, always, a colonial territory. They lived and moved between colonial regimes, local authorities, religious spheres of influence, and linguistic ecosystems. To concentrate on Tanganyika/Tanzania and Zanzibar is to make the story manageable, to focus on connected projects of codification. Language use and language policy in colonial Kenya and Uganda were very different from those in Tanganyika prior to the interwar period, and they began diverging again almost as soon as an interterritorial institution for standardization was established.[58] This meant that Tanganyika often had an outsized influence on Standard Swahili; and as standardization is never-ending, so too would this book be, were its geographic scope as wide as its temporal one.

CHAPTER OUTLINE

Chapter 1, "Note-Books and Slowly Accumulating Vocabularies," introduces the missionaries and African adherents of the UMCA, an Anglican missionary society that arrived on Zanzibar in 1864.[59] It begins with an examination

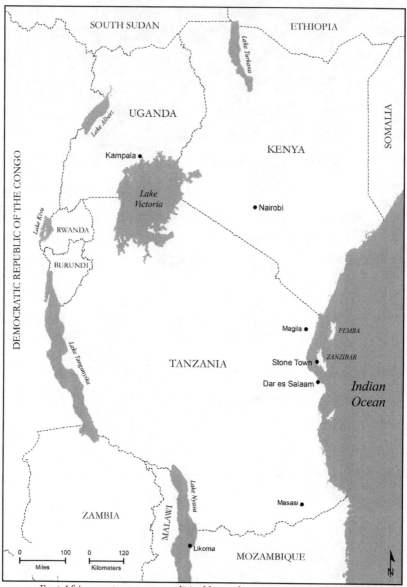

MAP 0.1. East Africa contemporary political boundaries. Brian Edward Balsley, GISP.

of the linguistic antecedents to the UMCA, including the work of Johann Ludwig Krapf (1810–81) and Johannes Rebmann (1820–76). The story then moves to the Universities' Mission at its Zanzibar headquarters, explaining why the mission leadership chose to concentrate on Swahili as its evangelical language. Working in the context of Kiunguja (the Zanzibar dialect of

Swahili), by the 1870s the UMCA had printed Swahili handbooks, biblical translations, and a collection of other publications. Turning to a series of letters between Revs. Lewin Pennell and Edward Steere, the chapter presents an initial instance of linguistic knowledge production in action. Through an iterative process of conversation, translation, printing, and then more conversation and retranslation, the missionary linguists and their East African interlocutors began to approach a standard written version of Swahili. This first chapter focuses on the period between 1864 and 1884, highlighting the fluidity of the first two decades of the standardization process, not only describing the logistics of the early stages of codification but also uncovering two of the communities emergent in the process—key to which were the mission's formerly enslaved students. For missionaries and converts alike, in this period Swahili served a short-term need for communication, evangelization, and "social rebirth."

Chapter 2, "*Msimulizi* and the Cultivation of the *Upelekwa*," covers the period between 1884 and the turn of the twentieth century, during which time the Universities' Mission began expanding its work on the mainland as well as imagining a longer-term life for its Swahili standard.[60] The chapter begins with a discussion of the demographic changes that resulted from the opening of new mission stations, as the student body gradually shifted from a majority of formerly enslaved to a majority of never-enslaved children. Along with the expansion of the UMCA's network from Zanzibar west to Lake Nyasa (Malawi), the chapter also explores the technologies of communication available to residents of eastern Africa at the end of the nineteenth century, including the power of the UMCA's printing press. Both of these changes—an expansion of the mission's reach and the availability of means of communication—facilitated the circulation of the mission's periodical *Msimulizi*, a magazine produced by African students and teachers at UMCA schools on both Zanzibar and the mainland. The magazine fostered a tangible sense of connection among adherents of the mission, both reflecting and fortifying the community of the *Upelekwa*—a Swahili term used to gloss the English word "mission," but which also contained within it the more expansive sense of community defined by religion, language, affective ties, and a sense of mutual obligation. Running parallel to the community-building project of the mission leadership, African adherents used their shared written language to build, maintain, and expand a network that extended from Zanzibar to the Great Lakes region, and even on to England. This chapter uses *Msimulizi* as a marker to trace the contours of that network.

Chapter 3, "German *Zeit* and Swahili Time," shifts briefly from the story of the Universities' Mission to that of the German colonial state, covering the period from the 1890s through World War I.[61] The chapter begins by exploring tensions between political expectations in Berlin, colonial language polices on the ground in German East Africa, and the linguistic research of German scholars (especially Carl Meinhof in Berlin and Hamburg), exposing the tug-of-war between specific, short-term pragmatism and generalizable universalism inherent in German engagement with Swahili. In East Africa, the German use of Swahili as an administrative language represented yet another community in construction: in this instance, a bifurcated community of rulers and ruled, with Swahili as an intermediary between the two. Meanwhile, the Universities' Mission continued thinking on a grand scale, beginning a series of revisions to its biblical translations, aiming for enduring, standardized versions of its most important texts—it is with the establishment of a mission Translation Committee that standardization begins its transformation into an actors' category. World War I, however, disrupted all these projects, in essence removing the Germans from the equation of Standard Swahili, while also demonstrating the resilience of the *Upelekwa*. The language of the UMCA's African adherents acted as a lifeline for a community trying to survive during the war and rebuild after it, a process that necessitated unanticipated shifts in power between European missionaries and African adherents.

Chapter 4, "Interlocutors in Interterritorial Codification," focuses on the Inter-Territorial Language Committee (ILC), the body established by the British colonial governments of East Africa to act as the official organ of Swahili standardization. First meeting in 1930, the ILC on one hand exemplifies the short-term, pragmatic imposition of linguistic (to say nothing of political) imperialism. But the plans of the ILC to revise existing dictionaries, encourage African authorship in Standard Swahili, and create interterritorial agreement about language policy all took a longer-term perspective. Even and especially in Tanganyika, a mandate over which Britain was ostensibly only holding trusteeship in preparation for self-rule, Swahili was expected to be the most important language for many decades to come, and standardization regarded as a necessary step toward that codified future. This balance of short-term and long-term planning was driven by the ideal of a written standard of Swahili—an outcome which everyone knew would always be just beyond grasp. A close examination of the ILC also reveals that the top-down, official line of standardization was only one part of the story of Swahili in the 1920s, 1930s, and 1940s. Focusing on the revision of the standard dictionaries, the chapter uncovers the extent to which the ILC relied on the participation of a host of interlocutors from around the region. The tension between these twin impulses and outcomes—to pronounce while asking for help, and to empower while trying to control—is the focus of this chapter.

Chapter 5, "The East African Literature Bureau: Creating Creativity in Standard Swahili," explores the shift from standardization to "creation" in the official mind of colonial East Africa, embodied by the establishment of the East African Literature Bureau (EALB) in 1948. Through essay competitions, the publication of books in Standard Swahili and other East African languages, and the printing of the Swahili-language magazine *Tazama*, the EALB attempted to "produce literature" in Standard Swahili. The bureau evaluated creativity in various, often ambiguous ways, concerned first and foremost with "suitability" for "the African reader." As with the ILC, the Literature Bureau set a precarious balance between responding to the demands of its East African readers and trying to prescribe their needs. This tension created sites of both constraint and opportunity—an opportunity of which some authors, including the celebrated Shaaban Robert, took advantage, using Standard Swahili and the boundaries imposed by the EALB for their own creative purposes. And while the Literature Bureau was undoubtedly a part of Britain's propaganda apparatus in East Africa, its demands for East African participation in its project of literature production opened the door for greater and greater East African demands to participate.

Such appeals are the subject of chapter 6, "Rumblings of Unanticipated Demand." With the post–World War II rise of developmentalist colonial states across the continent, colonial powers realized that maintaining their territories would necessitate some modicum of reform—that long-term planning for empire would require short-term changes. This new sensitivity to the demands of colonial subjects for things like improved social services and increased political participation coincided with more vocal calls, at first, for change within the colonial system and, eventually, for an end to that system. This chapter explores in particular two sets of demands that were connected to language—the interterritorial demand for libraries and the Tanganyikan demand for the translation of laws into Swahili—demonstrating that alongside the now-classic political history of debates about citizenship and subjecthood, there is a history of debate around language and literature that only grew anticolonial in the mid to late 1950s and early 1960s.

In all of these ways, starting in the 1950s and continuing through the independence era, Standard Swahili became more national—more Tanganyikan and then Tanzanian. But standardization also facilitated the use of the language globally, for new projects of community-construction. Standard Swahili became a rallying point for some, and a focal point of criticism for others. The history of Standard Swahili is therefore not one story but the connected stories of multiple communities contributing to knowledge production, each of which this book deliberately reconstructs on its own terms while reintegrating them into a new composite. The reader will, I hope, come away with an appreciation for the immensity of the work completed, the messiness hidden behind the standard moniker, and the powerful drive for linguistic commensurability that created a portable Standard Swahili.

1 ⁓ "Note-Books and Slowly Accumulating Vocabularies"

Their spirit sickens at the thought of the pile of note-books, and the slowly accumulating vocabularies.

—Rev. John Farler to Rev. H. P. Liddon, 1878

ANYONE WHO has struggled to learn a new language will recognize themselves in Rev. John Farler's description: the process generally comes with no little degree of tedium, frustration, and self-consciousness. And we must imagine that this sense of discomfiture would be all the more acute without the textbooks, dictionaries, and lesson plans available today for nearly any language one could want to learn. Such was the case for the early missionaries of the Universities' Mission to Central Africa (UMCA). They arrived on Zanzibar with few written resources aimed at Europeans seeking to learn Swahili; by 1884, the mission had printed, among other material, three editions of a Swahili handbook, a collection of Swahili folktales, and a translation of the New Testament. This chapter uncovers how the missionary linguists compiled these tools, pointing to their reliance upon various East African interlocutors.

For missionaries in many historical contexts, language learning was a prerequisite to evangelization. Teaching and preaching one's faith to others necessitated some degree of "mutual understanding" in a common language.[1] Initial language learning was often quickly followed by the translation of the Bible into the local language. In his study of Swiss missionaries undertaking this task in southern Africa, Patrick Harries asserted that "ascribing a sign to a phoneme is therefore not just a case of putting sounds to paper or, as is popularly thought, transcribing or 'recording' a language. Merely in terms of phonology and orthography, transcribing a language requires the taking of a number of decisions and a good deal of common agreement."[2] In few cases, however, did missionary linguists in Africa seek common agreement from as diverse a set of interlocutors as did the Universities' Mission. Because of the particular geographic and evangelistic circumstances of the UMCA—headquartered on Zanzibar, focused on the conversion of formerly enslaved people, but with an eye trained on the mainland—the mission leadership quickly realized that it could not build its community around a single "tribe" or ethnic group. And with Swahili, already a regional lingua franca, the missionaries believed that they could escape the choice of either privileging one of the mother tongues of their adherents or communicating in a European language. For though Swahili was the first language of few, it was related to many of the languages in the region, and it had speakers from the sultan's court on Zanzibar to the shores of Lake Nyasa (Malawi) and up and down the coast. In such circumstances, the UMCA's process of standardization was necessarily influenced by interlocutors from a range of ethnicities, religions, and linguistic backgrounds, creating a standard that was intentionally and often in fact "supra-ethnic."

The various linguistic influences per se on the mission's version of Swahili are not central to this story—that is, I do not seek to uncover the fingerprints of Makonde or Yao or Shambala speakers on Standard Swahili. Nor do I seek to pinpoint the "origin" of Standard Swahili—the language did not move directly from the UMCA's language handbooks to the textbooks in use today. Rather, I am interested in uncovering processes, to demonstrate how the diversity of interlocutors limited the UMCA's power of linguistic and ethnic invention.[3] The teaching and learning was mutual and mutually acknowledged, a power dynamic rarely emphasized in studies of early colonial Africa.

After an overview of the UMCA's initial years, this chapter offers a series of three-dimensional descriptions of the missionaries' main linguistic interlocutors, presenting the "who" of standardization. Next, I piece together the iterative process that resulted in the publication of translations, grammars, and dictionaries—thus uncovering the "how." And finally, I explore how two different but overlapping projects of community-construction became imbricated via the codification of Swahili; namely, parallel to the construction of an evangelical missionary community, the formerly enslaved students of the mission undertook a project of "social rebirth," attempting to build new social ties after the ruptures of enslavement. This section offers a glimpse of the "why" of standardization. Starting in 1864, these two projects of community-building became entangled: the missionary impulse to evangelize in the long-term worked alongside the formerly enslaved person's inclination to quickly re-create social ties, and these desires converged on Swahili.

Before beginning down this path, however, I must first concede that, for the mid to late nineteenth century, "standardization" cannot be classified as an actors' category; neither the priests and teachers of the UMCA nor their East African students and colleagues used the term. For the individuals described below, language was a pragmatic issue, needed for translation and communication (and evangelization); few were interested in linguistic codification for its own sake.[4] And yet by the publication of the third edition of Edward Steere's *Handbook of the Swahili Language* in 1884, the Universities' Mission and its adherents were using a relatively standard form of Latin-script Swahili—the form that, in the 1920s, would be explicitly adopted as the basis of Standard Swahili. Perhaps incidental, a shared linguistic register was nonetheless the undeniable outcome of the mission's community-construction, and the result of linguistic knowledge produced by recognized experts and supposed "nonexperts" alike. In these first two chapters, then, "standardization" is an analytical category. In examining this early stage of what would become standardization as an actors' category, however, we can quickly dispense with the notion that Standard Swahili was simply a colonial-era imposition. The process of codification began well before formal colonial rule, and it was iterative, labor intensive, and reliant upon a host of African interlocutors.

EUROPEAN SWAHILI STUDIES PRIOR TO 1864

Over the course of the nineteenth century, Swahili had risen to the status of a regional lingua franca, thanks in large part to the trade routes that crisscrossed eastern Africa. Because many of these caravans were funded by coastal merchants who, after the 1830s, fell under the authority of the Omani sultan at Zanzibar, that island's dialect (Kiunguja) was the most often heard along the interior trade routes and in market towns. It was utilized by merchants, suppliers of goods in the interior, and increasingly by the enslaved people being brought from the interior to the coast to be traded as commodities.[5] As Thomas McDow has described this era, "Human mobility [voluntary and forced] . . . broadened the boundaries of the Swahili-phone world."[6] The point should not, however, be overstated: while Swahili patently became a lingua franca in parts of the interior, there was still commercial advantage to be had by speaking local languages, as demonstrated by Stephen Rockel's study of professional porters along east-central Africa's caravan routes.[7]

Nevertheless, recognizing the language's versatility and potential profitability, by midcentury a handful of Euro-American merchants on Zanzibar had produced Swahili wordlists—collections of phrases removed from grammatical study and with the goal of simple communication.[8] The first European attempt to systematically study and record the grammar of Swahili is generally attributed to Johann Ludwig Krapf, a German missionary working for the Britain-based Church Missionary Society (CMS).[9] After spending the first years of his missionary career in Ethiopia, in the early 1840s Krapf began working in Mombasa. By June of 1844 he reported to the CMS leadership that he had begun seriously studying Swahili and was translating the book of Genesis into that language. The missionary traveled throughout the region for the next six years, learning languages and helping the CMS establish a station at Rabai. During this time Krapf also began compiling a Swahili-English dictionary.[10] In the course of his work, Krapf (and his colleague Johannes Rebmann) made two decisions that would affect future efforts to standardize Swahili. First, they decided to write the language using the Latin script.[11] In official usage, Arabic-script and Latin-script Swahili would continue to exist side by side until the early years of the twentieth century, and unofficially, Arabic-script Swahili has never disappeared; but starting with Krapf, European linguists produced their research almost exclusively in the Latin script. A second consequential decision was Krapf's choice to base his Swahili grammar and dictionary on the Mombasan dialect of Swahili (Kimvita). He and Rebmann considered the residents of Pate, Lamu, Malindi, Mombasa, and Tanga to speak "the best and most original dialect of Kisuahili itself," and to "claim pre-eminence over the inhabitants of Zanzibar and Pemba."[12] This decision dug a trench between the linguistic work of the CMS and the UMCA, pitting Kimvita and Kiunguja and their missionary proponents against one another in the British colonial imagination. As sociologists of science Susan Leigh Star and Martha Lampland have argued, standardization may be a recursive process, but "small conventions adopted early on are both inherited and ramify throughout the system."[13] This was undoubtedly the case with the linguistic decisions of Johann Krapf.

Despite dialectical disagreement, Krapf's studies were nonetheless important written resources for Steere and his colleagues trying to learn Swahili on Zanzibar. In 1850, for instance, Krapf published both a comparative vocabulary of East African languages as well as a Swahili grammar.[14] One of his most defining works, however, was *A Dictionary of the Suaheli-Language*, published posthumously in 1882, one year after his death. Steere examined Krapf's dictionary in manuscript form, and the two were aware of one another as both fellow workers and rivals.[15] For his part, Krapf expressed hope that others would build upon the foundation set by both his grammar and dictionary, leading to "the same linguistic perfection which has been attained in other continents by continuous and persevering activity."[16] Yet Krapf did not claim to be part of a formalized project of standardization, writing, "I had in the beginning no other intention but to concentrate and round up in a succinct sketch those grammatical matters which I considered correct and tenable."[17] Elsewhere he concluded, "A standard Suahili Lexicon must not be expected in the present century."[18] In this framing of the work ahead, Krapf regarded the project of standardization as necessarily piecemeal, a universal effort not linked to any single mission society, academic institution, or European state—a vision of codification that quickly became subsumed by more specific projects of community-construction.

THE UMCA AND SWAHILI

"There remains the East Coast of Africa," wrote Bishop William Tozer in 1864, "of which Zanzibar is the acknowledged capital, and I have no doubt myself that it presents a very favourable position for us to occupy."[19] Three years before, Tozer and his missionary colleagues had set out from England to establish a station in central Africa, rounding the Cape of Good Hope and ascending the Shiré River toward Lake Nyasa.[20] In the oft-repeated origin story, they and their Anglican sponsors had been spurred to action by a speech given by David Livingstone to the undergraduates at Cambridge. After a disastrous beginning in the interior, however, the company had retreated to Cape Town, and Tozer was now contemplating a new home base.[21] As the bishop waited anxiously for approval from the mission's Home Committee, he took the step of moving operations to Zanzibar, landing at this Indian Ocean entrepôt on August 31, 1864. The missionaries established their headquarters in Zanzibar Town at a house rented from the sultan, and soon thereafter began acquiring property both in and outside of town, anticipating a growing religious and educational infrastructure.[22]

Zanzibar in the 1860s was indeed the "acknowledged capital" of eastern Africa and the western Indian Ocean. On this archipelago—whose main islands are Unguja (often referred to as Zanzibar) and Pemba—merchants, sailors, travelers, and immigrants from all over the world jostled elbows. Ivory and enslaved people arrived on Zanzibar via the caravan trade and were exchanged for cotton cloth from America, dates from the Arabian Peninsula, or other commodities or currencies.[23] The Indian Ocean slave trade in particular had consequences for the UMCA. Though abolitionism was one of its founding principles, for the first several decades of the mission's existence it filled its schools and its pews with formerly enslaved people. Both the missionaries and the sultan believed that the UMCA would have little luck evangelizing among his Muslim subjects, and so they rarely tried—an unspoken agreement that persisted for decades.[24] Until 1873, when the British government and Sultan Barghash signed an anti-slave-trade treaty that closed the market on Zanzibar, the mission received individuals from slave dhows seized by the sultan for some legal violation. Following the 1873 treaty, the Royal Navy began patrolling the coast for illicit traders; upon seizing now-illegal cargoes of enslaved people, the ships would drop groups at Zanzibar and other ports, some of whom ended up in the care of the Universities' Mission.[25] In this way, formerly enslaved individuals made up the bulk of the mission's students and adherents until the mid to late 1880s when the mainland stations began producing students and converts.

Despite the mission's early and enduring orientation toward the mainland as a mission field, Zanzibar was the site of its major institutions and the central hub of the mission community well into the twentieth century. On Zanzibar itself there were three main mission sites: first, in the neighborhood of Mkunazini in Zanzibar Town, were located the mission house, the hospital, Christ Church cathedral (completed in 1877), and a rotation of schools over the decades. In 1871, the mission purchased a parcel of land at Mbweni, a seaside neighborhood just a few miles south of the town. Mbweni included the shamba (farm) for adults, and, after 1874, the girls' boarding school that housed young women received from the Royal Navy patrols and, eventually, the daughters of Christian parents from the farm. While the focus of the curriculum was religious teaching, some reading and writing, and domestic skills, the Mbweni school also trained the future female teachers of the mission.[26] In 1887, an industrial wing opened for instruction in small-scale trades.

Also located just outside of town was Kiungani, where a house and school were established in 1866. Kiungani quickly took a central place in the mission's educational system—and in the imagination of its members—and stayed there for many decades to come. It began as a boys' boarding school, both a high school and a teacher-training college. Then in 1884 the UMCA began offering theological training at Kiungani—investment in the mission's great hope for an African clergy and the ultimate Christianization of east-central Africa. Students came from all over the mission field to study at Kiungani, in either the teaching or clerical branches.[27] In light of the growing emphasis on the theological college, by the mid-1880s the mission had moved its male industrial students—those not training to be teachers or clergymen but rather being taught various trades—from the high school to a building in Mkunazini. The year 1901 marked the opening of the Boys' Industrial House at Ziwani, on the edge of Zanzibar Town, and then in 1903 the industrial house and its students were finally moved to Pemba.[28] The institutions on Zanzibar also included a nursery school at Kilimani, a choir school, small schools in Bububu and a handful of other villages, and, from 1897, the house and farm on Pemba.

Though the Universities' Mission did take in some adults, it focused (like so many missionary societies) on teaching and baptizing children. The schools were therefore regarded as a crucial part of the evangelical apparatus. All students associated with the mission received at least an elementary education that included religious teaching and some reading and writing; and besides the youngest students at the later-established schools on the mainland, Swahili was the medium of instruction, as well as a subject of study, in every classroom. Following elementary classes, female students could continue on to teacher training; likewise, male students could go on to high school and teacher training or, for the select few, theological college. Only at those higher levels would students have been systematically exposed to English-language instruction; it was Swahili, not English, that was required for full participation in the mission community.

Alongside the educational trajectory were the processes of baptism and confirmation, marking students' entry into the religious community of the Universities' Mission and, concurrently, the Anglican Church. Infants or very young children who were placed into the care of the mission were baptized immediately. Potential adherents who were older had to first serve as catechumens (sometimes referred to as "hearers"). This was a period of formal training for baptism, during which time catechumens attended services, and it was generally followed by a shorter, more intensive period of preparation just prior to baptism. Boys could go on to become readers—lay people selected to teach and lead worship—or even subdeacons. On the next-highest rung of the clerical ladder were deacons, who were ordained members of the clergy; the first African adherent to be ordained a deacon was John Swedi in 1879. The highest clerical position to which a young African man could aspire in the late nineteenth century was the priesthood. In 1890, Cecil Majaliwa became the first African adherent to be ordained a priest, an event that was reported with jubilation to all the mainland stations and for which all the students on Zanzibar were given two full days off of school.[29] While the European members of the Universities' Mission always emphasized the importance of an African clergy—arguing that they could better evangelize among fellow Africans and that eventually the church would be turned over to local control—this was envisioned as a far-off transition. Yet the pipeline that sent adherents and students into teaching and the clergy served as the backbone of the mission, as well as the ribcage of its expansion, as the variegated community latched on to this structure. Evangelization and education were intricately intertwined, and Swahili was central to both endeavors.

Therefore, before the tasks of conversion and schooling could begin in earnest, the missionaries of the UMCA had to learn a new language.[30] There is a high level of linguistic diversity in east-central Africa: the region is home to speakers of Bantu languages (such as Swahili, Bondei, Shambala, Zigua, Sukuma, Nyamwezi, Ngindo, Yao, and Makonde), as well as non-Bantu languages (including Somali, Maasai, and Malagasy).[31] Despite this vast assortment of mother tongues, there are also relatively high levels of mutual intelligibility across languages and of multilingualism among speakers.[32] Anecdotally, the formerly enslaved students who arrived at the mission came into contact with a wide range of these languages from their places of birth, during their journeys to the coast, and after arriving at Zanzibar. Such a multilingual context was not unusual in Africa, and much has been written about missionary knowledge production and its consequences for this language diversity.[33] But the case of the Universities' Mission and Swahili does not quite fit into those conventional narratives. The European language-learners of the UMCA found themselves in a context in which there was a firmly established, spoken lingua franca by which one could effectively communicate over a wide geographic range. Swahili, furthermore, had a centuries-long history of written literature in the Arabic script.[34] In this time it had also been used to communicate a monotheistic religion (Islam) that shared many characters and concepts with Christianity. While some later missionaries would denounce Swahili, particularly Kiunguja, because of its association with Islam, Steere considered this to be a distinct advantage for his mission's own biblical translations.[35] Though a High Church Anglican society—with ritual and theological links to Catholicism absent the authority of the pope—the UMCA wanted adherents to be able to read scripture on their own, a characteristic most often associated with Protestant missionary societies; on Zanzibar this emphasis dovetailed with the mission's belief that by learning about both Christianity and Islam, its adherents would not only be able to resist, but possibly to convince Muslims to change their faith. Though such intellectual persuasion happened only extremely rarely, it underpinned many of the missionaries' preoccupation with language. And the UMCA's early linguists—who from the moment of their removal to Zanzibar intended to return to the mainland as quickly as possible—saw that Swahili could be *the* tool of communication at stations from Zanzibar all the way to the Great Lakes. As Sara Pugach has argued: "Above all else, nineteenth-century Protestant missionaries considered language the most practical means of disseminating the gospel. Religious concerns therefore guided them to philology."[36] It was this kind of utopian or universalistic pragmatism that drove the early linguists of the Universities' Mission.

Meanwhile the mission's early classes of students, though generally not first-language Swahili speakers, had often encountered the language somewhere on their forced march to the coast, and they became some of the missionaries' most important language teachers. Swahili thus became the lingua franca of the UMCA schools, and students within the mission system were taught to read and write in that language. It is difficult to establish what languages the students would have spoken to one another in private conversations, or what kind of code-switching went on at the mission stations. But it is clear that, though mother tongues no doubt survived, students very quickly incorporated Swahili into their repertoire, and the language was a crucial component of their social rebirth. The question, however, remains: How did the missionaries and their students achieve a written standard of Swahili that could be used as a medium of instruction and examination, evangelization and social rebirth? This is the process to which we now turn.

THE LINGUISTIC INTERLOCUTORS OF PENNELL AND STEERE

When Tozer was appointed bishop in 1862, Rev. Edward Steere, then rector at a small parish in east-central England, decided to give up his position and join his friend in East Africa.[37] Steere lived and worked mainly on Zanzibar for the rest of his life, serving as the mission's third bishop from 1874 until his death on August 27, 1882. He spearheaded the mission's linguistic work, combining evangelical zeal with skill in language learning and a reportedly affable nature. In June of 1868, Steere was joined in his work by Rev. Richard Lewin Pennell. Pennell taught at Kiungani and died on Zanzibar in July of 1872. Over the course of the latter's four years with the mission, the two men carried on a remarkable correspondence regarding Swahili translations. They were two of a kind, discussing at great length the intricacies of words both obviously important and seemingly trivial. Many of the letters held in the UMCA collection in Oxford are undated but must have been written between August 1868 and March 1872 while Steere was on leave in England.

Pennell and Steere's main sources of linguistic information were their local interlocutors on Zanzibar.[38] In Isabel Hofmeyr's words, "The basic unit of production in the mission arena was a 'first-language' convert and a 'second-language' missionary."[39] And while few of Pennell's interlocutors were first-language Swahili speakers, they were certainly more familiar with the language than were the English missionaries. This circle of language teachers included men such as Abdul Aziz, Hamisi wa Kai, Kassim, Ali, Masasa, Muhammed bin Khamis and the students at Kiungani (often referred to collectively as "the boys").[40] These groups held different stations in island society, and Pennell ascribed varying levels of linguistic authority to each, but as a collective they unmistakably shaped the translations produced by the missionaries. The correspondence between Pennell and Steere reveals the reliance of the UMCA teachers on their students and other interlocutors, as well as the meticulous decision-making that defined the initial process of codification.

ABDUL AZIZ

Pennell and Steere regarded Abdul Aziz ('Abd al-'Aziz al-Amawi) as the most learned of their interlocutors. Born in present-day Somalia in 1838, by age sixteen Abdul Aziz worked in a judicial role at Kilwa on behalf of the sultan. Shortly thereafter he was brought to Zanzibar to serve as a *qadi,* an Islamic jurist.[41] He was an active Muslim scholar, teacher, and community leader.[42] Abdul Aziz also reportedly conducted sharp debates with the UMCA Christians. In a biographical entry, historian Abdullah Saleh Farsy noted that Abdul Aziz wrote several responses to sermons given by Bishops Tozer and Steere and Rev. Godfrey Dale.[43] "Indeed, there has not been an alim [Islamic scholar]," Farsy wrote, "who has proven so effective in carrying on a debate with the missionaries at Zanzibar as did Sh. Abdu'l-Aziz, for his arguments were the most effective and they were not merely boasting and noisemaking. They were like a gun: whatever stood before them could not escape their destruction."[44] These thrusts and parries, however, constituted an intellectual rather than personal contest, and despite being their greatest rhetorical antagonist, Abdul Aziz carried out many linguistic efforts on behalf of the mission.[45] His most noted contribution to the UMCA's biblical translations was his work with Pennell on the Gospel of Saint Luke and the translation of several psalms. In the *Bible Society Monthly Reporter* of July 1882, Steere reported:

> A very interesting translation of the Gospel of St. Luke was
> made by one of our members, Mr. Pennell, with the aid of a learned
> Sheikh in Zanzibar, named Abd'ul Aziz. He translated from the
> Arabic, and Pennell checked the version by the Greek. The Sheikh
> also translated for us the first sixteen Psalms, but in so very learned
> and strange a dialect as to be of no practical use. This version of St.

Luke is a mixture of very learned and very common-place expressions, as Pennell often objected to a phrase he could make nothing of, and then they appealed to the bystanders, who suggested what first occurred to them.[46]

Abdul Aziz was at one end of the spectrum of the mission's interlocutors: Steere and Pennell thought him a bit too inclined to the "Mombas dialect," which they found overly poetical and little understood by most people on Zanzibar.[47] Yet the priest recounted visiting the sheikh every day at one o'clock to work on translating St. Luke; Pennell would then "before beginning have any difficulties [from the previous day's work] explained. I have particularly asked to make it easy for 'wajinga' [fools] to understand, and I think he really succeeds as I fancy most of the words are familiar."[48] Abdul Aziz also gave Pennell and Steere access to a committee of linguistic assistants, as translation sessions at his home often turned into conversations between four or five men.

Despite complaints about his occasional incomprehensibility and verbal ticks, Pennell and Steere recognized gratefully the assistance volunteered by the busy *qadi*.[49] In appreciation, they presented him with an Arabic copy of *Arabian Nights,* inside of which Pennell transcribed a note of thanks, written in Swahili with Arabic characters: "Richard L. Pennell gives Sheikh Abdul Aziz many greetings and requests that he accepts this book. Indeed, he thanks him very much on account of his having helped to translate the Gospel, the Good News of God, and he sincerely prays that God give him the reward of faith and the deliverance of Jesus when he returns on the last day to judge those both alive and dead. Amen."[50] The transcription reflects a relationship of debate and conversation: the *qadi* provided Pennell and Steere with the words they sought, and they clearly discussed both linguistics and theology. Despite occasional frustrations, the letters demonstrate mutual respect—Pennell, Steere, and the mission as a whole recognized the invaluable help they received from Abdul Aziz; he meanwhile seemed to value his relationship with the mission, asking after Steere while the priest was away and occasionally joining mission celebrations.[51]

KASSIM, ALI, HAMISI WA KAI, MASASA, AND MUHAMMED BIN KHAMIS

The next set of interlocutors included men named Kassim, Ali, Hamisi wa Kai, Masasa, and Muhammed bin Khamis, all residents of Zanzibar.[52] The missionaries relied on them to, they believed, access Swahili as understood by the general public on the island. These interlocutors made "enquiries in town" about certain words, reporting back to the missionaries about which were best understood, and which were most likely to be misunderstood.[53] They bridged the gap between the highly educated linguistic example of Abdul Aziz and that of the mission students with their various levels of experience with the language.

Pennell mentioned all these men regularly in his correspondence with Steere. For particularly important concepts, he gauged the fit of one man's translation by testing the responses of one or more of the others, seeking a common ground. In one instance, he wrote to Steere: "Abdul Assiz, Cassim, and Ali all give 'basiri' as an exact equivalent to our word 'evangelise', bishara as = 'Gospel' and 'mbasiri' to evangelist."[54] In another case, Pennell warned Steere about the use of the word *kusimika* ("to erect, to set up, to stand").[55] "It means to erect," he wrote, "but appears to be restricted to sexual intercourse. I recollect once using the word in class and the boys [i.e., the Kiungani students] clearly thought it a wrong word. Cassim today did not like to tell me the meaning, but Ali did."[56] Pennell also used this group to check the language of Abdul Aziz; referring to a group session at the *qadi*'s house where the translation of St. Luke was the topic of conversation, he wrote, "But between them [Aziz and his guests] and Masasa and Cassim I hope to get a vernacular translation intelligible to the people."[57]

The only bit of real biographical information that we have about a member of this group is for Hamisi wa Kai. In an early appearance in Pennell's letters, Hamisi wa Kai was sick, barely able to leave his home, and Pennell was planning to visit him and pick up a letter intended for Steere.[58] Over the course of their correspondence, Hamisi advised Pennell on, for instance, the causative form of *kujua* ("to know") and offered up fables for translation.[59] In a later letter, Pennell relayed the following story to Steere:

> Hamisi wa Kai has fallen through; when we thought all was settled, he told us he must wait for Pere Etienne's [of the Catholic Holy Ghost Fathers] return from Bagamoyo as he was engaged with him till the end of the month. About a week since he told us that Pere Etienne had paid him a year's salary in advance and there were six months yet to run, but that he wanted to repay Etienne the money and attach himself to us. We told him we could not hear of this without Etienne's full concurrence. He did not at all like the idea of my calling on Etienne, but I did and found that Hamisi had been as closely connected with them as Masasa is with us for nine years, and they were naturally not a little annoyed at what they thought was our trying to filch away a useful servant from them. Hamisi has not acted right in the matter at all.[60]

Pennell consequently cut ties with Hamisi wa Kai, this despite that fact that, according to Steere, he and Muhammed bin Khamis were able to offer examples of the "best and purest language of Zanzibar."[61] In fact, prior to the falling-out, Steere mentioned his "[indebtedness]" to Hamisi wa Kai in the preface to his 1870 *Handbook of the Swahili Language*, describing him as "a very intelligent young Swahili, who always comprehended better what a foreigner wanted to know, and explained more clearly what was difficult, than any one else I met with while in Zanzibar."[62] In the same preface, Steere also acknowledged the assistance he had received from Muhammed bin Khamis, with whom Steere had spent many Saturdays "asking him about his language," making lists of nouns, adjectives, pronouns, and verbs that eventually found their way into the *Handbook*, and to whom he "owe[d] all that is best in my knowledge of African tongues."[63] Pennell's letter also alluded to Masasa's close ties to the mission, implying that he was a servant attached in some way to the UMCA. This supposition is reinforced by Steere's reference in his volume of *Swahili Tales* to stories related to him by "Masazo, who was for a long time our cook and house steward" and who offered tales in "a dialect spoken by a class less refined and educated."[64]

Along with evidence of their linguistic opinions and the scarce biographical information, Pennell's letters hint at affection, or at least cordiality, between these men and the missionaries. "Cassim begs to be kindly remembered to you and Mrs. Steere," Pennell wrote, and "Abdul Aziz and your other friends are constantly asking after you."[65] Or in another letter: "Kassim sends you many salaams and wishes to send you a mark of his love but there is no boat."[66] In 1866, Steere lent Kassim six dollars, which he repaid in just four days.[67] In a postscript to one letter, Pennell passed on the message, "*Kassim na Ali wanakupa salamu nyingi. Wanaketi karibu sana.*" ("Kassim and Ali give you many greetings. They are sitting very close.")[68] The fact that the postscript was written in Swahili, while the body of the letter was in English, suggests that these latter two wanted to be sure that their message was passed on correctly and insisted that Pennell write it in Swahili. Or perhaps Pennell shifted languages to literally convey to Steere the words of his greeters. In any case, the postscript demonstrates the easy familiarity with which the missionaries and their interlocutors interacted, and the intermingling of languages within those interactions.

THE KIUNGANI STUDENTS

The final group of interlocutors consisted of the students at Kiungani in the early 1870s, often referred to in the letters as "the boys." Kiungani was the main school for male students; the name itself is a phrase meaning "in the outskirts," and some referred to the area as Kiinua Miguu (or Mguu)— "lift your feet"—because of its location about two miles, much of it uphill, south of Zanzibar Town. For the first few years on Zanzibar, the UMCA moved its students around as it acquired land and buildings; the land at Kiungani was purchased in 1866 and the house occupied in 1868. The male students moved there in 1869, at which point the college—dedicated to St. Andrew—officially opened.[69]

In the early 1870s, there were anywhere between forty-five and one hundred scholars in residence at the school, and these students were the final check on the missionaries' translations into Swahili, the success or failure of which was determined by observing whether or not the students understood them.[70] Coming as they did from assorted linguistic backgrounds, with various levels of exposure to Swahili and its dialects, the students were simultaneously learning and helping to create the mission standard through their reactions to translations. Pennell also occasionally referred to actively translating with the help of his students: "You have sent us the Epistles and Gospels of the Trinity season from the 14th Sunday. I and the boys have translated the other Sundays of the season, all the collects, Advents, Christmas, and its satellites."[71] Usually, however, he either tested translations by reading them to a class and gauging the students' reactions, or by asking about specific words or phrases. For instance, Pennell reported to Steere that he had changed his translation of Matthew after reading it to "the boys" over the course of a few months.[72] Steere likewise described his "Swahili discourses to the boys and girls" as "preparation" for preaching in town.[73] If a translation was widely understood in the classroom, then the missionary linguists could be reasonably confident that it would be understood in Zanzibar Town, and—hopefully—across great swathes of east-central Africa.

Pennell also observed *how* the students read the translations that he and Steere prepared. For instance, the discussion about how best to write out Swahili verbs—which consist of a root and prefix or suffix as required—was still unsettled during their correspondence. Tozer, for instance, proposed inserting hyphens between each part of the verb, a suggestion that was ultimately dismissed.[74] As Pennell wrote to Steere: "The Bishop [Tozer] and I have had many talks about how the reading long Swahili words may be made easier. The boys clearly look for the verb, and often take up a syllable and make guesses. I don't mean George, Francis and John but some of the younger ones but even these three find a difficulty."[75] The classroom was thus a testing ground for the mission's translations, just as it was the intended site of their utilization. At the time, George Farajallah, Francis Mabruki, and John Swedi were three of the most advanced students at Kiungani: they each spent nearly two years studying in England and were eventually ordained as subdeacons (Swedi and Farajallah in February 1870, and Mabruki shortly thereafter).[76] In 1879, John Swedi was made a deacon—"the first fruits of the College."[77] Swedi and Farajallah served as pupil-teachers at Kiungani, and Mabruki worked for a time at Mbweni before being appointed to Magila on the mainland.[78] At the outset of their educations, Bishop Tozer wrote to Steere: "I am reading the Acts now daily with George, John, and Francis, and it is refreshing to see how well they take it all in."[79] No doubt Tozer was pleased at their reception of both the spiritual lessons *and* the Swahili translation of these biblical passages. If these three scholars struggled to read a translation, as Pennell's comment about writing verbs indicated, it was a clear sign to their missionary teachers that it needed alteration. Pennell's letter is also an important reminder that the students, though many spoke better Swahili than the missionaries, were learning to read it, in the Latin script, for the first time. The language learning was mutual.

On the surface, the Kiungani experience was highly structured. The wake-up bell sounded at 5:30 a.m., dragging the boys from their beds to sweep the dormitories and courtyard with just enough time to appear in line an hour later for roll call. This was followed by morning prayer and breakfast (boiled potatoes), another roll call, then bathing in the sea. School began at 8:30 a.m., with the first session lasting until 10:45 a.m., followed by a second session from 11:00 a.m. to noon. Lunch consisted of rice, boiled meat, and sometimes fruit. School ran again from 2:00 p.m. until 3:30 p.m., then finally from 4:00–5:00 in the afternoon. Students had free time until dinner (boiled grain) at 6:30 p.m., then "they [would] dance and sing and sit by extemporized fires in the dark in the back yard, or turn over pictures and papers and books in the room" until the bell rang again to announce evensong. After leaving the chapel the younger boys were sent to bed, while the older students could stay up until 9:30 p.m.[80]

Inside the classroom, however, the rigidity sometimes gave way to linguistic experimentation, and even a reversal of the roles of teacher and student. We have already seen how the reaction of the class warned Pennell against *kusimika*. He likewise questioned another translation after their continued insistence that *kukoma* ("to cease, desist, stop") was a "bad word" (in the sense of being an improper choice), and he took into account their advice about when to use *kuzimia* ("to faint") over *kuzima* ("to extinguish").[81] In such moments, Pennell heeded the recommendations of his students. Other times, however, he dismissed their suggestions. In one letter, for instance, Pennell wrote, "The boys seem never to have heard the verb 'zuka' applied to the rising of the sun. I do not attach much importance to this, since it was quite clear that 'zuka' though well known was not one of their ordinary words, and of course their vocabulary would be rather restricted, and to some extent corrupt. One sees from these boys how easily they adopt words from other languages: for instance, 'kuchenja' which began in play is almost as often used as 'badili.'"[82] The experience of enslavement and displacement forced a certain level of linguistic flexibility upon the students of Kiungani, and the prospect of learning Swahili, or altering their use of the language, would not have been an unfamiliar adjustment. Combinations that served the purpose of communication such as *kuchenja* (linking the Swahili verb marker *ku* to a modified version of the English verb "change" in place of the Swahili verb *kubadili*) indicate such linguistic flexibility.

Yet at times the students insisted that a translation was wrong, thus molding the missionaries' translations. Pennell and Steere's main audience was, after all, their students, and the missionaries were ready to go through multiple iterations in order to find a satisfactory translation. As Pennell wrote to Steere, "To be of any value translations must not be done in a hurry, and for a long time to come we must be ready to go over our work again and again. All sorts of mistakes are sure to creep in."[83] The UMCA missionaries knew that they were not uncovering the single, unadulterated language of a unified "tribe," and they expected that their interlocutors might sometimes disagree. To approach mutual understanding, then, Pennell and Steere attempted to triangulate a range of linguistic advice. And while this lent some power of creativity to the missionaries, it also endowed their interlocutors with unusual power to check their inventions.

ITERATIONS TOWARD STANDARDIZATION

We can trace more precisely the influence of the missionaries' linguistic informants by comparing Pennell's letters to several publications compiled both during and after his correspondence with Steere: *A Handbook of the Swahili Language* (from 1870, 1875, and 1884); A. C. Madan's 1894 English-Swahili dictionary; and Madan's 1903 Swahili-English dictionary.[84] The first editions of the *Handbook* were written in the midst of the conversations that Pennell and Steere had with their students from 1864 through its publication, whereas Madan's dictionaries serve as a control—with them we can see which of the interlocutors' offerings stuck and which did not.[85] This comparison of the letters with the publications reveals specific instances wherein the linguistic interlocutors—from the learned *qadi* to the formerly enslaved students—shaped the Swahili used by the UMCA. At times they added to the lexical options, at other times they limited them. The group of interlocutors was a microcosm of the wider (linguistic, social, political, and religious) ecosystem of eastern Africa, and their pushing and pulling at the work of the missionaries resulted in a version of Swahili that was available for use by multiple communities-in-creation.

There are several examples of key words used in early UMCA translations that emerged from Pennell's discussions with the individuals described above. One such is the word *kanisa,* translated in today's Standard Swahili with the English word "church." Pennell wrote to Steere explaining that, according to Abdul Aziz, the word was borrowed from Arabic and could be understood in multiple ways: as a (Christian) church, a (Jewish) temple, or a thatched or open-air building. "The idea clearly is a place of gathering," Pennell wrote, and it necessitated a qualifier such as *ya Wazungu* ("European" or "foreign" or "Christian") or *ya Wayahudi* ("Jewish") in order to specify if it was being used as a particular place of worship.[86] In Steere's handbooks, the word *kanisa* appeared with the simple definition "church." Madan's 1894 English-Swahili dictionary included *kanisa* as a possible synonym for "church" or "temple," whereas "synagogue" was defined as *kanisa la kiyahudi.* By 1903, Madan's Swahili-English dictionary defined *kanisa* as "synagogue, temple, church," encompassing the word's widest possible meaning. Pennell and Steere thus used Abdul Aziz's conditional endorsement of *kanisa* as an understandable translation for "church," and only decades later did Madan re-expand it. In most UMCA publications the word was used without qualifier to mean a Christian place of worship, thus adopting part of Abdul Aziz's advice while ignoring the sheikh's insistence that an added qualifier (e.g., *ya Wazungu*) was needed.

The interlocutors also discussed how to translate the word "priest." Pennell and Steere argued against the use of the terms *mkohana* and *kahini* because of Kassim's warning that they were equivalent to "soothsayer" or "traditional healer" (the Swahili words *mchawi* or *mganga*).[87] In the same letter Pennell contrasted Kassim's view with that of Hamisi wa Kai: "I have asked Hamisi the meaning of mkohana; he tells me a person of great learning. This word then rather expresses a qualification very desirable, almost indispensable in a priest, but does not represent his peculiar office that of being appointed in things pertaining to God, a representing before men the mediatorial office of Christ."[88] Pennell went on to ask "whether it would not be better to introduce a strange word altogether and define it to the Catechumens than run the risk of using a Suahili word, [which] has one fixed meaning entirely different from the idea intended to be conveyed."[89] Again, in another undated letter, Pennell wrote: "I find from all quarters that 'Mkohana' means conjurer, or at the very best a clever person. I dwell upon this word thinking it most essential that people should not connect the two ideas of 'Priest' and 'Conjurer.'"[90] In this case, Kassim and Hamisi's advice was wholly adopted and *mkohana* was scratched. In its place the mission linguists adopted the word *kasisi,* borrowed from Arabic. "Knowing nothing of Arabic," Pennell ruminated about the choice, "I cannot say how far the word 'kasisi' used by you in your translation . . . would cover the idea of [for instance] a Jewish priest."[91] In the end, the UMCA adopted *kasisi,* used interchangeably with *padre* or *padiri,* as the word for "priest."[92] Thus one Bantu word—*mkohana*—was rejected in favor of two borrowed words.

The list goes on of terms that Pennell learned in conversation with this group, from the crucial and always complex conversation about how to translate the concept of the Holy Trinity, to more mundane words such as *somo* (to mean a close friend) and *mkutano* ("assembly").[93] At a certain point—and especially if there was disagreement among their interlocutors—the missionary linguists would simply make a decision and proceed with that. Nonetheless, the fingerprints of Pennell and Steere's conversational partners are readily apparent in this handful of examples. They begin to show us the laborious process undertaken by the mission linguists to define a version of Swahili that was widely accepted by speakers from all regions and walks of life. Such a process relied on the formerly enslaved students, the intellectuals and laborers, the Zanzibaris and mainlanders, and the Christians and Muslims with whom the missionaries interacted.

THE PRINTING PRESS

Key to the process of standardization was the mission's early use of a printing press, established very soon after Tozer and Steere's arrival on Zanzibar. I will explore the printing office in more depth in chapter 2, but it is important to note here that, early on, the mission used its press to print multiple iterations of its translations. In March of 1865, Steere was already writing about printing on Zanzibar; he had learned how to run a press while in law school and took charge of the work.[94] The first things to be produced on the mission press were drafts of biblical translations and pieces of what would become *A Handbook of the Swahili Language.*[95] These initial drafts were circulated among mission staff and other knowledgeable parties as well as in the mission's classrooms. "The principle we go on in these things," Steere explained, "is first to print an edition of our own, to circulate it, to get it criticised and corrected, and then, when it is complete, we are able to ask our friends in England to print the whole of it."[96] Over the course of the next several decades, the Zanzibar press continued to print such works—religious, linguistic, and pedagogical—along with pamphlets and reports in both Swahili and English. The fact of their printing lent these materials an air of authority, and thus also to the Swahili utilized therein.

The Society for Promoting Christian Knowledge (London), the British and Foreign Bible Society (London), Clarendon Press (Oxford), and Bell & Daldy (London) also printed some of the UMCA's Swahili translations and other works.[97] These included translations of the Gospels, the Psalms, and the entire New Testament (Bible Society); a Book of Common Prayer, Old Testament reading lessons, and an Anglican catechism (Society for Promoting Christian Knowledge); and the first two *Handbooks* and a volume of *Swahili Tales* (Bell & Daldy). Parts of all these works were first published on the mission's Zanzibar press, only sent to outside publishers after they had reached a degree of finality. The very fact that the mission was willing to spend time and money on multiple iterations of printed translations reinforces the idea that this process of standardization was a coproduction between teachers and students. If the missionaries of the UMCA felt confident that they would be able to divine the "pure" form of a language through observation—or even conversation—alone, they would certainly not waste paper and ink on multiple translations to be cross-checked by their students and other interlocutors. Knowledge production here had been consciously expanded beyond a cadre of elite outsiders and locals.

The *Handbook* was one of the crowning achievements of the mission's first years on Zanzibar. The first edition was published in 1870; Part I contained detailed grammatical explanations and examples, and Part II consisted of a Swahili-English vocabulary and several appendices. Though Steere intended the *Handbook* to outline Swahili as spoken at Zanzibar, the UMCA linguist also hoped that it was "not to be regarded as though its utility were confined to the islands and the narrow strip of coast of which this language is the vernacular, but much rather as the broad foundation on which our labors in the far interior must for many years be built up."[98] His vision was to elaborate a Swahili that could be used throughout the mission field as it expanded from Zanzibar. This is what made the African interlocutors so crucial to the UMCA's standardization efforts: rather than championing an ideal form of Swahili, whether or not such a dialect can be said to ever have existed, Steere and his colleagues sought widespread comprehensibility, and they could only attain such linguistic knowledge by talking, and listening, to a broad range of Swahili speakers.

SOCIAL REBIRTH AMONG MISSION STUDENTS

The process of standardization taking place at the UMCA schools on Zanzibar was iterative and broad based, with influences moving from the top-down, bottom-up, and horizontally across the social spectrum. But why, one still might ask, did these diverse interlocutors *want* to participate in the process? This final section explores in particular the motivations of the formerly enslaved students. For Pennell, Steere, and their colleagues, the impetus is clear: their mission was to evangelize, and they needed a language with which to do so. The first generation of students and adherents were meanwhile occupied with a slightly different program. In one sense, these children and young people had no choice; recently "liberated" into the care of the mission and with few other options, they were used as test subjects in the classroom and they needed Swahili in order to get by.[99] However, there are indications that the students were engaged in a more deliberate project of community-building—that they were attempting to reconstruct a social network within the available framework. The mission's evangelical project was, at first, incidental to individuals' determination to make a home within the mission community. And in order to gain full access to that community—to be "socially reborn"—students arriving at the UMCA schools had to help create a language that they could share. In this way, the mission's Swahili standard became nearly as central to their social and affective network as was Christianity.[100]

In Orlando Patterson's classic analysis, enslavement constitutes "social death."[101] The enslaved individual is sundered from family and friends and moved far away, prevented from reproducing his or her lineage. But the historian's analysis cannot stop here. "Social death" necessitates "social rebirth"—humans will not live as socially dead individuals.[102] As Patterson himself framed it, a slave's very natal alienation, their social death, made them "acutely sensitive to the realities of community."[103] The process of social rebirth began as early as the middle passage of slavery, whether by sea or land, long or short.[104] For the formerly enslaved students of the UMCA, one can trace their efforts to re-create social ties through the conversion narratives that the mission periodically collected and printed in various publications, including *Central Africa, African Tidings,* and the series *Stories of Africa.*[105] In 1887 the mission also published an extended collection of student narratives edited by lay teacher A. C. Madan: *Kiungani; or, Story and History from Central Africa.*[106] Along with various languages, the narratives show the students encountering a variety of people on the way to the coast. Slave traders, slave owners, enslaved people, non-enslaved people, Europeans, and Africans walked in and out of their stories, and the conversion narratives describe these relationships forged in transit, some of which were carried over into school life.

The method of assembly differed from narrative to narrative. For instance, mission teacher Alice Foxley, one of the most prolific collectors, went through several attempts to gather the story of Panya, which was presented in both *African Tidings* and *Stories of Africa* (No. 1). Not long after arriving at the mission in 1893, Panya (seemingly a favorite student of Foxley's) offered up a story for a sponsor back in England; that tale included a talking bull. "Well, I have that story all written down," recounted Foxley, "and as a piece of African folk lore it is very interesting, but as the story of Panya it seemed to me to lack the stamp of truth."[107] At a later point, Panya became quite ill, during which time, Foxley remembered, "very gradually, she began to talk about the past. . . . The story she told me then, will never be written down in its misery. But the men and women who heard these stories, can never forget them."[108] After recovering from her illness, Panya became a voracious reader of Swahili books. "And last Lent," concluded Foxley's introduction to the narrative, "when I was thinking of the things I had left undone, I remembered Panya's story, and I gave her warning I should expect it to be ready in a week. And one night I sent for her. . . . And very carefully and thoughtfully she began, and the second night we finished. And that was how Panya's story came to be written at last, and you shall hear it all in good time."[109] As with several of the narratives, this description implies that Panya told her story while Foxley wrote it down. The following issue of *African Tidings* included the narrative, written in the first person. Foxley's description of her relationship with Panya reveals one of the possible dynamics that could exist between narrator and collector: that of gentle but unmistakable coercion.

In contrast to Panya, her classmate Fayida began writing her own narrative for inclusion in *African Tidings*. Partway through the text, an editor's note explained: "As far as here, Fayida wrote herself in Swahili; she had a great wish to write her own story, but she had a great deal of work, and I found she had not time to do it and her work properly, so she told me the rest and I took notes."[110] The note demonstrates both Fayida's sense of ownership of her story, as well as the fact that she was far enough advanced in her studies to compose a written narrative in Swahili. Such hints about students' participation in the production of their own narratives suggests that the published stories were products of their own memories and recounting, granted the translating and editing undertaken by the missionaries. The narrators played to their audience, but also to their own agendas: the stories were neither wholly formulaic nor totally unfiltered.

In terms of language, nearly all the narratives that appeared in *Central Africa, African Tidings*, and *Kiungani* were written or spoken originally in Swahili and then translated by a native English speaker into that language. Most of the students were not native speakers of Swahili. What might their mother tongues have been? Along the coast opposite Zanzibar alone were at least three languages cited in various UMCA documents: Bondei, Zigua, and Zaramo.[111] Moving further south there would have been, among others, the Ngindo, Makonde, Yao, and Makua languages. We know that the mission printed vocabularies for Shambala, Nyamwezi, Yao, Bondei, Makonde, and Zigua. On the march to the coast, the students might have encountered any of these; they may also have come into contact with non-Bantu languages including Arabic, Maasai, Somali, or Malagasy.[112] Depending upon the time spent in any one place, they may have picked up some of these languages, as recounted by one narrator in *Kiungani* who learned the Yao language while living in a town on the shores of Lake Nyasa.[113] After coming to the mission, some of the students could not remember their mother tongues, while others certainly did. Another narrator from *Kiungani* even translated the Gospel of St. Luke into the Zaramo language, which he had spoken as a child.[114] As for Swahili, one student remembered trying to learn it at Kilwa, while another explained that when he arrived at Kiungani, "I understood [the other students] speaking in Swahili, and now I have forgotten my own language."[115] Multilingualism was common for nineteenth-century East Africans (as it is today). Encountering such a wide range of languages in one epic journey from inland home to coastal market, however, was unusual, and the narrators were very aware of linguistic boundaries and noted when they entered unfamiliar territory. In his own study of a collection of African "narratives of enslavement," Pier Larson noted, "If place and kinship were more restricted in their geographical scope, language marked out wider social boundaries of familiarity and belonging. . . . Encounters with those who spoke captives' languages along the polyglot routes of the African slave trade were welcomed and emphasized in narratives, suggesting the depth of feeling about displacement."[116] This awareness of linguistic change, which culminated in the learning of the mission's Swahili standard, was a central component of the social rebirth experienced by the formerly enslaved students.

Besides the awareness of linguistic change, another striking feature of the narratives is their use of the first-person plural: many students referred to the slave caravans as "we" and explained what happened to "us" along the way. Even as the size of the group waxed and waned and the individual storyteller was sold and resold, individuals often described the group as a connected unit. And within this unit, some remembered specific "companions," "chums," and "friends."[117] These relationships made the journey more bearable, but also more heartbreaking if those individuals were taken away. Fayida, for instance, recounted finding and losing a brother on the journey to the coast. She also later "remember[ed] well the night Panya came" to join the caravan.[118] The account of a narrator from Madan's volume is a poignant example of both the formation and sundering of social ties experienced during enslavement. Of an early leg of the forced march, the young man recounted:

> It took us quite a journey to reach their town, and while we were on the road they deceived me, and said, "You shall go back to the place you came from," because the man who sold me had been like a father to me, for I was at that time but a little fellow, like M–(eight or nine years old), and I did not know I was really in slavery, till these people came. I was very sad, because I had left all my companions whom I had come with, and I thought over this, and was very sorrowful. I kept on thinking and thinking, and fancying, "I shall never get to a quiet, settled place, where there is no more going away and being sold over and over again." I kept on brooding over this, and I could not get my food down; yet some of those people pitied me, but I refused to eat. I used to say I had had enough, because I was very, very sad indeed; and, besides, I had no one to play with.[119]

This loneliness was assuaged by the caravan's accumulation of enslaved people: "At last we arrived at a place where there were a very great many Arabs; indeed, there was a whole caravan there. When we had arrived, we stayed a very long time, while a number of our fellow-slaves were brought, and then sold and bought on the spot. . . . Here I was happy, because there were many of us, and not as at first, when I was all alone by myself."[120] After being sold again at this market town, the boy found himself with others who would later become his classmates: "After I had been there some time, three other boys now in the Mission were brought there, N—M—, W—E—K—, and H—M—, who is now at Mkunayini [Mkunazini]. It was here that they found me. We were four altogether. After we had remained there a long time, our master sold us all together, and we were all bought together by two Arabs. The Arabs were Arabs from the Comoro Islands. We travelled on, and came to a place where we met several more playmates. It was there we met C—P—."[121] And finally, after their dhow was intercepted by an English warship, the author accounted for each of the individuals with whom he arrived at the mission:

> We were A—A—, and C—P—, and N—M—, and W—E—K—, and myself, and three boys who went to Mkunayini, and there were two boys who have died. Then we were taken to Mkunayini, and four boys remained at Mkunayini, and we were brought here (i.e., to Kiungani): I, and W–E–K–, and N–M–, and C–P–, and (as I said)

myself. Here we remained, all of us boys, while two women went to live at Mbweni village and one girl at Mbweni House, and three men went to Mbweni village. This is the whole number of those who came with me, and this is the end of my story. These are my wanderings.[122]

Like the narrator of this passage, many of the contributors to the *Kiungani* volume were careful to list the names of those who arrived with them on Zanzibar. One even encouraged the reader to look at the mission register to verify the dates of their arrival and eventual baptism.[123] No matter how welcoming the missionaries and students at Zanzibar might be to new arrivals, those who traveled together also experienced the first steps of social rebirth together, and this was an important connection.

Few of the bonds evinced by the conversion narratives took the form of either ethnic or fictive kinship ties; early on in their school careers, friendship was the crucial relationship for the UMCA students. Stephanie Smallwood has pushed back against simplistic discussions of ethnic ties among enslaved people, "as if people who *could* talk to each other can be assumed to have *wanted* to talk to each other."[124] Friendship was a relationship of choice, and while the shared experience of enslavement and schooling facilitated such bonds, they were not an automatic result. Elisabeth McMahon reluctantly uses the term "networked kin" to describe these relationships, just as crucial to the process of social rebirth on Pemba as on Unguja.[125] The oft-used term "fictive kin," she argues, wrongly implies that ties of blood or marriage were the only real, or meaningful, social ties that a historical actor could have: "For the ex-slaves, there was nothing fictive about these relationships that bound people together."[126] McMahon points to instances when formerly enslaved people housed, protected, and stood up for their friends in difficult times; the UMCA students, too, built lasting relationships that were crucially important both socially and economically. The Swahili word *mzishi* exemplifies the importance of friendship: the word, as defined in Steere's 1870 *Handbook*, means "a burier, one who will see to one's funeral, a special friend." I cannot imagine a more poignant expression of the importance of friendship. The UMCA friendships were not only essential in grave situations, of course. The students also played and danced and fought and learned with one another. "Friendships were a survival strategy to mitigate the vulnerability of life," McMahon reflected, "but they also made life more enjoyable."[127] At the UMCA schools, the mission students continued to lay the foundations of a community, a social network that would support many of them—just as they would shape and sustain it—throughout their lives.

In the stories he examined from across the continent, Larson found that the "structure of African narratives of enslavement often reveal their authors' sense of original placement and subsequent uprooting."[128] And indeed, deracination is a part of the narratives of the UMCA students—many of whom then went on to describe the rerooting that occurred within the mission community. One example comes from the narrative of Korale Urelia, who was born near the mission's station at Newala, enslaved, and eventually brought to Mbweni. Her teacher reported that she "always held out herself that she never *was* sold. . . . She could not remember the time when she was not a Christian."[129] Urelia's case is useful because, while she claimed to not remember her enslavement (and she may in fact have been too young to remember much prior to her mission life), she also expressed a desire to return as a teacher "to her own people."[130] Her inability to remember her original home, that is, did not stymie her wish to return. Writing in *African Tidings* about Mkunazini, another missionary teacher recounted, "The girls do not like us to call them by their Swahili names, if we do, they say, *'Am I not baptised?'*"[131] Without entering into a discussion about trauma and memory, it is instinctually understandable that some of the students might focus on their new community, not wanting to recount their enslavement or their family lives, while others were likely too young to remember their homes.

Some students, though, were able to remember and did want to recount their histories. One Kiungani teacher noted that students would collect together and exchange stories about their families and their forced marches to the coast.[132] These memories were important ingredients in the social rebirth of some mission students, and occasionally details about them appear in the narratives. For instance, in the story of Safi, printed in *Stories of Africa,* the young girl had been a slave in Zanzibar Town but was turned out of the home after falling ill. After a time at Mbweni, where the mission took her in, she announced to her teachers and classmates that she would like to be called Ndunda: "[Her] mistress had called her Safi, but at home her mother had called her Ndunda. . . . So she asked to be called in the Mission by her old home name, for she realised that her slavery was left behind and she wished to lose every trace of it."[133] This child did recount her enslavement, and purposefully memorialized her pre-enslavement life, all while consciously trying to plant herself in the mission community. Similarly, a student whose story was printed in *African Tidings* reflected at first on the change between enslavement and his new life with the mission; but in concluding his narrative, the author also looked backward, reflecting, "I think by this time my relations have come to ransom me, but they have not found me. No doubt they are searching everywhere for me. No doubt, too, my father has cried when he finds that I, his child, am not there."[134] These are just a few examples of many confirming that some UMCA students could remember the various stages of their lives, that they could long for home while embracing their new realities, and that they would recount their stories for one another and, sometimes, for publication. At the UMCA schools on Zanzibar, the formerly enslaved students began the process of reconstructing their social networks. It was also at the Zanzibar schools that these same individuals participated in the codification of a standard written Swahili, the language that would come to shape their literate world.

~

The initial phase of codification culminated in 1883 with the publication of a Swahili translation of the entire New Testament. It was a compilation of all the previous translations, imbued with the input from the various interlocutors, which, now put together, had to agree in terminology, spelling, and grammar. It is true that both the New Testament and the Old Testament that followed in the 1890s were revised multiple times in the decades thereafter. But the initial printing reflected all that had come before, all the conversations that had taken place in the first two decades of the mission's existence. Ten years later, in 1893, a committee that included Cecil Majaliwa and Peter Limo, two African clergymen, produced a revised New Testament. This became the first translation to officially acknowledge African assistance. Eavesdropping on the written conversation between Pennell and Steere, however, it quickly becomes clear that East Africans of diverse backgrounds contributed to the process of standardization all along. Formerly enslaved students and Muslim Zanzibaris supplied the vocabulary, checked the missionaries' mistakes, and with their collective linguistic knowledge shaped a shared version of Swahili. All acted within the particular circumstances of the colonial transition, facing the constraints imposed (and possibilities opened) by linguistic, religious, political, and social structures in flux, as the slave trade dwindled but did not die, and when no one yet knew where all the chips would fall. In extending the history of Standard Swahili back into this transitional period, we uncover the who (diverse interlocutors) and the how (iteration after iteration) of codification, and we can begin to get a sense of at least one of the whys (social rebirth after enslavement). The product of these converging interests was, by the mid-1880s, a relatively standardized version of Latin-script Swahili. Next, we turn toward the mainland to explore how the mission's students and adherents disseminated this standard throughout the mission's East African network, expanding their own project of community-construction as far west as Lake Nyasa.

2 ∽ Msimulizi and the Cultivation of the Upelekwa

Duniani hapana furaha walla huzuni siku zote. Ndugu habari kidogo za furaha na huzuni. ("In this world there is neither happiness nor sadness every day. Brothers, here is a little bit of happy and sad news.")

—*Msimulizi*, October 1891

IN THE late summer of 1888, Owen Makanyassa directed his corps of printers as they set to work at the printing press of the Universities' Mission to Central Africa. They laid out the type, stretched the paper, and rolled ink onto the pages of the inaugural issue of *Msimulizi* ("The Narrator" or "The Reporter"), a Swahili-language magazine written, printed, and read by the African students and teachers of the mission. After Makanyassa—who had been enslaved as a young man, "liberated" at Zanzibar, and worked at the mission press since 1867—collected the work of his printers, the first issue was sent out via the mail steamers that plied the coast, beginning its journey along an intellectual and affective network that was built and maintained by the mission's African adherents.

This chapter continues the pre-nineteenth-century history of Swahili standardization, examining how the African and European adherents of the Universities' Mission to Central Africa (UMCA) carried the language as codified at Zanzibar with them as they traveled the mission's expanding mainland network. Over the course of the 1880s, as the East African slave trade began to slowly grind to a halt, the demographics of the mission schools started to change. The project of social rebirth in which the formerly enslaved students were engaged evolved into a determination by never-enslaved students to maintain and expand the *Upelekwa*—a Swahili neologism used to gloss the English term "mission," but which also contained within it the more expansive sense of a community defined by religion, language, affective ties, and a sense of mutual obligation.

This chapter begins with a description of how the UMCA grew its network of mainland stations in the 1880s and early 1890s, a network through which people, letters, and news circulated from Zanzibar as far as Lake Nyasa to the west and England to the north. This expansion resulted in a demographic shift at the mission schools on Zanzibar. As the mission opened more mainland stations, the student population began to include more young people from the mainland who had never been enslaved; like their formerly enslaved counterparts, these students had varying levels of exposure to Swahili prior to attending mission schools. And while the influx of new students strengthened ties between Zanzibar and the mainland stations, it also forced the mission to implement a two-pronged language policy. However, even as the UMCA community grew more geographically diffuse in the late nineteenth and early twentieth centuries, Swahili remained central to the process of socialization, now as the established and relatively standardized language of the mission.

After describing this demographic shift, the chapter moves to examine one medium through which the UMCA adherents utilized this written standard of Swahili as a part of their project of community-building: *Msimulizi* was a bimonthly Swahili-language magazine that circulated between the mission's various stations. As Derek Peterson and Emma Hunter have argued, "The historical convergence of language standardization and print technology allowed for the fast expansion of print vernaculars and the cultivation of readerships that recognized a particular language as their own cultural property. This is why newspapers were so exciting to their readers. They had the revolutionary power to create solidarities and convene communities."[1] *Msimulizi* served as just such a social and linguistic reinforcement for the community of the UMCA, coming even earlier than the newspapers referred to by Hunter and Peterson. Through *Msimulizi*, the far-flung members of the Universities' Mission carried on a regular written dialogue using their shared standard of Swahili. And as people and writing traveled along the mission network, the African adherents of the UMCA began to elaborate the notion of the *Upelekwa*, the vision of a community that could encompass both the formerly enslaved and never-enslaved, European and African, practicing and nonpracticing members of the mission. The *Upelekwa* was a network that was intentionally inclusive and continually expanding, while also recognizing distinctions between members and nonmembers—as required by the parallel goals of community reinforcement and evangelization.

Benedict Anderson, who regarded print vernaculars as a decisive step in the direction of modern nationhood, recognized the paradox of a nation as "both a *historical* fatality and as a community imagined through language," and therefore something "simultaneously open and closed."[2] One can, after all, theoretically learn a language and join the imagined community, "no matter how difficult in practice they make it."[3] But the paradox of the open and closed, or the public and private nature of language does not, necessarily, build toward a history of protonationalism. As Deborah Coen argues, using Anderson's framework and paying careful attention to the tools that made new scales of community conceivable, "political imagination was not confined to the spatial scale of nation-states and the temporal scale of their historical memory. In all, there was a wide variety of ways to envision relations between the individual and the state, between nation and empire, between the small scale and the large."[4] In nineteenth-century East Africa, too, intellectuals both elite and subaltern envisioned their community on different scales at different times.[5] There was nothing inevitable about the constitution of this Swahili-literate community: the mission's advantage in printing technology did not simply yield a unified language which in turn created a unified, exclusionary community. Rather the mission from its very beginning sought a language of widespread inclusion, and discussions about the *Upelekwa* that took place in print demonstrate how the idea had to be deliberately constructed.[6] By examining the production and circulation of *Msimulizi*, we can track the spread of the mission's written standard and examine the connections created between its far-flung stations, as the magazine helped "disconnected people feel themselves to be co-travelers."[7]

THE MAINLAND EXPANSION OF THE UNIVERSITIES' MISSION

Ever since withdrawing to Zanzibar in 1864, the leadership of the Universities' Mission always intended to return to its original site of evangelical work, namely, "Central Africa." The first mainland station was established at Magila, in what would become northeastern Tanganyika. Masasi, in the southeast, became the site of the next major mainland settlement in 1876. And the mission finally reached Lake Nyasa in 1885, setting up a station on Likoma Island.[8] As the mainland stations became more firmly established, the mission surrounded them with a series of central schools, fed by the smaller outstations where students received an elementary education;

some students were then sent on to Zanzibar. Around the turn of the century, the mission opened both teacher-training and theological colleges at Likoma so that students from the lakes region no longer needed to travel to Zanzibar for the highest levels of education.

The Universities' Mission was not the only Christian missionary society at work in east-central Africa in this period. The UMCA had been preceded on Zanzibar by the Catholic Holy Ghost Fathers, who moved their operation to Bagamoyo in 1868.[9] Among the other Anglo-Protestant missions active in the region were the Church Missionary Society (working in the Mombasa area and upland, as well as in Buganda); the Free Church of Scotland and Church of Scotland (which opened stations on the western and southern shores of Lake Nyasa, and south into what would become Nyasaland); and the London Missionary Society (working for a relatively short period of time in the lakes region). German Protestant societies included the Berlin Missionary Society, the Bethel Mission, the Moravians, and the Leipzig Missionary Society; these were concentrated mostly in the region north of Lake Nyasa.[10] Each of these organizations contributed to the religious, linguistic, and political context in which the UMCA operated, though the focus here will be on the Universities' Mission and its linguistic contributions, which were made particularly powerful by its focus on Swahili and the productivity of its printing press.[11]

While the mainland branch of the mission is crucial to this part of the story, it is also important to note that for missionaries and African adherents alike, Zanzibar remained the hub of this expanding world. It was to Zanzibar that students from mainland schools went for further education; it was to Zanzibar where new missionaries arrived; and it was through Zanzibar that correspondence for the entire mission passed. Linguistically, too, even as the UMCA printed grammars and biblical translations in the languages surrounding its mainland stations, Swahili retained its paramountcy, especially for written communication. In contrast to many of the other societies working on the mainland in the 1880s and 1890s, which emphasized other local languages, the UMCA had committed to the use of Swahili, and made a concerted effort to codify it.[12] While they did agree that people should initially be preached to in their local languages, the missionaries of the UMCA also believed that to concentrate their efforts on Swahili would be the most effective means of spreading the gospel, as well as of creating a unified church across a large area.[13] Thus, despite some vernacular preaching and teaching at the mainland stations, Swahili was central to the UMCA strategy, and it circulated along with the mission's adherents from Zanzibar to Lake Nyasa.

By the late 1880s and early 1890s, formerly enslaved individuals no longer made up a majority of the students at Kiungani.[14] Instead, never-enslaved children from the mainland began to outnumber their formerly enslaved counterparts, and the passage of students between mainland and islands consequently increased in volume. This second generation of students did not generally undergo the same process of "social rebirth" as their predecessors, but their socialization within the mission community, as well as their increasing role in its expansion, all necessitated the use of the mission's Swahili standard.

The numbers were never very large, as they had never been with the formerly enslaved students; to give a sense of scale, from 1871 through 1931, some 1,185 young men attended St. Andrew's College, first at Kiungani and then at Minaki.[15] Until the twentieth century, when the UMCA began offering advanced education at several mainland schools, missionaries would bring back to Zanzibar between three and ten students with every trip.[16] Yet from the moment the UMCA began operations at Magila in 1869, an alternate pool of potential students opened. Masasi was established in 1876–77, and by that year small numbers of mainland students from the region were already coming to Zanzibar. Reverend Chauncy Maples wrote of a group in March of 1877: "Altogether the visit of the four [students] gives one every encouragement for the future of Kiungani as a school for up-country free boys."[17] Already by the 1870s, that is, the vision for Kiungani had begun to shift, or at least began to accommodate mainland students. This effect was compounded by the fact that the slave trade, by the mid to late 1880s, was undoubtedly tapering off (though by no means completely at an end). In 1884, HMS *London* was relieved of its duty patrolling the coast.[18] In 1888, British and German naval forces blockaded the coast, enforcing an embargo on the trade of munitions of war and of slaves.[19] Of course smuggling continued, but without the concerted patrols to capture illicit traders, there would be fewer and fewer formerly enslaved students to fill the UMCA's classrooms. Kiungani had always been intended as a training center for African evangelists to be sent to the mainland, and by the 1880s, increasing numbers of students born free on the continent came to the school for education, then returning to what the UMCA hoped would be an expanding mission field. By 1899, the mission's English-language periodical, *Central Africa*, reported that of one hundred boys at Kiungani, only fifteen had been formerly enslaved.[20]

The expansion of the mainland work, and the shifting demographics of the Zanzibar schools, led the UMCA to adopt a two-pronged language policy. The initial, oral evangelization of new areas was conducted in as close to the local languages as the missionaries could come, often with the help of African adherents with knowledge of these vernaculars.[21] "It is quite true that for general purposes Swahili is useful everywhere," reflected Rev. Herbert Woodward, "but when it comes to teaching religion the native tongue is of the greatest importance. Some Europeans find it difficult to realize this. Of course it is a trouble to have to learn a second or third language—but it *pays*."[22] Missionaries feared that teaching the youngest students on the mainland in Swahili would result in the mere repetition of the words of the teacher rather than absorbing the intended lesson.[23] The mission produced translations, handbooks, and readers for the various languages of its mainland stations, including Chinyanja, Yao, and Nsenga.[24] Some church services, too, were carried out in local languages.[25]

As soon as possible, however, and especially in the classroom, the mission stressed the use of Swahili. Reverend Chauncy Maples, though applying himself to the study of Yao in order to be able to speak to his congregants at Masasi, regarded Swahili as "the language of the future for all these parts."[26] The 1890 teaching manual *Mambo ya Chuoni na Kawaida za Mafundisho* ("School Affairs and Standards of Teaching") dealt with reading and writing in Swahili and English only, and the latter, the preface stressed, was taught almost exclusively at Kiungani and by English schoolteachers.[27] Formal education in the mission system therefore began with Swahili. Whether it was introduced first as a subject of study, or abruptly transitioned to the medium of instruction, likely depended upon the particular teacher in the particular classroom. Vernacular teaching, however, would have been oral and reserved for the newest students. This was partly a recognition that the mission simply did not have enough manpower to master the local languages of all its stations, nor could it create translations for every language spoken in its expanding mission field.[28] By the turn of the century, therefore, the UMCA all but insisted that its new staff members learn Swahili, if possible before even coming to East Africa.[29] There was also an ideological underpinning to the emphasis on Swahili: the mission leadership believed that only through "a common home, a common language, a common training, a common cause, work, and hope, a common religion with common means of communication" would the mission build a strong community that could sustain itself over wide separations in time and space.[30] This was no doubt a utopian view of an everlasting community, but the UMCA put this ideology into practice in its classrooms. Swahili was the language of instruction at the central institutions both on Zanzibar and the mainland, meaning that any student who went beyond the most elementary levels of education would be taught to read and write in it. As the Kiungani student Yohanna Abdallah wrote to an English correspondent in 1894: "We are so many boys in this house, and of different tribes, Yaos, Makuas, Boondeis and Nyasas; but we all speak Swahili language."[31] Swahili was also, therefore, the language of focus for UMCA translations and publications, and in practice it became the connecting language between the various linguistic groups under the mission's umbrella.

Back on Zanzibar, by the 1890s the industrial school students had been removed from Kiungani and installed in a different building. "Gradually," wrote mission historian A. E. M. Anderson-Morshead, "Kiungani has assumed the position of a training and theological college,—the boys have ceased to be chiefly freed slaves (indeed, lately no more such boys have been taken), but are mostly picked boys from upcountry schools."[32] Then, not long after the separation of the industrial and teacher-training students, a discussion arose as to whether the theological and teacher-training school should be kept on Zanzibar or moved to the mainland, closer to the main source of its population. One of the central arguments against the change was that Zanzibar was "neutral" territory, and that various "tribes" would be less likely to mingle well, or even to come in the first place, if the school were placed in a specific ethnic territory.[33] Bishop Frank Weston remarked in one letter that "tribal customs are forgotten in Zanzibar" and in another described Kiungani as "neutral ground."[34] Simplistic notions of ethnicity aside, the schools on Zanzibar simultaneously played host to the mission's linguistic diversity and became a site of linguistic unification for the mission students. For it was not that local customs, or even languages, were forsaken by the second generation of students; rather, they needed to learn the language of their new classrooms. Students and former students then carried Swahili as taught by the UMCA back with them, whether on school holidays or for permanent postings at mainland stations. Of course, vernacular fluency in various mainland languages was one of the advantages of taking in students from all over the region, and Kiungani graduates did much of their preaching in local languages. But they were steeped in the culture of reading and writing in Swahili, the language central to the construction of the *Upelekwa*.

THE TECHNOLOGY OF COMMUNICATION

In the latter decades of the nineteenth century, the available technologies of travel and communication were simultaneously major sources of constraint and extraordinary pathways of mobility. This period, as many have written, witnessed significant technological advances that for many parts of the world seemed to accelerate time and shrink space. And yet, as On Barak has shown for turn-of-the-century Egypt, acceleration was uneven, and while technology such as trains and telegraphs objectively sped communication, things could seem comparatively (sometimes purposefully) slow.[35] This was certainly the case for east-central Africa, where the promise of rapid transit and communication raised hopes that were often dashed by persistent experiences of delay.

Communication was one of the foremost concerns of every letter writer on Zanzibar. Mails coming and going, mails delayed, fluctuations in postage prices, supplies collected or lost, telegrams received and sent—these were topics of constant repetition in both missionary and British consular correspondence. Though Zanzibar was a relatively well-connected place, the technological and logistical links were still tenuous at best. The opening of the Suez Canal in November 1869 cleared an important pathway between Europe and the Indian Ocean, expanding trade and communication. Messages to Zanzibar were generally relayed through Bombay, Aden, or the Seychelles, via the Canal or the Cape. The sending and receiving of mail during the mission's early years was catch-as-catch-can, with merchants, missionaries, or officials sending mail with whichever steamer would bring it in the right direction.[36] By 1872, a mail steamer from Aden, run by the British India Steam Navigation Company, was (theoretically) to reach Zanzibar every month.[37] The Germans, too, began a regular mail service between Hamburg and Delagoa Bay, which collected mail from Zanzibar, as well as a coastal service between several East African ports.[38] An August 1891 article in the mission periodical *Central Africa* detailed all the improved methods of reaching the mission's various island and mainland stations via British, German, and French ships.[39]

The advent of the telegraph dramatically shrank the distance between stations, and between Europe and Africa. Zanzibar received a telegraph station in the 1870s, the same decade that cables began crisscrossing the Indian Ocean.[40] As the "Home Jottings" section in the May 1884 issue of *Central Africa* reported, "Our friends in Africa are not out of reach; one afternoon lately we telegraphed to Zanzibar, and had the reply delivered by 6.30 p.m. the same day!"[41] At Blantyre—the town and mission station founded by the Church of Scotland mission just south of Lake Nyasa—a telegraph office opened in 1895. "This is a grand thing for the [Universities'] Mission in many ways," reported *Central Africa*, "as it brings us within the possibility of communicating with our friends on the Lake in a week if any urgent necessity should arise."[42] Of special importance to the UMCA, moreover, was the fact that the first message sent out from the Blantyre telegraph office was transmitted by a former mission student from Likoma.[43]

Despite steamships and telegraphs, however, lines of communication between England, Zanzibar, and the mainland could be tenuous. Expected ships went missing or were delayed with no explanation; letters and packages were damaged; ships caught fire or had accidents; and mail was left behind in other ports.[44] That the Nyasa mail was being "sent daily" in 1890, according to *Central Africa,* signaled that communication between the Cape and Quelimane was so irregular that mail could only be sent "as opportunity occurs."[45] Indeed, communication with the mainland stations could be even more difficult than between Zanzibar and England. Besides seasonal rains that made overland travel precarious, political upheaval sometimes hindered communication.[46] Delays occurred, for instance, at the introduction of a pass system as Germany exerted power in its new coastal territories.[47] Besides the Germans, local African authorities sometimes prevented easy passage to missionaries as the century wound to a close.[48] The consolidation of European control over eastern Africa did not at first ease the missionaries' obsession with communication, nor that of their adherents.

From the mission's early years on Zanzibar, the unfettered passage of mails was regarded as a "measure of common humanity," and its correspondence is rife with longing for communication from home.[49] "We are the unluckiest people in the world in our Mails," wrote Steere to his wife in 1865.[50] Steere's sister Anne referred in her diary to "the mystery that now hangs over all our correspondence," and Pennell wrote to him of the "chronic state of excitation about letters."[51] Helen Tozer recounted that "every one was worn and harassed by a wet season and by the utter absence of home news," while her brother wrote resignedly, "We have had another of those long postal gaps, to which we ought to be accustomed by this time."[52] After another long delay, Steere wrote with his typical wry humor: "A few newspapers have since come down from Bombay which leads us to believe that England still exists, but we shall be very glad when we get more definite information."[53] News could assuage the loneliness and feelings of separation, but its absence led to weariness and disappointment. "Thanks for your letter," wrote Eleanor Bennett to Rev. Duncan Travers, "I do so like to hear from England, and I think one's longing for letters increases as time goes on."[54] Correspondence was uncertain, and the missionaries lived and breathed by the news that came from home and from their sister stations. African adherents, too, were determined to maintain the important connections that they had built at the mission's schools. What good was social rebirth, after all, if that community dissolved once one left school?

In the midst of these precarious technological and logistical links between England, Zanzibar, and the mainland stations, there emerged the regularity of the production of *Msimulizi*. The magazine became a vehicle through which students and former students shared their news, their joys and despairs, wants and needs, stories and poems. The bimonthly arrival of *Msimulizi* was an event of central importance in the lives of many; and into their lives it brought a regular reinforcement of the mission's Swahili standard, reiterating for those scattered all over eastern Africa the importance to their community of reading, writing, and a common language.

MSIMULIZI, OR, THE NARRATOR

Returning to the printing office and the work of Owen Makanyassa: the inaugural edition of *Msimulizi* was printed in October of 1888 and sent out to the various stations of the Universities' Mission. Starting from Zanzibar, the magazine would have first reached Magila, in the hilly region of the Usambara Mountains. It would then have come ashore some eight hundred kilometers south, where it was ultimately carried up a road lined with fruit trees to the station at Masasi. Finally, eventually, a boat would have arrived at Likoma, about four hundred kilometers west of Masasi; among the food and firewood unpacked onto the sandy harbor would have been several copies of *Msimulizi*. Despite traveling hundreds of kilometers, over sea and land, at times stuck at ports or delayed by rains, sometimes waterlogged or otherwise degraded by the elements, over time the bimonthly arrival of *Msimulizi* became an expected event, the magazine a regular caller that made immediate the community of adherents scattered all over east-central Africa. But it was not just by appearing every other month that *Msimulizi* managed to collapse time and space, figuratively putting the readers of the magazine into the same room as its authors. A crucial factor was that *Msimulizi* was written in the Swahili that had become central to the community of adherents—this was the language that they and their predecessors had helped to standardize, and that now connected them all along the mission's intellectual network.[55] The processes of community-construction and language dissemination were mutually reinforcing developments that spanned the turn of the twentieth century.

The magazine was introduced to the wider public in the January 1889 issue of *Central Africa*. The article announcing *Msimulizi* read "A School Magazine, in Swahili, has appeared at Kiungani called 'Msimulizi,' (The Reporter). It is edited by one of the native teachers, Swithun Ulumana, assisted by several others as 'Correspondents.' It is printed at the Mission Press, Kiungani, and promised every two months at present, in time for the up-country mails."[56] The intention was to foster ties between the mission stations and those connected with the mission both past and present, and it would print news especially "bearing on the progress of Christianity in Africa."[57] The article applauded the "*esprit-de-corps*" demonstrated by the "native lads" involved in the inaugural issue. *Msimulizi* would appear every other month, from October 1888 through August 1896; each issue was generally about sixteen pages long.[58] The magazine displays a high degree of linguistic uniformity over the course of its eight-year run, from the structure of the greetings down to the grammar and vocabulary of the contributions. Of course, the editor and his assistants polished the articles for publication, but the assumption was that all contributions would be in a readable condition and written in Swahili.

Students and teachers on Zanzibar and the mainland divided the work of compiling the magazine: each station chose an *Mletaji habari* (a "supplier of news" or correspondent; pl., *waletaji*).[59] This individual was tasked with collecting and writing up the news of their area and sending it to Zanzibar. This correspondence was then collected by the *Mtengenezaji wa Msimulizi* (the "arranger of *Msimulizi*" or the editor; pl., *watengenezaji*). Every two months the *Mtengenezaji* and his staff would "collect news from here in Unguja, of Mkunazini and Mbweni and Kiungani, and also to get news of the areas of Boonde and of Nyassa and of Newala and the cities over there, and to print it here at Kiungani and make it into a small book."[60] The Zanzibar press printed the magazine, which was then sent out to the various stations. The subscription cost six pice (a fraction of a rupee) per year to cover printing and shipping.[61]

The *Barua ya Kuelezea* ("Letter of Explanation") that opened the first issue in October of 1888 explained that *Msimulizi* was modeled on school magazines in England aimed at both current students and alumni.[62] It was at heart a newsletter, reporting school exams, teaching appointments, and football matches with the same diligence as religious rituals, services, and holidays. The content of the articles was mainly secular—births, deaths, marriages, famine, war, comings and goings—but obviously run through with expressions of faith. It was meant for an internal audience, for fellow UMCA members in Africa, rather than as an evangelical or fundraising tool like the English-language *Central Africa* or *African Tidings*. The everyday content of the magazine, meanwhile, meant that the mission's version of written Swahili permeated the everyday life of its readers and contributors—*Msimulizi* was thus a vehicle for the dissemination of the mission standard as well as a tool used by adherents to reinforce the community that they were building. Examining the magazine, it becomes clear that Swahili was not confined to religious services, nor just a means of communication with Europeans. Rather, it defined the community of adherents, and this definition was reinforced every two months with the arrival of *Msimulizi*, the written language of which connected students and adherents across eastern Africa, engendering a worldview that was at once widespread and closely knit.

BUILDING THE UPELEKWA

Upelekwa was one of those words that gave me pause the first time I encountered it in *Msimulizi*.[63] Its constituent parts I could grasp, but the combination was unfamiliar. As I continued to encounter the word, its definition in context seemed straightforward: the authors used it to translate "mission," specifically a Christian mission. And indeed, the various dictionaries and translations produced by the UMCA linked the idea of Christian mission to the verb stem *-pelekwa*. Steere's 1870 and 1875 handbooks included the form *mpeekwa* as a definition for "missionary," while the 1884 version added *mpelekwa* as "a person sent, missionary."[64] Madan's 1894 *English-Swahili Dictionary* gave *upelekwa* as one possible definition for "mission," while his 1903 *Swahili-English Dictionary* defined *mpelekwa* as "a person sent, a messenger."

The term *upelekwa*, however, appeared with regularity first in *Msimulizi*. And while it was used to translate the English word "mission," a closer look at the parts of the Swahili word suggests a greater significance. First the verb stem: *-pelekwa*. This is the passive construction of the verb *-peleka* ("to send, cause to go, transmit, take to"). The prefix *u*, however, can be used to change nominal, adjectival, or verbal roots into abstract concepts. It can be used, for instance, to create an abstract noun from an adjectival root, like *uhuru* ("freedom") from *huru* ("free, independent"); likewise, the prefix can turn a verbal root, such as *-penda* ("to love") into a noun, *upendo* ("love"). It can also denote the English-language notion of "-ness," as in "Swahili-ness" (*Uswahili*) or "Kenyan-ness" (*Ukenya*), that is, the qualities or characteristics associated with being Swahili or Kenyan. For the term *upelekwa*, the *u* prefix changes the verbal root—"to be sent, caused to go"—into a noun encompassing the intangible quality of "being sent" or "sent-ness," of "being caused to go," in this case into the mission field in order to spread the gospel.[65] In *Msimulizi* the word was generally capitalized, indicating that it was being used to refer to a specific community—that is, members of the UMCA who were sent from England to Zanzibar, for instance, or from Zanzibar to one of the mainland stations.[66] This community was not constrained to any particular location; rather, the mission community, scattered as it was, was one collective entity, connected by the sense of being sent or caused to go.

The magazine, when referring to the UMCA, would often use the phrase "*Upelekwa wetu.*" A simplistic translation of this would be "our Mission," but embedded within the phrase are some important insights into exactly who were the central actors in this particular project of community-building. *Upelekwa wetu*, being both capitalized and including a marker of possession, hints at a sense of ownership on the part of the contributors, the students and teachers from the mission's schools. Moreover, the concept of the *Upelekwa*, with its connotation of inherent unity based on the quality of "being sent," demonstrates the feeling of shared community emanating from the mission stations. It was a community that was (ideally) both all-inclusive and clearly defined, locally practiced and universally expandable; it included all generations of mission students and looked toward those who were not yet a part of the community; and it paralleled the missionaries' evangelical project, but was undertaken by the African adherents of the UMCA.

The term *Upelekwa* appears some thirty-five times in *Msimulizi*'s initial forty-eight-issue run, including in the first issue's introductory editorial. Explaining the purpose of the magazine, the *Mtengenezaji* Swithun Ulumana wrote: "Because when we are finished staying here at Kiungani we are scattered here and there, every person to his work, we are staying very far apart, trying to do the work of our Mission [*Upelekwa wetu*]. And a person living very far away does not often have the opportunity to write to all of his friends who live in various places, that is, he is only able to get a very little bit of their news. Thus our charge is a fitting one, to bring the news of people and news of what has happened in every town of this Mission of ours [*Upelekwa wetu*]."[67] Subsequent references generally followed suit, with contributors writing about the *miji* or towns of the *Upelekwa*, the "*kazi ya Upelekwa*" ("work of the Upelekwa"), "*killa Station ya Upelekwa*" ("every Station of the Upelekwa"), "*desturi zote za Upelekwa wetu*" ("all the customs of our Upelekwa"), or the annual St. Bartholomew's Day celebration of "*kubatizwa wa kwanza wa Upelekwa wetu*" ("the first baptism of our Upelekwa").[68] The simultaneous consistency and nonspecificity of the references to the *Upelekwa* gave readers the space to identify in their local situations a connection to something bigger, an idea of community that could encompass a fairly wide range of smaller community-building projects.

The *Upelekwa* could even handle distinctions in ethnicity, a factor that complicates the UMCA's own narrative of the diminishment of ethnic identification, in part through its "supra-ethnic" language of Swahili. In 1890, for instance, the contributor from Mlolela (near Chitangali and Newala in the southeast) wrote: "We have accepted with great joy and are very proud for having received a Priest from our own tribe rather than you staying in all the other cities of the *upelekwa*."[69] Cecil Majaliwa, the first African clergyman to be ordained priest by the UMCA, had indeed been born in the Yao-speaking region of the south, and so the community at Mlolela felt a particular proprietary relationship with him. This celebratory ethnic distinction, however, did not hive the community at Mlolela off from the *Upelekwa*—both the UMCA and its shared Swahili standard may have been "supra-" or "multiethnic," but not blind to ethnic difference. The *Upelekwa* had to be carefully constructed to contain multiple constituencies, all claiming membership in a community that could encompass potential "divergences in understanding" of what exactly marked it as a connected unit.[70]

THE LITERARY STRATEGIES OF MISMULIZI

Besides use of the term itself, in what other ways can we see the concept of the *Upelekwa* at work in *Msimulizi*? The authors and contributors used three strategies in particular: the personification of the magazine, the use of familial language, and the careful reporting of individual comings and goings. Turning first to personification: the second editor, Hugh Mtoka, was the first to write *as* the magazine, penning articles from the point of view of *Msimulizi* itself.[71] Three of his introductory articles were written "by" the magazine, with titles like "*Anena Mwenyewe! Msikieni!*" ("He speaks himself! Listen!") and "*Mimi hapa Msimulizi!*" ("I am here, the Msimulizi!").[72] In the first piece of this genre, which opened the second issue, Mtoka—writing as the magazine—explained, "Thus I am happy that in every place my friends have received me with happiness, and told me, come, friend, come again, every two months come to our homes and report to us. So for this reason I have come again this second time, and this journey I come freely like the first, so that you receive me like a gift, but the third journey, apologies sir, you will want to pay one pice (or six pice per year) because my journey is expensive, it can't be avoided."[73]

Mtoka intended for the object held in the hand to "speak" directly to the reader. And how could one deny such a close confidant something as trivial as a subscription fee? It was a shrewd tactic to be sure. But beyond explaining the importance of paying for the magazine, Mtoka put its Swahili words into the minds of its readers, while simultaneously reminding them that it would return. Likewise, in the eighth issue, Mtoka (again personifying the magazine), began familiarly with the question, "Hey, Sir, how are you?" ("*Ee Bwana wee, u hali gani?*") He then went on to describe his travels between the mission stations, invoking the scattered community and *Msimulizi's* own role in connecting it: "I have arrived from time to time in each city of our Mission, I have chatted with many people, and I have been happy to get the news of their fellows from all around, because indeed I gave them much, until they see me now as a friend to be looked after. Even when I am here on Unguja—because I was born, you know, on the island of Unguja—the

Correspondents do not miss sending me their news, they do not forget me, except maybe once or twice I have been passed over."[74] The article concluded with "*Bassi somo, maneno hayo, ni yangu; nami nashughulika sana, kwani sharti niwafikie watu kama 350 killa safari—hatta Ulaya nafika kwa watu wapata 20. Bass uwe rathi, bwana, mimi hapa Msimulizi wako.*" ("Well my dear friend, these words, are mine; and I am very busy, because I am required to reach about 350 people each journey—even in Europe I reach 20 people. So, with your pardon, Sir, I am your *Msimulizi.*")[75] That final line can be interpreted as a formulaic farewell—"I am," or "I am yours"; but the very formulation indicates, again, the sense of ownership and responsibility felt by contributors and readers toward the magazine and its community. In such editorials, *Msimulizi* "spoke" to speakers of, for example, the Bondei and Makonde and Zigua languages, people from the linguistic communities surrounding the mainland stations; but it explicitly spoke to all of them as "theirs" through the medium of Swahili.

Mtoka's article also offers the first indication of the actual circulation numbers of the magazine. And while there were around 350 subscribers, including African teachers as well as advanced students, *Msimulizi* likely reached a wider audience. We know, for instance, that the editors were constantly reminding subscribers to pay their dues and urged readers to purchase their own copies. It seems that people often shared the issues, and the *Mtengenezaji* chastised them for it.[76] Jonathon Glassman described a similar tactic used by newspapers in Zanzibar in the 1950s, whose editors tried to shame their readers into buying their own copies. But this did not stop readers from sharing newspapers or reading them aloud at "the hangouts on city streets where vendors sold small cups of strong coffee and in the eating houses. . . . Thus, even the illiterate could participate in the arguments that ensued."[77] Perhaps *Msimulizi,* too, was read aloud at mission stations and other gathering places, increasing the circulation of its news and its language. This is especially believable given its conversational style, and the real-time exchanges of riddles, news seeking, and other appeals. *Msimulizi,* meanwhile, physically followed subscribers as they moved from station to station, "speaking" to readers with an uncanny sense of immediacy. In myriad ways, then, the mission's Swahili standard crept into both the oral and literate cultures of the UMCA network.

At times, the correspondents would reply to the personified articles of *Msimulizi,* holding a conversation on delay. At the most basic level, most every contribution (following the suggestion of the *Mtengenezaji*) started with a variation of the greeting "*Salamu sana,*" and some concluded with a farewell of "*Kwa heri*" or "*Salaam.*" Other conversations spanned several issues. One such discussion began in 1891 with an appeal from George Swedi, the third editor, in which he bemoaned the state of the correspondents' submissions. He then went on to (good-naturedly?) criticize a magazine that UMCA members at Likoma had just begun printing called *Mtenga watu* ("Divider of people" or "Causer of discord").[78] Swedi was responding to an article penned by Clement Kathibeni in the June 1891 issue of *Msimulizi*, in which he explained that the press at Likoma was developing rapidly; the printers there had already printed and sent out samples of *Msimulizi wetu* ("our *Msimulizi*"), and Kathibeni asked readers to subscribe to the new magazine.[79] Swedi responded: "But what? Should an elder be defeated by a child? Because the child I have is named '*Mtenga watu*' and he displays a bit of ostentation, he draws attention to himself, he is a show-off, so what am I the old man to do? I love him. Is he not my child? Is he not good? But he must remember to respect his father. And a father must not be angered by his child. He must just admonish him."[80] John B. Mdoe (a later editor, writing in his role as *Mletaji habari* from Magila) responded to Swedi's jibes in the October issue. At Magila they had also begun printing a magazine, called *Maongezi na Maarifa* ("Conversation and Knowledge").[81] Mdoe wrote in *Msimulizi*: "*Mtengenezaji* of *Msimulizi*, how are you? But have you seen that *Maongezi na Maarifa?* And we must stand up friend, it is not proper that the father '*Msimulizi*' and the child '*Mtenga watu*' must walk by themselves, it is necessary that they have a clerk, and this clerk should be proper and he must dress well to surpass the master and his child, so that they do not despise him. Our printing press continues sir until *Maongezi na Maarifa* is abandoned, please read it, and you will recognize it."[82] A friendly rivalry that was perhaps underpinned by some journalistic competition, this exchange is just one example of the conversations that occurred within *Msimulizi*.[83]

The real-time exchanges also took less light-hearted forms. In the April 1896 issue, for instance, Petro Musa—the *Mletaji habari* from Mwiti—shared the good news that "*ndugu yetu mmoja*" ("one of our sisters"), a student of Mbweni who left the mission to follow "worldly ways" ("*kufuata ulimwengu*"), had returned along with her husband.[84] In the following issue, however, Musa reported that "*ametoka kuufuata ulimwengu tena*" ("she had left again to follow worldly ways").[85] He continued: "*Kwa hivyo nasikitika sana kwa kuwa nalisema kama atakuwa mtu wa kuonekana tena huko Unguja, lakini sivyo.*" ("Therefore I am sorry because I said that she would be a person who would be seen again there at Zanzibar, but it is not to be.")[86] Another heavy-hearted report came in the June 1892 issue, in which a writer from Lake Nyasa wrote to inform the readers of the magazine of a tragedy that occurred in part *because* of the exchange of news. In February of that year, the residents of a station near Lake Nyasa received word that one of their students had died at Zanzibar. On receiving the news, the boy's distraught parents confronted the local teacher, Augustine Ambali. The confrontation came to a peaceful end, but soon afterward the boy's father grew ill and died. "Thus there is much sadness for this woman," wrote the reporter, "thinking about the news of her husband and thinking about the news of her child, but we do not know what will transpire, because we hear from time to time that this woman wants to kill herself and it is only people that have restrained her."[87] This is an extreme example of the power of information to change lives. There were more mundane exchanges, like requests for new teachers or supplies, the reporting of someone's arrival at a new station, or information about the regional political situation and its effects on movement or safety. In multiple ways, the exchange of news—happy, sad, or quotidian—had real consequences for the lives of the UMCA's adherents.

Along with the conversational structure of the magazine, the use of familial terms within its pages explicitly tied the magazine's readers together. Anne Marie Stoner-Eby touched upon such vocabulary in her investigation of the UMCA teachers in the Rovuma region around Masasi, examining the use of the word *ndugu* ("sibling," "kin," "relative," "comrade").[88] The use of this familial term, she argued, created a sense of the UMCA community as children under the same mother. The importance of "family, clan, and village" had not been undermined, but rather the concept expanded to include all UMCA Christians.[89] *Ndugu* appeared constantly in *Msimulizi*, in just the ways described by Stoner-Eby.

The magazine was also sprinkled with other familial terms, including the words *jamaa* and *kundi*. *Jamaa* means "a number of persons gathered or connected together, family, society, company, assembly, gathering, meeting."[90] The word was used in most cases in *Msimulizi* to refer to a specific person's family, as when mainland students would return home to visit "*jamaa zao*" ("their families"). It was not unusual, though, to use the word to refer to the broader "family" of the station, the mission, or even the "family" of Christians, as with "*Ninathani mtapenda kusikia habari ya jamaa wetu mmoja Mmasihiya*" ("I think you will like to hear the news of our single Christian family").[91] Paul Kasese, the *Mleteji habari* from Masasi, combined multiple sentiments of *jamaa* in his description of an anticipated visit from the bishop: "My dear *mtengenezaji* many greetings. After greetings I offer you the news of these days. Truly our brothers, as you know, in each Station of our Mission every year indeed there is the happiness of every Christian, for the reason that our family is welcomed into the greatest of Families. There is no need to speak of it to you, because you know well my meaning."[92] Kasese referred to the family of the station, of the mission, and of "every Christian." His Masasi station was linked to all these levels through the circulation of *Msimulizi* as well as by the bishop's visit. In *Msimulizi* one can find reference to the "*jama ya Kimasihiya*" ("the Christian family"), the "*jamaa wa Mbweni*" ("the family of Mbweni"), "*jamaa yetu . . . 'Chama cha Paolo Mtume'*" ("our family . . . the Guild of St. Paul"), and the "*jamaa huko Unguja*" ("the family there on Unguja").[93] The notion of family at every level—nuclear, station, mission, and Christian—permeated *Msimulizi*.

Kundi is another word that appeared frequently in the magazine. *Kundi* means "a group of (usually living) things together, crowd, troop, flock, herd." *Msimulizi* contributors used the term in multiple senses, from "*kundi la mbuzi*" ("herd of goats") to "*kundi la Kimasihiya*" ("Christian flock").[94] The latter was the most common usage, often employed in reference to baptism or confirmation: "*wakatiwa mikono, na kuwaaga watu wasikiao na waana-funzi kwa kuwaonya wawe siku zote na shauko ya kutaka nao kuingia katika kundi la Wamasihiya*" ("they were confirmed and said goodbye to the people listening and the students by warning them to show every day their desire to enter into the flock of Christians").[95] Another issue reported that an adherent from the Mbweni farm, who had drifted away from the church, "*ame-lirejea kundi lake la Umasihiya*" ("has turned back to his Christian flock").[96] Students were urged "*kuwa kundi moja*" ("to be one flock").[97] The repetition of this word reinforced the idea that the UMCA community was a collective, connected group. It also clearly referenced the biblical idea of Christians as a flock of sheep led by Jesus, their shepherd. Using *kundi* or *jamaa* to refer to the station, the mission, or to fellow Christians, the *waletaji habari* blended these layers together, creating a strong sense for their readers of affiliation across time and space.

Alongside the personified articles and the familial language, the reader can get a sense of the strength of the *Upelekwa* connections nurtured by *Msimulizi* in the careful track that the correspondents kept of the movements of individuals throughout the region. A contributor from an outstation, for instance, would report when a person or group left; the receiving station would often tell of their arrival; and, finally, the original station would happily announce when someone returned. Even in instances not tracked so thoroughly, readers were kept abreast of many of the movements and life developments of their fellow adherents. At times the *waletaji habari* relied on travelers to bring them news before it was sent to Zanzibar and then printed in *Msimulizi,* as when a traveler brought to Miwa "*habari za jamaa huko Unguja. Tukafarajika*" ("the news of our family there on Unguja. We were comforted").[98] Of course big events, like the ordination of Peter Limo in 1893, often passed first through telegraph and then through the magazine.[99] In such instances, too, the news would often prompt the granting of a holiday—a day off from school and work because of an event that happened at another station.[100] Keeping track through *Msimulizi* was often the best that old friends and classmates could hope for. "*Sijui kama watakutana mbele tena*," wrote Samwil Chiponde from Newala, "*Hiyo ndio taarifu nikuleteayo kwa mkono wangu.*" ("I do not know if they will meet again in the future. This is indeed the report that I bring to you with my own hand.")[101] Face-to-face reunions, meanwhile, were a joyful surprise. "*Na nilipowaona rafiki zangu,*" recounted correspondent A. M. of a journey from Zanzibar to Magila, "*nikafurahiwa sana sana.*" ("And when I saw my friends I was made extremely happy.")[102] Certain occurrences defined existence at the UMCA stations—the baptisms and confirmations, schooldays and holidays, births and deaths. The *Upelekwa* was strengthened by these shared experiences, both actually shared and vicariously shared through the magazine.[103]

The *Upelekwa* encompassed England, too, as distinct from but also naturally connected to the African branches of the mission. And while neither missionaries nor their African adherents were blind to the racial constructions that became increasingly entrenched in the late nineteenth century, the writers of *Msimulizi* did not use the concept to subordinate Africa and Africans. England may have been the source of denominational authority, of white missionaries, and of certain material goods, but *Msimulizi's* contributors gave examples of the assistance that Africa could offer to England, writing naturally of their own responsibility for their fellow believers on that other faraway island. For instance, at an 1891 meeting of the Guild of the Good Shepherd—an association of female teachers created on Zanzibar in the 1880s—the women decided that rather than giving their annual collection money to a mainland station as they had the year before, they would donate it to St. Alban's parish in Holborn, England, in order to pay for breakfast for the parish's poor children.[104] *Msimulizi* reported on another effort in December 1891: after a gathering of teachers and clergymen, Peter Limo and Samuel Sehoza requested that readers who wished to do so send a small offering to Zanzibar, which would then be sent on to England in order to erect a memorial for Mary Townshend, a former teacher and nurse on Zanzibar who was buried at Ziwani.[105] These examples disrupt our conventional understanding of the power dynamics that existed between converts and missionaries, Africa and England. The increasingly obvious influence of Britain in late nineteenth-century East Africa could, however, not be ignored, and this, too, comes across in *Msimulizi*.[106] Though the missionaries claimed that their only loyalties were to God and their flock, Great Britain also commanded fealty. In a very few instances, a missionary would contribute an article extolling the virtues of British governance.[107] The *waletaji habari,* too, recognized England's influence over the politics of their stations (never mind their trouble with the Germans). The contributors to *Msimulizi* were obviously aware of the increasing presence and power of the British on Zanzibar especially, and of European states more generally in the region.

Understanding the *Upelekwa* worldview is crucial to understanding the nature of the process by which the UMCA's written Swahili standard pervaded the territory between Zanzibar and Lake Nyasa. The language, though based on the Kiunguja dialect, was not foisted upon the mainland stations and the people inhabiting them. Rather, readers and writers from all over the mission field participated in the creation and reinforcement of the community and thus the circulation of its written Swahili. This was the power of the mission's standard: its initial codification drew upon people of various linguistic backgrounds; students and adherents then built ties to the UMCA through their social rebirth within the mission community; and finally, through the circulation of people and of *Msimulizi* beginning in the 1880s, this same standard permeated the region in written form as adherents carried it along the routes of communication and travel.

But it was not the simple fact of linguistic uniformity that gave *Msimulizi,* and future publications like it, the power to create a collective reading public; just as the twentieth-century texts examined by Emily Callaci cannot be considered merely evidence of Dar es Salaam's changing urbanism, but were themselves "*constitutive* of urbanism," so at various moments did the editors and contributors to *Msimulizi* not simply reflect but actually call into being the very community on which they reported.[108] The active participation of readers and contributors drew them into the conversations taking place in print, marking a community that was defined more by expansion and inclusion than the narrow and more rigid boundaries of nationalism often associated with the rise of printed languages. These conversations helped create a broad sense of shared belonging—what Karin Barber has described as the "simultaneous rootedness and billowing expansiveness" of a reading public.[109] The adherents of the UMCA used Swahili both to draw the mission's constituents into closer congregation and, ideally, to expand that very congregation.[110]

THE PRINTING PRESS, PART II

The influence of the UMCA's Swahili standard outside of the mission community is partially a story of the power of printing. We have already seen hints at the rivalry between the mission's printing presses at Likoma, Magila, and

Zanzibar. We also know from chapter 1 that the press on Zanzibar had been at work since almost the moment the mission arrived on the island, producing iteration after iteration of translations during the early phase of standardization. The printing office on Zanzibar also took in outside work for pay, from labels for soda-water bottles to programs and notices for government and private businesses, thus turning it into a lucrative site of "industrial education."[111] A report from A. C. Madan, printed in *Central Africa* in January 1884, noted: "The Kiungani trade receipts are almost entirely earned for us by Owen [and] Christease, who [have] received and done a great deal of work for the town this quarter. We have not yet been obliged to refuse any job, despite the departure of [the European printing manager] Mr. Hayman."[112] The printers were a close-knit unit with special privileges and responsibilities, and their output of multiple translations in the early years of the mission contributed directly to the standardization of the mission's Swahili. Steere paternalistically acknowledged this fact, reflecting, "We are indebted to those who came to us as little ignorant slave boys whom we taught to handle the types and the press, and to print for the benefit of their brethren all those valuable and invaluable works."[113] Though the printers did not control the content of the mission's publications, the work could not have been done without them. Regulars such as Makanyassa kept the mission's printing press going, so that even when Madan appealed again and again for English printers to oversee the work, the press continued to produce.[114]

And in the late nineteenth century, the Universities' Mission created an overwhelming amount of printed Swahili-language material relative to its missionary competitors, both on its own presses and through European firms.[115] Madan described the mission's dominance in the translating, printing, and supplying of Swahili material throughout the region in an 1884 letter to Reverend William Penney, in which he discussed the UMCA Swahili prayer book, printed by the Society for Promoting Christian Knowledge: "What has been done here . . . is to give Prayerbooks on application to any Mission in this part of Africa, and only to sell to persons who are not connected with missions. . . . The C. M. S., the London M. S., the Scotch Missions, even the French in some degree, draw on the stock, by the dozen."[116] That is, the UMCA supplied Swahili prayer books throughout the region to missions of various denominations. Likewise, in 1890, the missionary William Bishop reported that the Church Missionary Society (CMS) in Uganda "have sent for a large supply of books and have cleared us of Swahili New Testaments."[117] He also noted that there had been "a run" on the Swahili *Handbook* and the short exercise book compiled by Steere and published in 1882. If the CMS, centered in Buganda where Luganda was the mission's most important

THE MISSION PRINTING OFFICE, WITH MR. MALLENDER AND ASSISTANTS.

FIGURE 2.1. UMCA Printing Office on Zanzibar. Bodleian Libraries, University of Oxford, *African Tidings* no. 56 (June 1894), UMCA Box List A-F: A1(IV)B. Reprinted with permission of the United Society Partners in the Gospel.

spoken language, was scrambling for Swahili New Testaments, then we can see how truly the UMCA dominated the Latin-script printing and translation scene of eastern Africa in the late nineteenth century.

While acknowledging the printing advantage of the UMCA at least into the 1890s, however, the mere printing of lots of material in a relatively standardized version of Swahili was alone not enough to guarantee its staying power. Rather, the Swahili standard of the UMCA was well-placed to eventually become *Standard Swahili* because it was imbricated in multiple projects of community-construction and community-maintenance, projects that wove it into the linguistic fabric of eastern Africa. But in the late nineteenth century, neither political nor linguistic outcomes were set in stone.

⁓

The constituents of the *Upelekwa* were the adherents of the UMCA, those united by the act of being sent, by their religious calling; they were also, as we have seen, pulled together by their language and sense of mutual obligation.

Though the process of social rebirth had begun with the first generation of students arriving on Zanzibar—those who participated in the early phase of standardization—it was not until the UMCA began expanding its operations on the mainland that the community of adherents needed to formulate a way of including newcomers while maintaining a distinct sense of connectedness. The idea of the *Upelekwa* allowed for this project of fluid boundary setting, and one can trace the elaboration of this idea through the student-run magazine *Msimulizi,* written in a shared standard of Swahili.

By mining the literary techniques of the magazine and tracing the travels and correspondence of the UMCA's African adherents along a network that stretched from Zanzibar to Lake Nyasa and even on to England, we begin to see the contours of a project of community-construction that was imbricated but not synonymous with other processes taking place during the same period, including the European-driven, Anglican evangelical project; the nascent German colonial project; and the long-running project of trade along the caravan routes—patterns of exchange that lent their pathways to the adherents of the UMCA. Though the number of UMCA members was tiny relative to the population of east-central Africa, they exercised an outsized linguistic influence, and by the late 1880s they were envisioning a long-term expansion of their community across the region. With access to the mission printing press, connections to English patrons, evangelical zeal, and their own mission to build and stay in touch with and through the *Upelekwa,* these formerly enslaved and never-enslaved individuals, students, teachers, printers, cooks, carpenters, and others played an integral role in a process of linguistic knowledge production that reverberated across the decades. Though the Swahili that was central to the *Upelekwa* went on to become the basis of the language used by the colonial regimes of East Africa and ultimately the independent country of Tanzania, the mission adherents were thinking far beyond the borders of any future nation-state. Their project was both constrained and facilitated by the turn-of-the-century context of eastern Africa, which engendered a vision of community made up of multiethnic, Christian, Swahili literates—a community that was intimately connected even as it was continually expanding.

Though the concept was expansive, however, the *Upelekwa* did have limits: UMCA adherents worried about the *washenzi* ("barbarians" or "heathens") who still surrounded their stations; they were concerned about their Muslim neighbors and those who might be attracted to that religion; and they were all too aware of the denominational, national, and racial differences that seemed so important to their European counterparts. These groups were left out of the conceptualization of the *Upelekwa,* as were those fellow adherents who had "fallen away." Derek Peterson has posed the challenging question: "What other communities got imagined, in and out of print?"[118] Finding the stories of those left out is a much more difficult task than tracing the boundaries, fluid as they were, of the idea. The community of adherents was neither monolithic nor without friction; indeed, it was the very diversity of the community that necessitated the deliberate construction of the *Upelekwa* in all its expansiveness, its definition, its concreteness, and its malleability. For, as Karin Barber emphasizes, "African-language texts did not *only* consolidate sub-national ethnic identities" but could also be marked by a "wavering address, shifting its horizon from very local to supra-national" with a "capacity to convene publics on several different scales at once."[119]

What would happen as the mission and its adherents waded into the twentieth century, and the consolidation of the mission's mainland network came up against the increasingly obvious presence of the German colonial state in eastern Africa? Did the colony subsume the *Upelekwa?* Certainly the historiography of the Maji Maji war, for instance, would suggest that supra-ethnic social and political ties did survive into the German colonial period. This is what makes tracking the idea of the *Upelekwa* a worthwhile task: not necessarily because the word occurs more frequently than, say, *kundi* or *jamaa;* not because it structured subsequent political frameworks; but rather explicitly because it was *not* adopted by the colonial or postcolonial states—it was a path not taken. "But that fragility and situationality," as Emma Hunter argues, "does not mean that [such ideas] were not powerful while they lasted."[120] The next chapter will explore a period of social and political disruption that foreclosed some possibilities while opening others, during which time Swahili permeated new communities and became a subject of official debate.

3 ∼ German Zeit and Swahili Time

Saa ndiyo kazi, kazi hufanywa kwa saa kama huna saa utachelewa kwenda kazini nunua saa. ("Time is work, and work is measured by the hour, so if you don't have a clock you'll be late getting to work. Buy a clock.")

—Advertisement in *Kwetu,* April 1938

THE TURN of the twentieth century was, in an absolute sense, nothing special. A new year, another Christmas celebration or month of Ramadan, a fresh school term, the next monsoon season—the mundane experience of a calendrical turnover. And yet the years surrounding 1900 were also a time of significant change for many people living in eastern Africa—transformations occurred that caused timelines to splinter and proliferate as individuals began to think about their communities, and their languages, in different ways. The German administrative use of Swahili, parallel to but not contiguous with the use of Swahili within the *Upelekwa,* associated the language with a very different community-building project: that of *Deutsch-Ostafrika.* And during the period of early colonial rule, Swahili print media began to slowly expand, growing from and then beyond the example of *Msimulizi* to circulate along networks put in place by the regimes of eastern Africa. Many of these new publications entwined the notions of "civilization" and "progress" with an explicitly linear, forward-moving temporality. According to the first issue of the agricultural journal *The Shamba,* for instance, which was produced on Zanzibar under the auspices of the British colonial *Gazette for Zanzibar and East Africa*, "a newspaper is something more than a condition of progress. It is an indication that a certain amount has already been made, and it is also an earnest of future exertions. A community does not as a rule indulge in the luxury of a paper unless it has accomplished something worth writing about, and is voyaging towards prosperity. We, to a certain extent, may be said to have taken time by the forelock."[1] While the German and British colonial regimes emphasized linearity both temporal and "civilizational," there were communities that moved slightly out of lockstep with colonial "progress." The adherents of the Universities' Mission to Central Africa (UMCA), for instance, continued to maintain and slowly grow their own community using their written Swahili standard, surviving the devastation of World War I and facing the prospect of postwar rebuilding with the language as a crucial connecting thread.

Emma Hunter has argued of the German and early British colonial periods that "competing political priorities could coexist with a desire to work towards shared ends."[2] It is to just such overlapping projects that this chapter attends, visions that encompassed various scales of community over time and space, beginning with an examination of German colonial rule and German linguistic scholarship. Though colonial administration certainly expanded Swahili's sphere of influence, the German government declined to take up any official project of standardization. The chapter then turns back to the UMCA, examining how the mission leadership began to envision the consolidation of a standard that would last for all time, while constituents of the *Upelekwa* wrote letters that passed along the entire UMCA network, using Swahili to maintain and expand their community.

GERMAN COLONIAL LANGUAGE POLICY

Names such as Carl Peters, Otto von Bismarck, Hermann Wissmann, and Julius von Soden are among the central characters in the historiography of German colonialism in East Africa. Peters forced the hand of a reluctant Chancellor Bismarck, who hosted the future colonial powers in Berlin in 1884–85. Wissman then took over the "effective occupation" of the territory that would become German East Africa, sparking and then suppressing the Bushiri uprising in 1888–89. The Maji Maji war of 1905–7, overseen by von Soden, represented another major historical and historiographic marker of the period, after which the colonial administration of the territory became more concerted.[3] And while German colonial rule was relatively short lived, it was nonetheless dramatically consequential for many residents of eastern Africa. There were periods of violence, famine, and epidemic disease, all accompanied by shifts in the social, political, and economic balances of power across the region. In terms of language, the German colonial administration utilized Swahili, and thus conveyed a certain prestige to it, but the German colonial state never created an official apparatus for or policy of standardization. Thus, for the history of Standard Swahili, the consequences of German colonial rule were ambiguous. German administration brought Swahili speakers to places they had never been before and infused the language with a new element of power. At the same time, colonial language policy vacillated between the promotion of German and Swahili, dividing the linguistic attention of administrators, teachers, students, and colonial subjects alike. While German academics were among the most influential Swahili scholars in Europe during the late nineteenth and early twentieth centuries, the constant tug-of-war between Berlin, Dar es Salaam, and the individual interests of mission societies and local communities precluded official linguistic consensus.[4]

In the 1890s, as Germany began to build its administrative infrastructure in East Africa, it inherited two existing networks: the *akida* system of the Zanzibari sultanate and the network of missionary societies (German and non-German) that dotted the region. German colonial rule grew from coastal centers where Swahili was the well-established lingua franca.[5] Using Swahili-speaking *akidas* from these centers of power as intermediaries meant that, as administrative control expanded into the interior, the language (both spoken and written) followed along.[6] In contrast, the network of missionary societies at first exerted a linguistic counterforce to the wholesale adoption of Swahili as the language of German administration. Many of these organizations (particularly those of Protestant denominations) insisted that local vernacular languages were the only way to effectively preach the gospel and insisted on using these rather than Swahili (let alone German) in their schools. This only began to change in the 1910s when the administration offered grants-in-aid to mission schools that met certain qualifications, including language of instruction. These grants were meant at first to encourage the teaching of German, though policymakers eventually agreed to extend support to Swahili-medium schools as well—after which point many mission societies began to concede to that language.[7]

In Berlin, meanwhile, some politicians were intent that German be used throughout the colony and East Africans taught the language as quickly as possible.[8] This insistence was partially born of the belief in German cultural superiority and the concomitant desire to construct a culturally contiguous colonial empire. It was also partially driven by the perceived association of Swahili with Islam: some German lawmakers feared that support for the former would only encourage the spread of the latter. Indeed, through the turn of the twentieth century the government endowed a "Fund for the Spread of the German Language," which subsidized institutions throughout Germany's colonial empire, including the aforementioned funding for mission schools.[9]

While a German-language colony might have been held up as the ideal in Berlin, officials both at home and abroad agreed that the most important goals were efficiency of administration and to prevent the encroachment of the English language on German territory—both of which tipped the scales in favor of Swahili. Alongside pragmatism and nationalist rivalry, overt racism underpinned some of the arguments in favor of Swahili, including those who saw Africans as unworthy of using German, and others who sought to deny colonial subjects the power that came with mastery of the metropolitan language.[10] Officials in Dar es Salaam thus faced the conundrum of how to balance the pressures coming from the Reichstag with the intransigence of some missionary societies, all the while carrying out administrative tasks as efficiently as possible—a combination of interests that most often found suitable compromise with Swahili.[11] This state of affairs encouraged a modicum of language training for colonial officers: the Berlin Seminar for Oriental Languages began offering Swahili classes in 1888, for example.[12]

Besides the *akida* system, German promotion of Swahili can be traced most easily in its colonial education policy. The government school at Tanga was established in 1892, where the medium of instruction was Swahili (German was taught as a subject). Swahili speakers from Tanga and other government schools like those at Bagamoyo and Dar es Salaam went on to staff the upland schools built after 1905. Meanwhile, in 1904, Paul Blank, headmaster at Tanga, launched a monthly Swahili-language newspaper: *Kiongozi* ("The Leader" or "The Guide"). Much like *Msimulizi,* the newspaper was compiled at the school using news collected by *waletaji habari* who were scattered over an ever-widening swathe of German East Africa.[13] Students at Tanga did the printing, and by 1908 the print shop had a staff of fifty, producing some two thousand copies per issue. The contents of *Kiongozi* were largely didactic, proffering advice and analysis on topics ranging from agricultural production and medicine to poetry and local and world news.[14]

As Fabian Krautwald has demonstrated, a newspaper like *Kiongozi* represented neither a totally free press nor a simple mouthpiece of government propaganda.[15] Despite contemporary insistence as to the light touch of censorship, the oversight of German teachers was constant and, one must imagine, palpable for the East African student workers.[16] Yet participation in the production of the newspaper served as a central marker of identity for these government-educated, Swahili-writing colonial subjects. As Kraut-wald asserts, "The bearer of news' [*waletaji habari*] command of Latin script allowed them to access a privileged universe of knowledge. The socialization in government schools cast a long shadow. In the 1940s, the remaining German-educated teachers at Tanga still formed a group apart. The longevity of this community partly resulted from having been connected through *Kiongozi*'s audience."[17] And while the reliance of the German administration on this community of East African students, teachers, and writers uncovers certain frailties of colonial power, it is undeniable that *Kiongozi* echoed the government's linear notion of progress, dividing German East Africa between agents of that progress and "*washenzi.*"[18]

What did this tangle of interests, motivations, and policy decisions mean for the process of standardization in the early twentieth century? First, and most unambiguously, came the official insistence on Latin rather than Arabic script.[19] Beyond this official decision, however, the German administration did not take a stand on standardization qua policy; Derek Peterson has described German colonial attempts to codify Swahili orthography and spelling as "desultory."[20] Even Marcia Wright, in her emphasis on the "local roots" of German colonial policy, admitted "the question may legitimately be raised to what degree the Germans and others overestimated the infectiousness of Swahili as a lingua franca."[21] And despite occasional nationalistic protestations to the contrary, Swahili-medium schools in German East Africa initially relied on the orthography and texts of Steere and the Universities' Mission, even after German officials began producing school primers of their own.[22]

Under German colonial rule, then, Swahili became the default language of governance on the ground with little official thought given to its present or future shape and long-term status. For the duration of the German colonial period in East Africa, the linguistic question was never settled: Was Swahili a "stop-gap until German could take over" or did it represent the linguistic future of the region?[23] Ultimately, as Ann Brumfit has argued: "No official sanction for Swahili ever came from Berlin. . . . Adaptations had to be made on an ad-hoc and unofficial basis."[24] Therefore, while Swahili was central to German colonial administration, the effect of that administration on the process of standardization was equivocal at best.[25]

AFRIKANISTIK AND AFRICAN LANGUAGE STUDIES IN GERMANY

The divides within German policy did have some influence on scholarship, as the metropolitan sites of African language studies felt pressure to choose between a vision of longer-term, slower-moving research for the sake of academic understanding, and of research that could be used, quickly and easily, for the pragmatic needs of colonial officers. The figure of Carl Meinhof embodied the tension between academics and pragmatics, demonstrating how linguistics in early twentieth-century Germany was a divided camp. Sara Pugach has told Meinhof's story in great detail, tracing his move from an informal language school in the small town of Zizow, to the Seminar for Oriental Languages in Berlin, to the Colonial Institute in Hamburg.[26] The former institution, intended initially as a school for interpreters, exemplifies the pragmatic strain in German linguistic studies.[27] Of course, this was not a hard-and-fast rule, and the Seminar produced academic output as well.[28] And yet Meinhof, with his interest in developing comparative philological techniques, felt constrained by the pragmatic imperative in Berlin; he jumped at the chance to move to the newly constituted Colonial Institute in 1909, where he held Germany's first-ever chair in African languages. In Hamburg, Meinhof and his colleagues were given the freedom to combine linguistic, anthropological, and colonial studies and practice.[29] And with his own department, a phonetics laboratory, and a journal—*Zeitschrift für Kolonialsprachen*, or *Journal for Colonial Languages*—Meinhof had powerful tools at his disposal to shape African studies, including linguistics, in Germany, as well as to build a global reputation as an expert on African languages.

Benedict Anderson described the nineteenth century as a "golden age of vernacularizing lexicographers, grammarians, philologists, and litterateurs," and indeed, Meinhof was preceded by prominent scholars of language, including in East Africa Johann Krapf, Carl Büttner, and Carl Velten.[30] Into the twentieth century, German scholars (including Meinhof's protégé and colleague Diedrich Westermann) were at the forefront of the relatively young discipline of comparative philology, linguistics, or *Sprachwissenschaft*.[31] Using analogies from the natural sciences and particularly evolution (in 1863 the philologist August Schleicher claimed "that comparative philology not only corroborated Darwin's argument, but anticipated it"[32]), German linguists created linguistic "family trees" that purported to show predictable transformations of languages across time and space, claiming that each had a specific set of "natural" or "organic" surroundings.[33] By conceiving language change through a teleologically "evolutionary" lens (a distinct misreading of Darwin's variational theory, according to Joseph Errington), change over time moved straightforwardly from less "advanced" languages to their more "advanced" cousins. Such data, the comparativists claimed, could thus be used not only to uncover the origins of ("advanced") European languages and, perhaps, of humankind itself, but also to illuminate the sociocultural characteristics of speakers of any language around the world.[34]

Sara Pugach describes this as "cultural and linguistic racism" that "classified humanity according to grammatical, lexical, social, and religious criteria."[35] And though the transition was slow, the utopian pragmatism that drove many missionary linguists in the nineteenth century (as we saw in chapter 1) began in the early decades of the twentieth century to give way to a new kind of pragmatism: one concerned with the building of national identity at home as well as justifying (and administering) colonial rule abroad.[36] If African languages and their speakers were "trapped in the historical present," as Meinhof and others believed, then they could be used "to plumb the depths of the European past." And thus "the idea that the antiquity of African languages was what made them so vital to philology became a hallmark of arguments for their importance to the German colonial project."[37]

In terms of the history of Standard Swahili, German linguistic scholarship provided building blocks but no blueprint. In the preface to his 1903 *Swahili-English Dictionary*, A. C. Madan cited Steere, Krapf, and Sacleux as foundational sources; he also mentioned the increasing number of Swahili manuscripts that had come to his notice "due to the industry and scientific enthusiasm of German colonists and scholars."[38] But for Meinhof and most of his colleagues, even when they had been recruited to train officials being sent to Africa, the standardization of a single dialect was never the aim—rather, they believed in developing students' ability to communicate through comparative means, ideally with the basics that would allow officials to pick up any number of Bantu languages.[39] And once officials arrived in East Africa, communication was the standard by which they were judged, rather than adherence to a particular version of the language. Thus, just as German colonial language policy was driven by realities on the ground, so German linguistic scholarship refrained from championing one Swahili dialect over another. Turn-of-the-century German linguistic scholars were, therefore, neither totally academic nor totally pragmatic; or rather, the discipline's pragmatism could be evaluated differently.[40] Their work was conducted within this tension between Berlin and Hamburg, and between colonial officials and academically minded colleagues.[41] The professionalization of linguistics influenced colonial policy only to a limited extent—though officers deployed to places like Dar es Salaam were well-versed in the cultural-racial conclusions drawn from such studies—and the theories driving linguistics in Hamburg and Berlin, or Paris and London for that matter, could of course only do so much to control actual language use in colonial spaces.[42]

The period of German rule, as well as German conceptions of linguistic *Zeit*, were an amalgam of short-term and long-term timelines: looking back into the deep past for "origins," looking forward to the day when the German language would triumph, and all the while worried about the immediate, efficient administration of a burgeoning colonial empire. Time also, in a sense, ran out on the German colonial project; as John Iliffe has argued, "Germany's African empire did not last long enough for an administrative theory to gain acceptance."[43] This incoherence affected language policy in German East Africa, increasing the use of Swahili but without standardization as a driver of action. A similar intermingling of timelines would confront British administrators in the 1920s, but by then the political context and ideology of colonial administration had changed enough to encourage the official creation of a Swahili standard.

THE TRANSLATION COMMITTEE OF THE UMCA

In contrast to the relatively haphazard nature of German language policy, the Universities' Mission—which at the turn of the century spanned German and British territories in eastern Africa—maintained its focus on Kiunguja and attempted very consciously to finalize the standard versions of its most important texts. By the early years of the twentieth century, the UMCA had produced Swahili dictionaries and grammars, biblical translations, schoolbooks, and the first-ever Swahili-language periodical (*Msimulizi*). Up to this point, the process of standardization had been relatively broad based, drawing on a variety of constituents who were interested in codifying the language for diverse reasons. As the century wound to a close, however, the mission leadership began thinking along more permanent lines, embarking on several concerted attempts to revise (ideally for the last time) the translations of the Old and New Testaments, Hymnal, and Prayerbook. And as they started thinking about a final version of these Swahili works, the project moved from an open-source strategy to one that was driven by a panel of experts—namely, the Translation Committee, established in 1893.[44] This shift in the method of knowledge production reflected the changing political balancing act of the early colonial period, as well as a change in the temporal mindset of the mission linguists. By the turn of the century, the main interlocutors discussing the standardization of Swahili were no longer an admixture of Zanzibari Muslims, formerly enslaved students, and missionaries but rather the small group of European and African specialists who made up the Translation Committee.

The committee was first established at the 1893 synod on Zanzibar and reconstituted in 1896 with Revs. Godfrey Dale, Edward Palmer, Cecil Majaliwa, Peter Limo, and H. W. Woodward, and lay teachers A. C. Madan, Walter King, Samwil Chiponde, Ackworth Machaku, and Acland Misenga.[45] The two most important revisions undertaken at this time were of the New Testament—first published in 1883, it was revised and reprinted in 1892–93 and again in 1905 and 1921—and the Book of Common Prayer (the Prayer-book), which was first published in the 1880s, then revised and reprinted in 1896, and again in 1907–8.[46] During this same period, Madan published his two dictionaries: English-Swahili in 1894, and Swahili-English in 1903.

In July of 1897 the mission's English-language periodical *Central Africa* reported on a speech by Bishop William Richardson in which he described the standing work of the Translation Committee: "Now we have complete translations, you know, of the Old Testament, the New Testament, and the Prayer-book, but those who know about these things have thought that the time has come for a revision. . . . In order to be very watchful in all things that are printed and published in Swahili, there has been a committee appointed of those who know the language out there to watch over and edit linguistically . . . all publications that come from the Mission presses in Swahili."[47] The committee's portfolio was broad, indicating the removal of standardization from the normal workload of the mission and its transformation into a specialized task.

In the prefaces to his dictionaries, committee member Madan was simultaneously self-effacing and self-aggrandizing, declaring, "The Present Editor knows the Swahili of Zanzibar well enough to know that he does not know it well."[48] Yet he considered himself to be singularly qualified to prepare the dictionaries, correcting the works that had come before, "while making such a selection from them as suited his plan and accorded with the experience of eleven years' residence in Zanzibar."[49] That Madan's two dictionaries would, as we shall see, go on to serve as the basis of Standard Swahili, he could never have anticipated; he was openly torn between comprehensiveness and practicality, between his own expertise and his distinct sense of inadequacy. By his own admission, Madan believed that "at present," orthographic standardization was "impossible."[50] But that phrase—"at present"—contains within it the entire temporal ideology of the UMCA's Translation Committee. It was the same ideology that would drive the efforts, decades down the line, of the official British colonial standardizers. Standardization was a goal continually just beyond reach, but linguists both official and unofficial believed that the attempt to move ever closer to comprehensiveness and codification was a valuable endeavor.

Though the committee had been given responsibility for revision and standardization, it did feel some compunction to have its work verified by a broader audience. When it came time to begin retranslating the Prayerbook, for instance, pieces of the new version were sent to all the mission stations so that "Priests, and others competent to give an opinion, may send in any criticisms of the new renderings or suggest further changes which their local experience has shown them to be desirable before the complete work is finally printed."[51] Committee member Godfrey Dale, expressing a familiar nervous anticipation of readers' comments, wrote from Mkunazini: "Yes, it was a relief to see the copy of the revised Prayer Book. But as in duty bound I gave it to the Bishop and he has not told me of any misprints yet."[52]

Without having full copies of every version available, it is difficult to systematically analyze what kind of revisions occurred, either with the Prayerbook or the New Testament. Vocabulary and orthography were two main areas that remained under contention. Word substitutions, for instance, cropped up across the various versions of the Prayerbook: *orodha* or *kawaida ya* exchanged for *taratibu* to indicate the contents; *kipa imara* instead of *kutia mikono* for confirmation; and spelling changes such as *Anjili* to *Injili* ("Gospel").[53] The point to be made, however, is that with the establishment of a Translation Committee, standardization began to be transformed into an actors' category, with an explicit drive for codification and creation of official linguistic "expertise" (alongside a continued reliance on unacknowledged experts). Translation and revision had been institutionalized for the first time on the ground in East Africa, through a committee whose tendrils reached forward and backward in time, and inward and outward for data. As Bishop John Hine wrote in his Pastoral Letter of 1905, "We have to draw from all sources, cultured and uncultured, seeking to render the words so as to be clear and intelligible not to a small section of the people but to them all. . . . No alteration either great or small has been made without the greatest deliberation and care, and every suggestion or criticism made by the clergy or teachers on the Mainland has received the fullest consideration, before being either accepted or rejected."[54]

In this period, the UMCA also began to envision linguistic standardization across denominational boundaries. Specifically, the mission leadership tried to bring its biblical translations and those of the Church Missionary Society into alignment. One clear difference that arose between the two societies was the translation of "Jesus Christ" into Swahili. Initially the Universities' Mission had used the phrase *Isa Masiya*. Starting prior to the publication of the 1907 Prayerbook, however, the mission switched to the phrase *Yesu Kristo*, and the transition upset the translators of the Church Missionary Society (CMS). Hine referred to this opposition in a letter to Home Secretary Duncan Travers, writing:

> Evidently he [a CMS correspondent] thought the latter rendering was a new departure instead of being 10 years old and universal in all Christian missions in E and Cent. Africa except Uganda [where the CMS also worked]. Uganda alone now uses Isa Masiya and

Mombasa alone uses Jesu Masihi. Does the Most Reverend think that all the R.C. missions, the Lutherans, the Swedish, the Moravians, the Scotch Presbyterian and the Friends wh. all use Yesu Kristo as well as U.M.C.A. will alter their practice because Uganda writes Isa Masiya and Mombasa writes Jesu Masihi? It is C.M.S. who ought to fall into line with the other Xtian missions: not v.v. I have written at length to the Most Revd. about this.[55]

Hine clearly felt himself in a position to speak for all the missionary societies in eastern Africa, but this crotchety confidence was combined with the desire to create a united linguistic front. The CMS, with its own storied history of Swahili learning and translating, was the only society to attempt to oppose the UMCA's Swahili translations.[56] But in 1906, the *Yesu Kristo* debate came to a close when the bishops of Uganda and Zanzibar, along with other interested parties, met at Lambeth Palace in London, seat of the archbishop of Canterbury. "After much discussion," Hine reported, "it was agreed that our UMCA Prayer Book should be printed forthwith by S.P.C.K., with the form 'Yesu Kristo' throughout, but with an explanatory note stating that this was equivalent to the old form 'Isa Masiya.'"[57] The controversy generated over the translation of a single (albeit rather central) phrase, and the resolution of the conflict in favor of the UMCA, presaged the vehemence and eventual outcome of future debates about Standard Swahili.

The reasons behind the UMCA's switch from *Isa Masiya* to *Yesu Kristo* were never discussed on paper. Madan's 1903 Swahili-English dictionary included an entry for *Isa,* defined as "a proper name, not uncommon in Z[anzibar]. Also the only name for Jesus Christ known to Mahommedans,—often with the addition *bin Maryamu.*"[58] Perhaps, then, the mission linguists decided to switch to *Yesu Kristo* in the belief that it would have a clearer meaning for readers—to set this particular Christian *Isa* apart from the *Isa* of Islam and of daily life on Zanzibar. In any event, there was among the UMCA membership a willingness to revise—with an eye toward a timeless standard. As soon as the new Prayerbook was issued, Hine reflected on the translation: "No one I suppose regrets the introduction of the form 'Yesu Kristo' in place of 'Isa Masiya': none of our people ever thinks now of using the older form."[59] Ironically, it seems, in the effort to achieve a timeless, widely understood standard, nothing was sacred.

THE AFRICAN PRIESTS OF THE TRANSLATION COMMITTEE

The African members of the Translation Committee were among the elite of mission society. Ackworth Machaku and Acland Misenga were teachers,

Samuel Chiponde a future priest, and Cecil Majaliwa and Peter Limo had already been ordained. The participation of all five men in the work of the committee demonstrates one of the ways in which standardization began to emerge as an actors' category around the turn of the century: translations were no longer to be the product of testing in the classroom and contributions sent to *Msimulizi* but were now overseen by the mission's top figures, both European and African.

The biographies of Majaliwa and Limo offer particularly pertinent examples. Cecil Majaliwa was the first African to be ordained priest by the Universities' Mission, in 1890.[60] He came to the mission as a former slave, received his schooling at Kiungani, and rose through the ranks from reader to deacon to priest, at the same time learning to read and write in the mission's Swahili standard. In 1884, Majaliwa spent a year in England, at St. Augustine's College, Canterbury.[61] His career took Majaliwa and his family (he married Lucy Mgombeani in 1879 and they eventually had nine children) back and forth from Zanzibar to the mainland, where he also learned to speak Yao.[62] In 1892, he even translated an Altar Book into the Yao language.[63] In fact, Majaliwa began his work as a translator even earlier than that, beginning with a Swahili translation of "Agathos and other Stories" in 1882.[64] He wrote English well, and by 1893 his mastery was such that he was requesting "a good Eng.-Greek lexicon" in *Central Africa*.[65] The work of the Translation Committee fit right in with Majaliwa's hobby; he was proficient in the two main languages of the mission (Swahili and English) and on an even footing with his European counterparts on the committee. Despite a few late-career scandals, Majaliwa recovered his position and lived out his life in the Mbweni neighborhood as *Mzee* (Elder) Padre Majaliwa.[66]

The second African priest who was a member of the Translation Committee was Peter (Petro) Limo. Limo's early life unfolded very differently from Majaliwa's. Unlike his formerly enslaved classmate, Limo was born to a powerful family in the Magila region.[67] While he later remembered the influence of Islam in his early life, Limo attended a mission school at Umba as a young boy, and he was baptized and finished his elementary schooling at the Magila station. He moved to Kiungani in 1886 to train as a teacher.[68] In 1889, Limo traveled to England, where he studied for three years at the Dorchester Missionary College, funded through appeals in *Central Africa*.[69] While in England, Limo spoke at various fundraising meetings, perfecting his English and bolstering support for the mission.[70] When he returned to Zanzibar in 1893, he was ordained as a deacon, and in 1894 he became a priest. Mission publications variously lauded Limo as the "first free born native to be so raised" and "the first Bondei to receive Holy Orders."[71] His ordination, like

Majaliwa's, was celebrated throughout the mission, and schoolchildren were given holidays and special treats.[72] Soon after his ordination, Limo married Blandina M., a pupil-teacher at Mbweni who had also studied in England.[73] He had expressed a desire that his future wife "be a help to him in his work, and very much wished her to be really well educated."[74] Peter and Blandina went to work at Kwa Kibai, a new station near Magila. They also spent time at Mkuzi, Misozwe, and Korogwe (all in the Magila region). Limo's final posting on the mainland was to Kwa Magome, to which he moved in 1909. The work there went on until Limo was imprisoned, along with other African clergy, by the German army in 1916.

Like Majaliwa, Limo began his work as a translator very early in his career, helping Rev. John Farler complete a translation of the Gospel of St. Matthew into the Bondei language in 1887, and working on a Bondei Prayerbook the following year.[75] According to Farler, Limo could speak "English, Swahili, Bondei, a little Hindustani, as well as writing in Arabic characters," into which he transliterated a version of St. Matthew in 1891.[76] His English was highly proficient, despite his insecurities about it: "I should like very much to write to the African Tidings [an English-language mission periodical] but I always afraid of my English, you see it must be very good one to make people understand what you mean in writing."[77] He was central to the Translation Committee's revision of the Swahili New Testament, staying at Zanzibar after the 1896 synod to participate in the work.[78]

Limo, Majaliwa, and their counterparts on the Translation Committee were among the elite of the mission society, highly educated teachers and clergymen who were given official status as standardizers. Their work with the Translation Committee erases any idea that linguistic knowledge production, even after the turn of the twentieth century, was wholly in the hands of European missionaries and academics. But their participation does little to illuminate the wider embrace of the mission's written standard of Swahili; to uncover a sense of this, it is helpful to follow the African adherents throughout the *Upelekwa* who used the language as their personal means of communication.

LETTERS FROM AFRICANS

Among the archival boxes held in the UMCA collection at the Weston Library in Oxford there is a file labeled, rather offhandedly, "Letters from Africans." It contains fifty-six letters sent from Africa to Europe in the late nineteenth and early twentieth centuries, some of them part of ongoing correspondence and others seemingly one-off missives. Even taking into consideration the coincidence of preservation, these letters could have

begun to proliferate only around the turn of the century: their production necessitated that a requisite number of students had been through
the mission's Swahili-language education system and then been scattered
among the mainland stations. This collection of letters demonstrates the
ways in which African adherents used their Swahili literacy to emphasize
their membership in the mission community, reinforcing the *Upelekwa* that
had been established during the late nineteenth century.[79] As the twentieth century dawned, their Swahili literacy served as a tool for ensuring the
community's survival through periods of violence, famine, sickness, and the
ever-tightening straps of European colonial rule.

The largest set of correspondence in this collection consists of the
letters of Agnes Sapuli, a female teacher and member of the mission who
lived in southeastern Tanganyika, and who wrote some twenty missives
that eventually wound up in this archival box in England.[80] Agnes's life, as
seen through her letters, reveals the contours of a transcontinental network that interlaced the stations of the Universities' Mission, from Zanzibar
to Lake Nyasa and even on to England. It was a network built upon religion, to be sure; upon affective relationships within and between genders,
unquestionably—but these central elements of the community were linked
across time and space by the mission's written Swahili standard.[81] Swahili was the language that spanned the mission's scattered stations, each
embedded in its own linguistic milieu. Swahili was also the language that
crossed generational, educational, and ethnic boundaries within the UMCA
community.

Agnes Sapuli wrote these letters to her English sponsor, Rev. Cyril Child,
between 1898 and 1912. Almost all the letters include both the original Swahili and an English translation; Andreana Prichard suggests that the Swahili
versions were dictated by Sapuli and written by an amanuensis, which is
possible, given the different handwriting apparent in the letters. It is also
possible, of course, that the letters were copied at some later time, perhaps
in the process of translation.[82] Ajanjeuli Achitinao (who would be baptized
as Agnes) was born in the early 1880s at Chitangali, a village in the region of
the UMCA's Masasi station. She entered the mission's records in the 1890s
via the pen of Cecil Majaliwa, who came to Chitangali first as a teacher and
then, in 1890, as the mission's first African priest.[83] Cecil's wife Lucy started
a day school for girls, and Achitinao was one of her students; according to
Majaliwa, Achitinao could not yet be baptized because she was too young
to withstand pressure from her parents and their "wicked heathen customs."[84] In 1895, Achitinao and her family moved to Chiwata, and two years
after that, a missionary wrote to Rev. Child about "your girl Ajanjeuli."[85] By

that time, she was officially a sponsored student, whose education would thenceforth be paid for by Rev. Child's St. Agnes Church in Kennington Park, London. That same missionary priest reported, "She is delightfully promising, age about 14—bright—clever so much above the average that she is a sort of pupil teacher under Hugh's wife at Chiwata."[86] Achitinao was still unbaptized, but the priest hoped to do so by Christmas of 1897, and asked Child if he would like her to take the baptismal name of Agnes, after Child's parish church.[87]

It was in 1898 that Achitinao began writing to Child herself, reporting in one of her first letters that she had indeed been baptized and given the name Agnes.[88] This was the beginning of a chain of correspondence that continued for more than a decade. Agnes's letters displayed the simultaneous normalcy of communication at long distances and the uncertainty of those communicative links. "I hope you will get this letter before or close to Christmas," she wrote in November of 1899.[89] Agnes had to account for the time it would take to get her letters to Masasi, let alone from there to the coast to catch a mail steamer. She explained in another letter: "Tell Miss Clara Garnett hello and that I will write her a letter for the second mail, today I am very rushed because tomorrow is the post at Masasi and here our place is a bit far from Masasi."[90] From there, letters would be carried to the port city of Lindi, to be sent on to their various destinations via Zanzibar or, after the 1890s, the steamer service put in place by the German colonial administration. As always, however, weather, political upheaval, accidents, and other mishaps could disrupt this flow of correspondence. Yet Agnes, like her fellow African letter writers, relied on these connections to communicate with the mission center at Zanzibar and with her English patron.

Just as Agnes began writing to Child, she also became engaged to Francis Sapuli, a student of the Chitangali school who had trained as a teacher on Zanzibar. The couple was married in 1900 (in the interim both of Agnes's parents had died) and they settled at Mwiti, where they taught at the mission school.[91] In September 1901, Agnes gave birth to her first child, a daughter who was baptized Rose Annie Sapuli.[92] Over the course of her life, Agnes gave birth to six children, but only Rose Annie and John Owen (born in June of 1912) survived past childhood.[93]

Agnes and Francis Sapuli emphasized literary education for their children. They sent Rose Annie, their eldest child, to a mission boarding school at Masasi when she was ten years old.[94] A year later, Agnes reported on her daughter's progress: "Now she knows how to read and write and sew a little bit."[95] When she was able to write well, Agnes continued, Rose would send the children of the church a letter of her own.[96] Rose did eventually write a letter, in Swahili, to the students at St. Agnes, offering up small bits of news about her own school and her family, and concluding, "I want to get your letters and as for me this is truly the first letter I have written to you in my own hand."[97] Her brother John Owen also attended school: though his education was interrupted by World War I, in 1924 he entered the Central School in Chiwata. For religious and likely also secular reasons (such as job and marriage prospects), the Sapulis placed great importance on their children's literacy and specifically, based on Rose's letter, literacy in the mission's Swahili standard—the language that connected them to all aspects of the mission community.

In 1910, Francis became a reader—a lay evangelist—and he and Agnes moved multiple times in the Masasi region as Francis embarked on this new work.[98] The Sapuli family was in Chilimba when World War I came crashing down on eastern Africa, and Agnes's letters cease to appear. Sapuli in fact survived the global war only to fall ill and die during her seventh pregnancy, on August 9, 1918. Francis wrote to Child (in English), giving an account of Agnes's last days. He grieved, but wrote that he drew consolation from her piety in the face of death, recounting, "Oh! she died in faith indeed . . . so your prayers which you prayed for her for many years, I can say without hesitation that God had heard it."[99] Francis's letter brought to an end the remarkable correspondence between Agnes Sapuli and Child, a correspondence that had traveled along the UMCA's transcontinental network from two of its extreme ends.

Agnes's life as reflected in her letters to Child displays the type of "affective spiritual community" described in the work of Andreana Prichard.[100] She carefully sent greetings to specific members of Child's parish, asking after their health, the news of the Church of St. Agnes, and of Child himself.[101] "What news these days there in Europe?" she inquired casually in 1900.[102] In their home, she and Francis prominently displayed a photograph of Child's church. "It reminds me every day of my friends of St. Agnes," she wrote of one such photo.[103]

She also promised to send a photograph of herself and her family at the soonest opportunity.[104] After the war and Agnes's death, in 1919, Francis wrote to Child saying that he would like to dedicate his church at Chilimba to Saint Agnes's parish, "for our thanksgiving to you, as you know that for your alms and prayers to us we done our work. So tell our friends of St. Agnes."[105] This was a symbolic but clearly very meaningful exchange for Francis. The network outlined by the Sapulis' letters spanned mainland East Africa, Zanzibar, and England; it was a community made up of fellow worshippers, of patrons and clients, students and teachers, family members and friends. But how exactly did Swahili fit into these affective connections?

FIGURE 3.1. St. Agnes Place at Kennington Park, London. Photo by author.

FIGURE 3.2. St. Agnes
Church, rebuilt after
World War II. Photo
by author.

Agnes Sapuli's first language was likely Yao, Makua, Makonde, or one of the languages of southeastern Tanganyika. When she began writing to Child, Agnes was a teenager and had attended school for about eight years. Her fluency in Swahili is indicative of the emphasis placed on that language at the UMCA schools, even on the mainland.[106] Though she (and her husband) would have taught and preached in the Makua, Makonde, or Yao languages while working at mainland stations, their interactions with European missionaries and non-Makua/Makonde/Yao speakers, as well as Francis's education at the theological college on Zanzibar, would all have taken place in Swahili. And Swahili was the language of choice for Agnes's communication with her main epistolary correspondent. Her husband, Francis—who was himself a good English writer—likewise turned to Swahili when he had much to say. In 1924, after a two-year stretch without sending a letter, Francis wrote to Child (in Swahili): "The reason I do not write this letter in English today is because I need to be able to write a lot, so that you can know how I have been since leaving Hegongo."[107] Through such letters, we can begin to see how Swahili served as a connecting thread of the *Upelekwa:* the affective relationship between Agnes Sapuli and Child was maintained through Swahili, and without this flexible but durable thread, the transcontinental network might have stretched to breaking.

A WORLD WAR AND ITS AFTERMATH

In March of 1904 a familiar sight rolled off the press at Zanzibar: a pamphlet announcing, "To all Kiungani fellows, greetings, and after greetings I inform you that I have come to stay!"[108] It was the first issue of the second run of *Msimulizi,* under the joint editorship of Revs. Frank Weston and Samwil Chiponde. The magazine had not, in fact, come to stay—it ran for only five issues, until February 1905. And, appearing eight years after its last nineteenth-century issue, the familiar voice of *Msimulizi* found itself forced to reflect on changed times. Such reflection was made most explicit in an anonymous article that spanned two (planned for three) issues, titled "*Ya Kale si ya Sasa*" ("The Past Is Not the Present").[109] The article followed two hypothetical journeys from coast to interior, one, "*ya kale,*" which included dangerous robbers and animals, starvation and dehydration, and a low survival rate; the second, "*ya sasa,*" was taken comfortably on a steam train. "So what do you think?" asked the article's author. "The past is not the present. All matters of the past have disappeared leaving only the present. And of the present-day countries, all are peaceful, from the coast to Buganda."[110] An uninspired interpretation of "progress," perhaps, yet none could escape the fact that East Africa's landscape—physical and political—had indeed changed since the magazine's first run. But if the author of "*Ya Kale si ya Sasa*" was keenly aware of the alterations wrought by colonial encroachment, he or she could never have anticipated the outbreak of World War I and the ruptures it would bring to the region.[111] The consequences of the war were devastating for countless communities across the continent, the Universities' Mission included. For the mission's African teachers on the mainland, the war brought imprisonment and physical violence. For those who escaped imprisonment, the war brought disease and famine, requisitions of food, cloth, paper, and other necessities, and for many men, impressment into work as porters.[112] In German territory, African clergy and teachers often took sole charge of mission stations upon the imprisonment of the British staff, and many African clergymen were also imprisoned.[113] Thus the war's effects on the mission community were double-edged: in some aspects it was torn apart—physically, communicatively, and spiritually—but these disruptions forced those who remained to strengthen their ties. And in some cases, the war put the African members of the mission into unprecedented positions of authority, both spiritual and secular. World War I and the period of rebuilding that followed was a time of heightened power for African leaders of the mission, a moment that came just as the British colonial state began to crowd the UMCA out of the standardization arena.

One could write an entire book about the experiences of the UMCA congregations during the war, but I must resist that temptation here. In November of 1918, German General Paul von Lettow-Vorbeck led his troops to Abercorn in Northern Rhodesia, surrendering to the Allied forces there. By that time, the British occupation of German East Africa was largely complete, and the European and African teachers and clergy of the Universities' Mission had all been released from German prisons and were beginning to return to their stations. The mission faced a "Now what?" moment of immense proportions: huge swathes of the mission's infrastructure had been destroyed, especially in the mainland portions of the Zanzibar diocese; the steamers of Lake Nyasa had been requisitioned by the British army; and large numbers of students and adherents had lost years of education and religious reinforcement due to imprisonment, impressment, or simple lack of access to schools, teachers, and priests. Many had died, and survivors continued to suffer from famine and the postwar outbreaks of diseases such as influenza and smallpox. Though the signing of the armistice was obviously an occurrence of great joy for the members of the Universities' Mission both in England and Africa, it was also a moment of reckoning for the mission that confronted the massive task of rebuilding, as well as renewed pressure to expand its work. "The war is over," reflected Bishop Cathrew Fisher of Nyasaland. "The end has been so bewildering in its suddenness that it is difficult to face the next stage. We have been saying 'after the War' so steadily and so regularly and so long, that now it really is after the war, it is almost difficult to realize that we need do so no longer."[114]

The four years of despair had divergent consequences for the mission and its work of evangelization. On one hand, many Christians experienced a crisis of faith, and in some areas, especially in southeastern Tanganyika, Islam gained a number of converts.[115] On the other hand, the removal of most European missionaries during World War I put African teachers and clergymen into unprecedented and unanticipated positions of both spiritual and secular power.[116] Rather than representing a drastic change of course—the mission had always relied on African interlocutors and knowledge producers, and had looked to a future African-led church—the immediate post–World War I years sped up the timeline.

And despite the magnitude of the task and countless reasons for pessimism, the on-the-ground leadership of the mission approached the prospect of rebuilding with surprising optimism. Schools reopened, churches were rebuilt, and life returned to a semblance of normalcy even in the hardest-hit areas. In fact, the mission leadership presented the rebuilding process as an opportunity for expansion, especially into territory formerly worked by German missionary societies.[117] New stations were built, including at Milo (on the northeast coast of Lake Nyasa) and Mkushi (in Northern Rhodesia), while some parishes and archdeaconries were reapportioned to more evenly distribute adherents and clergy. The optimism came through most clearly in accounts of the spiritual steadfastness demonstrated by the mission's African adherents during the war, often in the absence of any reinforcement. Article after article in *Central Africa* praised their resilience in the face of this European-caused destruction.[118] Archdeacon William Percival Johnson visited the stations around Lake Nyasa and reported that the teachers had carefully kept the registers of catechumens and hearers: "Some of the books were battered and torn but there was not a page lost."[119] While the war had uprooted the mission's carefully laid plans and leveled some of its classrooms and churches, the missionaries, at least, had to make themselves see its silver lining: "But we can thank God with all our hearts because the war has shown to us most vividly what marvelously sterling stuff these native teachers are made of."[120] Soon after the war ended, Bishop Frank Weston ordained seven priests, after an accelerated track through deaconship to the priesthood.[121] This postwar Africanization policy was above all a necessary strategy to fill positions for which there were not enough English recruits, rather than a strictly progressive move on the part of the Universities' Mission. But the purported recommitment to an "African church" did solidify the place of Swahili in the missionary imagination as a necessary tool for evangelization.

As we have seen, since the UMCA had begun establishing stations on the mainland in the 1870s, the mission had followed a two-pronged approach to language in its schools and churches. Initial evangelization and schooling were conducted in local languages (or as close as the missionaries could come). As soon as possible, however, the medium of instruction switched to Swahili.[122] This policy persisted into the interwar years; by the time a student arrived at one of the mission's central diocesan schools, the medium of instruction would have been Swahili.[123] An article published in 1919 in *Central Africa* neatly summed up the mission's language policy: "The ideal seems to be for hearers [i.e., those who were informally learning about Christianity from the mission] to be taught in the vernacular, and for catechumens [i.e., those training specifically for baptism] gradually to learn Swahili. . . . Probably the Swahili language will ultimately triumph over the other dialects."[124] Even at the new station of Milo, in the sphere formerly worked by German missionaries who preferred local vernaculars over Swahili, one observer noted that the latter was "more or less spoken in the villages, and if taught in our schools it would soon be the *lingua franca* of the parish and obviate the necessity for endless translations."[125] Facing the very obvious turning of a new page following the war, the Universities' Mission continued to emphasize Swahili as central to its community's linguistic identity, even (perhaps especially) as that community slowly continued to grow.

~

The first two decades of the twentieth century was a period marked by both great change and notable continuity. Politically there was the consolidation of colonial rule, including the administration of German East Africa and the British protectorate on Zanzibar. There were two major conflicts in the territory that would become Tanganyika (Maji Maji and World War I), and the aftereffects of those wars. In the period between 1885 and World War I, the German colonial administration had declined to take up the project of language standardization in a concerted, official way, though the language was used in its schools and offices around the territory. Meanwhile, the UMCA had created a body—the Translation Committee—tasked with revision, explicitly aiming for permanent, standardized versions of its Swahili texts. For each of these communities in East Africa, Swahili was the common denominator.

Within the longer history of Standard Swahili being traced here, we see the effects of structural constraints—the German colonial administration, the Translation Committee, and wartime deprivations and incarceration—as well as of grassroots possibility—the letters connecting east-central Africa to Zanzibar or England. The standardization efforts of the early twentieth century toggled between such short-term and long-term efforts, and between unofficial and highly controlled projects, presaging the processes that would continue under British colonial administration, with several communities-in-creation converging on a single but expansive linguistic project.

It is true that, whether we are talking about the teachers and students at German government schools, or the UMCA and its African adherents, we are talking about a slim minority of the population of East Africa. And as Derek Peterson has reminded his fellow historians, "The interpretation of vernacular literature in Africa and elsewhere has been clouded by assumptions about the organic connection between authors and their communities."[126] The contributors to *Msimulizi*, for instance, did not speak for a single, uniform community—these were people divided by location, education, vocation, and countless personal distinctions. Yet the persistent use of Swahili, particularly in writing and print, put the UMCA's version of Kiunguja into the position to be taken up by the official British project of language standardization. After decades of individual and regional uncertainty, the idea of imposing a standardized language emerged as a potential tool of order, appealing to the colonizer to be sure, but not entirely anathema to the interests of some among the colonized. Thus, the Swahili standard of the UMCA emerged in a position of power through a combination of coincidence and conscious decision-making, pragmatism and utopianism. Everyone was improvising in this period of reconstruction, and though Swahili was not predestined to become the British administration's language of choice, nor was it a wholly unlikely candidate. Swahili had long been a language of power, deployed in different ways and by different people at various times, by some with more and some with less authority. And beginning in the 1920s, the language was folded into official British efforts to govern their newly configured colonies of East Africa.

4 ~ Interlocutors in Interterritorial Codification

IN MARCH of 1932, a frustrated army captain filed an official complaint with the British Civil Service Commission in London. Captain J. B. Cooper of the Gloucestershire Regiment had served with the King's African Rifles in East Africa and was seeking a post as interpreter of Swahili. Cooper, however, had failed his language examination, and subsequently wrote to the Commission claiming that "he was not examined, as he had requested, in 'Standardized Ki-Swahili' which he asserts is 'now in use as the official master language in Tanganyika, Uganda and Kenya.'"[1] The complaint worked its way up through the system to the head of the Civil Service Commission, L. C. H. Weekes, who spoke with the commissioners on the ground as well as the examiner who had conducted Cooper's exam, none of whom could clarify his questions about "Standardized Ki-Swahili." Weekes then wrote to the Colonial Office, indicating that he and his colleagues "would be glad if they could be informed what this consists of and for how long it has been in official use."[2] In a draft reply, the Colonial Office wrote up a brief history of the establishment of the Inter-Territorial Language Committee in East Africa, noting that a standard dialect had been adopted in 1925 and that in 1928 a resolution was passed "that in all Government examinations held after the year 1932, spelling other than that of the Standard Swahili be not accepted."[3] This resolution was subject to the approval of the four territorial governments concerned, and in 1931 the government of Kenya had decided "to continue to permit the Languages Board to exercise the greatest latitude in the matter of spelling of Swahili used in Government examinations."[4] Of course, such flexibility could have helped Captain Cooper in his quest to become an interpreter, but in this case it seems that the linguistic ambiguity had scuttled his ambitions. Weekes finally wrote back to the War Office to the effect that Standard Swahili, while a recognized entity, would only become "obligatory" for all four territories (Kenya, Tanganyika, Uganda, and Zanzibar) at the end of 1932, "and that, if [Cooper] presents himself thereafter for examination in Swahili, the examination will take place in the standardized language."[5] Cooper's complaint and the responses it received reflect the concerns of the main actors in standardization in the 1920s, 1930s, and early 1940s—namely, What shape would Standard Swahili take and who should have the authority to decide? How to get four colonial territories working together on the nitpicking work of orthographic, lexicographic, and grammatical standardization? And, finally, was investment in this linguistic tool—Standard Swahili—worth all that effort?

The Inter-Territorial Language Committee (ILC) was the official governmental body in charge of linguistic decisions regarding Standard Swahili. Conceived in 1925 and meeting for the first time in 1930, the ILC was soaked in worries about time. In the short-term, the territories of Tanganyika, Kenya, Uganda, and Zanzibar needed textbooks for all school levels; they needed a medium of instruction for classrooms; and they needed to be able to tell civil servants how to study for required language exams. In the long-term, the members of the ILC felt that English could only serve these purposes in the distant future, so their responsibility was to decide upon a durable, uniform way of writing Swahili. As one member of the committee insisted, while using Standard Swahili would initially be awkward for some, especially those accustomed to other dialects, such sacrifice "does not amount to much when weighed against the great benefit, due to standardization, which will accrue to millions who use this language now and to the unborn millions *who will use it in the future*."[6] In the vision of the ILC, as we shall see, standardization was never absolute, never perfect or complete, but it was the consistent goal that drove linguists and civil servants alike.

The ILC was also torn between the top-down nature of its project—to police a language standard of its own creation—and its need for assistance from East Africans, low-level bureaucrats, and missionaries from around the region. Standardization, even in its most official and concerted version, was never solely top-down nor bottom-up, never just a short-term fix nor a permanent solution. In the 1930s and 1940s, practicality bumped up against perfection, idealism against bureaucracy, and confusion against clarity. To examine these counterposing forces, this chapter focuses on the ILC and in particular its production of three dictionaries—Swahili-Swahili, English-Swahili, and Swahili-English.

Dictionaries, for all their reputation as dust-collecting decoration, can actually reveal a great deal about both power and time: their production starts with vast amounts of information gathering, sifting, and organization; it requires countless decisions that are then concealed behind the comforting pattern of alphabetic entry, etymology, and confident definition. Once in published form, dictionaries promise a synchronic snapshot of the lexical richness of a language, while simultaneously linking it diachronically, first backward, to the language's "naturally occurring" words and definitions, and then forward, trying to leave room for future shifts in meaning.[7] This is the dictionary's highly revealing "essential tension": the attempt to encompass both the "traditionalist" and the "iconoclast."[8] It is a remarkable, almost utopian tool, combining practicality with idealism by systematically and comprehensively containing, in an easily accessible way, the building blocks of an entire means of communication. As Rev. A. B. Hellier remarked in the early days of the ILC: "I am not interested in what must be, but what is, and when we find a variety of usage we ought to formulate a rule wide enough to cover all the variations."[9] Even the most optimistic of standardizers would have to concede the impossibility of Hellier's proposal, and yet this ideal drove much of the work of the ILC in its first twenty years of existence.

A close study of the ILC, its Swahili dictionaries, and the reception of standardization in parts of the Swahili-language press in the 1930s and 1940s exposes the multitude of timelines, incentives, people, and ideas involved. Dictionaries, as Derek Peterson has asserted, are "fundamentally dialogical," and in this chapter I seek to uncover such dialogues, sometimes more and sometimes less one-sided.[10] Beginning with an overview of the post–WWI British administrations in East Africa, the chapter then turns to the establishment of the Inter-Territorial Language Committee, starting with the 1925 Education Conference in Dar es Salaam, before turning to the ILC's dictionary projects and the Swahili-language press in Tanganyika.

BRITISH COLONIAL ADMINISTRATIONS IN EAST AFRICA

Following World War I, the League of Nations distributed German colonial territories in Africa to other European powers as "mandates." In this way the former German East Africa became Tanganyika Territory, under the control of the British Colonial Office.[11] In the meantime, the East Africa Protectorate had become the Crown Colony of Kenya, while Uganda and Zanzibar maintained their protectorate statuses. Each colonial territory offered different sets of administrative challenges: Kenya had to deal with a relatively large and powerful population of European settlers; Uganda officials had the centrality of the kingdom of Buganda to contend with; Zanzibar was ostensibly under the rule of the sultan; and the Tanganyika administration felt some pressure to live up to the League of Nations mandate and its emphasis on the "well-being and development" of the indigenous population.[12] Besides different administrative obstacles, the place of Swahili also varied in each of the British East African territories in the 1920s and 1930s. Generally speaking, Kenya administrators questioned the dialectical decisions of the ILC; Uganda officials generally favored the use of English as the protectorate's unifying language; and on Zanzibar, administrators faced relatively strong demands for Arabic and South Asian languages to be accommodated in schools and official publications. From the beginning, officials in Tanganyika Territory championed the cause of interterritorial language unification on the basis of a standardized version of Swahili, at times over the intransigence of their cross-territorial colleagues. This meant that Tanganyika often disproportionately influenced the work of the ILC.

As we have seen, the German colonial regime had adopted Swahili for most administrative purposes, so the language was already well-positioned to serve in the same role for Britain. Much like the German decision to utilize Swahili, the British decision was ultimately made out of a combination of pragmatics (it would take a long time to establish widespread English-language literacy across the territory, and creating infrastructure in all the local languages would be expensive); racism (the idea that East Africans did not "deserve" or should be kept away from the benefits of English literacy); and in the case of Tanganyika, a nod toward the League of Nations ideal of "development" along local lines. Just a few years into mandate rule, meanwhile, the Tanganyika administration had been chastised by the American Phelps-Stokes Commission and the Colonial Office for sluggishness in embracing "adapted education" policies—criticism which Governor Donald Cameron was determined to meet with educational reform.[13]

ESTABLISHMENT OF THE INTER-TERRITORIAL LANGUAGE COMMITTEE

To that end, on October 5, 1925, fifty people gathered in Dar es Salaam to begin planning the future of education in Tanganyika. Attendees included government and missionary representatives. Cameron opened the conference, and then left the proceedings under the control of his Director of Education, Stanley Rivers-Smith. Over the course of eight days, the conferees listened to papers presented on various topics pertaining to education. In the afternoons, the participants broke off into subcommittees to prepare reports on specific issues. The most prominent subcommittee was

FIGURE 4.1. 1925 Education Conference in session. From "Conference between Government and Missions, Report of Proceedings, Dar es Salaam, 5th to 12th October 1925." Columbia University Library.

the Committee for the Standardisation of the Swahili Language. After four days of deliberation, the committee submitted its report, which began by emphasizing the reach of Swahili and therefore its suitability as a medium of instruction. The committee recognized the need to choose a standard for this language of multiple dialects, and the report's first resolution laid to rest any remaining dialectical controversy, declaring "that the Zanzibar dialect with such modifications as may be required be adopted as the Standard form of Swahili."[14] More specifically, "that if permission could be obtained for their revision, the Exercise book and Hand book (grammar portion only) by Bishop Steere would be the most suitable for adoption as a standard grammar, and Madan's Dictionaries as a standard work."[15] With these two short resolutions, the Zanzibar dialect (Kiunguja), as codified by the Universities' Mission to Central Africa (UMCA) and its adherents over the course of some six decades, became the basis of *Standard* Swahili.

The committee had settled on Kiunguja in the belief that it was the most widely understood dialect. In fact, they believed its use in East Africa to be expanding, as opposed to the "confined and local use" of the Mombasa dialect (Kimvita), the only other dialect that had been seriously in contention.[16] Frederick Johnson, who would become the first secretary of the

Inter-Territorial Language Committee, claimed that though the differences between the dialects were slight, they were "just sufficiently [different] so to cause books to be printed in that of Mombasa to present a certain amount of difficulty to the natives, especially the less educated ones, of Tanganyika Territory and Zanzibar," while on the other hand "the Mombasa natives as well as those living up country in Kenya would find no difficulty in reading and understanding books printed in the Zanzibar dialect, or a modification of it."[17] Whether or not these statements reflected actual sociolinguistic reality in 1925, this was the perspective of those who would go on to organize the Inter-Territorial Language Committee.[18]

The choice of the UMCA's standard, based on the Zanzibar dialect, did not go altogether uncontested. The main dissenters included partisans of Kimvita, and at a follow-up meeting in 1928 the proceedings reportedly became emotional when the Kiunguja decision was confirmed. As Ronald Snoxall (later a secretary of the ILC) recounted, "The late Canon Crawford [of the Church Missionary Society] had to be led from the room in tears."[19] Wilfred Whiteley, another future ILC secretary, would reflect that "the bitterness which this decision engendered was slow to subside."[20] Part of this bitterness stemmed from the fact that there were no representatives from either Kenya or Uganda present in Dar es Salaam; nevertheless, in 1925 the conference participants quickly confirmed the proposals of the Standardisation Committee and the decisions were communicated to administrators in all of Britain's East African territories.[21] Over the next five years, the four governments confirmed the choice of the Zanzibar dialect as the basis of Standard Swahili, and various proposals circulated between the Conference of the Governors, Directors of Education, and other officials within Britain's East African administrations, setting the parameters of the committee's work.

Before the ILC's first meeting, however, the four governments had to agree on where the committee should be headquartered—a question with both logistic and linguistic considerations. Rivers-Smith recognized that Nairobi might be more convenient for all involved, but he wished to headquarter the organization in Swahili's "natural environment of the coast."[22] F. J. Durman, Tanganyika's acting chief secretary in 1929, agreed but considered Mombasa "to be unsuitable owing to the influence of the Ki-mvita dialect."[23] Meanwhile, the Secretariat on Zanzibar was pushing for Mombasa, while the Uganda government wanted the headquarters at Nairobi because of its centrality. In the end, the committee headquarters were placed at Dar es Salaam, though the first meeting was held in Nairobi. Another decision made prior to that meeting was the appointment of a secretary to head the ILC. The position of chairman would rotate among the various hosts of the annual meetings, but the secretary would set the longer-term agenda, so the choice was significant. Consensus fell rapidly upon Frederick Johnson, the superintendent of education for Tanganyika—so rapidly, in fact, that Johnson was appointed to the position while on leave, apparently without having been officially offered (or officially accepting) the job.[24] He complained briefly about the salary being offered, though his acceptance seemed a foregone conclusion. Subsequent correspondence before the first meeting shows that Johnson was also concerned about the selection of two African clerks to work in his office, and particularly whether they would be entitled to remain members of the African Civil Service.[25] Johnson was especially anxious about the appointment of Rawson Watts, inquiring soon after accepting the job as secretary when Watts would be available for transfer to his office, eventually succeeding in having him moved from the Department of Education to the ILC.[26]

With the secretary and his office in place, the first meeting of the Inter-Territorial Language Committee occurred on April 26, 1930. The ILC consisted of sixteen members, two official and two nonofficial from each of the four territories.[27] Though the attendees at the 1925 conference had resolved that "native representatives be included in their number," there were no Africans appointed to the ILC until 1939. In that year, the committee amended its constitution to officially include non-European members, and the first three East Africans invited to join were Sheikh Mbarak Ali Hinawy, Sheikh Abdulla Muhammad el-Hadhramy, and Stephano Mgalawe—though because of wartime travel restrictions, they were not able to attend their first full committee meeting until 1946.[28] The permanent staff included the secretary, four readers (one per territory), and two African clerks.

At the first ILC meeting, several short-term objectives were discussed, including the production of books in Swahili, particularly of textbooks. The ILC quickly approved a procedure for the submission of works for review: after the four Directors of Education approved the content of a proposed textbook, the manuscript would "then be submitted to two of the Readers of the Committee for perusal from the point of view of language only."[29] This was the birth of the ILC imprimatur, which would adorn the title pages of books for years to come. Another urgent goal of the committee was the revision of Madan's Swahili dictionaries, and at this first meeting a subcommittee was appointed to begin that process. Until the dictionaries could be compiled and published, the committee resolved to circulate lists of words to publishers, government officials, and mission societies, both to encourage consistency and to solicit suggestions. "By these means," the meeting report noted, "a definite move has been made towards uniformity."[30] Following up on this suggestion, in October of 1930 the first issue of the ILC *Bulletin* was published, which compiled lexical suggestions from readers and the secretary for public perusal.[31]

The third meeting of the ILC took place on Zanzibar in 1932. There the committee members finalized a proposed constitution, a copy of which was then sent to the four governments for approval; the final document was published in 1934.[32] The evolution of the ILC constitution reveals some of the tensions inherent in the organization's philosophy of standardization. For example, the draft constitution stated: "The central aim of the Committee shall be to promote the development of the Swahili Language into an adequate medium for the expression of thought."[33] In one copy, a reader left a single exclamation point in the margin next to this clause, simply expressing surprise, insult, and/or disbelief at the idea that Swahili was not already "an adequate medium."[34] The final version swept this disparaging phrase under the rug, stating rather aseptically, "The central aim of the Committee shall be to promote the standardisation and development of the Swahili language."[35] The conversation continued, however, in the footnotes, in which it was conceded that "the Committee recognises that while such development should and must be mainly the work of those to whom Swahili is the mother-tongue, much initial European help is necessary."[36] Ambiguity of authority was thus baked into the very constitution of the ILC.

The committee did not, however, always shy away from fundamental questions about standardization—though it attempted to defend its approach at every turn. In 1934, a contentious set of articles was published in the *Bulletin,* opening with this question: "*Is the Inter-Territorial Language Committee working on the right lines?*"[37] The first article, titled "Modern Swahili," was written by an anonymous officer working in the education department of Kenya. It is worth quoting at length, for the article touches upon several contemporary and lasting criticisms of the ILC:

> We have standardised Swahili and in the process Swahili seems to have become a new language. While, doubtless, all are ready to admit that Swahili, like any other language is bound to develop and grow, in form, idiom and vocabulary, as a result of the impact of the civilisations of the immigrant communities, yet surely the development must come from the Swahili mind, and must not be superimposed on them from without. But that is just what we have tried, and are still trying, to do, with the result that we are in the somewhat ludicrous position of teaching Swahilis their own language through the medium of books, many of which are not Swahili

in form or content, and whose language has but little resemblance to the spoken tongue.[38]

The author not only criticized the ILC for being "in too great a hurry to get the books written and published," but questioned the very idea that a committee made up of nonnative-speakers should try to influence the language at all.[39] He concluded the article with specific linguistic criticisms, using examples pulled from ILC-approved books, arguing that while they might be grammatically correct according to committee standards, "grammatical accuracy however, does not of itself constitute a language, and it is perhaps this very exaggerated application of grammatical rules that has led us away from the real Swahili language, and made us substitute something which at its best is lifeless, though intelligible, at its worst both lifeless and unintelligible. . . . It is the language that makes the grammar, not the grammar the language."[40] This was more than a disgruntled Kimvita partisan airing his grievances; the officer was calling into question the very project of Swahili's standardization by the committee.

Among the works referenced by the Kenya officer was an article published in the Arabic-Swahili newspaper *Al-Islah* ("The Reform") founded in 1932 by Sheikh al-Amin Mazrui, a Muslim scholar from Mombasa.[41] The *Bulletin* included an extract from the newspaper written in June of 1932, from an article titled "*Madhara ya Harufu za Kizungu kwa Lugha ya Kiswahili*" ("The Harm of Latin Script to the Swahili Language").[42] The author took the colonizers to task for imposing the script onto Swahili, "*kama kwamba hatuna harufu zetu*" ("as if we did not have our own script").[43] This shift significantly changed the pronunciation of the language, Mazrui argued, and most harmfully, it penalized students who did not want to write in Latin script. The concern about language and the education system was essential: while members of the ILC would claim again and again that they remained open to different styles of Swahili, and that they wanted to cede control of the language to East Africans and allow it to change as necessary, this continually bumped against their determination to set the language taught in schools across the region.

The next item in the same issue of the *Bulletin* was a response to "Modern Swahili" written by Canon Gerald Broomfield, an ILC member and UMCA priest working on Zanzibar.[44] The heart of Broomfield's defense came midway through the article: he and his Kenya counterpart concurred that the "development of Swahili must be, primarily, the work of Africans themselves. We all agree about this, and it has been stated many times."[45] However, they must also agree, he urged, that "every advance in knowledge, and every advance in systematic thought, necessitates change and development in the language which is to be the vehicle, and means of expression, of that knowledge and philosophy."[46] It was in this arena of linguistic "development," Broomfield argued, that the ILC could and should contribute. The first field of work that he envisioned for the ILC was the compilation of dictionaries and grammars. The second realm of ILC labors was to be the lexicographic expansion of Standard Swahili. "Ideally," he admitted, "it might be better to make no suggestions at all, and just wait for Africans to evolve new words when they felt the need for them, but life is not long enough."[47] The final field of work requiring European assistance, according to Broomfield, was the correction of manuscripts prior to publication, paying particular attention to differences in dialect. Here Broomfield touched upon the fundamental question of how much uniformity was required of a standard language:

> It is quite obvious that the time has not come when all our books can be produced in one identical form of the language. One has to bring them into agreement so far as is possible without creating too much ill-feeling.... Kiunguja must be the basis, but, as it seems to me, all the main dialects will contribute something to the future. Further, Swahili is developing everywhere, and, if left to itself, will develop in different ways in different localities. New words, etc., are needed, and they are being evolved or borrowed. It is the function of the I.L.C. to pick out the more satisfactory forms, and encourage their use everywhere.[48]

Throughout his response, Broomfield never questioned whether or not official standardization was necessary; assuming that it was a worthy project, he argued that, at least initially, it required Europeans to be carried out properly.[49] He concluded his defense of the ILC by holding out a hand to the author of "Modern Swahili," writing, "The truth is that the standardization and unification of a language is an extraordinarily difficult task, and those who undertake it will be popular with nobody.... None of us thinks himself infallible. We are all very anxious to learn. If the author of the memorandum would send notes on words, idioms, etc., for publication in the Bulletin, then we should all have the benefit of his knowledge."[50]

The inclusion of the "Modern Swahili" article and the *Al-Islah* extract indicates that, to a certain extent, the committee was open to criticism and encouraged broad-based participation in its project of standardization—though of course Sheikh al-Amin Mazrui was never invited to submit to the *Bulletin*. As Broomfield's response makes clear, short-term requirements were at the forefront of the ILC's concerns, backed by a belief in the long-term benefits of linguistic commensurability. And while these complex questions were in the air in 1934, they did not stop the committee from putting its imprimatur inside the front covers of books, nor from turning its attention to the revision of the dictionaries.

REVISION OF THE DICTIONARIES

To the ILC, the revision of the existing Swahili dictionaries was central to the project of standardization, and much other work was deliberately put off until after their completion. Indeed, this sense of finality surrounding the dictionaries led some to ask whether the ILC should be dissolved once they were published, believing that this would "complete" the standardization of Swahili. Of course, the printing of a dictionary did not, could not, finalize standardization, an operation whose endpoint was always elusive. It is the process by which these dictionaries were created, and the ideas behind them, that is of interest here, for the construction of the dictionaries epitomized the mixture of long- and short-term thinking, top-down and bottom-up direction, and utopian and pragmatic aims inherent in any project of language standardization. And when one reads through the papers of the ILC, the confidently top-down approach of the committee clashes quite obviously with the distinct sense that language is one of the few things that no body—governmental or otherwise—can completely regulate. The ILC leadership recognized the limitations of their understanding and control, linguistic and otherwise, and they solicited expertise and assistance from a wide range of speakers and writers of the language, at least for a time. The tension between these twin impulses and outcomes—to pronounce while asking for help, and to empower while trying to control—are what make the ILC dictionaries crucial subjects of examination.

Dictionaries were in fact on the agenda of the ILC's very first meeting in 1930, when a subcommittee headed by Stanley Rivers-Smith and Gerald Broomfield was appointed to begin the project.[51] The first obstacle to be navigated was obtaining the rights to A. C. Madan's English-Swahili and Swahili-English dictionaries from Oxford University Press (OUP), which had first been published in 1894 and 1903, respectively. The ILC also determined to compile a Swahili-Swahili dictionary from scratch. In obtaining permission from the OUP, the committee faced a linguistic question that bumped up against a legal one—namely, can one compile a dictionary without reference to other dictionaries?

Rivers-Smith had begun corresponding with the OUP regarding Madan's dictionaries in the late 1920s, and the press had expressed two hesitations: first, as far as they could tell in 1929, no "uniform orthography nor standard dialect had been finally accepted in East Africa as a whole," which meant there was no guarantee that these dictionaries would be lasting; second, Madan's dictionaries had apparently only recently made back their original production costs, so the press insisted on financial backing from the East African governments in order to take on the printing of revisions.[52] At the 1931 ILC meeting, the committee resolved that they could not agree to underwrite the risk of the publication with a subsidy or guarantee of sales, but did commit to further communication with the press.[53] The correspondent at the press, meanwhile, made it clear to the committee that "if an attempt is made to have a new Swahili dictionary produced by another publisher it will be regarded as an infringement of the copyright of Madan, which the Press will resist."[54] The ILC faced a difficult conundrum: the OUP would not print the revisions without some kind of financial guarantee, which the committee could not offer, but the ILC could not look elsewhere for a publisher because the OUP would interpret this as a violation of copyright. One British official fumed, "Such an obstructive attitude on the part of a Press which is, I believe, intended more for the dissemination of learning than for private profit is somewhat surprising."[55] He continued that, if such a view was truly accepted, "it would be impossible, once a dictionary of any language had been published, for any other dictionary of the same language to be produced by a different publisher, and I think we ought certainly to obtain legal advice on the question."[56] Would it be possible to avoid legal conflict with OUP if, for instance, the compilers "[eschewed] the sight, even of the outside cover, of Madan's book during their work"?[57] The crux of the matter from the committee's point of view was to determine how much they actually needed to rely on Madan's dictionaries for their own revisions; there were, after all, other dictionaries available that could serve as the starting point.

It took another two years for the ILC to reach a deal with the OUP.[58] The terms included the details of the printing (cloth-bound bindings, two dictionaries of six hundred pages each), the financial arrangements (to be printed at the expense and risk of the press with a royalty of 10 percent to be paid to the ILC after the sale of the first three thousand copies), and the stipulation that the committee was not to publish any abridged version of the dictionaries without the press's consent. The drawn-out negotiations, however, had not prevented the ILC from earnestly commencing the work of putting the dictionaries together, a process that very quickly moved beyond Madan's texts as members of the dictionary subcommittee began collecting words and definitions for inclusion in the revised dictionary. In fact, by the time of the first meeting, the ILC had already compiled thirty pages of amendments to Madan's Swahili-English dictionary. "These amendments," according to a 1931 memorandum, "do not attempt to deal with the meanings of the words given in the dictionary but with the spelling of words only. It will be realised therefore that revision such as contemplated will practically amount to the compilation of a new dictionary. However, being a dictionary, in the nature of things, it must contain all or nearly all the words found in Madan, with the addition of many others recorded since. The explanations of the words, however, will in many cases be different from those found in Madan."[59] These early discussions were fraught with temporal tension: the ILC focused on a foundational text, imbuing it with a sense of linguistic timelessness; on the other hand, when "revision" becomes "rewriting," there is an obvious recognition of change over time, and of the short-term necessity of working toward a long-lasting solution.

To that end, with those thirty pages of internally generated amendments in hand, the ILC turned outward, soliciting words and definitions from around the region. Under Johnson's signature on ILC letterhead, the committee sent out a circular letter to all four Directors of Education.[60] The letter asked the directors to distribute the request for assistance to officials throughout their territories. These administrators were then to allocate letters of the alphabet to government officials, missionaries, or other knowledgeable individuals within their jurisdiction, in order to collect words and their definitions from across the region.[61] The process was not innovative but rather a technique used from Turkey to Germany and beyond for various dictionary projects.[62] In East Africa, too, individual compilers were assigned letters and told to create a slip of paper for each word, which would be sent back to the ILC to be slotted into a comprehensive index. Informants were also asked to address particular subjects based on their personal interests. Finally, the committee requested that individuals share "any notes on Swahili philology which may have been made."[63] Madan's work was to serve as the template, with any omissions or errors corrected by this broad-based effort.

The crowd that was being sourced with this letter, of course, was a minority of the total Swahili speakers in the territory, and it was made up almost entirely of Europeans. In this sense, it was a limited effort. The committee did recognize this shortcoming in its strategy and therefore directed recipients of the circular: "It should not be taken for granted that the explanations and uses of words found in existing Swahili dictionaries are correct, every possible means should be taken for arriving at the correct explanations and meanings, and natives should be consulted freely. It should however be remembered, that direct questions seldom elicit satisfactory explanations, and it will be necessary to set traps frequently, to see what the natives say when taken unawares."[64] For the subject collections, as well, the compilers were encouraged to expand their own expertise, "to watch the various things the men and women do and to ask what they are doing, and then to verify information received from different sources."[65] Theoretically, then, the data collected for the new dictionaries would come from a pool of supposed "experts" as well as presumed "nonexperts," witting and unwitting contributors, combining official and unofficial knowledge production.

At the 1932 annual meeting, the dictionary subcommittee reported on the progress of its information collection, recording, "Valuable notes have been received from the Revd. Canon Dale, formerly of the Universities' Mission to Central Africa, Zanzibar, and Dr. Werner, formerly professor of Swahili and Bantu in the University of London. Mr. J.H. Vaughan of Zanzibar, has submitted a list of Swahili names of various birds, and Mr. E.G. Staples of Uganda, supplied some useful comments on a list of trees and shrubs which was circulated amongst the Directors of Education for submission to competent authorities."[66] The knowledge production happening here included well-known experts in the field (Dale and Werner among them) as well as broader "authorities." As for the assigned letters, the committee had received "U from Umuungu to the end of U. [from] Mr. L.W. Hollingsworth, of Zanzibar. V, w, y and Z. [from] Mr. L.A.C. Buchanan, Zanzibar." Both of these collections would be "re-allocated later for further comments from other Swahili scholars."[67] By 1934, they had received "Mu to the end of M, from the Rev. K. Roehl, Dar-es-Salaam." But still nothing had been received for "A, B, CH, D, E, F, G, H, I, J, K (to kiungulia), N, O, P, and T," and so Johnson himself had taken over those letters.[68] As information flowed (or perhaps trickled) into the ILC headquarters, the committee printed lists of words, at times for internal circulation at the annual meetings, at other times to be published in the *Bulletin*. Issue No. 8 from May 1935, for instance, included a "Revised List of Swahili Equivalents for Words and Terms." The list's introductory comments read: "In the lists circulated in previous Bulletins there are many words which are already contained in Madan's Swahili-English dictionary with the meanings approved by the Committee. These were submitted for verification with the object of obtaining uniformity of terminology in text books, etc. . . . The following is the revised list which *supersedes all previous lists*."[69] And so it went for several years, each new list superseding its predecessors, each awaiting confirmation by "experts" from all quarters.

The committee had begun working along the same lines with the preparation of the Swahili-Swahili dictionary, circulating to the ILC readers lists of words with definitions in Swahili. They quickly discovered, however, that the readers could not serve on the front lines of this work, being already swamped with the review of manuscripts, so the preparation of the Swahili-Swahili dictionary was handed over to the "Secretary and [his] Staff."[70] This early turning over of the work to Johnson actually meant, however, that the Swahili-Swahili dictionary advanced more quickly than the two revisions, and it was published in June of 1935 as *Kamusi ya Kiswahili yaani Kitabu cha Maneno ya Kiswahili.*[71] By November, the Dar es Salaam Bookshop had sold out of its stock.[72]

According to an announcement about the dictionary's publication, the Sheldon Press had included a blank page at the end of each letter "for noting additional words and to allow these words to be included in a reprint without unduly upsetting the paging of the book."[73] And in the preface to the dictionary, Johnson wrote, "I will be very happy if any person who sees any mistakes within will send me notice in order that the mistakes be removed, and if those knowing Swahili words that are not included will send me notice so that they be included later when the book is printed a second time, which is to say that will indeed be what enables us to compose a 'Dictionary' befitting the Swahili language."[74] The expectation of revision was therefore incorporated into the very production of the dictionary—it was recognized as a codified work-in-progress rather than as the final word.

Work on the Swahili-English and English-Swahili dictionaries, meanwhile, dragged on. According to the 1936 annual report, the ILC was receiving proofs of the Swahili-English dictionary in installments, and the press would endeavor to have them all delivered early in the next year.[75] Laying blame on the OUP, the report continued: "It is unfortunate that such great delay has occurred—it will be remembered that the manuscript was sent to the publishers in October 1935—as, although it may be possible for the Secretary to correct the first proofs before he proceeds on leave at the end of February, 1937, the subsequent page proofs will either have to be dealt with by him while on leave, or be held until he returns in October."[76] The English-Swahili manuscript, meanwhile, was "practically complete" and would (aspirationally) be sent to the press before Johnson's leave.

DEATH AND NEW LIFE IN 1937

In the event, Johnson was not able to complete the revisions after returning from leave, for he died en route at Aden on March 12, 1937. The choice of a successor was at once straightforward and complicated. The simple part was choosing who should be the next secretary: consensus formed rapidly again, this time around Rev. B. J. Ratcliffe, a former missionary with the United Methodist Free Church who had been an education officer in Kenya since 1933. Ratcliffe had also served as an ILC reader since 1930.[77] The complications entered the picture when it came to completing the work of the remaining two dictionaries. The question of continuity bubbled to the surface: Would Ratcliffe be able to take on the work of correcting proofs during the transition, or should the ILC hire someone else to finish the task? Gerald Broomfield was the someone that certain members had in mind: staunch defender of the ILC, he had also been involved in the negotiations with OUP and worked with Johnson during the compilation phase. The committee did not want Johnson's sudden death to derail the already delayed completion of the dictionaries, and some felt that Broomfield's continued involvement would supply the stability necessary to finish the project. A few members even suggested that Ratcliffe's appointment should be put off until Broomfield finished the dictionaries. Others felt that hiring Broomfield was unnecessary when they had a perfectly well-qualified secretary in Ratcliffe. The issue widened certain interterritorial fissures, with Tanganyika adamant that Broomfield be involved, Kenya insistent that this was a waste of resources, and Uganda and Zanzibar toggling between the two. By December of 1937, Ratcliffe had essentially silenced the debate himself, writing in a letter to the Tanganyika Secretariat, "I have come to the conclusion that there is no necessity to put the proof-reading of the remaining letters of the Swahili-English dictionary into other hands. . . . The publishers might now be requested to return the remaining copy 'S to Z' to this office and the proof reading proceeded with at once. The printing of the 'page proofs' can then be pushed forward and the production of the dictionary thus be expedited."[78]

Within the correspondence pertaining to Ratcliffe, Broomfield, and the future of the dictionaries, we get occasional glimpses of the person who forged ahead with the work while the ILC leadership squabbled. In a letter from April 1937, W. Hendry, the Director of Education for Zanzibar, wrote to the secretary of the Governors' Conference, weighing in on the hiring of Broomfield. "In correspondence with the Director of Education Tanganyika," Hendry noted, "I have ascertained that the office work of the Inter-Territorial Language Committee is being carried on by the clerk Pedro, who has instructions to refer any difficulties to Mr. Williams or Mr. John of the Education Department, Tanganyika Territory."[79] Hendry informed the secretary that he had sent the final proofs of the Swahili-English dictionary to the press, "stating that Pedro will do a first correction of the outstanding galley-proofs, and asking them to hold up all final proof reading till we make arrangements for a competent person to undertake the work."[80] Pedro himself (his full name was Pedro Msaba or Mzaba) corresponded with the press, writing on behalf of the ILC to request the return of the galley proofs of the Swahili-English dictionary.[81] And in 1941, an ILC memo recorded that "the death of Petro Mzaba is a great loss: he was a faithful and valued servant of the Committee."[82] The simultaneous recognition of Pedro's work on the dictionaries and the nonrecognition of his "competency" is, no doubt, telling of the general ILC attitude toward their East African employees. While in the coming years Africans would be appointed to the ILC as official members, this respect was reserved for a select few African linguistic "experts." Yet the work of Pedro Msaba, the longtime clerk and proofreader, exemplifies the reliance of the ILC on African interlocutors at every stage, and indeed, Johnson thanked him (along with fellow clerk Rawson Watts) in the prefaces of all three dictionaries.

The year 1937 was a consequential one for the ILC beyond the death of its first secretary, for it also marked a new lease on life for the committee itself. Already several years into the revision of the dictionaries with no definite end in sight, the fate of the ILC hung in the balance. There had been hints of dissension as early as 1933 when Kenya threatened to pull its financial support. Just a few years later, the discussion regarding the ILC's future struck on some fundamental questions. In the summer of 1935, the secretary of the East Africa Governor's Conference reported, "The Kenya Government considered that the main object of the committee—standardisation—would as far as possible at present, have been attained with completion of the revision of Madan's dictionaries."[83] The report continued, "It appeared, therefore to the Kenya Government, that when the dictionaries were in final form, there would be little need for the retention of the Committee at the cost involved, and that any essential work in connection with its functions could be carried out at the annual conferences of Directors of Education. That Government accordingly suggested that the Committee should be suspended or abolished and that the 30th June 1936 would be a suitable date for its discontinuance."[84] The Tanganyika government reacted vociferously to the proposal, declaring, "The suggestion that the Committee should be regarded as an ad hoc body having as its particular task the 'standardisation' of Swahili and that that task was such as could be described as complete at some fixed date was, as far as the Tanganyika Government is concerned a new one."[85] Officials in Dar es Salaam became so exercised that they submitted a memorandum of their own, written in November 1935: "Standardisation is only one of the aims of the Committee: the other being of equal importance, i.e. the development of the language. In any case, even if the raison d'etre of the Committee is the production of dictionaries, the date suggested for its dissolution, the 30th of June, 1936, is premature, as the various dictionary projects are not likely to be completed until much later."[86] The memorandum continued for two pages, picking apart Kenya's proposal based on both prior agreements and financial considerations, but focusing on the linguistic "harm" that would be caused by the dissolution of the ILC:

The publication of the dictionaries will put an end to a part of the Committee's task. It will not, however, put a term to the development of the Swahili Language, and the dictionaries themselves will require periodical revision. . . . Swahili is a living tongue. It is the principal medium of education and of all communications between Government and governed, and it will continue to expand and adapt itself to new needs and changing conditions. Its growth requires the continuous guidance of a central definitive body until it has moved so far beyond the influence of local peculiarities that it is able to stand alone without external assistance.[87]

Tanganyika's call to arms convinced Uganda to reverse its prior support of Kenya, while Zanzibar had opposed the Kenya suggestion from the beginning.[88] At a meeting of the territorial Directors of Education in February 1936, the issue was effectively put to rest in favor of the Tanganyika view. The directors concluded that "in order to ensure the spread of standardized Swahili through the medium of books written in approved orthography an inter-territorial Swahili Committee will continue to be necessary for some years after the publication of the dictionaries."[89] The Governor's Conference confirmed the view of the Directors of Education at its June 1936 meeting, citing cost considerations in the production of textbooks and official publications, the uniformity of language examinations, and the need for literature as among their reasons for supporting the continued existence of the ILC.[90] This averted crisis offers another glimpse into the organization's philosophy of standardization, to which the dictionaries were no doubt central. The ILC did not, however, regard their production as the culmination of language standardization. The next steps, as indicated in this flurry of memoranda and reports, included the "development" of Standard Swahili, in part through the production of literature in that language—a topic to which we turn in the next chapter. This debate about the purpose of the committee also uncovers the long-term considerations of standardization hidden among the short-term exigencies of dictionary creation. References to the "living tongue" or the "living language" of Swahili mark a recognition that, while present uniformity was necessary for things like textbooks and examinations, standardization would always be chasing linguistic change.

COMPLETION OF THE DICTIONARIES

The ILC's Swahili-English and English-Swahili dictionaries were finally published in 1939, more than nine years after the start of the negotiations with OUP. Back in 1935, the committee had asked the bishop of Zanzibar,

Rev. Thomas Birley, to write a forward for the Swahili-English dictionary, "as the Universities' Mission to Central Africa has taken such a large part in the development of Swahili literature."[91] The committee also "unanimously decided that the words 'Compiled by the Inter-Territorial Language Committee of the East African Dependencies under the direction of Frederick Johnson, late Secretary of the Committee,' be printed on the title page of the revised dictionaries."[92] The English-Swahili dictionary dedication, meanwhile, read "To Krapf, Madan and Steere, whose work for the Swahili language should never be forgotten." Madan's name even appears on the title page of both works, which are described as "Founded on Madan's English-Swahili [or Swahili-English] Dictionary."[93] This framing of the dictionaries reveals a committee that was all too aware of previous scholarship, that respected foundations, and that sought sources of stability and expertise. But in 1939, after the culmination of nearly a decade of work, some members of the ILC were already looking ahead and anticipating change, as we have already seen with the inclusion of extra pages in the Swahili-Swahili dictionary. A 1936 report pertaining to that work referred to another provision for change that had been taken from the very moment of its publication: "In accordance with the arrangements made with publishers, the type of this dictionary which was published in 1935, was kept standing for one year, at the end of which any alterations and additions were to be made so that plates could be prepared and the type re-distributed. Amendments and improvements have been sent to the publishers, and approximately 600 words have been added. The new edition will not be available until the present edition is exhausted."[94] The same plan was implemented for the Swahili-English dictionary, to save the type for future corrections. By the time that dictionary appeared, however, war in Europe had intervened, and in October of 1939, E. C. Parnwell of the OUP had to regretfully inform the committee that the press could no longer hold on to the type:

> Since that arrangement was made, however, there have been two important changes in circumstances. First of all it was not possible for the editors to take due notice of corrections received before even the book had been printed; so that the type as it at present exists is far from perfect, and the cost of perfecting it would be very high. Secondly, the outbreak of war creates an awkward position with regard to type. Metal is more precious and there is great urgency to distribute all the type that can possibly be distributed. Failure to do this will render the publisher liable to high rent charges for standing type. With regret we have had to decide therefore that the

type of these dictionaries may not be kept standing after the end of November. If before then you care to let us have particulars of any very important corrections we will do our best to alter the type before moulds are taken.[95]

Ratcliffe replied in the only way he could: "Under the circumstances and exigencies of the war there would seem to be no help but to acquiesce to the suggested course of action and to distribute the type after the end of November."[96] But Ratcliffe's response did not address Parnwell's first point—namely, that the committee had submitted corrections to the dictionary so quickly that the type was already imperfect! The ILC's own office copies of all three dictionaries were printed in interleaved style so that additions or changes could be noted for future editions, and the 1940 *Bulletin* stated frankly that "although we are extremely grateful to our late Secretary and his associates for the vast amount of work that has been done in preparing these dictionaries it is quite obvious that a revision will have to be made in a few years' time, especially in view of the Committee's intention to preserve and encourage the literary use of all well-established Swahili vocabulary."[97] The ILC readers were understandably exacting in their scrutiny of the dictionaries, calling attention to multiple errors.[98] The minutes of the readers' 1943 meeting, for instance, included a memo which argued that the "arithmetical terminology" of the dictionaries was unsatisfactory according to math teachers in the territories, and they proposed a conference to bring teachers together "so that the best list of terms may be compiled and adopted."[99] Outmoded almost from the moment they were published, the dictionaries embody the temporal tension within the ILC's standardization project. Each dictionary marked a *moment* of standardization, and they were to serve as tools of both learning and evaluation for many decades to come; yet they were also expected to change along with the language that they reflected.

How, then, did the ILC envision the "completion" of standardization? As we have seen, for some in the Kenya administration the dictionaries did represent the end goal. Tanganyika officials, in contrast, were adamant that standardization was not *only* a linguistic question but also necessitated the dissemination of that standard, in part through schools and in part through the production of reading material in a reasonably uniform linguistic form. Absolute uniformity, however, was never the goal. At its annual meeting in 1939, the committee discussed the role of the readers as set out in its constitution, calling for their attention to be "directed to the fact that it is not the accepted policy to foster any one form of Swahili to the exclusion of all others, but rather to encourage the literary use of all well established Swahili idiom and vocabulary under a common orthography."[100] One critic, Rev. A. R. Pittway from Kenya, accused the ILC of just such exclusivity: of being "arbitrary" and "too mechanical," and approaching standardization with a "stereotyped nature" that "savours of the surgical rather than the linguistic mind."[101] Rev. A. B. Hellier came roaring to the defense of the committee in the *Bulletin,* accusing Pittway of "[throwing] out epithets like 'arbitrary' and 'mechanical' in a wholly irresponsible way."[102] Even in terms of spelling, Hellier insisted, the ILC was only too aware "of the complexities involved, of the very obvious fact that a *living* language does not submit to arbitrary treatment. . . . Moreover, the Committee felt that although standardization implies unification this need not be overdone, and that to allow some latitude was advisable if not actually necessary, provided again that the latitude was not overdone either."[103] Returning to the dialectical debate, Hellier wrote, "I can only assure Mr. Pittway, and all who use the Kimvita dialect, that nobody wishes to prevent them from doing so or would dream of denying their perfect right to do so."[104] And yet, Hellier conceded, certain "modes of spelling" *were* rejected by the committee, uses "which are now not so much forbidden as deprecated."[105] This "deprecation" of certain orthographies inarguably drew lines between Standard and non-Standard uses of Swahili. Yet the goalpost was continually shifting, and even Hellier had to admit that "they could not get away from exceptions, which are liable to intrude themselves into every rule that can be formulated."[106]

THE QUESTION OF PARTICIPATION

Among all the listed attendees at the 1925 Education Conference at which the ILC was established, there were only two East Africans, both former members of the Universities' Mission.[107] As we know, Samuel (Samwil) Chiponde had been a teacher, editor, member of the Translation Committee, and priest; in 1925 he was serving as "native interpreter" for the High Court in Dar es Salaam and was also a member of the standardization subcommittee at the conference. Leslie Matola was a former mission teacher who had taken a job at a government school.[108] The participation of Chiponde and Matola presents a productive puzzle. For on one hand, the 1925 Education Conference exemplifies the exercise of arrogant colonial authority: the intent of the meeting was to decide upon the language that people across the territory should use to read, write, and learn, with only token input from African interlocutors. In their recorded comments from the meeting, both Chiponde and Matola spoke in favor of an official process of Swahili standardization. Chiponde reflected on his time on the UMCA Translation

Committee and the work left to be done, work for which, he said, "I believe all of us are responsible."[109] He likewise balanced a short- and long-term view of standardization, recognizing the inconvenience it might cause some readers and writers, but calling on them to "bear in mind that the fruits of this Conference are more for the future of Africa than for the present."[110] Matola's comments echoed those of his colleague, urging the prospective members of the ILC to "think of the future of these isolated tribes and teach them Swahili as a language in which they may converse with all other tribes in Tanganyika."[111]

The presence of Chiponde and Matola at the 1925 conference was, however, also testimony to an ongoing reality confronting the European members of the ILC: they needed the help of African interlocutors. In a chapter centered around the institutional mindset of the ILC and its mainly European members, the discussion of African participation may seem tacked on as an obligatory sidebar. There is no doubt that African interlocutors were valued less within in the official channels of standardization of the 1920s and 1930s than they had been in the 1870s and 1880s, when "standardization" was not yet an actors' category. There is no getting around the fact, moreover, that East Africans were not granted leading roles in the ILC until the eve of independence. Yet the ILC members knew that, at the very least, the adoption and dissemination of an official standard necessitated a degree of buy-in from Swahili speakers. They also needed the help of African clerks and translators to carry out the logistics of producing a bulletin, preparing revised dictionaries, and other types of office work. Moreover, many members of the ILC prided themselves on their relationships with local intellectuals and regularly sought their input, if only according to the committee's timetable. From its very inception, therefore, the ILC experienced the tension between top-down and ground-up impulses—the start of a pattern in which demanding assistance would lead, eventually, to demands for the right to participate.

Yet there are hints of the ILC reliance on African participation at every stage. There was the circular letter promulgated by Johnson in 1930, asking for contributions from colonial officials, teachers, and missionaries, in which he suggested that "natives should be consulted freely."[112] The option of hiring Swahili speakers was written into the committee's constitution, and in 1932 Augustino Ramadhani and Muhamad Salim Halil were brought in to work with a committee tasked with reviewing the original list of Swahili words and glosses circulated to ILC members.[113] There are the examples of Pedro Msaba and Rawson Watts (along with Sayyid Majid Khalid), among a select group who "read drafts of the [Swahili-Swahili dictionary] from start to finish giving [Johnson] lots of fitting explanations and advice," while a handful of East Africans from Zanzibar and Tanganyika offered feedback on specific sections.[114] The *Bulletin* also conveyed some sense of collaboration, including instances in which English members of the ILC described interactions with groups of African interlocutors, from students to teachers to acquaintances, people whose advice was used to form linguistic opinion on various questions.[115] There are also a few examples of direct East African contribution to the *Bulletin* prior to the independence period. Abdulla Mohamed el-Hadhramy compiled a list of Swahili intensifiers, which was printed in issue No. 13.[116] Issue No. 19 from November 1945 included contributions from Oswald Mhando, S. Joel Mdundo, and Amour Ali Ameir, a reader from Zanzibar.[117] In the following issue, from July 1947, A. S. Lubwama, M. B. Msimbi, and J. Kasaja, all assistant education officers from Uganda, wrote a letter supporting an earlier editorial pertaining to the orthographic standardization of other East African languages.[118] All these examples reflect the kinds of participation asked of and provided by African interlocutors: some worked for the ILC or engaged with it as interested amateurs; others were the students, teachers, scholars, and acquaintances with whom European contributors spoke about linguistic questions, sometimes soliciting direct feedback, at other times simply gauging reactions in order to decide on a lexical or grammatical point. Meanwhile, the ILC was not the only body that felt responsible for promoting and maintaining a "correct" form of Standard Swahili; this was also a concern taken up by readers of and contributors to the burgeoning landscape of Swahili print media being produced in eastern Africa.

SWAHILI NEWSPAPERS AND THE "DAFTARI YA USTAARABU"

In 1923, readers in Tanganyika were enthusiastically greeted by a newcomer on the newspaper scene: *Mambo Leo* ("News of the Day"). "In years past," the opening issue declared, "you all were acquainted with a friend of mine, his name being *Kiongozi*. Now, he has passed away. You all know how pleasing he was in conversation. Well, I am his heir, and I hope to please as much as he did."[119] Indeed, *Kiongozi* had "passed away" in 1916, another victim of World War I.[120] Yet the Department of Education in Britain's newly acquired territory of Tanganyika explicitly hearkened to the German paper in the opening pages of its own journalistic endeavor; the direct, conversational style of its editorials, meanwhile, borrowed from the long-standing techniques of periodicals like *Msimulizi*; both characteristics rooted it within a legacy of Swahili-language print media. The monthly paper quickly gained popularity, reaching a circulation of nine thousand in the early 1930s, and fifteen thousand by the end of the decade.[121]

The transformations of concepts such as *ustaarabu* ("civilization"), *maendeleo* ("development"), *uraia* ("citizenship"), and *taifa* ("nation-state"), particularly through politics and the print media in East Africa, have been thoroughly examined by scholars such as James Brennan, Emma Hunter, Katrin Bromber, and Jonathon Glassman.[122] Embedded within the contemporary discussions of such concepts was an assumption that "development"—whether of a civilization, a race, or a nation-state—must and would unfold along a forward-moving path. It is therefore not so surprising that a government periodical such as *Mambo Leo* expressed certainty that "*Afrika ya kesho*" ("the Africa of tomorrow") need only find the correct "*ufunguo*" ("key") that would unlock "*ustaarabu.*"[123] Meanwhile, Emma Hunter has described how seriously the producers of *Mambo Leo* took their role "in policing 'correct' Swahili."[124] The establishment of the ILC was front-page news in 1925, and the editor called on readers to follow the conventions of the newspaper, which would thenceforth be taking its cues from the committee.[125] *Mambo Leo*'s support of the ILC is, again, not particularly remarkable—the newspaper was after all an official organ of government.[126] It is perhaps more surprising, however, to see similar discussions in the newspaper *Kwetu* ("Our Home"), which appeared in 1937 and was charismatically edited by a resident of Dar es Salaam, Erica Fiah. The countertempo here is subtle, but present: while official outlets like *Mambo Leo* encouraged identification with the colony or, at broadest, the empire, journalist-printers like Fiah at times encouraged identification with a Swahili-literate community, regardless of political boundaries.

Born in Uganda in the late 1880s, Erica Fiah moved to Nairobi as a young man, joined the Carrier Corps during World War I, and then settled in Dar es Salaam. In 1936, he founded the Tanganyika African Welfare and Commercial Association (TAWCA).[127] Fiah started *Kwetu* the following year, intending for it to serve as the official organ of the association, but the newspaper soon grew beyond the rather constrained influence of the TAWCA.[128] *Kwetu* appeared (approximately) every eighteen days, a deliberate interval chosen to avoid the expense of officially registering under the terms of the Newspaper Ordinance. As Fiah bemoaned in various fundraising appeals, he produced the paper largely on his own, work which included printing it using an old, hand-operated "Japanese press."[129] *Kwetu*'s contents were ever changing, but always included local and international news (sometimes pulled from other periodicals), a contribution from Fiah, and a section entitled "*Viongozi wa Kwetu*" ("Guides of *Kwetu*"), which featured letters to the editor from around the territory. The paper's circulation was between seven hundred and one thousand copies per issue, with the wartime appetite for news helping to boost its numbers in the late 1930s and early 1940s.[130] Politically, Fiah (and thus the newspaper) was often critical of the colonial government, while being un-failingly loyal to the British Empire. *Kwetu* appeared less and less frequently after the end of World War II, and it ceased publication altogether in 1951.[131]

When it came to the notions of "civilization" and "progress," Fiah and the contributors to *Kwetu* were certain of one thing: no matter what might cause "*ustaarabu kupiga hodi Tanganyika*" ("civilization to knock on Tanganyika's door"), newspapers would be there to open it.[132] More than that, Fiah con-sidered *Kwetu* itself—as printed on the first page of nearly every issue—to be "*Ufunguo wa Ustaarabu*" (the "key to civilization"). Not only did the paper keep the Swahili-reading public "well informed" about developments local, regional, and global, but it actually (like its predecessors *Msimulizi, Kiongozi,* and even *Mambo Leo*) helped to create that literate community.[133] Fiah conceived of his newspaper as a "*baraza*" through which any writer could address the govern-ment, thus emphasizing East Africans' participation in their own governance years before the idea of an independent nation-state of Tanganyika had gained any widespread traction.[134] In the meantime, Fiah stressed, there was the free press, which was as fundamental to a country's well-being as its network of roads. As he explained in one editorial, "Printing in a country is something like infrastructure, for example: if there is no road to Dodoma and Tabora to purchase cattle, we won't have meat in Dar es Salaam. If a person tries to pass through the bush he will be attacked by lions, etc. If the people of any country do not have their own newspaper, they are the same as a country without roads."[135] Only those communities that supported a free press, Fiah contended over and over, would be written into "*Daftari ya Ustaarabu*" (the "Ledger of Civilization"), a register whose most important language was Swahili.[136]

And if, as one letter writer described it, *Kwetu* was indeed the "*ulimi wa Taifa*" ("tongue of the Nation"), then it seemed only natural to Fiah and many of the contributors to *Kwetu* that they, too, take up some of the responsibility for patrolling the developing standard of Swahili.[137] Or, rather, it was a con-stant worry of the editor that he could not *better* control the shape of the Swahili printed in the paper. Fiah included frequent apologies for mistakes in spelling (in both Swahili and English), explaining that the work had to be done quickly and without assistance. As the harried editor wrote in 1941, "*Mtu si Mashini*" ("a Person is not a Machine").[138] Given how thinly Fiah was spread (and likely, too, as a political expediency), he disavowed any respon-sibility for the contents of the section "*Viongozi wa Kwetu,*" including not just the opinions expressed but also the linguistic style therein.[139] Yet this state of affairs clearly pained him, and Fiah fastidiously printed corrections of spelling errors, occasionally taking it upon himself to change the spelling of a contribution before it was published.[140] He harped on his contributors to write—neatly—with ink, to keep their letters short, and to conform to widely accepted spellings. Any nonconforming letter, on any of these fronts, "*haitaandikiwa katika Kwetu*" ("will not be printed in *Kwetu*").[141] In late 1938, Fiah seems have become fed up with the shoddy state of some contributions and wrote an editorial directly addressing the "*Maandishi ya Barua*" ("Writing of Letters"). In it he upbraided the authors, asserting that to rush the writing process—to not take care "from start to finish"—was a clear indication that "*hutaki ustaarabu*" ("you do not want civilization").[142]

But how exactly did Fiah judge the linguistic "correctness" of the contributions? His yardstick was, in fact, the ILC and (after their publication) its dictionaries. The arrival of the latter was announced in the newspaper with great excitement, the advertisement directing readers, "If, as you know, education has no end, it behooves every person who would like to increase his education to make an effort to procure these books."[143] Fiah took this to heart, using the dictionaries in his own editorial work. In the aforementioned admonition to letter writers, for instance, he referred to the word *Saidina,* which appeared in the 1935 *Kamusi ya Kiswahili* as a *neno jipya* ("new word"): its meaning approximated the more familiar words "*Sayidi, Saidi au Seyidi; kwa lugha ya Kiingereza Sir (Bwana).*"[144] "We have written a letter to the Director of Language," Fiah wrote, "asking him to explain to us the difference between these words."[145] The appearance of the 1939 dictionaries provoked more questions along these lines: the spelling of the term of honor—*Seyidi*—generally used in the newspaper's letters-to-the-editor section was transformed into *Saidi* and given the definition of "lord, master." Meanwhile a term suggested as a gloss for the English word "sir," which had previously been spelled *Habibi,* appeared in the new dictionaries as *Hababi.* Hewing to the new standard, Fiah affirmed that "*sasa tutatumia neno Hababi badala ya Seyidi*" ("now we will use the word Hababi rather than Seyidi").[146] Contributors followed suit, addressing nearly all of their subsequent letters to "*Mtengenezaji Kwetu, Hababi.*" Fiah encouraged writers to consult the *Kamusi* so that they would not "forget syllables and letters" and urged them to purchase not only the ILC dictionaries but also Gerald Broomfield's *Sarufi ya Kiswahili* (published in 1931).[147]

Despite his apparently enthusiastic use of the ILC dictionaries, Fiah's editorials also make clear his belief that Swahili was the responsibility of East Africa's *watu weusi* ("Black people") and that its development, use, and control could not be left entirely to the *Wazungu* ("Europeans"). He welcomed European help with dictionaries and matters of grammar but, after all, "*Waswahili ni sisi*" ("we are the Swahili").[148] And though Swahili was not his own mother tongue, Fiah recounted the effort he dedicated to learning the language, because he believed it to be *"ufunguo wa Ustaarabu hapa Tanganyika"* ("the key to Civilization here in Tanganyika").[149] Swahili was the language that could connect all East Africans with one another *and* with which they could communicate with government. The language thus deserved to be used with honor and care within the pages of *Kwetu*. But, again, Fiah's sense of responsibility—and his projection of that responsibility onto his readers—did not cause him to eschew the efforts of the ILC. Rather he regarded himself and other East Africans as active collaborators in that work: in the same editorial in which Fiah urged letter writers to take care "from start to finish" while composing their contributions, he concluded by asserting, "Therefore the time has come for us to attend to this language. Read the Swahili Dictionary page IV."[150] What was Fiah referring to here? The editor of *Kwetu* and admirer of Swahili and its standardizers was also, apparently, an incredibly close reader, for this is a reference to the last page of the Swahili-Swahili dictionary's preface, written by Frederick Johnson, in which the late director of the ILC had expressed (in both Swahili and English) that he "shall be grateful to receive corrections, additions, and suggestions."[151] Fiah took Johnson at his word, pointing to this passage to galvanize his readers to see themselves as co-workers in the standardization of Swahili, and to do so in an active way—namely, by writing contributions to his paper.

I should stress, too, that Fiah and his likeminded readers shared the ILC's vision of short-term codification combined with long-term flexibility. In *Kwetu* were published several letters that spoke favorably of languages borrowing from one another and changing over time.[152] Furthermore, wrote one commentator in a contribution titled "Telling Time," "people have mixed with one another, so why should we be surprised about the mixing of languages?"[153] In 1942, one B. Salim from Arusha kicked off a heated exchange with his contribution entitled "Good English" in which he asked why youths who boast about knowing English frequently mix in words from African languages when they speak it.[154] Salim's question prompted two answers: one from a writer in the Rufiji River valley who argued that it was no mistake to mix Swahili and English because the former is used by many different ethnic groups and is therefore necessarily a mixture, just as English has borrowed Swahili words such as *safari*.[155] The second response came from A. Amon in Kimamba, who concluded, simply, that "the mixing of English with our languages is not a mistake: it's habit."[156]

⁓

As we have seen, the ILC came in for criticism from its earliest days, whether because of its choice of Kiunguja, its push for rapid production and uniformity, or its slowness and simultaneous desire for immediate change. Several committee members admitted later in life that, in retrospect, too much emphasis had been placed on uniformity in the early days of the ILC. On his retirement from the committee in 1952, Ronald Snoxall wrote, "Until consistent forms of spelling and grammar had been evolved perhaps it was inevitable that one dialect should be abased and another exalted. At the time it all seemed so tragically final and one of the most valuable tasks which the Committee has accomplished has been to show that the eclipse of the Swahili dialects other than Kiunguja was not and could not be final. Tolerance and understanding have come with age and that is as it should be."[157]

Other critiques went beyond linguistic questions, linking standardization to the colonial project and thus attacking its moral and ethical roots. To the moral question, all that the stalwart ILC defender A. B. Hellier could reply was "that the Committee were, and are, an honest and responsible body of men who have put a great deal of hard work into a tough job and have taken pains to collect evidence and to weigh decisions, without partiality and at the same time without fear of criticism."[158] An answer which was really no answer at all. Snoxall and others came close to retrospectively conceding that putting European members in sole control of the official project of standardization had been ill-advised, couching their admissions in pleas to necessity. "I feel that in spite of the opposition in the earlier days to the work of the Committee," Snoxall reflected, "and the complaint that a number of Europeans were setting themselves up as the highest court of appeal on questions of Swahili, Africans and Swahili speakers would now agree that the initiative had to be taken by someone, and that the Europeans had to start the ball rolling. The subsequent history of the Committee has shown that it is natural and necessary that the members of the Committee of whatever race, creed or colour, must meet on the common ground of their interest in and love for the Swahili language."[159] Too little too late, one might argue, given that it took over a decade for the committee to welcome its first few non-European members. As one commentator argued in *Kwetu* in 1940, "Building Swahili is the work of the native inhabitants whose own language it is."[160]

The project of standardization, and the specific decisions made by the ILC, remained a matter of debate for decades to come, well after the independence of Tanganyika, Zanzibar, Kenya, and Uganda. Sometimes this took the form of polemic, such as Abdallah Khalid's *The Liberation of Swahili from European Appropriation*, published in 1977 by the East African Literature Bureau in Nairobi.[161] Some authors have been more considered in their critiques; Shihabuddin Chiraghdin and Mathias Mnyampala, for instance, acknowledged the colonial-era origins of the ILC and its successor organizations, noting that "the purpose [of the committee] was to ease the administration's work rather than benefitting the indigenous people of these countries."[162] They point to the cruel irony of mother tongue Swahili speakers being told in school that their language was wrong, or that Europeans knew more about what suited the indigenous people of East Africa than the indigenous people themselves.[163] This was the "imperial arrogance" that John Mugane has highlighted.[164] And yet, Chiraghdin and Mnyampala reminded readers in 1977, dialects had been an unavoidable part of standardization from the very start, through the presence and pressures of East African speakers and writers. "These dialects," they wrote, "are truly the nutrients of the standard language; its fertilizer comes from within them."[165]

In his *New Horizons in Kiswahili,* Ireri Mbaabu likewise addresses the argument that Standard Swahili is inherently colonialist.[166] While Standard Swahili was no doubt a product of the colonial era, he argues, "it is no more colonial than the civil service institution or the educational set up and other institutions which we inherited from the Colonial Government. The things we have inherited from the colonial past form part of our history. The fact that we retain functional set-ups like the ones mentioned above is no indication that we cherish the colonial era or that we are brainwashed."[167] Some have argued that such inheritances are, in fact, distinctly (neo)colonial.[168] But it is Mbaabu's use of the term "brainwashed" that jumps out to me, bringing to mind Ngũgĩ wa Thiong'o's *Decolonising the Mind.*[169] For Ngũgĩ, the imposition of European languages in colonial settings was violent and psychologically traumatic, particularly as it was inflicted on children at schools. He argues that vernacular languages, in contrast, are connected to the history, culture, and social structures of their respective communities and are therefore invaluable and worthy of use for all purposes. This is why Ngũgĩ famously gave up writing fiction in English after the publication of this book.

But where might Standard Swahili fit into Ngũgĩ's worldview? Is it a foreign imposition, or a vehicle of organic creativity and community strength? In *Decolonising the Mind,* he criticizes the contradictory orthographies introduced into Africa by different colonial interest groups, seeing it as a tactic of "divide and rule" to keep the majority of people illiterate while creating a class of civil servants. He argues that colonial states were interested in systems of writing African languages so that "the biblical message of subservience, the administrative orders for labour and taxes and the military and police orders for killing recalcitrants, reached the native messengers as directly as possible."[170] And yet, in his chapter on the novel, Ngũgĩ insists that "the social or even national basis of the origins of an important discovery or any invention is not necessarily a determinant of the use to which it can be put by its inheritors. . . . Nowhere is this more clear than in the area of lan- guages. It is the peasantry and the working class who are changing language all the time in pronunciations, in forming new dialects, new words, new phrases and new expressions."[171] Why then, Ngũgĩ concludes, should the Af- rican writer not appropriate the form of the novel—or, for our purposes, the standardized language? Indeed, Ngũgĩ's embrace of an ongoing process of commensurability, of lexical expansion and experimentation, comes across clearly in an example used to show the connection between vernacular lan- guages and the inner, emotional lives of their speakers. "This may in part explain why," he muses, "technology always appears to us as slightly exter- nal, *their* product and not *ours*. The word 'missile' used to hold an alien far- away sound until I recently learnt its equivalent in Gĩkũyũ, *ngurukuhĩ*, and it made me apprehend it differently."[172] The concept of "missile" was certainly not something from the deep past of Gikuyu life, and yet, Ngũgĩ insists, find- ing a Gikuyu term for the new technology changed his relationship with it.[173] And though Standard Swahili sits uncomfortably in the center of a Venn diagram encircling vernacular and nonvernacular languages, Ngũgĩ is nev- ertheless a champion of the language.[174] He celebrated the translation of his novels, encouraging "communication between African languages" including Standard Swahili.[175]

This chapter has followed a process of codification that began in the 1920s at the behest of the British colonial states of East Africa. In this period, and particularly with the creation of the three Standard Swahili dictionaries, the temporal tensions inherent in the project of standardization are easy to see. Standard Swahili was simultaneously expected to hew to linguistic an- tecedents, to be immediately useful for myriad purposes, and to be lasting far into the future. The official nature of the ILC's work, meanwhile, should not obscure another tension within the project—namely, the committee's reliance on African assistance even as it pronounced what was and was not Standard. The next chapter examines the transition from standardization to dissemination and the colonial states' attempts to build a literary canon, exemplified by the establishment of the East African Literature Bureau. As we shall see, what may have started as a project driven by the administra- tive focus on "suitable" literature written in "good" Swahili, was carried on by East African writers both famous and anonymous—it is to the idea of creativity that we turn to next.

5 ～ The East African Literature Bureau

Creating Creativity in Standard Swahili

IN 1972, Professor Ali Ahmed Jahadhmy, a scholar of Swahili at the University of California, Santa Barbara, wrote to J. W. T. Allen, former secretary of the East African Swahili Committee (successor to the Inter-Territorial Language Committee [ILC]) and retired director of the Institute of Kiswahili Research at the University of Dar es Salaam. Trying to raise the spirits of his friend who had suffered a series of professional setbacks, Jahadhmy wrote, "I am not surprised that you are assailed right and left; do you know why? Because many of the so called pundits of our language are content with talking; doing never! ... If you had people like Wilfred Whiteley and the other despicable so called linguists, they would work for the destruction of our classics, one of the few real treasures still left with us."[1] Jahadhmy's vitriol lays bare a division in Swahili studies that had first developed in the colonial period, a division between the professed standardizers and the self-styled literature creators. "The so called Swahili fundis are not even fundis when you examine them closely," Jahadhmy concluded. *Fundi,* a Swahili word meaning "craftsman" or "artisan," became derogatory in the professor's letter. The "so called linguists" were highly skilled, as is the *fundi,* but in Jahadhmy's eyes they had squandered this skill by using it to standardize rather than create;

they were highly competent builders, but they were neither artists nor even architects.² The letter from Jahadhmy to Allen reveals the deep emotions stirred up by the standardization project, emotions that simmered even a decade after independence in East Africa. The distinction between the "*fundis*" of Standard Swahili and the inspiration of the "classics" came to the fore starting in the 1940s, when the colonial administrations began to shift from a focus on codification to an emphasis on creation—specifically, the creation of "literature" in Standard Swahili, an effort placed under the auspices of the East African Literature Bureau (EALB). Meanwhile the Inter-Territorial Language Committee found itself teetering on the edge of dissolution, prompting a shift in focus from standardization to research, encompassing Swahili in all its forms. Still, when it came to governmental support and encouragement, the ILC found itself eclipsed by the EALB and its prerogative to "produce literature" in Swahili and other African languages.³ It is with this split between the ILC and the EALB, between codification and creation, that this chapter begins.

The same tensions that were at the center of the ILC's project of standardization persisted in the work of the East African Literature Bureau: the EALB was yet another interterritorial organization caught between its aim to dictate standards while requiring assistance from all corners. The EALB aimed not simply to promote literacy across the East African territories, but to stimulate "creativity" in African languages including, most centrally, Swahili. But a distinct irony beset the bureau's mission as it set out to regulate creativity, a force uncontrollable almost by definition. The very terminology employed by the bureau—to "produce" literature—hints at an industrial, almost mechanized approach. This is not language typical of conversations about "literature," itself a term torn between the ideals of exceptionalism and exemplariness, of tradition and innovation. And while the East African Literature Bureau could judge the creative forces that it had unleashed, and it could try to fill space with government-approved literature, the story of the EALB includes the now-familiar tug-of-war between control and empowerment, oppression and opportunity. The bureau sought to create a canon, believing that it was starting with a clean slate. But neither the long literary history of eastern Africa—both written and oral—nor the desire of East African authors to create on their own terms, could be entirely suppressed. Much like its predecessor the ILC, the EALB found itself in a position of great temporal tension, at once looking back to "traditional" or "classical" forms of Swahili literature, while encouraging African authors to create "modern" literary works.

This chapter explores, too, the possibility that the constraints imposed by the bureau, which encouraged adherence to a standard language and prescribed forms of literature, actually facilitated the creativity of some authors. As On Barak has argued about the relationship between "standard time" and "Egyptian time" in colonial Egypt, "Egyptian clocks . . . did not parody time by ignoring it."[4] Rather, politicians, artists, and nationalists of all stripes *used* the notion of punctuality—at times invoking it, at times by deliberately undermining it—to their own ends. And, as Barak stresses, "to realize unpunctuality's potential, an accurate clock was indispensable."[5] The existence of a standard, that is, gives creative people something to push back against.

The Swahili essay contests instituted by the ILC and continued by the EALB offer a useful bridge from which to examine the split between the two organizations and their underlying ideologies. The chapter then shifts its focus to the Literature Bureau, revealing the organization's tendency to prescribe "African needs" despite claims to be simply responding to "African demands." The EALB's valorization of creativity sat uneasily next to its mandate to produce literature. Meanwhile, the constraints of the bureau's position as a colonial agency did not prevent East Africans from taking advantage of the possibilities it offered—from the famed writers Shaaban Robert, Ngũgĩ wa Thiong'o, and Muhammad Said Abdulla, to the less-well-known contributors of manuscripts and essays, to the unnamed typists, assistants, and editors who kept the EALB humming. While institutions such as the Literature Bureau *demanded the participation* of people like these in its literary efforts, the colonial administrations of eastern Africa soon found themselves facing *demands to participate* from colonial subjects, often along linguistic or literary lines. This chapter explores the efforts of the EALB to respond to the demand of readers and writers, while recognizing that it often took it upon itself to prescribe needs.

THE ESSAY COMPETITIONS OF THE INTER-TERRITORIAL LANGUAGE COMMITTEE, 1935–48

The third article of the ILC constitution tasked the committee with "Giving encouragement and assistance to authors whose native tongue is Swahili."[6] At its annual meeting in January 1935, the members of the committee (still an all-European affair) committed to mobilizing on that intention by creating a Swahili essay competition. The contest was comprised of two parallel annual competitions, one for essays written on precirculated topics and one for "free essays," with an initial prize of £10 for each. The prompts posed for the 1935 competition were "The History of a Crop"; "What changes have occurred in your clan and tribe since the year 1914?"; "Missions"; and "Give an account of the observance and significance of either Id-Il-Fitr or Christmas."[7]

These were typical of the set subjects, which were generally semi-historical or semi-ethnographic in nature.

At the following annual meeting in February of 1936, the competition subcommittee reported on the first round of essays, noting that the Directors of Education had chosen the best entries from their respective territories, which were then sent up to the ILC for judging; over the next several years, hundreds of submissions would be vetted by the Directors of Education.[8] The 1936 report stated that the "essays were, on the whole, of a fair standard," though the committee never articulated an exact basis for its judgments. In 1939, the committee added a new component to the annual ritual, referred to as the "Swahili Authorship Competition."[9] Authorship implied a more ambitious undertaking than simple essays, and the new branch of the contest aimed at "further stimulating the literary gifts revealed in the Essay Competition."[10] In setting the parameters of the authorship competition, the committee noted that "although the utmost freedom should be allowed in the choice and treatment of subject, the manuscripts should possess literary merit."[11] Regarding this criterion—literary merit—the report on the first authorship contest was only slightly more detailed than those that had come before: "In all, eighteen manuscripts were submitted, for the most part of very considerable merit and revealing a certain literary gift which if encouraged and cultivated holds the promise of an increasing output of Swahili literature through native authorship."[12] The report included a summary of the top four manuscripts submitted, with first prize going to Thomas Mbotela for his piece *Habari za Maisha ya Wenyeji—Wakamba,* a history/ethnography of the Kamba ethnic group from south-central Kenya.[13] Of Mbotela's work the committee noted, "On the whole the Swahili in which the manuscript is written is good. The author describes native customs vividly and gives the impression that but for the limitations imposed by the conditions of the Competition more might be said: it is not long-winded or irrelevant and holds the interest of the readers throughout."[14] Mbotela was a student at the Government African School in Machakos, Kenya, a quintessential intermediary figure. His writing was simultaneously held up as necessary and even good "from the point of view of native authorship," while also being criticized for its apparent haughtiness regarding certain Kamba customs, "a failing," the committee noted, "which is fairly common in the transition period through which the East African is passing."[15] Mbotela and others like him, it seems, could be neither "evolved" nor "authentic" enough. The ILC did, however, want Mbotela's work to be published, and the manuscript was circulated among the wider committee for comments on "orthography and style."[16] The runners-up to Mbotela, meanwhile, were given "words of commendation and encouragement to continue their efforts in literary production and offering advice in possible improvement of style."[17] Here we begin to see the committee's dual concern for linguistic "correctness" and compositional "style"—two concepts only ambiguously defined throughout the reports.

In 1941, the authorship competition took in twenty-six manuscripts, with the winning entry coming from Daudi Yongolo, who was associated with the Teachers' Training School of the Moravian Mission in Tabora.[18] The judges described Yongolo's work as "a very interesting 'life sketch of the Wanyamwezi' from birth to death. The author touches upon almost every aspect of life and the book is written in an easy and pleasant style. The Swahili used may be said to be uniformly good throughout."[19] What seems to have set Yongolo's ethnographic work apart, however, was the committee's sense that "in his treatment of all these varying phases of progress from the 'old' to the 'new' the author maintains a reasonable and well balanced statement avoiding undue denunciation of the older ways of life and the laws by which they were governed; passing easily over to the present time which inevitably he compares with the old to the advantage of the new."[20] Yongolo successfully threaded the needle where Mbotela had failed, satisfying the committee's desire to see tradition respected but put in its proper place. His work would eventually be published in the Literature Bureau's "Custom and Traditions" series, which prized this balance between ostensible tradition and modernity.[21]

While literary merit was judged on an unspoken balance between past and future, the ILC encouraged its essay contestants to think about progress toward *ustaarabu* ("civilization") as moving along a linear timeline. In 1947, for instance, Salum Kombo won the authorship contest for a piece that would later be published as *Ustaarabu na Maendeleo ya Mwafrika* ("Civilization and Development of the African").[22] In this slim four-chapter volume, Kombo outlined what he believed civilization consisted of and how East Africans could achieve it individually and, thereby, collectively. Progress, the author emphasized early on, moved stepwise and forward in time. Notice the temporal markers in the following passage: "The African of the distant past [*juzi*] did not know the value of tribe and therefore did not take heed of anything more than his kinfolk. The African of yesterday [*jana*] progressed forward a little bit getting to know the value of tribe instead of only clan, and in taking yet more steps forward, the African of today [*leo*] greatly honors the nation more highly than tribe or clan, and this is a good indication that he has taken large steps forward in civilization and in his relation to world affairs."[23] Forward in time and outward from the local: according to Kombo, this was the path that East Africans needed to follow toward "civilization." Among the concrete steps laid out in *Ustaarabu na Maendeleo*, from investment in farming to health education, Kombo emphasized the importance of reading and writing. He used two hypothetical scenarios to drive home the importance of literacy. In the first, an old man in the countryside needed to write to his son, living in the city, to request financial assistance; the *mzee* cannot read or write, so he asks a local youth to draft the letter on his behalf. Seeing the opportunity for a quick scam, the young man changes the wording of the letter, listing himself as the financial intermediary, and makes off with the money intended for the old man. Kombo's second story involves a man who, traveling alone, comes to a fork in the road; tacked to a tree is a note warning of an injured (and dangerous) lion down one of the paths. Unable to read the sign, and assuming it was "just some nonsense of the Europeans," the traveler chooses the leonine path and is killed.[24] "And now," Kombo summarized the two parables, "it must be made clear that these two losses—being robbed of money and suddenly losing a life—would not have happened but for the inability to read."[25] Literacy, he emphasized, did not only benefit those trying to be hired for work, but helped a person along every walk of life.[26]

Kombo's argument serves as a ready transition to the story of the East African Literature Bureau, which published his piece in 1950. For if the ILC essay and authorship contests were a part of the "dubious enterprise," as V. Y. Mudimbe describes it, of colonial regimes promoting literature in African languages, the desire of the EALB to direct creativity in Standard Swahili pushed that enterprise into new realms.[27] And yet, as Mudimbe also asserts, such literature should be considered "as an expression of African condition."[28] For even within the bounds of a government-sponsored writing contest, authors could "[take] on a power which could ultimately be used against foreign ideologies."[29] So it was with the authors who contributed to the ILC authorship competitions or who would later publish their work under the auspices of the Literature Bureau.

THE SPLIT BETWEEN THE ILC AND THE EALB

Though the full committee did not meet from January 1939 until March 1946, it maintained most operations during World War II, carrying on "research, adjudication in competitions and manuscript reading" largely through correspondence.[30] During the war, Swahili had been encouraged—at times enforced—as the lingua franca of the British army in eastern Africa, increasing the number of Swahili-literate individuals in the region. It was therefore with the end of the war, and the impending demobilization and return home of those East African soldiers, that the notion of a literature bureau was seriously raised.[31] In 1945, the East African Governors' Conference invited Elspeth Huxley to the territories to look into the possibility of setting up such an organization.[32] After her visit, she completed a report that lay the foundation for what would become the East African Literature Bureau. Opening the report, Huxley cautioned that the stakes were high:

> Everyone I consulted expressed the opinion that the demand for literature was very great, was rapidly increasing and was far ahead of the supply. If sufficient good and desirable literature is not supplied to meet the growing demand it is clear that either bad and undesirable literature will fill the gap, or the gap will remain largely unfilled, in which case children who, at public expense, have been taught to read will quickly relapse into illiteracy.... Literature, by reason of its relative permanence and cheapness, will undoubtedly remain one of the most important means of enlightenment and persuasion.[33]

A literature bureau, Huxley and others believed, would contribute to the "development" of East Africa and East Africans; this was the post–World War II spin on the "civilizing mission," to create "good citizens" of the colonial state.[34] In her report, Huxley noted that, while some East African languages still lacked an agreed-upon orthography, the ILC had largely achieved this for Swahili.[35] Therefore, Huxley recommended that the ILC should be "fitted into the new organisation," perhaps as a "useful nucleus of translators."[36] The report presaged the shift of official emphasis from codification to creation, with the ILC shoved to the periphery—a division of labor that was finalized with the creation of the East African Literature Bureau in 1948.[37]

The actual work of setting up the EALB was put into the lap of Charles Granston Richards, who served as the literature secretary for the Church Missionary Society in Nairobi. Richards was initially appointed as an adviser to the bureau for a limited term, but he would go on to serve as head of the EALB until 1963. Richards, too, believed that the creation of the Literature Bureau would necessitate changes in the organization and aims of the ILC. His own report, submitted to the governors in 1947, proposed reducing the membership of the committee, which would focus on technical questions pertaining to Swahili and act as the "reference regarding new words to be adopted into the language."[38] Richards also suggested that the ILC "would be the body which would meet professors of linguistics visiting Africa for their various purposes"—a truly damning fate![39] The members of the ILC had no choice but to concede to the changes, which meant among other things giving up the review of manuscripts as well as the organization of the essay and authorship contests to the EALB.

The 1951 ILC *Bulletin* described these adjustments to its readers, reporting on a meeting attended by both Richards and ILC representatives where it was "unanimously agreed that the Inter-Territorial Language Committee should continue to function ... as a separate linguistic unit distinct from the East African Literature Bureau and that in all matters of Swahili research and orthography it should officially be recognized as the authority in Swahili publications: the committee being academic and the bureau concerned with the provision of books."[40] This issue of the *Bulletin* reads like a retrospective, mixing nostalgia with a touch of defensiveness about the committee's accomplishments:

> An orthography has been forged for common use by the Education Departments of the East African territories in all schools for the African: the various Departments of Government service in producing translations or original works have adopted the orthography thus produced by the Inter-territorial Language Committee: official examinations in Swahili are conducted in accordance with linguistic rules as published by the Inter-territorial Language Committee. Publishers in Europe, America and other parts of the world have come to rely upon the Imprimatur granted by the Inter-territorial Language Committee. ... In all these lines the members of the Inter-territorial Language Committee have contributed by freely giving of their scholarship and time and so they pass on a heritage of work faithfully done, a foundation upon which the East African Literature Bureau can safely build and a pattern which the many Swahili writers of the present and future time can follow.[41]

The following *Bulletin,* which appeared in August of 1952, went so far as to claim that the shrinking of the ILC and the contraction of its duties was "a development for the good" because it represented a "[whittling] down to a small body of keen experts" who no longer had to concern themselves with contests and business meetings.[42] But the closing remarks of Ronald Snoxall, elected chairman of the 1952 annual meeting, undermined this magnanimity:

> Often it has seemed to those of us with a deep love for the Swahili language that its value has been belittled in high places and that there has been insufficient understanding of the work which the Committee has done. Certain it is that the Committee has

carried on a continuous fight for existence with the money which has appeared to be grudgingly allocated to it. In assessing its value it is admittedly difficult to do justice to the imponderable reasons such as the need to maintain and develop the beauties of Swahili speech and idiom and the richness of its vocabulary, for such values can never be easily weighed against the expenditure of money, but even from a more mundane and hard-headed point of view it would surely be folly to disregard such a civilizing, unifying and beneficial instrument of policy as the Swahili language. I wish the Committee a long future not of struggle but of success, and may the bulletin circulate Swahili scholarship far beyond the bounds of East Africa.[43]

In that same year, the offices of the ILC were transferred to Makerere University in Kampala, where Wilfred Whiteley would serve as both a lecturer and committee secretary—developments which further emphasized the ILC's removal from the center of interterritorial coordination in Nairobi.[44] Finally, in 1954, the *Bulletin* was renamed the *Journal of the East African Swahili Committee,* marking "a shift in outlook towards longer articles intended as much to titillate the interest of scholars as to stimulate response from the practical student of the language," a goal of little interest to the colonial administrations.[45] The ILC, rechristened the East African Swahili Committee (EASC), would persist in various forms through the independence period, evolving into the current-day Institute of Kiswahili Studies at the University of Dar es Salaam.

THE GENERAL LITERATURE BRANCH OF THE EALB

As director of the EALB, Richards proposed dividing the work of the bureau into five branches: textbooks, periodicals, libraries, general literature, and distribution/business management.[46] For the general literature section, the bureau focused at first on producing books in Swahili, Luganda, Luo, and Gikuyu; more languages were added to its repertoire as time went on. Richards assured the Governors' Conference that the EALB would not compete with commercial publishers but would rather direct manuscripts to them, only taking on the publication of works deemed of immediate necessity or of an "experimental" nature.[47] The bureau itself was described as an "experimental" affair, funded initially for only five years, in part via the Colonial Development and Welfare Act. By the early 1950s, however, EALB partisans were arguing that it had become "a vital social service," deserving of more funding.[48] And as the bureau got down to business, the authorship competitions started to lose their centrality to the work. The EALB's Annual

Report of 1950 noted, "To 'build up an indigenous school of authorship' was one of the Bureau's terms of reference, and this is being done continuously. Authorship competitions have aroused some interest, but the entries have not been of a high standard. Better work has come from literary-minded Africans who have written asking for help."[49] So while the competitions would continue to be used to "stimulate authorship," Richards and his colleagues at the bureau began to feel that other methods of reaching out to authors, including lectures at schools or directly soliciting writers for specific works, would produce better results.[50]

The EALB did not have its own printing press, but it did have its own imprint, the Eagle Press.[51] The name alluded to a parable attributed to James Aggrey which recounts the story of an eagle that had been raised alongside chickens, thinking itself one of them; after being shown the sun rising on the horizon, however, the eagle finally flies—the idea being that literature in African languages would finally help readers to "fly."[52] Books printed with the Eagle Press imprint were financed by the bureau's Publishing Fund. Through 1952, 915,949 volumes of 154 titles were published with Eagle Press, of which 366,613 were sold; meanwhile 300,000 volumes of 127 titles had been published by commercial presses.[53] The Annual Report of 1955–56 calculated that the bureau was producing an average of sixty new titles every twelve months.[54] While by mid-decade demand seemed to be accelerating, in earlier years some bureau staff worried that the EALB's production was outstripping demand, declaring that they had helped so many authors succeed in getting published that the EALB had "reached a phase when there is no alternative but to delay or refuse acceptance of manuscripts."[55] By 1953, the bureau's Advisory Council encouraged "caution" in its publication program, insisting "that there should be still more emphasis on distribution."[56] The Literature Bureau relied, especially in the early years of its operations, on existing bookshops, particularly those run by mission societies in Dar es Salaam, Nairobi, and Kampala.[57] These then provided smaller booksellers with their necessary supply. Concerns about distribution were, however, constant, with Richards reporting as late as 1960 that the "greatest single obstacle to publishing is the scarcity of bookshops sited and staffed to sell to the African public."[58] Distribution was important not only to make more books available to more people but also to gauge the tastes of readers. The 1960 Annual Report made that link explicit, arguing, "The fundamental error of this over-concentration on production and neglect of sales is that so much of what is produced is guided by theories of what will be popular instead of knowledge of the interests of the public."[59] Indeed, the files of the EALB throughout the 1950s are filled with book order forms, and the publication list grew with each passing year. And while report after report noted with apparent pride the bureau's success in stimulating the "desire to read for pleasure" among East Africans, the exact shape of that demand took time to come into resolution.[60]

RESPONDING TO DEMAND OR PRESCRIBING NEEDS?

"Demand" was one of the watchwords of the EALB. In its publications, its outfitting of libraries (on which more in chapter 6), and the content of its periodicals, the EALB was ostensibly responding to the demands of East African readers. Yet Huxley, Richards, and their colleagues believed that, before the bureau could effectively respond to demand, it needed to *create* it. In fact, the bureau often took it upon itself to prescribe the "needs" of East African readers, treading a fine line between facilitator of publications and mouthpiece of colonial government.

By 1944 it was a commonplace that demand for reading material—whether textbooks for students or books and newspapers for adults—had been on the rise in East Africa and would increase exponentially after the war. The East African Literature Bureau was established in direct response to that anticipation, and its members conceded that the first years would be spent feeling out the market—an "experimental period" necessary to gauge demand. Huxley described the process as an "attempt to distil the essence of various impressions and opinions" about what readers wanted.[61] In a paper delivered after his retirement, Richards claimed "It must be stressed that publishing, to be successful, must come out of the life of the people . . . a publisher who is really in contact with the people he is seeing can be the essential spring of inspiration or point of reference."[62] Such remarks contain an obvious internal contradiction: a publisher should be sensitive to demand, on the one hand, and serve as a "spring of inspiration" on the other. And as it happened, the bureau's experimental phase only lasted for about two years, after which the 1950 Annual Report declared, "This experimental period has passed, and the emphasis now is on more selective publishing and on distribution."[63] The bureau's "selectivity" deserves examination: How were the selections made, and based on what criteria? The idea of fulfilling the demands of East African readers was a slippery one: there were schools that required texts, readers in remote areas who wanted books, and authors writing in multiple languages seeking an outlet for their work. At the same time, the EALB was a branch of the colonial administrations, each with its own set of ideas about what East African readers needed. The tension between responding to demands and dictating needs arose immediately, in Richards's initial report, which stressed, "It is understood that H. M. Government has decided that there shall be provided this abundance of reading matter, even if a stage is reached at which the supply is ahead of the demand."[64] The bureau, that is, would attempt to create demand by increasing supply, concertedly filling the space with, in Huxley's earlier words, "desirable" literature.

But what did the Literature Bureau deem to be both desirable *and* in demand? The 1955–56 Annual Report is a useful source of data because, at the end of that year, funding from the Colonial Development and Welfare Act was up for renewal; in his report, therefore, acting director J. C. Sharman (Richards was on leave) took time to reflect on the EALB's work since its founding, thus compiling useful statistics for the historian. First, some raw totals: in its first two years (1948–49), the bureau had produced (either under its own imprint or by shepherding titles through commercial publishing firms) 86,500 volumes and sold 13,286.[65] Those numbers rose steadily over subsequent years, and in 1955–56 the bureau produced 237,700 volumes and sold 295,895 (this included stock from previous years).[66]

The data on the genres of bureau-produced books offer a complex picture of what was the organization's bread and butter. In terms of total titles published, subjects like "History and Biography" and "Civics and Moral" led the way, followed by "Education General," "Health," and then a significant drop-off to "Fiction" and other pedagogical genres.[67] In terms of thousands of volumes published over the course of the eight years, the hierarchy changed only slightly: in this calculation, publications on the subject of "Health" led the way with 336,650 volumes printed, followed by "History and Biography" (282,800 volumes), "Civics and Moral" (248,550), and "Education" (236,950). While "Fiction" came fifth in terms of the percentage of titles published, it was only sixth in terms of volumes published.

Besides the range of genres, EALB publications were also written in a variety of languages, with Swahili representing the largest percentage. Between 1948 and 1953, 41 percent of the total books published were written in Swahili, 14 percent in Luganda, 14 percent in "Kenya vernaculars," 13 percent in English, and 10 percent in Uganda vernaculars other than Luganda, and 7 percent were bilingual in English and another language.[68] The language breakdown of volumes sold was similar, though the Uganda vernaculars represented 12.5 percent of the books sold while the Kenya vernaculars dropped to 9.5 percent.[69] In terms of authorship, European writers initially vastly outnumbered African writers. The table of publications from 1956 to 1957, for instance, included 75 titles (new and reprints), of which 59 were authored by Europeans and only 16 by Africans.[70]

Books adopted by education departments or for "community development" programs had a guaranteed audience, and so the curricula of government schools had an outsized influence on the content, the languages, and the sales of EALB books. At the same time, however, the bureau was under pressure to become self-sufficient as quickly as possible, which meant, simply, that it had to get good at selling books outside of government departments. This required, as we saw earlier, solving problems of distribution as well as assessing what would sell. The Annual Report of 1955–56 sounded a hopeful note on this front, claiming confidence in its ability to target its efforts and get books to potential readers.[71] Many of the bureau's statistics on reading came from its library system, which, while it might not perfectly predict the books that people would pay for, Sharman believed the bureau could use "as a guide to possible future experimentation." What did the bureau see when it crunched these numbers? The 1955–56 report asserted, "The indications are that when the public has access to a very wide selection of books, allegiances drift gradually from the frankly instructional type to the more generally entertaining. . . . Looking back over the last eight years' production, and having regard to the tendencies now emerging, it seems that we may now stand at the turning point." The pronouncement of having reached "a turning point" both in terms of the bureau's potential profitability *and* in terms of the general taste of readers raises again the question of demands and needs, of responsiveness and prescription.[72]

LITERATURE AND PROPAGANDA

It also perhaps raises a more fundamental question: Why would the colonial administrations of eastern Africa have desired a (partially government-funded) publication bureau? Emily Callaci has argued, "The history of novel and fiction writing in East Africa is linked with histories of modernizing ambitions of the colonial state, missionary communities, and nationalist intellectuals, who, in the post–WWII years, saw literacy and fiction reading in particular as a form of modernity, civic virtue, and development for Africans."[73] And the methods of achieving those aims—modernity, civic virtue, development—could flirt with propaganda, being inextricably linked to the growth of the developmentalist colonial state, including its racist and arbitrary side. The EALB participated in this project by censoring its publications and, sometimes, through the production of what can only be classified as government propaganda.

Richards did occasionally express ambivalence about the state-run publishing firm of which he was the head. In an interview conducted in 1976, a journalist queried the former director: "The East African Literature Bureau was government-funded and maybe government-controlled. Are you an advocate of state publishing?" to which Richards responded, "It is not something I care for myself."[74] Yet he had clearly shared many of the colonial state's ideas about development, ideas that were inflected by race and couched in the language of progress. In an earlier exchange from the same interview, the reporter asked, "Over the years you have been in publishing, have you seen missionary and other presses foisting western ideas and western attitudes on the public?" Richards replied somewhat defensively: "You use rather loaded words. When you talk about 'foisting' and 'western,' it sounds as if it is a planned policy of trying to westernize people: but if western people come and they think—I'm not necessarily saying they were right—that their ideas were good for everybody and endeavoured to communicate them, I think it is a bit hard to say they were foisting."[75] And yet, the policy of the East African Literature Bureau was *precisely* to, if not "westernize," then to "modernize" East African readers and writers—and to modernize them, of course, in ways the colonial government saw fit.

Censorship was one method by which the bureau tried to shape the written word in support of late-colonial ideologies. The suppression was rarely blatant, and most often took the form of decisions based on the "quality" of the writing, justified by a piece's supposed literary merit (or the lack thereof). Richards, for instance, wrote disparagingly of "'racial tension' writing," claiming, "I have not, myself, seen anything that seemed of lasting value . . . more like variations on a borrowed theme than real creations."[76] Race had been a sensitive issue for the bureau from the very beginning, and the colonial administrations of East Africa were clear on their power to control the content of printed material.[77] In the bureau-funded libraries, meanwhile, the director controlled which books would be stocked, paying particular attention "to books or subjects of a possibly controversial nature, i.e. religious, moral or political, which may require a 'policy decision.'"[78] Even in cases when censorship was discouraged, as by one district official from Tanganyika who urged that the bureau's output "should not be unduly censored before publication," there was tacit recognition that *some* censorship could and should be exercised.[79]

Independent newspapers, meanwhile, were one of the bureau's greatest worries. Huxley dedicated significant space in her report to the importance of an allied press, urging "nothing can poison relations between European and African, and between government and governed, so pervasively and quickly as a disaffected and irresponsible press."[80] She was hopeful that in East Africa the groundwork for a favorable newspaper scene had been laid with government-friendly, vernacular-language periodicals, including *Baraza* (published in Kenya) and *Mambo Leo* (in Tanganyika)—but she warned against complacency.[81] For alongside these stalwart periodicals, East Africa was also home to a robust independent Swahili-language press.

And the "dangers" of hostility or antagonism, Huxley suggested, "might be mitigated but not removed by censorship or suppression."[82]

Censorship, that is, was just one tool in the bureau's kit, and not the most effective when it came to shaping reading habits. Rather, Huxley contended, a hostile press could best be contained by "counter-irritants, e.g., by seeing that the truth—objectively, simply and forcibly stated—is made available to the people on the widest possible scale."[83] This was the most common strategy deployed by the EALB to inculcate "civic virtues" in its East African readership: filling the publication space with favorable material. One can read this impulse in a brief glance at the EALB catalog, which included many didactic titles in Swahili, such as the multipart series *"Mama wa Afrika na Nyumba Yake"* ("The African Mother and Her Home"), *"Mali ya Waafrika ni Nini?"* ("What Is the Wealth of Africans?"), and *"Ujiongezee Maarifa"* ("Increase Your Knowledge"), or volumes like *"Habari za Bendera iitwayo Union Jack"* ("The History of the Flag Called the Union Jack").[84] One could pull countless examples of similarly "edifying" works, written in all of the bureau's languages of publication.

Beyond its book catalog, the EALB sought to fill even more reading space by creating its own magazine. In his planning documents, Richards advocated for a periodicals branch as an integral part of the bureau, emphasizing its potential "to develop the habit of buying periodicals literature other than that based so lately on inter-racial animosity and distrust, conveying at the same time information and instruction in a popular and even entertaining form."[85] The subsequently appointed editor of the periodicals section, T. H. Maynard, echoed Richards, proposing that the publication could be used to explain "the various actions of Governments, the laws passed, the steps taken and what they mean to the African in helping in the development of his country. Handled in a careful manner it is felt that the suspicion of Government actions could be combatted and the periodical would contribute to internal security as well as to orderly development, by a dissemination of knowledge."[86] This is just about as good a description of propaganda as one could hope to read!

The EALB periodicals branch went through several iterations until the 1952 launch of *Tazama,* a Swahili-language weekly magazine published in collaboration with the *East African Standard.* The East Africa High Commissioners were hopeful that *Tazama* would "provide [readers] with useful and helpful material in place of the undesirable reading matter which is beginning to become available in increasing volume from other sources."[87] The bureau received supplementary support from the Colonial Development and Welfare Act for the first six years of publication. A Luganda-language

FIG. 5.1. Two "senior members of the Editorial Staff" of *Tazama*. EALB Annual Report 1951, Richards Archive PPMS12 2/19, SOAS University of London.

version—*Tuunulira*—was meant to follow closely on the heels of *Tazama*, though its production lagged and it did not appear until 1956. A year after its launch, *Tazama* had a weekly circulation of about thirteen thousand, growing to over nineteen thousand in 1955.[88] The EALB Annual Report from that year crowed, "A significant fact emerges. Each week more than 16,000 Africans are buying—and thousands more are reading—literature for enjoyment in their leisure-time that is neither the news material to be found in newspapers nor political in character."[89]

The content of *Tazama* included social commentaries (e.g., a 1954 article about appropriate dress in dancehalls); short fiction; letters to the editor; an opinion column; trivia and other contests; and lots of photographs, illustrations, and advertisements.[90] Much more could be written about the bureau's magazine, which came continually under fire for its style and was constantly on the brink of being abandoned by the territorial governments. But the point to be made here is that through *Tazama* one can clearly make out the uneasy balance struck between demand (for the magazine relied on sales to individuals and therefore popularity) and "desirability." Recognizing as much, in 1954 one Colonial Office commentator figuratively threw up his hands, declaring: "It is becoming fairly clear from our various efforts in the publishing world in East and West Africa that Govts are not good at running the popular press. Inevitably the Govts go in for 'uplift' which is, alas, not what the reader is prepared to pay for."[91]

THE EALB AND CREATIVITY

Even before the establishment of the Literature Bureau, the Inter-Territorial Language Committee had begun to open more widely the umbrella of Standard Swahili, and as the committee became more research oriented, non-standard dialects came officially under its purview.[92] In his 1952 report to the East African Swahili Committee, the first since its move to Makerere, Whiteley reminded readers that the ILC was no longer systematically reviewing manuscripts.[93] "Whether this is a desirable state of affairs or otherwise," Whiteley mused, "it is clear that manuscripts are being published without the Imprimatur without marked diminution of standards, though some diversity of style may be observed."[94] He continued to meditate on the question, deciding, "While it is necessary to adhere to established grammatical canons, it is yet desirable, in the course of the development of a language, that individuality should not be submerged in the interests of standardization. To make a comparison, while any building must be constructed on sound structural principles, this does not preclude the widest possible variation in architectural detail."[95] Whiteley's metaphor casts one's mind back to Jahadhmy's scathing criticism of the Swahili "*fundis*," including Whiteley himself. The ILC secretary was only too aware of the growing official distinction between codification and creation, and he did not want the committee to be seen as standing in the way of the latter.

This recalibration of codification did not come without growing pains; as the editorial staff noted in the 1951 ILC *Bulletin,* "There are those of us who deplore much of the change which has been introduced by so many writers of these days, departing from the principles of the language which are the essence of its beauty ... giving place to a journalese which neither expresses the soul nor the real mentality of the people."[96] It is terribly ironic to read European commentators lamenting linguistic changes supposedly violating "the soul" and "real mentality" of Swahili speakers. What they mourned, more likely, was their own confident sense of expertise. And despite lamentations, the Inter-Territorial Language Committee had been continually confronted by its inability to control language in use.

It was into this conundrum of codification and creativity that the East African Literature Bureau stepped in the early 1950s. Richards wrote in his initial proposal for the EALB that "it is emphatically the intention that the Organisation shall stimulate authorship as widely as possible."[97] The bureau staff rarely used the term "creativity"; rather, the default language was that of "production," betraying a mechanistic approach that is not instinctually congruous with creativity. The EALB, whether in the judgment of authorship competitions, assessing manuscripts for publication potential, or evaluating the popularity of its publications, did prize characteristics such as "imaginative,"[98] "traditional,"[99] "original,"[100] "indigenous,"[101] and "modern."[102] But it was never explicit about how such attributes were to be evaluated and how an author might best achieve them. How, for instance, could some submissions be described as "traditional stories" that were simultaneously "more or less original"?[103] Why were other submissions criticized for "a complete reliance on European remedies and methods" when adaptations of English novels had initially been praised?[104] In its first few years, the bureau sought to offer feedback to any author who submitted a manuscript, recognizing that if "[one] of the objects of the Bureau is to build up a school of indigenous authors ... the return of the MS. with a curt rejection slip as a means of shortening work" would be counterproductive.[105] In hopes of cutting down on the burden of feedback, however, the EALB published a series of leaflets on topics meant to assist potential writers.[106] The pieces, published in English, Swahili, and Luganda, were reportedly quite popular.[107] Subjects included "How a Book Is Published," "Some Forms of Writing," "Hints on Recording Tribal Custom," and "Hints to Translators."[108] The authorship leaflets, as the EALB referred to the publications, were regularly revised and reprinted, and Richards believed them to be "of considerable assistance in clearing the minds of authors on what they want to write and how to set about it."[109] The leaflets can also help the historian triangulate the bureau's vision of creativity, the definition of which was perpetually unsettled.

In what appears to be a mid-decade reboot, the authorship series kicked off with *Helps and Explanations for Authors No. 1: How a Book Is Published.*[110] This first issue offered an overview of the entities involved in publication (author, publisher, printer, and bookseller); the preparation of manuscripts; and the concept of copyright. Leaflet No. 2, *Some Forms of Writing*, opened by listing three questions on which prospective authors must "clear their minds"—namely, subject, audience, and form.[111] In choosing a topic, the pamphlet stressed the research side of nonfiction writing: "Remember there is no point in writing unless you are going to add to people's knowledge or understanding of the subject."[112] When writing fiction, on the other hand, imagination was key: "you need to have imagination and to be observant, so that your stories can become interesting, and your characters like human beings."[113] Leaflet No. 2 included a glossary in which "imagination" was defined as "the power by which you can make up stories and scenes and characters for yourself, out of your knowledge and observation of life and what you have learnt from books."[114] The authorial imagination should, however, root itself in tradition: "There is an African style of telling a story," the leaflet explained, "or conveying information, by using parables, to use a style like this, which will be readily understood because it is customary."[115]

Potential authors were encouraged to study the work of famous (Anglophone) writers, as well as anthologies of short stories or series of notable novels, even translations of "the great Greek classics."[116] Not until the discussion about writing autobiography was a single non-European author and work mentioned: Booker T. Washington's *Up from Slavery*. And here, too, were listed the first Swahili-language models, including *Uhuru wa Watumwa* by James Mbotela, and *Maisha Yangu* by Shaaban Robert.[117] The advice presented in Leaflet No. 5 on short-story writing, in contrast, was decidedly unhelpful on the question of where writers should go for inspiration: "You may be helped by reading some good short stories: or you may not want to read any at all."[118]

Amidst all the suggested techniques, a clear tension emerges between modeling and originality, imagination and expectation. Temporality was again at issue: while the ILC had wrestled with the question of linguistic roots and durability, the EALB tried to decide from where—and when—authors should seek their creative inspiration. In some cases, the emphasis was placed squarely on the past, on "tradition," including oral traditions. "The earliest literature of England," one leaflet explained, "was the writing down of such traditional tales; in writing these down, the African author may be helping to lay the foundations of an East African literature more surely than by any other form of writing, since they are, and will still be of the people. In East Africa the need for books on it is urgent, because so much of the lore of past ages is being forgotten."[119] It encouraged aspiring poets to "collect and publish the old songs sung by local bards," declaring that "the 'modern' poet will do well to study these and thus follow in the footsteps of his or her predecessors."[120]

But such a standard for measuring creativity (i.e., traditional "authenticity") was not universal, even within the EALB's own literature. "Possibly the most important thing of all," stressed the leaflet titled *Novels and Novel Writing,* "is to write in your natural manner. In a novel nothing is worse, nothing will more quickly turn it into a lifeless and dull affair, than the attempt to imitate some so-called 'good' style which does not come naturally."[121] The pamphlet concluded with this emphatic advice: "If your novel is to be good, it will have to be fresh and original, not an imitation of some other novel you have read."[122] Here, authenticity was tied to the originality of the work rather than to conformity with some idea of tradition. The author of the *Novels* leaflet went so far as to caution that, while writers should draw on their own life experiences and could even dip into history for inspiration, "if your imagination is to work freely, it must not be bound tightly to actual people and events."[123] These stark shifts in the advice for authors reflect the contradiction between the bureau's desire to build up a canon of literature to document and retain "traditional" forms of creativity and knowledge, and its valorization of individuality and innovation, a desire to build up a "modern" literature in African languages.

In 1961 the EALB received a grant from the Rockefeller Foundation to set up a Creative Writing Committee, which in turn sponsored a novel-writing competition.[124] In his memoir *Birth of a Dream Weaver,* Ngũgĩ wa Thiong'o (winner of the contest in 1961) recounts the excitement sparked among Makerere students at the announcement of the competition. The books published by the EALB, Ngũgĩ remembered, "were shorn of politics and issues that questioned the colonial order," but the Rockefeller competition represented "the bureau's first project that went outside its norm and tradition."[125] Another early winner of the novel-writing competition was Muhammed Said Abdulla with his piece *Mzimu wa Watu wa Kale* ("*Shrine of the Ancestors*").[126] Abdulla's novel, set on Zanzibar, tells the story of Bwana Musa and his companion Najum as they solve the mystery surrounding a gruesome murder: following the clues given by the possessed wife of the missing Bwana Ali, the detective and his assistant find the decapitated body of the missing man in the sacred grove of the ancestors, and then unravel the events that led to that point, much to the astonishment of the local police inspector. Abdulla would go on to write multiple detective stories featuring Bwana Musa, a character whom critics liken to the East African Sherlock Holmes—complete with an ever-present pipe and a capable if not-particularly-gifted assistant (Watson/Najum).[127] Indeed, Abdulla inserts the Baker Street detective's most famous refrain into the mouth of Bwana Musa, who responds (in English) to Najum's teasing reference to Holmes with "Simple, my dear Watson, quite simple. You know my methods."[128] The structural model for Abdulla's novel is clearly that of English detective stories, thereby drawing upon a "traditional" genre but one born outside of East Africa. Scholars of Abdulla's work have, however, stressed the ways in which the author masterfully wove the Zanzibari context into the detective form, creating characters true to his reality and that of his readers all within often fantastic plotlines.[129] As Emily Callaci observes of the genre, "While some aspects of crime thrillers—plot lines, character types, and aesthetics—might be portable and universal, the meaning of authorship and readership and the mode of producing and disseminating fictional texts cannot be taken as universal."[130] And indeed, Bwana Musa is anything but a knock-off Sherlock Holmes: he observes the subtleties of race and class on Zanzibar; he speaks with characters of varying accents (though Musa himself only speaks "pure Swahili");[131] he listens to spirits while rooting his investigation in logic and observation; and he offers philosophic takes on various topics. Abdulla went on to publish six novels featuring Bwana Musa, among other works, and is considered by many to be a "founding father" of popular literature in Swahili, and particularly of the highly successful detective genre.[132] His work, as exemplified by the contest-winning *Mzimu wa Watu wa Kale*, masterfully toed the blurry lines drawn by the EALB, which wanted authors to simultaneously model exemplary (generally English) literature, to root their work in the East African context, and to display individual imagination.

It is ironically in Leaflet No. 6, *Notes on the Writing of Poetry in English*, that one finds what is perhaps the clearest articulation of the bureau's overarching philosophy of creativity. In describing the assessment of poetry, the author asked, "Has the writer approached the language with the kind of disciplined excitement which poetry requires?"[133] How would the bureau readers know whether or not an author had approached their work with "disciplined excitement"? "There are really no rules about poetry," the piece concluded, "except that the result should be good. . . . If you write with passion, discipline and conviction we are bound to enjoy what you send."[134] In the end, it seems, the bureau's judgment of creativity operated on the "we know it when we see it" principle, seeking some undetermined balance between modeling and invention, emic and etic sources of inspiration.

SHAABAN ROBERT AND THE EALB

The East Africans who worked for the bureau, who contributed manuscripts, and who competed in the authorship competitions were many and diverse: they staffed offices, libraries, and schools in all four territories; they were adults and young people; they were good writers and bad writers; and they wrote in multiple languages. And the most talented among them used the expectations of the EALB to their own creative advantage, working productively within the context of social, political, cultural, and temporal tension inherent in their cooperation with the bureau. Here, I focus on one of the most famous contributors to the work of both the ILC and the EALB: Shaaban Robert. Robert's relationship with both organizations demonstrates one way in which an author could exercise creativity within the standard framework.[135]

Shaaban Robert's body of work and literary legacy have been examined by scholars across the disciplines; his reputation as one of the "fathers" of both poetry and prose in Standard Swahili—"the Shakespeare of Swahili literature" or the "undisputed Poet Laureate of the Swahili language"—is almost conventional wisdom.[136] Robert's role in the project of standardization and his prolific use of Standard Swahili also made him the object of some virulent criticism, referred to by one critic as a "yes-man and Oncle Tom" as well as a "docile African."[137] Such sentiments represent a critical misunderstanding of Robert's politics, and of his art. Through Shaaban Robert's pen, politics and language were simultaneously personalized and universalized, and Standard Swahili was the language with which he chose to write about the human condition. His was anything but an apolitical creativity: the writing was driven by a deep belief that "the minutest action, the most unassuming poem, the most delicate point of view, is always likely to grow and upset the order of things."[138] In search of self-actualization through writing, Robert composed in Standard Swahili and published under the auspices of government organs, using the constraints of the colonial situation to push at those very boundaries.[139] While the official bodies tried to depoliticize the work of Robert and writers like him, their readers could reinsert the politics; and Robert's decision to publish in Standard Swahili ensured that a wide range of East African readers could access his work.[140]

Shaaban Robert was born in 1909 near Tanga, and his writing career began in the early 1930s with letters to the editor and short pieces submitted to *Mambo Leo*. He worked for his entire adult life within the colonial administration, first in the Customs Service at Pangani, then the Department of Game Protection at Mpwapwa, and he retired as a clerk in the Tanga District Office.[141] His position as a civil servant circumscribed his involvement in party politics, but he was an early supporter of the Tanganyika African Association.[142] Robert's engagement with the ILC began as early as 1936 when his submission to the committee's essay competition won first prize in the set essay section, as well as the prize for best overall submission.[143] He submitted pieces in a few subsequent years, not sweeping the competition but regularly receiving honorable mention.[144] Robert eventually transitioned from participation in the essay contests to submitting full manuscripts for ILC review—namely, a translation of *Aggrey of Africa* (a biography of James Aggrey) that he sent to the committee in 1939 (it seems to have never been published).[145] When he died in 1962, Shaaban Robert was serving as ILC chairman (a rotating position), he had attended committee meetings in the 1950s, and had both contributed to and had his work reviewed in the ILC *Bulletin*. The *Bulletin* published an extensive "In Memoriam" section dedicated to Robert after his death, which included poems composed by admirers as well as his final speech delivered at Makerere University in November 1961, entitled "Swahili as Unifying Force in East Africa."[146] Alongside his work with the ILC, Robert also regularly interacted with the East African Literature Bureau: he served as one of Tanganyika's representatives to the bureau's Advisory Council between July 1951 and August 1952, and later from 1958 to 1960 (after which the council was dissolved).[147] The bureau sold his novel *Kusadikika,* a fantastical story about a dictatorial state located in the sky, through the Eagle Fiction Library imprint, and also facilitated the publication of his translation of the work of the Persian poet Omar Khayyam.[148] In the advertisement for the former, Shaaban Robert was described as "one of the most successful of [the] authors" to have been discovered through the essay and authorship competitions.[149] Yet despite the EALB endorsement, Ireri Mbaabu has described *Kusadikika* as an allegory "of colonised and oppressed people who are expected to 'believe' everything from the authority without question. . . . Shaaban Robert is encouraging the people of Tanganyika to fight for their political rights."[150] Several scholars have similarly pointed to the threads of dissent that run through Robert's writing. K. Inyani Simala argues that his poetry "depicts the colonial encounter and response at various levels other than the level of outright protest."[151] Ann Biersteker describes his famous "Kiswahili" as "an angry poem," a poem "about language and empowerment."[152] The "*titi la mama litamu,*" the sweetness of mother's breast, *is* Swahili, Biersteker reminds readers; it is the home language, the language of the oppressed, even if not strictly as a mother tongue.[153] Ngũgĩ wa Thiong'o even used the refrain to open *Decolonising the Mind*, emphasizing his case for African authors to proudly use African languages.[154]

Shaaban Robert worked for the government his entire adult life, which meant, for all but a single year, working for the British colonial administration. His letters to the editor of *Mambo Leo* were certainly not anti-British, but they did call on Tanganyikans to get involved and to think deeply about their relationships with their fellow man.[155] Later in life Robert enthusiastically supported Tanganyikan independence, describing in his second memoir how "my heart melted like snow under the sun over the many issues of the country, and I saw that it was my duty and honor to assist in coordinating and building, as others have done, so that [the country] might flourish."[156] Yet Robert's politics consistently connected the universal, or the national, to the personal; his politics and his writing encompassed both the ideological and the pragmatic. In the same paragraph wherein he described the experience of a heart melting with patriotism, for instance, the author admitted that he attended political meetings whenever he could but only "until the government forbade its servants to be party members and to participate in politics."[157] In a later discussion about Tanganyika's boycott of goods coming from apartheid South Africa, Robert wrote that the eyes of the world were on that country, decrying the human rights violations perpetrated against Black South Africans. In the midst of these reflections on universal human rights, however, Robert could not help but note that the boycott would hurt the sales of his books that were published by the press at Witwatersrand University.[158] But of course, Robert quickly corrected himself: "However, if a small contribution such as mine helped to bring about freedom and peace for the people of South Africa, this loss is small compared to the happiness of the victory that was expected to come for the people in the end."[159] The chapter continued along these lines, insisting that the victory over apartheid would not be victory for any one race, but for the pride of every nation in the world—before returning again to the level of the personal, concluding, "I was assisting in purchasing or in redeeming the greatness of mankind by my small sacrifice."[160] Xavier Garnier insists that this passage be read not as narcissism but rather literally, expressing a belief that every small act can build toward great change.[161] The global fight for justice was a very personal one for Shaaban Robert.

The same went for his art, which was personal while also seeking universality; for Robert, the very act of writing was at once exalted and quotidian. "Voluntary labor overcomes enslavement," he wrote, and "writing was my labor of choice."[162] He felt compelled to write all the time, from morning until night, whether poetry or articles or books.[163] And yet, central as writing was to his life—a compulsion that he could not resist, an act that gave him freedom—Robert was always clear that he expected to be paid for his work. For, in his words, "a writer is not an extraordinary person who can live by eating air and drinking fog."[164] For Shaaban Robert, politics and writing were at once personal and universal, ideological and practical.

In 1954, Robert published an examination of prose writing called *Kielezo cha Insha* ("*Index of Essays*" or "*Model Essays*").[165] His purpose in composing the book, as he wrote in the preface, was to assist students with their own writing. "The work of composing and writing is beset by doubts," the author sympathized with his readers; "Without a certain kind of guidance many people, who perhaps would have been better writers, give up hope, saying this education is only empowering a few people."[166] But his aim was not to suggest that every writer should conform to his suggestions. Rather than strict adherence to a specific idea of taste or beauty, Robert stressed process and practice: "A person must write many essays before they will be a good writer."[167] The meat of the book consisted of model essays, each marked so as to demonstrate to the reader (and aspiring writer) how it was constructed. He included various types of essays (there were sixty in all!) in order to avoid the impression that there was just one proper topic or way of writing. "A student should not be limited to one kind of writing," Robert wrote. "He must be given abundant opportunity. He has the option to choose whatever means he likes in his work."[168] Yet Robert's insistence on the freedom of new writers bumped up against his occasionally formulaic pedagogy, up to and including fill-in-the-blank pages on which readers could outline their essays using the organization provided.[169]

Robert included one essay entitled "*Lugha ya Watu Wote Afrika Mashariki*" ("The Language of All East African People").[170] In it he made the case that a shared language was necessary for national (and perhaps regional) unity, and that Swahili should play that role in East Africa. He offered methods by which the use of Swahili could be expanded, from using it in colleges and at regional meetings, to conducting more research into an expanded lexicon, to including Swahili subtitles in movie theaters. In the essay's conclusion, however, Robert conceded "*Hapana lugha iwezayo kuwa kamili.*"[171] ("No language can be made perfect.") That is to say, even this advocate of Swahili as a unifying force, a dedicated utilizer of Standard Swahili in his own work, recognized, in the midst of writing a handbook on essay composition, that standardization could never truly be perfect or complete. Yet Shaaban Robert, as with all the interlocutors involved in the various stages of codification and writing in Standard Swahili over the course of multiple decades, was driven to participate, even knowing that the project would never be finished. And his creativity arose within the constraints of both the standard language and the colonial context, in full awareness that—quickly or slowly, perceptibly or indiscernibly—inexorably, times change.

～

With the establishment of the East African Literature Bureau in 1948, the colonial governments of eastern Africa signaled a division between the projects of standardization and the production of literature in Standard Swahili. Administrative focus also expanded to include other East African languages, which the bureau considered to be in various states of codification. Between its essay and authorship competitions and its general literature branch, the EALB sought "creativity"—defined at times in comparison with English works, at times in terms of originality, and always with the ambiguous requirements of style and desirability. The East African Literature Bureau, like the Inter-Territorial Language Committee, was another site in which empowerment could be intertwined with oppression, and where constraint could foster opportunity. The intermediaries who contributed to and worked for the bureau experienced both extremes in their interactions with these institutions.

Though undergirded by government funding and precluded from competing with private firms, the EALB was fundamentally a publishing company, and it needed readers to buy its books. This necessitated an awareness of demand, even given Richards's recognition that the bureau would have to begin with "experimental" books that may or may not have an immediate audience. Responding to demand, however, was only one part of the EALB mandate. The other half inched closer to a prescription of "needs"—bureau officials asked themselves what it was that East African readers *should* be reading in order to inculcate the characteristics most valued by the developmentalist colonial state. These prescriptions sometimes took the form of censorship but more often meant filling the reading space with "desirable" literature, whether this be fiction, periodicals, educational manuals, civics books, or poetry. The balance of prescribing and responding could tip in one direction or the other given the needs of the colonial administrations. As the next chapter reveals, however, government insistence on broad participation in its linguistic projects—from standardization to the production of literature—created rumblings of unanticipated demands to participate on the part of colonial subjects. These demands, which began well before decolonization was on the horizon, eventually dovetailed with the nationalist project of the Tanganyika African National Union, as timelines began to converge on the issue of independence.

6 ～ Rumblings of Unanticipated Demand

IN 1937, Kihama Sangiwa, a teacher at a government school in Tanganyika, was killed in an automobile accident. Sangiwa's extended family consisted of fifteen people, and after his death they came under the legal and financial care of Sangiwa's relative, S. M. Mtengeti.[1] Mtengeti also worked for the government, as a clerk in the Provincial Office in Dar es Salaam. Mtengeti's new dependents included Sangiwa's son, Rajabu Kihama, who was set to enter school in 1939. The headmaster of the Moshi Government School, on the orders of the Director of Education, agreed to waive Rajabu's school fees in respect of his father's government service. Four years later, however, the headmaster reversed his decision, claiming that because another relative for whom Mtengeti paid fees had left the school, he should now be able to use his salary to pay the fees for Rajabu. Mtengeti sent appeals first to the Director of Education, then to the chief secretary, contending that the original agreement had implied that the fee waiver would apply to the whole of Rajabu's education; since 1939, as Mtengeti wrote, "my position with the care and maintenance of the deceased's family has not changed or either improved."[2] He was still a junior clerk, and the cost of living in Tanganyika had only risen in the intervening years.

Mtengeti's appeal to the Director of Education, however, went beyond the matter of making ends meet. In this letter, the clerk invoked the obligations of an empire toward its subjects—even of a state toward its citizens—arguing, "If, however, Sir, it is your inclination to withdraw your previous approval on the grounds stated in your letter under reference, I will philosophically accept your decision, but may add that if that is what is happening round the 'Globe' for the children of men who die for their State, many would hardly stand beside it."[3] In his response, the Director of Education ignored the potentially revolutionary nature of Mtengeti's argument, falling back on administrative protocol and insisting that the clerk could and therefore should pay the fees.[4] The chief secretary, however, recognized the power in Mtengeti's appeal and overrode the director's decision. Not only did Sangiwa, Rajabu's father, die "in circumstances which were admitted by Government to form grounds for the payment of compensation to his family," but more importantly "it is suggested that this is not the appropriate time to increase the commitments of Government servants if this can be avoided, and it is felt that in all the circumstances you may be disposed either to waive the fees or to remit one half of them."[5]

Why was the chief secretary so keen to appease a junior clerk like Mtengeti? As World War II came to an end in Europe, the colonial powers in Africa began to plan for the future, and while officials believed that empire would persist, many also realized that its longer-term survival would require some immediate changes. The decade after the war was therefore marked by the rise of "developmentalist" colonial states, as governments conceded some provisions for social services and even limited political participation to colonial subjects.[6] Materially, this shift included supplying certain "benefits" to those subjects, things including schools, libraries, and other institutions—against and within which East Africans began making demands of their own. And as the 1950s proceeded, many Africans around the continent began abandoning imperial timelines altogether, calling instead for concrete plans for independence. Alongside this now-classic political history of debates about citizenship and subjecthood in the run-up to independence, there is a parallel history of linguistic demands—demands which helped to throw a foot in the door of the eventual anticolonial struggle in East Africa, though they may not originally have had independence in mind.[7]

In the case of Rajabu's school fees, the Director of Education eventually agreed to instruct the headmaster at Moshi to charge only half fees to the boy's uncle. But the issue was still not fully settled: in 1945, Mtengeti wrote again to the headmaster at Moshi, copying the chief secretary. He explained that for two years the school had not sent him a bill, leading him to assume that the headmaster had ultimately agreed to waive the fees entirely. But the requests for payment had, it turned out, been sent to the Pare Tribal Council and the fees paid out of its Native Treasury; the council was now calling in the debt that Mtengeti had thus unknowingly accrued. "In reply to his letter," Mtengeti relayed to the headmaster, "I entreated the President [of the Tribal Council] to be good enough to continue paying the fees since the father of this boy was one of those local celebrities who did a lot to educate the majority of the many progressing Wapares [Pare people], and further the deceased was a man for whom the Native Treasury could have compunction to educate his son without hesitation."[8] In the time between sending that request to the council and receiving their negative reply, Rajabu had been sent away from the school until his fees were paid. The frustrated uncle requested that the headmaster deal directly with him in the future—losing faith, it seems, in the local indirect rule structure represented by the Pare Tribal Council.

This chapter explores the fabric of oppression and empowerment, subjugation and resistance, woven out of such threads of unanticipated demand. Language remains central to the analysis as Standard Swahili became not just a matter *of* debate but also the language *with which* to debate—to debate about the rights of colonial subjects, the obligations of the colonial state, and, eventually, about the very existence of that state.[9] As the East African administrations began to provide more and more services, they continued to insist upon the participation of colonial subjects. This insistence on *participation* only sparked demands for more widespread services and for more and more opportunity *to participate*.

Beginning with the interterritorial library system put in place by the East African Literature Bureau (EALB), the chapter then turns to Tanganyika and demands for the translation of colonial laws and ordinances into Swahili. The nation-state came into the equation only at the end of this period, as interterritorial governance began to fracture, sharpening the outlines of what would become the postcolonial states of eastern Africa. As this chapter also demonstrates, the Inter-Territorial Language Committee (ILC) and its successor organizations became increasingly "Tanganyikan" and then "Tanzanian," as did Standard Swahili. The language, however, was not destined to play this nation-building role; there is very little that is "natural" about any language policy, as evidenced by the persistence of advocates of the Arabic script into the 1940s and beyond. Rather, as we have seen throughout, Standard Swahili had been used for many different purposes over the course of many decades before the nation-state of Tanzania came into existence, and it had been used to articulate all kinds of demands. Nonetheless, by the 1960s, Standard Swahili had become an arrow in the quiver of Tanzanian nation-building.

Along with the production of books and periodicals, the East African Literature Bureau was also tasked with creating an interterritorial library service. As Charles Richards explained in his preliminary planning document, the service was another way in which the bureau could "[stimulate] both reading and the possessing of books."[10] Libraries quickly became a central part of the bureau's mission to widely circulate "desirable" reading material. Meanwhile, as we saw in the last chapter, the bureau used data collected from the libraries to assess readers' tastes and thereby better target its publication program. The EALB library system was, on one hand, a government-driven project of "development." On the other hand, however, it was built upon, and thrived because of, local demand across the territories.

There had been previous attempts to put territorial library systems into place—namely, by the Uganda government—but the service struggled to attract borrowers. The EALB library system began operations in 1950, funded by a £65,000 grant from the Colonial Development and Welfare Act for a period of six years; over that same period, the East African governments would need to contribute about £11,000 per year between them.[11] George Annesley was appointed head librarian and given the go-ahead to begin purchasing books, with an eye to building up a collection that could be circulated through rotating book boxes, with a concentration on rural areas. Books were ordered from England in October and November of 1950 and began trickling in by February of the following year. The interim period was spent setting up headquarters in Nairobi and branch offices in Dar es Salaam and Kampala, ordering equipment, and deciding where to send books. The first sites included secondary schools; police, prison, medical, or other offices; and training or social centers. In the first two years, Kenya set up thirty-nine libraries, Uganda fifty, and Tanganyika twenty-eight (Zanzibar came under the Tanganyika branch).[12] This was considerably fewer than the one hundred libraries per territory initially proposed, but the process was slowed by delays in finding staff and supplies.[13]

While each library had a degree of static stock, the bulk of the system consisted of circulating book boxes which were sent between the branch headquarters and the various local libraries. These book boxes were containers filled with volumes that could be shipped and then folded out into display cases—most reports referred to the book boxes themselves as "libraries." Each site received a new box two to three times per year, in order to keep the choices from becoming "stale."[14] In its first year of operation, the bureau ordered 18,000 books to build up its collections.[15] By 1953, Kenya had approximately 14,000 volumes in its system, Uganda 15,000, and the Tanganyika/Zanzibar branch approximately 11,000.[16] The book boxes were organized into three "Grades" based on the language of the books included. In Tanganyika the breakdown was between Swahili and English, with Grade A boxes containing more English books, and Grade C boxes a majority Swahili.[17]

Besides the book boxes, the EALB also oversaw a postal service for people who lived far from library sites. Patrons of the postal library service made a deposit of ten shillings to enroll in the system and could then choose one or two titles from the catalog, which would be sent (and then returned) in the mail for free. Distance and communication did pose obstacles for the postal library service—in Tanganyika, for instance, the only readers who had the chance to borrow more than one book per month were those living near the Central Rail Line.[18] A 1952 report from the Kenya library branch frankly listed the pros and cons of the postal service, the major disadvantages being the burden of paperwork on the branch headquarters, the cost of postage, and the unavoidable delays. But the advantages were seen to outweigh the difficulties: the postal service offered access to a far wider range of books than any single

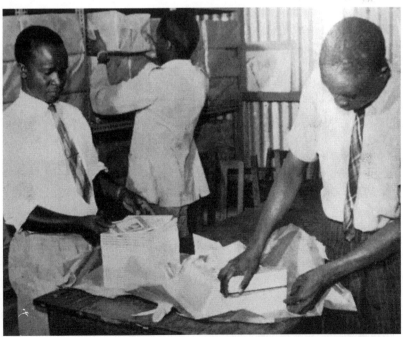

FIG. 6.1. Philip Wambua (left) and assistants, "In the Bureau's Despatch Department." EALB Annual Report 1956–57, Richards Archive PPMS12 2/24, SOAS University of London.

book box library; it served as effective publicity for the library service as a whole; "the serious student" could obtain much-needed textbooks; and the postal library service offered more valuable data about reading preferences.[19]

Uganda and Kenya were first to set up postal services, with Tanganyika following suit in 1953 (until then, Kenya had supplied books to borrowers in Tanganyika). By 1953, the bureau reported that between 1,000 and 1,200 books were issued per month through the postal service, with a total of 10,097 through September of that year. This was a significant increase over 1952 during which 7,814 books were issued for the entire year.[20] By the autumn of 1953, the Tanganyika postal service had seventy readers signed up with "more applications . . . coming in every day."[21] Uganda, in comparison, had a total of 391 readers using its postal system by September of 1953—and Kenya had 547 members already by the end of 1952.[22] In fact, by the end of that year the Kenya branch reported, "So great has been the response to this service that at one time it threatened to exceed our capacity to supply, and further publicity has been stopped for the present, until staff and bookstock can be developed sufficiently to cope with increased demand."[23] And indeed, the service kept growing: by mid-1956, Kenya had nearly 2,000 members and Uganda 1,500, "[proving] once more that a very great demand exists among Africans for books."[24] The Tanganyika/Zanzibar postal service grew more slowly, boasting only 300 members in 1956. By 1957, the Uganda postal library service had a wait list of five hundred people, for it had become "necessary to refuse new memberships, if standards of efficiency were to be preserved," and Tanganyika had grown to 424 members.[25] It was not until 1959, when increased postage costs forced the bureau to charge an additional fee and decrease the number of books sent out, that membership declined.[26]

The 1952 EALB Annual Report claimed that the most popular books borrowed were educational texts, especially instructional books on the English language, mathematics, and economics. "As yet," the report claimed, "only a few Africans read for pleasure, but there are signs that the number of these is increasing."[27] But the library service's own statistics from that year belie the notion that there was little reading for pleasure in East Africa: the 1952 numbers for Kenya showed the most popular genres to be "fiction, stories, novels," which accounted for about 15 percent of the total books issued by the postal service, followed closely by "social sciences; political science, economics, education, law, government," also 15 percent, and "applied science and useful arts; medicine, engineering, agriculture, trades, manufacture" with 14 percent.[28] Fiction was still most popular in Kenya in 1955, though "history, geography and biography" had slid into second position. The popularity of fiction kept growing, and by 1959 that genre accounted for nearly 31 percent of the total borrowings from the Kenya postal service.[29] The majority of the postal service requests were for English books—an indication perhaps of the type of reader who had the disposable income and desire to put down the ten-shilling deposit.[30] In Tanganyika and Zanzibar, however, where the library centers had more borrowers than the postal system, Swahili books were most in demand.[31]

Of course, the bureau's attempts to track demand—bumping up as they did so often against prescribing needs—could be convoluted. As a new interterritorial service, Richards stressed the experimental nature of the libraries.[32] Others referred to the inevitable "teething trouble" of the new endeavor.[33] Uganda had perhaps the best record keeping of the three branches, reporting in 1953, "An attempt has been made to instruct local librarians in the analysis by subject of books issued from the centres. By the end of the year it is hoped that all the centres will be sending in these analysed returns, or at least that they will send in their issue records to Kampala for analysis there. This should give a useful indication of the type of books most popular."[34] Of course Uganda had made the mistake, according to Richards and others within the bureau, of starting an earlier service with books that "were much too advanced and highbrow for most African readers," and thus had to "contend with the impressions left in the African reader's mind" as it recalibrated its offerings.[35] As with the bureau's publications section, the "suitability" of books was a major concern for library staff.[36] Despite lip service paid to "the special tastes and interests of Africans," it seems that the most important consideration when filling book boxes was that "no books contrary to the public interest or Government policy find their way into the libraries."[37] Yet the task of "[building] up the reading habit among Africans" did require making available books that people wanted to read, not only what the government wanted them to read.[38]

Before the bureau could effectively analyze reading tastes, however, it first had to determine which communities wanted libraries at all. On the interterritorial level, the Kenya branch developed most quickly: by 1952 there were nearly forty libraries in the territory which "with one or two exceptions . . . are all being well used."[39] A patchwork analysis indicated that each of these libraries issued between 20 and 220 books per month, with an overall estimate of 2,000–3,000 books issued per month from all the Kenya libraries combined.[40] That same year, Uganda reported that the territory housed fifty active library centers, many of them inherited from the previous library scheme.[41] In 1954, Richards reported that fifty-one libraries had been established in Tanganyika, and that the "number of borrowings up to the end of November, 1953, had totalled 11,454 which was an increase of 2,000 over the previous year."[42] By 1955, the Tanganyika branch had ninety-one book box sites which had issued 78,214 books for the year.[43] In terms of use, almost every report stressed that the borrowing statistics could not capture the number of patrons who came to the library centers to read but did not check out books, which by all accounts represented a significant number.[44]

When it came to predicting the success of any single library, Annesley and others at the bureau highlighted certain factors. First and foremost, the local librarian was considered of utmost importance.[45] The EALB relied on its local staff to run the libraries as well as to collect the ever-important statistics about library use, so whenever possible the bureau would give a training course in library management.[46] Some of the local librarians were paid for their services, which were generally only part time. A few EALB librarians went on to receive professional certificates in library science, including W. Kibwebwe from Uganda and John Ndegwa, who was crucial to organizing the library service in postcolonial Kenya.[47] This was all a part of Richards's plan to "[build] up a class of professional public librarians" who could eventually replace European staff, and he urged that EALB budget estimates "include salaries adequate to keep these men in the Service."[48] Besides the local librarians, Annesley believed that the success of a library site depended on "the senior officer on the spot, (e.g. the District Commissioner)," for, he felt, if "an African librarian is left entirely alone to run the library, without interest or encouragement by his senior officers, the issues tend to flag considerably."[49] The third leg of the stool was Annesley himself, or the central librarian whomever that might be in future, whose work included "maintaining interest by correspondence and personal visits."[50] The libraries also relied upon cooperation from the territorial governments and the various departments within them, in particular the Education and Social Development and Welfare departments, as well as the provincial administrations.[51] Even given a combination of all these factors, however, some libraries failed to attract borrowers. In the town of Morogoro in the Eastern Province of Tanganyika, for instance, the district commissioner submitted a despondent report about the local library, noting that of the few borrowers, the "bulk . . . appear to be conscripts from Standard IV."[52] The word "conscript" certainly leaps from the page here, an indication that the mere presence of a library, or even the admonition of students to use it, could not ensure success. Instead, there was genuine demand for libraries in some places, and it was this demand that determined the success of a library site.

In fact, the bureau's library system was substantially built upon local efforts. Elspeth Huxley had noted in her 1945 report that small libraries had been established in localities across all three territories and suggested that the Literature Bureau incorporate them.[53] Many of these local libraries had been established by "Native Authorities," the intermediary bodies of indirect rule set up across British colonial Africa. A local federation in the Maswa District of Tanganyika, for instance, "provided £40 in their Native Treasury estimates for 1934 to establish tribal libraries at their various headquarters," and bureau administrators believed that similarly "advanced" Native Authorities would be willing to support local libraries, which could be the building blocks of an interterritorial library system.[54] Richards, too, emphasized that the new library system would build upon existing local libraries, indicating that the first task of the central librarian would be "to tour the territories, studying the results of all library work for Africans already started."[55] In 1951, the government in Dar es Salaam solicited advice from the provincial commissioners as to where libraries could be established and the types of book boxes required at each site. Among multiple responses, those from Tanga and Arusha were two of several that mentioned the presence of existing, nongovernmental libraries or literacy programs. The provincial commissioner from Tanga reported, "The Chief has already started a small literacy scheme of his own at Vuga (without Government or N.T. funds) and the establishment of a library would therefore be appropriate both as a recognition of local initiative and demand and as a preparation for organised literacy measures in the future."[56] In Arusha, meanwhile, the Kilimanjaro Native Co-operative Union had already opened a library, and the provincial commissioner suggested therefore that the bureau library should be placed in another town.[57] Such local initiatives were central to the EALB plans for the library system, indicating where local authorities might be willing to assist with logistics and maintenance, as well as offer financial support.

The emphasis on local contributions was also an implicit acknowledgment that, in the not-too-distant future, the EALB might no longer be running an interterritorial library system; if libraries were to survive, each territory and its local authorities would need to be ready to take over. The Literature Bureau as a whole was initially only funded through 1956, so its constituent parts needed to start thinking ahead almost immediately. For its first six years, the library service was funded mainly by the Colonial Development and Welfare Act, in keeping with the underlying purpose of the program to "prime the pump" and assist governments with new programs.[58] The library system was thus set up such that there would be "a gradual devolution of financial responsibility" to the territorial governments.[59] In the late 1950s, the bureau also began to plan for the installation of more static libraries, particularly in cities and large towns; by 1959 these libraries, as opposed to the circulating book boxes, issued the largest numbers of books, thus rooting the system deeper in specific territorial spaces.[60]

FIG. 6.2. "The Bureau Library on a Saturday morning." EALB Annual Report 1960–61, Richards Archive PPMS12 2/27, SOAS University of London.

After having received a funding stopgap in 1956, by the end of the decade the bureau was on the brink of an exhausted libraries fund. At the last possible moment, officials in London agreed to send enough money to keep the interterritorial library system afloat, with the caveat that substantial reorganization take place, including long-term plans "for developing national (or central) library services."[61] The "national" at this time was still conceived of as a colonial entity, but the dissolution of interterritorial cooperation only reinforced national, eventually anticolonial, identifications.

The library service began as a system by which to expand the consumption of EALB-produced books. The libraries were also, no doubt, a part of the propaganda wing of the colonial administrations of eastern Africa. In 1950, for instance, one colonial official questioned the bureau's initial focus on rural book boxes, arguing, "Educated Africans (among whom must be counted potential trouble makers, as well as more responsible leaders of public opinion) tend to congregate in and around the larger towns, and I should have thought that the Bureau ought to have planned to reach these persons by means of literature."[62] The truth was, however, that in many cases the bureau was not executing a grand strategic plan, but was rather following on the heels of local demand for libraries. Some of these local initiatives happened at the behest of prison wardens, European school heads, and provincial and district commissioners, to be sure. But there were also libraries put in place by "Native Authorities" and "chiefs," kept running by local librarians or schoolteachers, and patronized by East African readers—beginning well before, and continuing long after, the Literature Bureau entered the arena.

TRANSLATION AND LAW

In 1948, Saadan Kandoro—a poet, organizer in the Tanganyika African Association, and future founding member of the Tanganyika African National Union—wrote a poem titled "Kitumike Kiswahili" ("Swahili should be used").[63] The poem included the refrain *"Kitumike Kiswahili, Baraza la Tanganyika"* ("Swahili should be used, the Legislative Council of Tanganyika").[64] The Legislative Council (LegCo), which had been formed in 1926, did not include any African members until 1945, and only then as "unofficial" members.[65] And when Kandoro wrote these lines, most African politicians in Tanganyika were calling for change *within* the colonial system—namely, representation on the LegCo, and, as in the poem, that Swahili be an official language of exchange in the council.[66] In this section, we move from the interterritorial level of the EALB to the territorial level of Tanganyika, exploring another kind of demand that was only eventually folded into the nationalist, anticolonial movement—specifically, demands for the translation of government regulations and ordinances into Swahili.

In the third verse of "Kitumike Kiswahili," Kandoro stressed the importance of legal translations:

Sheria zinapotoka, tuzisome bila ghali,
Ndipo tujue hakika, za haramu na halali,
Ili tupate zishika, na kuzitii kwa kweli,
Kitumike Kiswahili, Baraza la Tanganyika.

("When laws are issued, we should read them effortlessly,
Then we will know certainly, what is forbidden and what is legal,
So that we can grasp them, and obey them truly,
Kiswahili should be used, the Legislative Council of Tanganyika.")[67]

Kandoro was not the first to raise the issue of justice and translation, and the injustice of untranslated laws. When Britain took over Germany's former East African colony, accommodations for German-speaking residents became a matter for consideration. As late as 1933, for instance, the Meru Coffee Growers Association submitted a complaint to Governor Stewart Symes, accusing German speakers of shirking tax payments and using language as an excuse: "Because of persistent rumours that certain Germans have consistently refused to pay, first the Education Tax and now the Graduated Poll Tax, on the plea they do not understand English," the association appealed, "would it not be advisable for government to give wide publicity to the fact that English and Swahili are the two official languages of the country?"[68] Though the district officer in Arusha denied that German speakers were any more delinquent on their tax payments than were English speakers, the connection between language and the misunderstanding of laws—along with the Meru association's emphasis on *both* English and Swahili as official languages—indicates that language rights were considered a potential problem, and were a platform from which colonial subjects could make demands of the government.[69]

Despite the early relegation of German to nonofficial status, however, there *were* positions within the British administration devoted to translating German documents.[70] But for Swahili, one of the colony's two administrative languages, no such position existed. In fact, Tanganyika had no official policy of legal translation well into the 1950s. One unimaginative official wrote in 1930, "The matter is important, but it is difficult to see what easy way there is of securing that the natives generally are cognizant of the laws affecting them."[71] The solution seems, if not easy, then simple: as a first step, the laws should be translated. And indeed, demands for legal translations were ever present; in 1929, the chief secretary of Tanganyika conceded that "there was a very large number of well-meaning people who thought that the native was being seriously prejudiced because he could not buy a copy of the laws in Swahili."[72] Erica Fiah's paper *Kwetu* regularly raised the issue of linguistic access, suggesting that government meetings and deliberations touching upon Tanganyikan issues should be conducted in Swahili, and stressing that it was incumbent upon Europeans in government to know the language.[73] Or, as one contributor directly phrased it, "*Si lazima waseme Kiingereza tu, Kiswahili ni lugha kubwa ya Serikali katika nchi hii*" ("It is not necessary that they only speak English, Swahili is a major language of government in this country").[74] As such demands gained momentum into the 1940s, the colonial administration began making limited, ad hoc concessions, presaging the gradualist policies of political reform that characterized decolonization in Tanganyika. But the administration's hesitation to institute a blanket Swahili translation policy, even in the face of demand, is summed up succinctly in the minutes of a meeting of senior administrative officers in Dar es Salaam in 1929: "The general opinion of the Conference was that it was better, in the interests of the natives themselves, that the principal features of the laws affecting natives should be explained verbally, rather than that an attempt should be made to translate the laws into Swahili, though, in certain cases, a simple paraphrase, to be prepared in the office of the Secretary for Native Affairs, might be useful. The Conference considered that many dangers would arise if the translation of Ordinances, etc. into Swahili were attempted as the general practice."[75] What "dangers" did the colonial state envision as arising from translation? Many, as it turns out. Some at the highest levels of the administration worried that the translation and promulgation of laws could even bring the broader colonial project under scrutiny, "inevitably [creating] a demand for some form of general statement of the position of the African under the law."[76] Dangerous indeed: translation had the potential to pull the rug entirely out from underneath the colonial project. To avoid such eventualities, the translation of regulations and ordinances continued on an impromptu basis, sometimes left to African clerks, sometimes done by the ILC, other times completed by officers within the Department of Education or sent to missionaries, and sometimes done by the Information Office (later the Public Relations Office).

But the actual labor of translation was of secondary concern to Tanganyika officials, to be dealt with only after decisions were made about *what* to translate into Swahili. It was widely agreed that only the "salient features" of notices, regulations, and ordinances should be translated, those "affecting Africans."[77] These translations were therefore not intended to give readers of Swahili the opportunity to grasp all the workings of government, but merely to make clear those regulations whose translation "might help to disperse . . . ill-feeling" on particular matters such as land tenure, taxes, and so on.[78] One set of regulations considered for translation were those governing the "Native Subordinate Courts" in Tanganyika. As one colonial official argued in 1939, "From experience gained at Mwanza, Tanga and elsewhere of these N.S.Cs. it is obvious that the Liwalis, Kadhis, etc. [local African officials] have little knowledge of their duties in civil and criminal matters."[79] The officer proposed that the only "fair" solution to the problem was "that their legal duties should be made clear to them in the language that they understand. . . . I realise the difficulty of this matter but I am convinced that a Handbook in Swahili for N.S.Cs. is necessary if they are to function efficiently."[80] It was not until 1950, however, that "translations of paraphrases of certain Ordinances applied to Native Courts" were circulated to the provincial commissioners.[81] Other proposed (but not necessarily completed) translations included the Local Civil Service Regulations, the Native Authority Memoranda, and the UN Charter and Declaration of Human Rights.[82]

Besides questioning *what* to translate, some administrators queried the very capacity of Swahili to handle translations of legal concepts. The officials making decisions about translations were, on the whole, not well-versed in linguistic theory, and their arguments for the suppression of translation on the basis of Swahili's capability were unsophisticated at best. In January 1958, the *Journal of the East African Swahili Committee* (formerly the ILC) noted the failure of all four administrations to take advantage of the organization's linguistic expertise when it came to translation:

> Vigorous discussion was provoked by a suggestion that the Committee should establish facilities for translation work, to tackle the considerable demand which appears to exist among Government departments for translations of official documents. There was unanimous agreement that skilled translation was a necessity. . . . However, as the discussion proceeded it became clear that the practical difficulties of implementing the suggestion were formidable, particularly when it was realized that Governments tended to defer asking for translations until the last possible moment, and hence might actually prefer the system, or lack of system, whereby such work was given to whoever was willing to do it in his spare time.[83]

The administrations' lawyers, in particular, were desperate to avoid "getting ourselves into an awful tangle" because of misunderstandings arising from translation.[84] This issue also arose in neighboring Kenya, where one official bemoaned, "I cannot think for instance how such a phrase as 'culpable homicide not amounting to murder' could be put into Swahili. . . . The probable effect of which would be to convey to the native who tried to unravel it an impression that in certain circumstances homicide is a laudable action."[85] Legal language was difficult to decipher in English by English speakers, he continued, let alone in translation, and particularly by nonlegal experts.

Similar concerns continued to hold over the decades, though the pressure to offer Swahili translations did cause officials in Tanganyika to change their tone, conceding the desirability of translating legal notices while throwing their hands up at the perceived difficulties of doing so. One can see the dissimulation on display in 1953, referring to the request of the Kilimanjaro Native Co-operative Union (KNCU) for a translation of the UN Charter and Declaration of Human Rights: "The great objection to committing ourselves to a translation of these documents is the extreme difficulty of getting such an accurate translation of abstract ideas that it leaves no room for misunderstanding. But I doubt if we can say so to K.N.C.U. We should, however, avoid any suggestion that we are 'suppressing' them. . . . I would be inclined to reply with a simple negation—'that it is not Govt's intention to have them translated at an early date': and leave the next move with K.N.C.U."[86] Well into the 1950s, these concerns about Swahili's capacity to express legal concepts, as well as the "danger" of misunderstanding, were still being debated, even as translators both amateur and professional put the language to use for such purposes every day.

Another question raised by colonial administrators was whether there were enough literate readers of Swahili to make translation worthwhile. Were oral explanations, some officials asked, actually more effective in conveying information about government regulations? The institution of the *baraza*—a Swahili word meaning "verandah," "receiving room," "or assembly"—was central to this conversation. Both a physical location and a metonym encompassing the act of colonial officials meeting and speaking with local authorities and populations face to face, many officials pointed to the *baraza* as the best place to communicate, in spoken Swahili.[87] It was, according to senior officials in Tanganyika, "in the interests of the natives themselves" that regulations be explained orally rather than translated and published.[88] An assistant district commissioner in Kenya wrote somewhat defensively in 1930, "I wish emphatically to combat the suggestion that we deprecate translation of the laws because we wish to keep the native population in ignorance of them. It is necessary to say this because I know that such a suggestion has been made. It is definitely untrue. We feel that we can convey a much clearer understanding by means of conversations between the District Commissioners and the Native Headman, Elders and others at barazas and at informal meetings."[89] Over a decade later, Erica Fiah would contest such assertions, publishing in a special edition in 1941 (in both English and Swahili), "We respectfully submit that old and vague expression 'Native law and custom' should timely give way to a sound and universally known and WRITTEN native law."[90] Such demands grew louder over time, and when, in the mid-1940s, Africans were given representation on the Legislative Council in Tanganyika, the issue arose regularly. At a meeting of the Standing Finance Committee in May 1946, for instance, Chief Kidaha Makwaia—one of the first two Africans appointed to the LegCo—asked "whether important Government Notices could be printed in Swahili."[91] At the council meeting in July of that year, Makwaia pressed the matter further, asking, "Does Government realise the importance of having Government publications concerning Native Administration translated into Swahili for the general information of the African public? If the answer is in the affirmative, will Government see to it that this is done as soon as possible?"[92]

The administration's response to Makwaia in the moment was to dissemble, but his queries reverberated up the chain of command. That same month, the Information Department sent a letter to the acting Chief Secretary F. A. Montague, noting that the Director of Education and the social welfare officer both favored Swahili translations of laws, at least in summary form. "Now," the letter continued, "we have a similar suggestion by an African member of the Legislative Council—supported, I am sure, by several of his fellow countrymen."[93] The following year, the Tanganyika African Association held its annual conference where it, too, agitated for legal translations. The minutes of the meeting recorded:

> It was stated that the English law books used in East Africa are a great confusion to an African whose only medium of Communication is Swahili. He cannot shun what is blameable nor adhere to what is blameless. A way out of this confusion must be found if the law is to be justly administered to all people concerned. A greater number of convicts in East Africa is that of the natives. Presumably they become victims to the law because of their ignorance; at law ignorance is not an excuse. If this was the case the Conference unanimously voted that all law books in use in the East African dependencies should be translated into Swahili to justify the assertion that ignorance of law is not an excuse. Failing this the convictions passed on the Africans who know nothing of the English law are regarded as quite unjust.[94]

For Tanganyika's main African political party of the 1940s, language and the justice system were inextricably intertwined.

The issue hit close to home for officials working in the office of the social welfare organizer, who favored translation. In March of 1949 the organizer wrote to the chief secretary about a "case of extreme hardship which occurred through genuine ignorance of the Income Tax Law."[95] Seyyid Ali Khalid Barghash, who worked in the office as an assistant editor, was facing steep penalties for missed tax payments. He had paid his poll tax but had apparently been unaware of the income tax, which he paid as soon as he understood his obligation. The social welfare organizer asked that the penalties be waived, and he concluded the letter by asking, "I further request that the digests of legislation affecting the Swahili speaking population should be urgently prepared for publication in the local vernacular press."[96] By this point, the demands for translation were becoming less and less deniable, arriving as they were from multiple directions.

In May of 1949, following up on the demands of the Tanganyika African Association (TAA), Chief Secretary Montague drafted a reply that attempted to put off action until some future date. Referring to the requests made at the organization's meeting, "in which it was suggested that all law books should be translated into Swahili," Montague wished "to inform [the members of the Association] that Government has had this proposal under consideration for some time. As an initial step the revision and bringing up-to-date of the Native Courts Ordinance is contemplated, and thereafter it is hoped to publish from time to time a 'digest' in Swahili of legislation which affects the African community."[97] Prior to giving this response to the TAA, an officer in the Secretariat had circulated instructions to the territory's provincial commissioners. "This subject [of translating laws into Swahili] has been under consideration for some time," he wrote, "and various suggestions have been made for keeping the African informed of the laws to which he is subject."[98] It had become increasingly clear, he continued, that demand for translation would continue until some policy was put in place, despite the numerous difficulties raised by the issue. "As you are aware," the officer concluded, "a new Native Courts Ordinance is in course of preparation and as soon as it has become law … a new edition of Native Administration Memorandum No. II will be prepared and a suitable précis in Kiswahili of both Ordinance and Memorandum will be made. Thereafter 'digests' in Kiswahili of legislation affecting the African will be published from time to time."[99]

Yet the distribution of published translations took place only slowly and erratically. In response to a request from a district commissioner in the Southern Province, asking which ordinances would be translated for the year and if he could receive an extra copy, the member for local government in Dar es Salaam replied, "It is unlikely that any Swahili versions of Ordinances will be distributed during 1951."[100] Requests for translations kept pouring in, from groups like the Kisutu Ward Council in Dar es Salaam, the KNCU, and the provincial commissioner of Tanga province.[101] Resistance to Swahili translations nevertheless persisted. Non-African members of the Legislative Council were particularly vociferous in their opposition to the inclusion of Swahili in the governmental process—despite the fact, of course, that since the establishment of the Mandate, Swahili had been a recognized language of colonial administration, up to and including governmental funding for institutions such as the ILC and EALB. In 1950, the European members of Tanganyika's Committee on Constitutional Development rejected the idea that Swahili be introduced as a second language in the Legislative Council, "on the grounds that a bilingual state was undesirable, and that the Swahili language was incapable of adequate expression for the purpose."[102] The reaction seems dramatic in light of the fact that the committee's

African members had requested only "the right to speak in Swahili. It was not necessary that all papers, laws etc. would be translated."[103] The momentum for Swahili could not, however, be denied, and by 1950 LegCo reports were starting to be translated. The step was applauded in a letter written by P. S. E. Mhando to the *Tanganyika Standard,* which carried the connection between language and governance to its logical conclusion: "This announcement proves that it is quite possible to interpret the discussion and translate the records of the Legco from Swahili to English and vice versa, thus removing the only obstacle to the admission of more African members in the Legco."[104] Mhando's sentiments were echoed at the Conference of the Provincial Commissioners of Tanganyika, who had finally come around on the issue, recommending that Swahili "should be introduced as an official language in the Legislative Council."[105] The Secretariat's reply to that recommendation, however, hearkened back to prior prevarications, underlining the continued tension between governmental promotion of Swahili and its hesitation to commit to official bilingualism:

> Although Kiswahili is the lingua franca of the territory and has been adopted as the official vernacular for education and other purposes, it is still in process of development and the continual introduction of the new words is necessary to make it an effective medium for the exchange of views on modern complicated matters. . . . Its use as an official language in certain local government institutions and representative bodies is quite feasible, though even there its limitations are apparent. In the case of the Legislative Council there would not only be the inconvenience and delay of interpretation during debates but it would be necessary to provide precise official translations of laws and other complicated material into a language which is not sufficiently developed for the purpose and which would require such artificial manipulation as to make the result in many cases unintelligible to most readers.[106]

The government even went so far as to argue that most Tanganyikans would not favor the introduction of Swahili into the LegCo, because so many were eager to learn English—an idea belied by the demands of African LegCo members, among others. Yet resistance to Swahili translation continued—in 1954 one official suggested that "if Africans want to know the details of the Ordinances etc. they just have to learn English."[107]

By the end of the decade, however, such arguments could not stand. In 1958, the Tanganyika Government Printer published a pamphlet titled *Sheria za Serkali Kuu* ("The Laws of the Central Government"), which was reviewed in the East African Swahili Committee (EASC) *Journal* in both English and Swahili. In his English-language review, R. S. King opened with one of the questions that had plagued attempts to translate laws from the very beginning. "It is often assumed, and sometimes argued," King wrote, "that the niceties of modern law go ill if at all, into African tongues. Is this really true of a language with as wide a scope as Swahili?"[108] The language, King insisted, could encompass topics as diverse as seafaring, commerce, religion, philosophy, and diplomacy. "Today," King continued, "it is acquiring, without undue pain, the power to deal with science and politics. Is law a thing wholly apart?"[109] There were interpreters in courts across Tanganyika, he pointed out, who translated laws into Swahili every day, and the *Sheria za Serkali Kuu* was a necessary printed confirmation of that fact. King concluded his review by looking ahead, indicating that many more such translations would be necessary in the near future, even if English-language education began to grow in the territory: "Political development will make it necessary to issue more of these to explain, even if not to translate, laws and the more successful they are in achieving their political purpose, the more likely they are to prove Swahili capable and, in proving it capable, to make it capable of being a language of modern law and government."[110] The Swahili-language review of *Sheria za Serkali Kuu* was written by C. P Kabyemera, whose opinion of the publication was just as positive as King's, though he suggested a few specific changes to the translations.[111] Still, Kabyemera insisted, *Sheria za Serkali Kuu* would be of great value to Tanganyika's citizens.[112]

Language policy is one of the fundamental questions of governance, a baseline from which many other policies extend; and over the course of nearly forty years, the colonial administration of Tanganyika declined to formulate a policy of translating laws and regulations into Swahili. In the end, it took decolonization for these demands to be fully addressed, and as the colonial subjects of Tanganyika began to imagine themselves as citizens of an independent nation-state, language came to shape their community-in-creation. Swahili was made the official language of the Republic of Tanganyika (a position only reinforced with the 1964 incorporation of Zanzibar into the United Republic), and in 1963 the East African Swahili Committee reported that "the Minister for Justice has set up a Committee with the Hon. Secretary, East African Swahili Committee as its Secretary to work on a legal vocabulary which will later be used to translate the laws into Swahili."[113] That same year, the aforementioned minister of justice, Sheikh Amri Abedi, opened the annual meeting of the EASC by looking ahead at the linguistic tasks facing the newly independent country: "An example of what is needed is illustrated by the necessity to set up in the Ministry of Justice, my own

Ministry, a complete Translation Section, whose function is first to build up a vocabulary of legal terms and phraseology, before embarking upon the vast undertaking of translating the laws of Tanganyika into Swahili."[114] Until that moment, the arguments against translation had remained remarkably stable: there were questions about whether or not Swahili could be satisfactorily used to translate legal concepts; there were questions about whether Swahili would be the best language for communicating such information; and there were the ever-present "dangers"—the danger of misunderstanding, the danger of wasted effort, and the danger of protest. And yet, thanks to the continuous demand of East Africans, laws were translated, albeit on an ad hoc basis, across this entire period.

STANDARDIZATION AND THE ARABIC SCRIPT

Another group making linguistic demands upon the administration of Tanganyika was made up of those who read and wrote Swahili in the Arabic script (or most often a modified form thereof, referred to as 'Ajamī), and who wanted to be able to continue to do so in official venues such as government schools. While the lexical "de-Arabization" of Swahili was a theme in some European circles (e.g., the biblical translation of German missionary Karl Roehl, published in 1937), the ILC never described its work in these terms.[115] Rather the bureaucrat-linguists echoed their missionary predecessors in lazily dismissing the Arabic script as unsuited to Swahili pronunciation—an argument which ignored the ingenuity of Swahili speakers who modified the script in various ways to mold it to their communicative needs.[116]

Despite its official dismissal, however, 'Ajamī Swahili and its users could not be wholly ignored: in 1936 the administration of Tanganyika considered the inclusion of Arabic script in its lower-level Swahili examinations for administrative officers. Ironically, given what we have seen above regarding government's haphazard translation policies, the assistant secretary of Native Affairs, A. E. Kitching, also insisted that government publications should be published in both Latin and Arabic scripts.[117] As one of his colleagues put it, "Kitching feels very strongly that the Government is ignoring the Moslem population of the Coast and that a little more effort in the direction of furnishing information and advice in the characters most easily read by that population would be very much appreciated and would react to the benefit of both Government and the people."[118] The administration sought to purchase, and even considered creating, a manual that new colonial officers could use to learn the Arabic script, and ideally how it was used to write Swahili by the coastal communities of East Africa. Claiming a lack of suitable pedagogical materials, however, the matter was dropped in most official circles by 1940.

Meanwhile, on Zanzibar, the Arabic language itself became a topic of debate, particularly in the creation of government syllabi.[119] While Swahili had long been the unchallenged lingua franca of the island—its dialect serving, of course, as the basis of Standard Swahili—as well as a first language for many Zanzibaris, Arabic retained an important symbolic role. In 1953, John Rankine, the resident of Zanzibar, outlined the issues facing that territory in terms of education and language. He dismissed out of hand the idea of using Arabic, first, because he believed that the use of English across the East African territories should be the ultimate goal of the British colonial regime; moreover, Rankine reported, very few Zanzibaris "can speak or write Arabic with any ease or accuracy." However, he continued, "for a variety of reasons, religious, historical, political and, one might add, social, it has an importance which is not revealed by any statistical analysis. . . . My concern here is not with the rights and wrongs of this (it is clearly right that Arabs should take a pride in their culture and Moslems in their religion) but with the complication which it has in fact introduced into our educational syllabus."[120] Rankine went on to explain that from Standard III through Standard VIII, students at government schools on Zanzibar were learning three languages at once—Swahili, English, and Arabic—which he believed lowered the overall standard of English. He proposed changing the syllabus to circumscribe the teaching of Arabic in primary schools, turning it into an optional subject in secondary schools where it could fulfill "something of the same educative function as a study of the classics in European schools." Rankine recognized that "the matter is a delicate one for political and other reasons, and before any change of this kind can be introduced into the syllabus the ground will have to be very carefully prepared."[121] Despite dwelling on the question of Arabic and its effects on English in Zanzibari schools, Rankine revealed the underlying linguistic reality in his closing note: "I must apologise that so much of this letter is taken up with the question of Arabic teaching rather than English, but the two, as I have explained, are closely bound up together and must indeed be regarded as rival aspirants to the place of 'second language' in Zanzibar."[122] Yet Arabic remained a consideration for the colonial administration there, and the interterritorial organizations chipped in: the EALB provided Arabic books for the islands' libraries and, in the early 1960s, produced at least two textbooks for learning Arabic.[123]

Arabic-script Swahili, meanwhile, continued to play an important role in the lives of many coastal dwellers. We briefly encountered Sheikh al-Amin Mazrui in chapter 4, when an excerpt from his bilingual Swahili-Arabic newspaper *Al-Islah* was reprinted in the 1934 *Bulletin* of the ILC. Much of the excerpt centered around the question of script, emphasizing the "harm" ("*madhara*") done to Swahili by the Latin script and the "shame" ("*aibu*") of wearing a "borrowed coat" ("*kanzu ya kuazima*")—that is, the Latin alphabet.[124] He called on scholars and students writing in Swahili to eschew the Latin script, thereby setting a good example for the entire Swahili-writing populace. And while *Al-Islah* was printed in the Latin script (largely in the Kimvita dialect), Sheikh al-Amin had previously circulated a weekly pamphlet called *Sahifa* ("The Page") which was written in Swahili using an 'Ajamī script.[125] With his writing and publications, Sheikh al-Amin in fact embarked on a standardization project of his own, pioneering "the systematization of the Arabic script through the use of superscript and subscript diacritical symbols to make it more suitable for the writing of Swahili."[126] He also reportedly requested of the colonial government that both Latin- and Arabic-script Swahili be officially recognized, and that all Swahili-language books already published using the Latin script be re-released in Arabic script as well.[127]

Another twentieth-century figure central to the preservation and proliferation of Arabic-script Swahili manuscripts was Muhamadi Kijuma of Lamu, who was an invaluable interlocutor to well-known European scholars including Alice Werner and Ernst Dammann. This latter described Muhamadi Kijuma's style of writing Swahili in the Arabic script: "In my opinion M.K. had no rigid principles in respect of the pronunciation of such words. It seems to have depended on the extent to which the individual speaker was aware of the Arabic origin of the word and wanted to show this by his pronunciation.... Each writer had a certain degree of freedom. It would be interesting to know whether M.K. always used the same method, something which I am inclined to doubt, at least in respect of certain details."[128] But Kijuma, too, supported the idea of codification, calling on Harold Lambert in 1929 to organize a meeting in Lamu to discuss the matter.[129] The desire to standardize, that is, was not limited to proponents of the Latin script.

Yet Kijuma, according to Dammann, was "a representative of a transitional period. He still lived in the old tradition though he knew it was no longer working."[130] This reflected the views of an outsider to that tradition, to be sure, but Gudrun Miehe and Clarissa Vierke have noted that, by the 1930s and 1940s, scholar-artists like Kijuma were producing more work for "foreigners who cherished the idea of a Swahili culture" than they were for local use, as handwriting—where 'Ajamī scripts flourished—gave way to print and other modes of communication.[131] But 'Ajamī scripts have in no way disappeared from use: studies from West Africa report, for instance, that 70 percent of the population of Labé in Guinea Conakry is literate in Fuuta Jalon Fula 'Ajamī. The same percentage holds for Diourbel, Matam, and Podor in

Senegal, while 80 percent of the population in parts of Niger and Nigeria are literate in Hausa 'Ajamī.[132] Fallou Ngom has described the layered praxis of communication and record keeping among scholars in West Africa, who might write to one another in Arabic, speak in a regional lingua franca, but keep personal notes in an 'Ajamī script—including his father, who "recorded most of his life in Wolof Ajami," spoke Fuuta Jalon Fula with visiting scholars, annotated Arabic texts (a language he could not speak) with 'Ajamī notes, and whose "written legacy includes no page of Seereer, his mother tongue."[133]

In the more recent East African context, the figure of Ahmed Sheikh Nabhany exemplified the perhaps necessary versatility of Swahili scholars in the last half century. Nabhany, born in Lamu in the late 1920s, was a poet who operated in two scripts (Arabic and Latin) and three languages (Swahili, English, and Arabic).[134] He traveled in Africa, Europe, the Middle East, and the United States, received prestigious scholarships and honors, and advised PhD candidates in various fields, all while remaining a local force of linguistic, historical, and cultural authority.[135] As Kai Kresse has described, Nabhany's poetic work and scholarly consultations included two interconnected but divergent aims: that of preserving specific cultural knowledge via the Swahili language (most often in the Kiamu dialect), as well as that of advocating for the expansion of the Standard Swahili lexicon by coining words using the etymology of the language's dialects.[136] Nabhanay thus positioned himself as both conservationist and innovator, looking to the past for knowledge both cultural and linguistic in order to make Swahili (and the language's speakers) ready for the future, and addressing his poetry to an audience that included both the "insiders" and the "insider-outsiders" who make up the Swahili-utilizing community in its broadest sense.[137] The impressive balancing act practiced by Ahmed Sheikh Nabhany—not to mention his linguistic skills, wide base of historical and cultural knowledge, and dogged commitment to research and conversation—demonstrates one path by which the connections between Swahili in all its dialectical, spoken, and written forms can be strengthened.

The modes of writing Swahili used by scholars such as Sheikh al-Amin Mazrui or Muhamadi Kijuma were just two in a long line of innovative ways to mark the pronunciations of African languages with modifications to the Arabic script, not just in East Africa but around the continent. Meikal Mumin has referred to 'Ajamī-script writing as an "understudied literacy," a literacy whose depth and breadth (he and his colleagues have attested the existence of at least eighty indigenous African writing traditions) renders ridiculous any notion that "Africa was a continent without writing."[138] Mumin argues further that Africa does not "have history *despite*" a dearth of written sources, but rather that historians of Africa long lacked the awareness and appreciation of these collections of primary sources, as well as, often, the technical proficiency to understand them—a state of affairs that, it must be said, is changing thanks to the work of scholars such as Fallou Ngom, John Mugane, Coleman Donaldson, and many others.[139] Helmi Sharawy has outlined several projects launched across the continent in the last several decades to study and preserve Arabic-script manuscripts, from Mali to Zanzibar, Senegal to South Africa.[140] And outside of the realm of academia, the recognition of non-Latin-script literacy has consequences for governments and citizens alike: the official nonrecognition of such literacy is not only a problem for censuses and their results, but redounds to the resources available to people in the languages that they use.[141]

Though Arabic-script Swahili has not successfully made the jump to print media as have, for instance, Hausa or other West African languages written with 'Ajamī scripts, it is "still in use in the horizontal sphere," including private correspondence, poetry, or as an important marker of particular types of identity all along the coast.[142] Clarissa Vierke and Chapane Mutiua have, for instance, chronicled the long life of Swahili poetry in Mozambique, written in Arabic script and recited at special occasions—a context beyond what is traditionally considered the heartland of Swahili poetry.[143] In a volume published by the Institute of Kiswahili Research in Dar es Salaam, Abdu Mtajuka Khamisi—an advocate of Swahili as an international language—asked, "Therefore today in East Africa is there anyone who is able to come forward and say that the Swahili of today is his possession?" and—more to the point—"What would it even mean to make such a claim!"[144] Khamisi's incredulity must be taken to heart by admirers of Swahili across the spectrum, from its Latin-script standardized version to its every individualized 'Ajamī form: the recognition, study, and celebration of Swahili in all its modes should pull devotees together, not build walls between them.

⌐

Throughout the colonial period, East Africans made appeals of various kinds to their governments, including along linguistic lines for things like reading material, libraries, and the translation of laws. Some of these requests were met, while others were refused. Most initially called for change within the colonial system, and only slowly became anticolonial in nature. Charles Richards himself made the connection between the kinds of linguistic appeals that the EALB was created to meet, and their evolution into anticolonial demands, writing in his memoir, "As nationalism and the desire for independence grew there naturally grew up a literary expression of these inevitable results of imperial government. . . . This was an expected (by me, anyway) outcome of our pioneer work."[145] Meanwhile, both colonial officials and colonial subjects began to imagine the constituent territories of the ILC/EASC and EALB in a more and more atomized way, laying the foundation for *national* movements of colonial reform and anticolonial protest. Indeed, the interterritorial organizations themselves had anticipated their own eventual dissolution into territorial units: by 1954—the same year as the establishment of the Tanganyika African National Union—the Literature Bureau was already using the term "national" in reports about the library service.[146]

The EASC, for its part, became ever more national in its postcolonial existence. The committee transferred its offices from Makerere to Dar es Salaam in 1963–64 in part because the committee leadership believed that "it was better for this research to be done in a country like Tanzania where Swahili was joined at the hand with government rather than Uganda where it would have competed with Luganda."[147] By 1964, the committee had changed names yet again, to the Institute of Kiswahili Research (*Chuo cha Uchunguzi katika Lugha ya Kiswahili*)—marking its new form as an academic organization under the auspices of the University College, Dar es Salaam.[148] From that point on, as Ireri Mbaabu has described, the Institute "operated its affairs as a national rather than an East African Institute."[149] Standard Swahili, too, became more closely associated with Tanganyika/ Tanzania, though the *idea* of Swahili as a regional, Pan-African, and/or diasporic lingua franca remained seductive into the postcolonial period and has in some communities, as we shall see in these final pages, indeed been given such a role.

Conclusion

IN NOVEMBER 1961, the East African Swahili Committee (EASC; formerly the Inter-Territorial Language Committee) held its twenty-fifth annual meeting on the campus of Makerere University. In just a month's time, Tanganyika would gain independence from Great Britain with Julius Nyerere as prime minister; a year after that, Tanganyika would become a republic with Nyerere serving as president. In the minutes from the 1961 meeting, the committee included a resolution that read, "It was REGRETTED that Tanganyika had chosen to use 'UHURU' to mean both 'FREEDOM' and 'INDEPENDENCE.'"[1] The standard dictionaries of the ILC differentiated the two ideas, linking *uhuru* to the sense of "freedom from slavery, liberty, emancipation," while "independence" included a range of notions from political self-determination ("*kujitawala*") and the possession of economic means ("*-enye mali*"), to personal characteristics such as stubbornness ("*obstinacy*") or intractability ("*ugumu*").[2] And yet, no matter what the dictionaries said or the linguists preferred, *Uhuru!* was the political slogan on which the Tanganyika African National Union (TANU) had ridden to power, independence, and freedom of multiple connotations—in the light of which excitement the committee's rebuke appears futile at best, petulant at worst. Events had moved quickly past the standardizers: *uhuru* was "a word in motion" and the members of the EASC could only record their disapproval in the journal.[3] In this concluding chapter, I would like to sketch the travels of Standard Swahili, its speakers, and its writers since Tanganyika's independence. The portability of the language raised then and continues to raise questions about *which*

Swahili gets used *when* and by *whom*, and the duck-rabbit of standardization has yet to resolve into any single temporal or directional plane.

WHICH SWAHILI?

Soon after the formation of TANU in 1954, Julius Nyerere embarked on a "political *safari*" along with fellow organizers Bibi Titi Mohamed and Elias Kisenge, giving speeches and encouraging people across Tanganyika to join the party.[4] It was in this period that the "double-edged" nature of Standard Swahili became widely apparent, as the language adopted for colonial administration began to be used as an organizing tool for an anticolonial movement. While the political activism of the 1950s did not suddenly imbue Swahili with the capacity for resistance, its use by Nyerere and TANU linked the language inextricably to a *nationalist* cause. Nyerere proudly reported, for instance, that during his multiple speaking circuits around the country, he had only needed to use an interpreter twice (or maybe thrice).[5]

Swahili took on both symbolic and practical functions after Tanganyika achieved independence in 1961 and the union (*muungano*) with Zanzibar in 1964. This dual role was given clear political-ideological language in Nyerere's Arusha Declaration of 1967. The concept of *Ujamaa*—familyhood or "African socialism"—as articulated by Nyerere has received much scholarly attention.[6] In terms of language, the Arusha Declaration reiterated the central place of Swahili in Tanzanian political, cultural, and social life. In 1968, S. S. Mushi, the "Promoter of Swahili Language and Literature," gave a paper that explicitly linked creative work in Swahili to Nyerere's *Ujamaa* ideology. He started by outlining the conventional wisdom on nation-building: "Often times, when we talk of 'Nation Building,'" Mushi began, "we tend to imagine a group of people gathered for the purpose of making a road or a bridge, digging a waterchannel or a well, building a school or a hospital, or doing any other piece of communal or self-help work for the benefit and prosperity of the public."[7] Such images of the physical construction of the nation squared with Nyerere's policies of villagization and communal agricultural labor. "But," Mushi continued, "this list does not exhaust all that our men and women could do. There are other vital fields of activity, and which, perhaps, for one reason or another, have not appeared to us to be nation-building activities. One of these vital fields is the *Writing of Books*."[8] Mushi was reminding his listeners that the creation of literature in Swahili, once the official charge of the colonial state and its Literature Bureau, had been taken over by the independent government of Tanzania, and that this, too, was a part of the construction of a nation. Mushi's remarks coincided with the establishment of the National Swahili Council of Tanzania (*Baraza la Kiswahili la Taifa,* or BAKITA), the Society for Swahili Composition and Poetry in Tanzania (*Chama cha Usanifu wa Kiswahili na Ushairi Tanzania,* or UKUTA), and the National Swahili Council of Zanzibar (*Baraza la Kiswahili la Zanzibar,* or BAKIZA), which together promoted the use of Swahili in Tanzania along broad lines.[9] Jan Blommaert has argued that, evaluating the totality of *Ujamaa* policies from the 1960s through Nyerere's retirement from the presidency in 1985, "language was the only issue on which absolute clarity reigned; the connection between the new nation and its new language, Swahili, was a fixed trope that was never challenged: in the independent Tanzania, the national language would be Swahili."[10]

Bibi Titi Mohamed, however, remembered things a bit differently; in describing Julius Nyerere's first speech as a TANU leader in Dar es Salaam in 1955, she recounted, "So when Nyerere arrived, someone translated [from English to Swahili] for him. I've forgotten who. That's correct. Nyerere didn't know [Swahili]. I say in this matter I was his teacher."[11] This is at first an unbelievable claim, given that Nyerere would go on to translate Shakespeare's *Julius Caesar* ("*Juliasi Kaizari*") and *The Merchant of Venice* ("*Mabepari wa Venisi*") into Swahili, among other foundational speeches and writing in that language. Yet as noted by Susan Geiger, who recorded Bibi Titi's life history, the female activist's comment highlights the various registers of Swahili that were still in circulation in Tanganyika. Nyerere, who had been educated first in Zanaki and then English, had a "by-the-book" knowledge of Swahili, "correct and fluent, but lacking in familiarity with or appreciation of popular idiom, forms of delivery as expressions of particular meaning, ways of manipulating words and phrases to make people laugh, and so forth. In other words, Nyerere needed to learn how to talk to people; and Bibi Titi was a superb teacher."[12]

Nor should the universality of Swahili, of any dialect, be overstated. Emma Hunter found during her fieldwork conducted in the Mwanza Region that "elderly men who remembered the growth of the nationalist movement in the 1950s recalled that while Julius Nyerere would address crowds in Swahili, many of his auditors could not understand what was said, and for the majority small group discussions held in the Sukuma language afterwards were more important than public rallies in shaping local understandings."[13] The concerted literacy drives conducted by TANU in the postcolonial period also indicate that the ability to read Swahili was anything but universal, with the literacy rate estimated at around 16 percent in 1961.[14] Meanwhile, debates about orthography and grammar continued into the early years of independence, in forums both official and unofficial, including the letters-to-the-editor section of the independent but TANU-supporting newspaper *Ngurumo* ("Thunder").[15] But the Tanzanian government was nevertheless committed to educating citizens in Swahili, creating a terminal primary school curriculum in that language as well as the adult literacy campaigns, which, for instance, enrolled some 5.2 million Tanzanians between 1972 and 1975, with a subsequent two million passing the national literacy test.[16] Such policies created a genuine sense of Tanzanians as *Waswahili*, with a shared national linguistic identity.[17]

The same cannot be said for the other two territories that had constituted the EASC and East African Literature Bureau: Uganda and Kenya. The colonial government of Uganda had moved decisively away from Swahili after World War II, emphasizing English as a lingua franca alongside non-Swahili vernaculars.[18] After independence in 1962, Swahili was largely associated with the police and military, a situation only exacerbated during the reign of Idi Amin, though this has begun to change. In Kenya, Swahili had served a symbolic purpose for the Kenya African National Union, with its slogans of *Harambee!* ("Pull Together!") and *Uhuru na Kazi* ("Freedom and Work").[19] After independence in 1963, however, the country's leaders took a "laissez-faire attitude towards language," which divided the country socioeconomically and regionally between English, Swahili, and vernacular languages.[20] Various Swahili dialects, too, held more popular support in Kenya than in neighboring Tanzania, lending a sometimes "purist motive" to Swahili activists in the former.[21] Kenya is also the home of Sheng and Engsh, vernaculars based on Swahili that, while earlier associated with youthful Nairobi speakers, have been embraced by advertisers, media producers, and politicians alike.[22] Such a linguistic matrix provided stiff competition for Standard Swahili.[23] Yet while Kenyan emphasis on Swahili as a national language has waxed and waned, it inarguably serves an important purpose in that country's society, as author Binyavanga Wainaina reflected in his memoir: "In this part of [Nairobi], all three Kenyas live: city people who work in English making their way home; the village and its produce and languages on the streets; and the crowds and crowds of people being gentle to each other in Kiswahili. Kiswahili is where we meet each other with brotherhood."[24] And while we often talk about languages competing in a zero-sum game using violent terms such as language "death" or even "suicide"—and while language policies do carry serious stakes for the citizens of every country—closer to the truth might be Abdulrazak Gurnah's description of "learning to read" and write as "a process of accumulation" of various registers, or what Salikoko Mufwene describes as "mutual accommodations," a repertoire in which Standard Swahili, for many speakers, has a role.[25]

Meanwhile, the East African Swahili Committee had to find its place in the postcolonial world, the world of independent nation-states, of the East African Community, and of the Organization of African Unity. This included the move back to Dar es Salaam and transformation (in 1964–65) into the Institute of Kiswahili Research at the University College of Dar es Salaam, with Wilfred Whiteley as director. In the first issue of the *Journal* following the EASC's transformation into the Institute, Whiteley reflected, "While we respect and learn from the past we cannot live in it. We have to live in the present while planning for the future."[26] But often in the realm of language, as we have seen, future planning requires attending to the past, and the scholars of the Institute of Kiswahili Research quickly put the dictionaries of Standard Swahili back onto the agenda. In a matter simultaneously perceived as "urgent" and likely to "take a full ten years,"[27] the March 1966 issue of the *Journal* included an official announcement about the dictionary revisions, expressing a now-familiar admixture of fixture and fluidity: "Two points are illustrated here: firstly, lexicography is a never-ending task, the dictionary maker of to-day builds on the labours of his predecessors and his work will in turn need to be revised by others after him. The reasons for this are easily stated: language itself is constantly changing. . . . A dictionary, however adequate at its first appearance, becomes progressively less so as time passes, and for this reason most major dictionaries have permanent revision committees. The second point illustrated is that dictionary making is a long job and must be viewed in terms of years rather than months."[28]

The Institute returned to the compilation process of the 1930s, word slips and all: while the editors, led by J. A. Tejani, scoured all previous dictionaries as well as the word lists that the EASC had diligently compiled over the years, the Institute also called on individuals to submit contributions, with Whiteley stressing: "A Dictionary cannot be compiled simply by a small team of research workers. They are dependent to a very large extent on the co-operation received, not merely from scholars throughout the world, but also, and most importantly, from Swahili speakers within East Africa."[29] Two years into the dictionary revision, the Institute had collected over thirteen thousand cards from contributors, inviting more and anticipating the receipt of six thousand additional slips before the dictionaries would be printed—which, the new director George Mhina hoped, would happen within the next year or so.[30]

All did not, however, go according to plan. In fact, the process went on for many years and the first revision, that of the *Kamusi ya Kiswahili Sanifu*, did not appear until 1981. The *English-Swahili Dictionary* was published in 1996, and the *Kamusi ya Kiswahili-Kiingereza* did not appear until 2001.[31]

Politics, and particularly the deceleration of Tanzania's policies of "Swahi-lization" over the course of the 1980s and 1990s, certainly slowed work on the revisions.[32] Another key factor, however, was that such projects just take time. Dictionaries, grammars, books, libraries, curricula—the material components of standardization—these move slowly, using existing knowledge to plan for the future, all the while attempting to accommodate usefulness in the present.

WHOSE SWAHILI?

What did all of this time devoted to standardization actually buy? Two of the outcomes were commensurability and portability. Portability had been a characteristic of Swahili since at least the nineteenth century, when the language could be heard in the extracontinental African diaspora on the lips of merchants, enslaved people, and other migrants with deep connections to eastern Africa. But by the mid-twentieth century, Swahili began to find traction in perhaps unexpected places, made increasingly portable through the development of a tangible, commensurable infrastructure built of dictionaries, grammars, newspapers, literature, syllabi, et cetera. Such written resources are one part of the story of Standard Swahili's portability: the language was "shaped by millions of printed words into a 'concept' on the printed page and, in due course, into a model" as to whose "'it-ness,' as it were, no one ever after had much doubt."[33] But grammars and dictionaries alone did not consolidate Standard Swahili's portability: just like the idea of the nation as examined by Benedict Anderson, Swahili in all its forms has attracted passionate loyalty from various corners of the globe, including within parts of the Black American community of the United States.

Africa writ large rose into American political consciousness in the 1950s and 1960s because of Cold War considerations—namely, concerns to "secure" Africa from communism. The Kennedy administration, for instance, extended a modicum of goodwill gestures toward newly or nearly independent African nations, including programs such as the "African airlifts," which allowed hundreds of East African students to enroll in colleges and universities across the United States. (Such programs also offered a way to signal support for civil rights without, supposedly, alienating southern voters.)[34] It was in this period, the 1950s and 1960s, that African language programs at American universities began to find the support of the federal government, initially as a part of the National Defense Educational Act of 1958 (origin of the Title VI Foreign Language and Area Studies centers).[35] Swahili was, and still is, the African language (besides Arabic) that garnered the largest enrollment in American universities, and by a wide margin: from 22 students

nationwide in the fall of 1960 (the last year in which Yoruba had more en-
rollees), to 123 in the fall of 1962, 1,241 in 1998, and 1,593 in 2002.[36] And the
Swahili being taught in those classrooms was Standard Swahili. A pragmatic
decision perhaps, not unlike the teaching of Modern Standard Arabic in the
face of that language's many dialects, and a decision that can and has been
criticized on the grounds of comprehensiveness. Yet the portability of Standard Swahili placed the language at the fingertips of Black American civil
rights activists across the political and ideological spectrum.[37]

In 1968, the *Washington Post* reported on the opening of the Freedom
School—Shule ya Uhuru—an annex of Eastern High School in Washington,
DC.[38] The school, founded and run by a student organization known as the
Modern Strivers and sanctioned by the municipal school board, offered supplementary courses for students from Eastern who sought an education that
centered the Black experience, in the forms of history, philosophy, literature,
art, drama, current events, and community organizing.[39] The Modern Strivers came of age as the civil rights movement transitioned to an argument
for human rights, driven by the ideological and organizational forces of the
Black Power movement. The cultural nationalist side of the movement emphasized racial pride, in part through connections to Africa, hearkening to
the global Black experience shared by Africans from the continent and in
the diaspora. At the Shule ya Uhuru, teachers and students sought to shape
an education "geared for black students and directed to solving the problems of the black African nation inside and outside the United States."[40] Swahili became a central way for Black cultural nationalists to connect with the
African continent, an Africa that "at the level of geography, identity and consciousness," according to Keith Mayes, "had to be invented or re-invented by
black Americans for black Americans."[41]

Why Swahili? That is, why did major figures and organizations choose
to center their cultural revolution on an East African rather than West
African language, the region of descent for many Black Americans? Such
a question, as Ali and Alamin Mazrui phrase it, is "reminiscent of the
divide-and-rule policies of the colonial era," for it was Swahili's status as
a Pan-African language, not a "heritage" language, that attracted activists
and organizers including Maulana Karenga.[42] Karenga started the organization "US" in southern California in 1965; the name refers to the Black
community as "us" as opposed to "them"—that is, the oppressive white
majority.[43] While Karenga was certainly not the only activist to promote
Swahili, and while his organization was not without its critics, its found-
er's desire "to detail the theoretical underpinnings of his self-styled liberation strategy" is helpful in understanding the role of Swahili in the Black

cultural nationalist movement of the 1960s and 1970s.[44] Maulana Karenga's foray into community organizing and activism happened side by side with his study of Swahili, starting at Los Angeles Community College. "Swahili's ubiquity, at least in East Africa, attracted Karenga to the language," writes Keith Mayes; "What appeared most important was the language's continental origin and its regional coverage. If Swahili could serve as a national language for some continental Africans, then Karenga and US believed Swahili could serve as an unofficial lingua franca for culturally awakening African-Americans desiring to demonstrate African roots and assume a greater African posture."[45] Karenga himself explained, "[Swahili] is an African language and it is non-tribal; we are not interested in identifying with any one tribe but with African people."[46] Black Power activists consciously linked the struggle for human rights and self-determination in the United States with the similar struggles taking place on the African continent. Pan-Africanism thus became an ideological pillar for many Black cultural nationalists in the United States, and particularly the Pan-Africanism of Julius Nyerere, including his promotion of Swahili as a simultaneously supra-ethnic, national, and continental language. As Ali and Alamin Mazrui remarked, "It was as if Nyerere was anticipating the development of Swahili into a language of global Africa."[47] Whether because of Nyerere's blend of traditionalism and socialism, his support for militant groups fighting the white supremacist regimes in southern Africa, or his inclusion of Black Americans under the Pan-African umbrella, there existed according to Ali Mazrui a kind of "Tanzaphilia" among segments of the Black nationalist movement in America.[48] And despite tensions within and between Pan-Africanists and Pan-Africanisms, the centrality of Tanzania to both the ideology and action of Pan-African cooperation lent Swahili the flexible organizing power cited by Karenga.[49]

Besides the formation of US, Karenga is perhaps best known as the creator of Kwanzaa; the holiday, first celebrated in December of 1966, began as part of Karenga's "black protest calendar" and has now been widely embraced as a kind of "multicultural" celebration in the United States.[50] The name is inspired in part by the Swahili phrase *matunda ya kwanza* ("first fruits") used to describe harvest festivals; Karenga added an *a* to the word in order to, according to various accounts, link the seven principles celebrated during the holiday to the seven-day week; to differentiate it from the actual Swahili word; or to include an extra child in the first Kwanzaa celebrations.[51] Karenga also used Swahili to name the seven principles (*Nguzo Saba*) underpinning the holiday: *umoja* (unity), *kujichagulia* (self-determination), *ujima* (collective work and responsibility), *ujamaa* (familyhood/cooperative economics), *nia* (purpose), *kuumba* (creativity), and *imani* (faith). In the elaboration of Kwanzaa, Karenga used Swahili to link the human rights struggle of Black Americans to the "powerfully explosive continental and diaspora politics" then sweeping across Africa.[52]

John Mugane describes the language used by Karenga as "easily recognizable as taken from what is considered to be Standard Swahili," with some notable adaptations including the use of anglicized word order and plurals (e.g., *karamus* for "feasts").[53] During performances, for example, dancers in US's Taifa Dance Troupe would count off their steps with shortened Swahili numbers—that is, rather than "moja, mbili, tatu," the dancers would chant, "ja, li, tu."[54] While Karenga's organization did offer Swahili lessons in some communities, the "grammatical or syntactical minutiae of the language" was rarely emphasized in his activism; Swahili appeared mainly in the targeted use of words.[55] At institutions such as Shule ya Uhuru, too, certain Swahili words entered the vernacular of the students, with calls for *Umoja!* mixed naturally in with English writing.[56] And by the early 1970s, Swahili words had made their way out of the activist realm and into advertising campaigns in magazines like *Ebony* and *Jet.*[57]

Swahili also became, however, a serious part of the curriculum at the Freedom School and at colleges and universities across the country, thanks to pressure from students to create Black studies departments and to offer programs in African languages.[58] This was a part of what Eyamba Bokamba has described as "the re-appropriation of [programs in African languages]" by Black American activists, students, and intellectuals, from a national defense, Cold War–driven origin to a vital part of Black nationalist thought.[59] In 1973, the *Black Collegian* magazine, for instance, printed Swahili lessons, inviting readers to study the language that "besides being a tremendous asset for the unfolding movement of African cultural restoration . . . is an easy and delightful language to learn."[60] There is an earnestness to the lessons, an expectation that the collegiate readers of the magazine would devote time to the exercises and learn the structures of the language. The Swahili lessons of the *Black Collegian* underpin Keith Mayes's assertion that the constructedness of these links between Black cultural nationalism in the United States and the Swahili language did not make them any less meaningful or authentic: "In the sense that Kwanzaa takes from Africa, it is an old-world original import. In the sense that Kwanzaa takes from nowhere in Africa, but rather is created in Los Angeles, it is imagined."[61] So, too, with the holiday's adopted language: the portability of Standard Swahili allowed it to be brought into the civil rights and Black cultural nationalist movements, which then made the language their own.

In a talk given in June of 2021 to the members of the Swahili Heritage Trust in Mombasa, Ngũgĩ wa Thiong'o recounted a potentially embarrassing moment avoided. Some thirty-five years earlier, he had been invited to give a lecture at the BBC on the topic "Is English the language of the world?" Not aware that Prince Philip, patron of the nonprofit "English Speaking Union," was present in the wings, Ngũgĩ made the case instead for Swahili to be the unifying global language.[62] Though the prince lent an understanding ear, Ngũgĩ stood ready to defend his arguments: unlike English, Swahili was not associated with imperial conquest; it was spoken in East and Central Africa and growing in importance across the continent; and it was being learned by people around the world. Three decades later in Mombasa, Ngũgĩ reiterated his case for the widespread use of Swahili, asserting that it is the heritage of all Africans, not only those of the continent's eastern coast. While advocating strongly for the official adoption of Swahili in more realms, however, Ngũgĩ also warned against hierarchical thinking. "I implore all Swahili enthusiasts," he stressed. "Please let us not make Swahili sit on the seat where English once sat; a seat of condescension, requiring other languages to kneel down. We must abandon this system of ranks."[63]

One could read Ngũgĩ's remarks as a condemnation of Standard Swahili, construing its dictionaries and grammars as part of the obsession with *lugha hasa* ("exact" or "particular" language), which he rejects. But it seems to me that Ngũgĩ wants us to eschew linguistic hierarchies of all kinds. He wants us to stop regarding one language variety as more important than another either because it is "standard" or because it is "authentic"; because it is a mother tongue or a second language; or because it is spoken in the classroom or in the marketplace. Swahili has been and can be a powerful linguistic force exactly *because* of its availability on multiple planes to a multitude of speakers and writers. Ngũgĩ concluded his talk: "Therefore let us be proud of our mother tongues; let us be proud of Kiswahili as the national language; and on top of that let us add the knowledge of English or Mandarin or French or Yoruba, et cetera. These will only give strength to our proficiency and communication. But our foundation is made of our mother tongues and the language of the entire nation, that is Kiswahili. . . . Kiswahili can be the language of African Unity!"[64] In Ngũgĩ wa Thiong'o's vision, pride in one's own language does not foreclose language learning, linguistic borrowing, or creativity. These activities can and should be combined, with Swahili serving the particular role of Pan-African language of communication. And in some ways, Ngũgĩ's suggestions are already being implemented. In 2019, the

Southern African Development Community named Swahili one of its four official languages, the only non-European one on the list, and the South African Department of Basic Education has proposed offering Swahili as an optional subject of study. Already by 1998, Ali and Alamin Mazrui declared Swahili to be approaching a "*universalist* stage when the language has become the most widely used African language internationally and is becoming the medium of scientific discourse and technology."[65] And while Standard Swahili continues to be debated and shaped in eastern Africa, its resources have helped the language to become truly global, "a language alive" that continues to win speakers not through conquest but through participation.[66]

The history of Standard Swahili, several threads of which have been the subject of this book, is a history that must incorporate fluid geographies and multiple timescales, while also finding root in specific places and times. Some standards, Swahili included, achieve both geographic and temporal portability—never perfect or unchanging, but able to be adopted and adapted by a multitude of speakers and writers. Standard Swahili has empowered some, who have deployed it for creative or political purposes; it has oppressed others, whose linguistic repertoires are categorized, at times denigrated, as nonstandard. Even for the linguistically disenfranchised, Standard Swahili has at various times offered a powerful machine against which to rage. And while Standard Swahili always has been, and always will be, undergoing revision, it nevertheless offers a baseline of commensurability.

In this book, I have sought to capture the "duck-rabbit" moments—periods during which the short-term existed alongside the long-term, or when power and action moved from the top-down and bottom-up simultaneously. In considering the longer historical timeline alongside brief snapshots of the language's history, it becomes clear that Standard Swahili was not simply imposed on East Africans during the British colonial period. Nor, however, was it naturally transposed from nineteenth-century Zanzibar into the textbooks, dictionaries, and novels of the mid-twentieth century. The process involved decision-making and contingency, lessons imperfectly learned and others deliberately taught, and communities converging on the process for divergent reasons. Standardization was a shared goal and an acknowledged impossibility, driving the actions of real people across more than a century of East Africa's history, all of whom sought, and achieved, linguistic commensurability. My greatest hope is that this book will similarly serve as a baseline, a point from which other threads of this history can be followed. History, like language, is inescapably bound up with questions of time, embedded in a specific temporality while, if it is to go on living, constantly under revision.

Notes

INTRODUCTION

1. His name suggests that he had been born in the region of Lake Nyasa (Malawi), in the southwestern part of modern-day Tanzania or northern Mozambique; the origins of the name Owen are less clear.

2. Edward Steere, *Central African Mission: Its Present State and Prospects* (London: Rivingtons, 1873), 17, BDL, UMCA Box List A-F: A1(II)A. [Collection "UMCA Box List A-F" hereafter referred to as "Box List," housed at the Bodleian.] Zanzibar is the name of an archipelago off the east coast of Africa, the largest island of which is Unguja; Zanzibar, however, is often used to refer to the main island, a practice I adopt unless clarification is necessary.

3. For biographical information on Makanyassa, see Universities' Mission to Central Africa Annual Report 1871–2, 19, Box List: A1(I)A; Letter from L. Pennell to E. Steere, July 14, 1870, A1(III)C; "Missionary Life in Central Africa, by Geo. Wm. Mallender," Box List: A1(IV)B; and "The Register of the Old Boys of St. Andrew's College, Kiungani and Minaki, together with short notes of the History of the College, 1871–1931," BDL, UMCA SF Box List, SF No. 79 I-II.

4. Steere, *Central African Mission,* 18.

5. Recognizing the tug-of-war between "a terminology of authenticity" and "a terminology of intelligibility," I have chosen to follow the example of Alamin Mazrui and Ibrahim Noor Shariff in foregoing the use of the *Ki* prefix when referring to the Swahili language (i.e., Kiswahili), utilizing instead the English translation "Swahili." See Alamin Mazrui and Ibrahim Noor Shariff, *The Swahili: Idiom and Identity of an African People* (Trenton, NJ: Africa World Press, 1994), ix–x.

6. Letter from E. Steere, April 6, 1867, Box List: A1(I)A; Universities' Mission to Central Africa Annual Report 1871–2, 20, A1(I)A; Letter from A. C. Madan to W. Penney, October 26, 1885, A1(VI)A; *Central Africa* no. 13 (January 1884): 8; *Central Africa* no. 16 (April 1884): 74; and R. M. Heanley, *A Memoir of Edward Steere, D.D., L.L.D., Third Missionary Bishop in Central Africa,* 3rd ed. (London: Office of the Universities' Mission to Central Africa, 1898), 248.

7. Letter from E. Steere to J. Festing, August 1, 1874, Box List: A1(III)A.

8. Universities' Mission to Central Africa Annual Report 1871–72, 19, Box List: A1(I)A. Though the curmudgeonly Arthur Madan complained in 1885 that Makanyassa "[was] not accurate at all." Letter from A. C. Madan to W. H. Penney, October 26, 1885, Box List: A1(VI)A.

9. Universities' Mission to Central Africa Report 1876 (Oxford Google Books Project), 7; and *Msimulizi* no. 32 (December 1893): 709, BDL.

10. See, for example, Thomas Kuhn, *The Structure of Scientific Revolutions,* 4th ed. (Chicago: University of Chicago Press, 2012), 85, 112–15, 120.

11. "To the Supporters of the Central African Mission," Box List: A1(III)A.

12. W. H. Whiteley, "Ideal and Reality in National Language Policy: A Case Study from Tanzania," in Joshua Fishman, Charles Ferguson, and Jyotirindra das Gupta, *Language Problems of Developing Nations* (New York: Wiley, 1968), 327.

13. John Mugane, *The Story of Swahili* (Athens: Ohio University Press, 2015), 219.

14. Derek Peterson, *Creative Writing: Translation, Bookkeeping, and the Work of Imagination in Colonial Kenya* (Portsmouth, NH: Heinemann, 2004), 8.

15. Peterson, *Creative Writing,* 9.

16. See David Crystal, *The Stories of English* (New York: Overlook, 2004); and Jean-Benoît Nadeau and Julie Barlow, *The Story of French* (New York: St. Martin's, 2006).

17. Benedict Anderson, *Imagined Communities: Reflections on the Origin and Spread of Nationalism,* rev. ed. (New York: Verso, 2006), 42.

18. Anderson, 72–75.

19. Joseph Errington, *Linguistics in a Colonial World: A Story of Language, Meaning, and Power* (Malden, MA: Blackwell, 2008), 100–102. Errington incorrectly identifies Ranavalona as a king.

20. See Geoffrey Lewis, *Turkish Language Reform: A Catastrophic Success* (New York: Oxford University Press, 1999); Ilker Aytürk, "Revisiting the Language Factor in Zionism: The Hebrew Language Council from 1904 to 1914," *Bulletin of the School of Oriental and African Studies* 73, no. 1 (2010): 45–64; Elisabeth Kaske, "Mandarin, Vernacular and National Language—China's Emerging Concept of a National Language in the Early Twentieth Century," in *Mapping Meanings: The Field of New Learning in Late Qing China,* ed. Michael Lackner and Natascha Vittinghoff (Boston: Brill, 2004), 265–304; Tommaso Pellin, "The Sweet Revolutionaries: The Chinese Revolution in Grammar Studies and Henry Sweet," *Language and History* 54, no. 1 (May 2011): 35–57.

21. Derek Peterson and Emma Hunter, "Print Culture in Colonial Africa," in *African Print Cultures: Newspapers and Their Publics in the Twentieth Century,* ed. Derek Peterson, Emma Hunter, and Stephanie Newell (Ann Arbor: University of Michigan Press, 2016), 12.

22. Jan Blommaert argues similarly from a sociolinguistic point of view: Blommaert, *State Ideology and Language in Tanzania,* 2nd ed. (Edinburgh: Edinburgh University Press, 2014), 153–54.

23. For "constructed" languages such as Esperanto and Ido, see Esther Schor, *Bridge of Words: Esperanto and the Dream of a Universal Language* (New

York: Metropolitan Books, 2016); and Michael Gordin, *Scientific Babel: How Science Was Done Before and After Global English* (Chicago: University of Chicago Press, 2015), 105–58.

24. Mugane, *Story of Swahili,* 270.

25. Mugane, 215.

26. Rocha Chimerah, *Kiswahili: Past, Present and Future Horizons* (Nairobi: Nairobi University Press, 1998), 83.

27. Mugane, *Story of Swahili,* 40.

28. Letter from G. Dale to D. Travers, September 18, 1904, Box List: A1(XIV).

29. "Conference between Government and Missions. Convened by His Excellency the Governor, Sir Donald Cameron. Report of proceedings. Held at Dar es Salaam, 5th to 12th October 1925," (Dar es Salaam: Government Printer, c. 1926), 102.

30. "Conference between Government and Missions," 102.

31. John Iliffe, *A Modern History of Tanganyika* (New York: Cambridge University Press, 1979), 265.

32. "Conference between Government and Missions," 102.

33. "Conference between Government and Missions," 103.

34. Iliffe, *Modern History of Tanganyika,* 267; and Andreana Prichard, *Sisters in Spirit: Christianity, Affect, and Community Building in East Africa, 1860–1970* (East Lansing: Michigan State University Press, 2017), 147–48.

35. Iliffe, *Modern History of Tanganyika,* 266.

36. "Conference between Government and Missions," 22.

37. Deborah Coen, *Climate in Motion: Science, Empire, and the Problem of Scale* (Chicago: University of Chicago Press, 2018), 20.

38. Coen, 16.

39. Coen, 20.

40. On Barak, *On Time: Technology and Temporality in Modern Egypt* (Berkeley: University of California Press, 2013), 121.

41. Barak, 83.

42. Barak, 244.

43. Barak, 244.

44. See Erik Gilbert, *Dhows and the Colonial Economy of Zanzibar, 1860–1970* (Athens: Ohio University Press, 2005); and Thomas McDow, *Buying Time: Debt and Mobility in the Western Indian Ocean* (Athens: Ohio University Press, 2018).

45. Emma Hunter, "Print Media, the Swahili Language, and Textual Cultures in Twentieth-Century Tanzania, ca. 1923–1939," in *Indigenous Textual Cultures: Reading and Writing in the Age of Global Empire,* ed. Tony Ballantyne, Lachy Paterson, and Angela Wanhalla (Durham, NC: Duke University Press, 2020), 191; and McDow, *Buying Time,* 8, 271.

46. See, for instance, Karin Barber, ed., *Africa's Hidden Histories: Everyday Literacy and Making the Self* (Bloomington: Indiana University Press, 2006), and *The Anthropology of Texts, Persons and Publics* (New York: Cambridge University Press, 2007), 137–99; Emily Callaci, *Street Archives and City Life:*

Popular Intellectuals in Postcolonial Tanzania (Durham, NC: Duke University Press, 2017); Isabel Hofmeyr, *The Portable Bunyan: A Transnational History of "The Pilgrim's Progress"* (Princeton, NJ: Princeton University Press, 2003); Emma Hunter, *Political Thought and the Public Sphere in Tanzania: Freedom, Democracy and Citizenship in the Era of Decolonization* (Cambridge: Cambridge University Press, 2015); J. D. Y. Peel, *Religious Encounter and the Making of the Yoruba* (Bloomington: Indiana University Press, 2000); Peterson, *Creative Writing,* and *Ethnic Patriotism and the East African Revival: A History of Dissent, c. 1935–1972* (New York: Cambridge University Press, 2012), and "Vernacular," in *Critical Terms for the Study of Africa,* ed. Guarav Desai and Adeline Masquelier (Chicago: University of Chicago Press, 2018), 331–45; and Peterson, Hunter, and Newell, *African Print Cultures.*

47. Joseph Errington discusses the ways that deviations from standard speech, including notions of "accent" and "dialect," have become in some historical contexts "marks of personal deficiency" rather than simply "differences of usage." Errington, *Linguistics in a Colonial World,* 108. Jonathon Glassman, meanwhile, describes the ultimately dangerous racial/linguistic "chauvinism" that arose with the choice of Kiunguja as the basis of Standard Swahili. Glassman, *War of Words, War of Stones: Racial Thought and Violence in Colonial Zanzibar* (Bloomington: Indiana University Press, 2011), 88–89.

48. For more on the dialects of Swahili, see Derek Nurse, "A Tentative Classification of the Primary Dialects of Swahili," *Sprache und Geschichte in Afrika* 4 (1982): 165–205; Joan Russell, *Communicative Competence in a Minority Group: A Sociolinguistic Study of the Swahili-Speaking Community in the Old Town, Mombasa* (Leiden: Brill, 1981); and Mugane, *Story of Swahili,* 32–37.

49. Among a multitude of examples, see Clarissa Vierke, *On the Poetics of the Utendi: A Critical Edition of the Nineteenth-Century Swahili Poem "Utendi wa Haudaji" Together with a Stylistic Analysis* (Zurich: Lit Verlag, 2011); Rose Marie Beck and Kai Kresse, eds., *Abdilatif Abdalla: Poet in Politics* (Dar es Salaam: Mkuki na Nyota, 2016); and Xavier Garnier, *The Swahili Novel: Challenging the Idea of "Minor Literature"* (Suffolk: James Currey, 2013).

50. Johannes Fabian, *Language on the Road: Notes on Swahili in Two Nineteenth Century Travelogues* (Hamburg: H. Buske, 1984).

51. Anderson, *Imagined Communities,* 81.

52. Pier Larson, *Ocean of Letters: Language and Creolization in an Indian Ocean Diaspora* (New York: Cambridge University Press, 2009), 348.

53. The terminology surrounding the idea of vernacular, local, ethnic, or indigenous knowledge has been a matter of much debate. For a sampling, see Clapperton Mavhunga, *The Mobile Workshop: The Tsetse Fly and African Knowledge Production* (Cambridge, MA: MIT Press, 2018); Nancy Jacobs, *Birders of Africa: History of a Network* (New Haven, CT: Yale University Press, 2016); Abena Dove Osseo-Asare, *Bitter Roots: The Search for Healing Plants in Africa* (Chicago: University of Chicago Press, 2014); Helen Tilley, *Africa as Living Laboratory: Empire, Development, and the Problem of Scientific*

Knowledge, 1870–1950 (Chicago: University of Chicago Press, 2011); and "Global Histories, Vernacular Science, and African Genealogies; Or, Is the History of Science Ready for the World?," *Isis: A Journal of the History of Science* 101, no. 1 (March 2010): 110–19; William Beinart and Karen Brown, *African Local Knowledge and Livestock Health: Diseases and Treatments in South Africa* (Rochester, NY: James Currey, 2013); and Patrick Harries, *Butterflies and Barbarians: Swiss Missionaries and Systems of Knowledge in South-East Africa* (Athens: Ohio University Press, 2007).

54. Derek Nurse and Thomas Hinnebusch, *Swahili and Sabaki: A Linguistic History* (Berkeley: University of California Press, 1993), 1–2, 21–23. For more on the early linguistic history of Swahili and the social/cultural history of the Swahili coast, see Derek Nurse and Thomas Spear, *The Swahili: Reconstructing the History and Language of an African Society* (Philadelphia: University of Pennsylvania Press, 1985); John Middleton, *The World of the Swahili: An African Mercantile Civilization* (New Haven, CT: Yale University Press, 1992); David Massamba, *Historia ya Kiswahili: 50 BK hadi 1500 BK* (Nairobi: Jomo Kenyatta Foundation, 2002); and Abdul Sheriff, *Dhow Cultures of the Indian Ocean: Cosmopolitanism, Commerce and Islam* (New York: Columbia University Press, 2010).

55. See Nurse and Hinnebusch, *Swahili and Sabaki,* 21; and Mugane, *Story of Swahili,* 147–48.

56. See Mugane, *Story of Swahili,* 175–91, and "The Odyssey of ʿAjamī and the Swahili People," *Islamic Africa* 8, nos. 1–2 (2017): 193–216.

57. In the official realm, the debate about Swahili orthography was not so contentious for Swahili as it was for other African languages. The ILC rejected the "scientific," phonetic alphabet of the International Institute of African Languages and Cultures (IIALC) early on, so that while the spelling of specific words, and the creation of spelling norms and rules, *were* a part of official discussions, the alphabet never was. In fact, advocates for Standard Swahili often insisted that its orthography should be utilized by the standardizers of other East African languages. For some of those debates, see Derek Peterson, "Language Work and Colonial Politics in Eastern Africa: The Making of Standard Swahili and 'School Kikuyu,'" in *The Study of Language and the Politics of Community in Global Context,* ed. David Hoyt and Daren Oslund (Lanham, MD: Lexington Books, 2006), 185–214, and *Creative Writing,* 117–37. For a look at this debate in West Africa, see Isaac Adejoju Ogunbiyi, "The Search for a Yoruba Orthography Since the 1840s: Obstacles to the Choice of the Arabic Script," *Sudanic Africa* 14 (2003): 77–102. The history of science can also offer a useful framework for analysis on the topic of the compromises required of collaboration; see, for instance, Susan Leigh Star and James Griesemer, "Institutional Ecology, 'Translations' and Boundary Objects: Amateurs and Professionals in Berkeley's Museum of Vertebrate Zoology, 1907–39," *Social Studies of Science* 10, no. 3 (August 1989): 387–420.

58. For a concise comparison of Tanganyika and Kenya, see Peterson, "Language Work and Colonial Politics in Eastern Africa," 190–92. For language policy in Uganda, see Ireri Mbaabu, *Language Policy in East Africa: A Dependency Theory Perspective* (Nairobi: Educational Research and Publications, 1996), 93–114.

59. Portions of this chapter have appeared in Morgan Robinson, "Binding Words: Student Biographical Narratives and Religious Conversion," in *The Individual in African History: The Importance of Biography in African Historical Studies,* ed. Klaas van Walraven (Boston: Brill, 2020), 197–218.

60. Portions of this chapter have appeared in Morgan Robinson, "The Idea of the *Upelekwa:* Constructing a Transcontinental Community in Eastern Africa, 1888–96," *Journal of the History of Ideas* 81, no. 1 (January 2020): 85–106.

61. Portions of this chapter have appeared in Morgan Robinson, "La Belle Époque from Eastern Africa: An Individual Experience of the 'Globalizing' World, 1898–1918," *Journal of Eastern African Studies* 13, no. 4 (2019): 584–600.

CHAPTER 1: "NOTE-BOOKS AND SLOWLY ACCUMULATING VOCABULARIES"

Epigraph: "The Work of Christ in Central Africa, A Letter to the Rev. H. P. Liddon, By the Rev. J. P. Farler," (London: Rivingtons, 1878), 31, Box List: A1(IV)B.

1. "The Universities' Mission to Central Africa, A Speech Delivered at Oxford, By Edward Steere, LLD," Box List: A1(III)A.

2. Patrick Harries, *Butterflies and Barbarians: Swiss Missionaries and Systems of Knowledge in South-East Africa* (Athens: Ohio University Press, 2007), 157.

3. See Carolyn Hamilton, *Terrific Majesty: The Powers of Shaka Zulu and the Limits of Historical Invention* (Cambridge, MA: Harvard University Press, 1998); Thomas Spear, "Neo-Traditionalism and the Limits of Invention in British Colonial Africa," *Journal of African History* 44, no. 1 (2003): 3–27.

4. As Sara Pugach described missionary involvement in linguistic study, it was important "to usher potential converts into an international Christian community," the great equalizer that "would reincorporate Africans into the family of civilized man." Sara Pugach, *Africa in Translation: A History of Colonial Linguistics in Germany and Beyond, 1814–1945* (Ann Arbor: University of Michigan Press, 2012), 26, 57.

5. John Mugane, *The Story of Swahili* (Athens: Ohio University Press, 2015), 98–105.

6. Thomas McDow, *Buying Time: Debt and Mobility in the Western Indian Ocean* (Athens: Ohio University Press, 2018), 8.

7. Stephen Rockel, *Carriers of Culture: Labor on the Road in Nineteenth-Century East Africa* (Portsmouth, NH: Heinemann, 2006).

8. These wordlists included that composed by Samuel Masury, "A Vocabulary of the Soahili Language, on the Eastern Cost of Africa," *Memoirs of the American Academy of Arts and Sciences,* New Series, vol. 2 (1846), 248–52. Steere mentioned manuscript vocabularies "collected by Mr. Witt and Mr. Schultz, then representing the firm of O'Swald and Co. in Zanzibar." Edward Steere,

A Handbook of the Swahili Language, as Spoken at Zanzibar (London: Bell & Daldy, 1870), v. For an in-depth investigation of the genre of the wordlist, see Johannes Fabian, *Language and Colonial Power: The Appropriation of Swahili in the Former Belgian Congo, 1880–1938* (New York: Cambridge University Press, 1986).

9. Much of the following biographical information about Krapf is based on Shihabuddin Chiraghdin and Mathias Mnyampala, *Historia ya Kiswahili* (Nairobi: Oxford University Press, 1977), 54–56; P. J. L. Frankl, "Johann Ludwig Krapf and the Birth of Swahili Studies," *Zeitschrift der Deutschen Morgenländischen Gesellschaft* 142, no. 1 (1992): 12–20; M. Louise Pirouet, "The Legacy of Johann Ludwig Krapf," *International Bulletin of Missionary Research* 23, no. 2 (April 1999): 69–74; Pugach, *Africa in Translation;* and Joan Russell, *Communicative Competence in a Minority Group: A Sociolinguistic Study of the Swahili-Speaking Community in the Old Town, Mombasa* (Leiden: Brill, 1981), 42–51. See also J. L. Krapf, *Travels, Researches, and Missionary Labors, during an Eighteen Years' Residence in Eastern Africa* (London: Trübner, 1860).

10. The first manuscript of the dictionary was apparently destroyed by white ants, setting the missionary-linguist back several years.

11. For more on orthographic decisions vis-à-vis Swahili, see Caitlyn Bolton, "Making Africa Legible: Kiswahili Arabic and Orthographic Romanization in Colonial Zanzibar," *American Journal of Islamic Social Sciences* 33, no. 3 (2016): 61–78.

12. J. L. Krapf, *A Dictionary of the Suahili Language* (London: Trübner, 1882), xi. Rebmann apparently held that translators should reject the Zanzibar dialect because of its Arabic borrowings, whereas Krapf came around to the position that the Zanzibar dialect was a useful resource. See Krapf, *Dictionary,* xi–xii.

13. Martha Lampland and Susan Leigh Star, eds., *Standards and Their Stories: How Quantifying, Classifying, and Formalizing Practices Shape Everyday Life* (Ithaca, NY: Cornell University Press, 2008), 14–15.

14. J. L. Krapf, *Vocabulary of Six East-African Languages (Kisuaheli, Kinika, Kikamba, Kipokomo, Kihiau, Kigalla)* (Tübingen: L. F. Fues, 1850); and J. L. Krapf, *Outline of the Elements of the Kisuaheli Language, with Special Reference to the Kiníka Dialect* (Tübingen: L. F. Fues, 1850).

15. Krapf lived to see the first and second editions of Steere's *Handbook of the Swahili Language,* and to his eyes, Steere's work relied heavily on his own. Steere, for his part, was open about the influence that Krapf's dictionary had on his own *Handbook.* Krapf's dictionary and Steere's handbooks do present similar vocabulary with recognizably shared roots, despite some orthographic differences; yet both missionaries acknowledged that they were championing different dialects of the language.

16. Krapf, *Dictionary,* x.

17. Krapf, *Outline of the Elements,* 5.

18. Krapf, *Dictionary,* xi.
19. Copy of Letter from Tozer to Bishop of Cape Town, June 14, 1864, Box List: A1(I)A.
20. The origins of the Universities' Mission are well known and documented. For this introductory section, I rely on the official, published mission histories: A. E. M. Anderson-Morshead, *The History of the Universities' Mission to Central Africa, 1859–1896* (London: Universities' Mission to Central Africa, 1897), *The History of the Universities' Mission to Central Africa, 1859–1909,* 5th ed. (London: Universities' Mission to Central Africa, 1909), *The History of the Universities' Mission to Central Africa,* vol. 1, *1859–1909* (London: Universities' Mission to Central Africa, 1955); A. G. Blood, *The History of the Universities' Mission to Central Africa,* vol. 2, *1907–1932* (London: Universities' Mission to Central Africa, 1957), and *The History of the Universities' Mission to Central Africa,* vol. 3, *1933–1957* (London: Universities' Mission to Central Africa, 1962); and George Herbert Wilson, *The History of the Universities' Mission to Central Africa* (London: Universities' Mission to Central Africa, 1936).
21. For an in-depth account of this first attempt, see Landeg White, *Magomero: Portrait of an African Village* (New York: Cambridge University Press, 1987). The UMCA was initially co-sponsored by the universities of Cambridge, Oxford, and Durham in England, and Trinity College in Ireland.
22. Sultan Majid, incidentally, also gifted the mission with its first five formerly enslaved pupils, as well as "an eightday clock with chimes etc." Letter from E. Steere, November 11, 1864, Box List: A1(1)A. Years later, Sultan Barghash provided the UMCA with a clock for its church tower.
23. See, for instance, Edward Alpers, *Ivory and Slaves: Changing Pattern of International Trade in East Central Africa to the Later Nineteenth Century* (Berkeley: University of California Press, 1975); Rockel, *Carriers of Culture;* and Matthew Hopper, *Slaves of One Master: Globalization and Slavery in Arabia in the Age of Empire* (New Haven, CT: Yale University Press, 2015).
24. In the early 1870s, for instance, the UMCA ruffled feathers by trying to build a seawall along a disputed property line; an officer in the Foreign Office wrote to the mission leadership "that it would under the circumstances be more judicious to cease from endeavouring to complete the wall, as a persistence in such a purpose can only have the effect of irritating the Sultan and the Muslim Community among whom the Missionaries labour, and thus increase the difficulties of their position." Extract of Letter from T. V. Lister, ZNA, UMCA Records, CB1–15.
25. For more on "liberated Africans" in the Indian Ocean, see Hopper, *Slaves of One Master;* and Padraic Scanlon, *Freedom's Debtors: British Antislavery in Sierra Leone in the Age of Revolution* (New Haven, CT: Yale University Press, 2017)
26. For a full account of the training of female teachers at the UMCA, see Andreana Prichard, *Sisters in Spirit: Christianity, Affect, and Community Building in East Africa, 1860–1970* (East Lansing: Michigan State University Press, 2017).

27. In 1899, the theological college moved to Mazizini, another site on Zanzibar. Then, in 1925, St. Andrew's College moved to Minaki, close to Dar es Salaam. Kiungani also housed the printing press until 1897, when it was moved to Mkunazini. The mission eventually also established printing presses at Likoma and Magila.

28. Morgan Robinson, "Cutting Pice and Running Away: Discipline, Education and Choice at the UMCA Boys' Industrial House, Zanzibar, 1901–1905," *Southern African Review of Education* 19, no. 2 (2013): 9–24.

29. For reports on Majaliwa's ordination, see "Kuamriwa Kasisi Wetu Mweusi wa Kwanza," *Msimulizi* no. 9 (February 1890): 129–30, BDL; and Anderson-Morshead, *History* (1909), 182–83.

30. Joseph Errington has argued, "Faith drew so many to the work of conversion that missionaries count as the group which has produced the single largest body of knowledge about linguistic diversity around the world." Joseph Errington, *Linguistics in a Colonial World: A Story of Language, Meaning, and Power* (Malden, MA: Blackwell, 2008), 13.

31. For a comprehensive linguistic history of east-central Africa, see Derek Nurse and Thomas Hinnebusch, *Swahili and Sabaki: A Linguistic History* (Berkeley: University of California Press, 1993). For a broader overview of Bantu languages, see Derek Nurse and Gérard Philippson, eds., *The Bantu Languages* (New York: Routledge, 2003).

32. Nurse and Hinnebusch, *Swahili and Sabaki,* 34; and Nurse and Philippson, *Bantu Languages,* 1.

33. See, for instance, Terence Ranger, "Missionaries, Migrants and the Manyika: The Invention of Ethnicity in Zimbabwe," in *The Creation of Tribalism in Southern Africa,* ed. Leroy Vail (Oxford: James Currey, 1989), 118–50; Harries, *Butterflies and Barbarians;* and Errington, *Linguistics in a Colonial World.*

34. For more on Swahili written in the Arabic script, see Mugane, *Story of Swahili;* and John Mugane, "The Odyssey of 'Ajamī and the Swahili People," *Islamic Africa* 8, nos. 1–2 (2017): 193–216.

35. For other examples of the UMCA's willingness to occasionally incorporate local and/or Islamic influences into its own work, see Anne Marie Stoner-Eby, "African Clergy, Bishop Lucas and the Christianizing of Local Initiation Rites: Revisiting 'The Masasi Case,'" *Journal of Religion in Africa* 38, no. 2 (2008): 171–208; and G. Alex Bremner, "The Architecture of the Universities' Mission to Central Africa: Developing a Vernacular Tradition in the Anglican Mission Field, 1861–1909," *Journal of the Society of Architectural Historians* 68, no. 4 (December 2009): 514–39.

36. Pugach, *Africa in Translation,* 37.

37. Much of the following is taken from R. M. Heanley, *A Memoir of Edward Steere, D.D., L.L.D., Third Missionary Bishop in Central Africa,* 3rd. ed. (London: Universities' Mission to Central Africa, 1898).

38. They did occasionally turn to other Europeans for help; see, for example, Letter from Pennell to Steere, November 2, No year, Box List: A1(III)C.

39. Isabel Hofmeyr, *The Portable Bunyan: A Transnational History of "The Pilgrim's Progress"* (Princeton, NJ: Princeton University Press, 2003), 14.

40. The missionaries' spelling of these names sometimes varied; I have adopted the most-commonly used forms from Pennell's letters.

41. Abdallah Salih Farsy, *The Shafi'i Ulama of East Africa, c.1830–1970: A Hagiographic Account,* trans. Randall L. Pouwels (Madison: African Studies Program, University of Wisconsin–Madison, 1989), 44–50.

42. Abdul Aziz was a member of the *Qadiriyya,* a Sufi tariqa, and later in life he formed his own tariqa called the *Nuraniyya.* See Valerie Hoffman, "In His (Arab) Majesty's Service: The Career of a Somali Scholar and Diplomat in Nineteenth-Century Zanzibar," in *The Global Worlds of the Swahili: Interfaces of Islam, Identity and Space in 19th and 20th-Century East Africa,* ed. Roman Loimeier and Rüdiger Seesemann (New Brunswick, NJ: Transaction Publishers, 2006), 263–65.

43. It is unknown whether any of these writings survive; Farsy had not seen them. Farsy, *Shafi'i Ulama,* 44.

44. Farsy, 44.

45. See Hoffman, "In His (Arab) Majesty's Service," 263–64; and Anne Bang, *Sufis and Scholars of the Sea: Family Networks in East Africa, 1860–1925* (New York: Routledge, 2003), 95.

46. "The Bible in East Africa, By the Right Rev. Dr. Steere, Bishop of Zanzibar," *Bible Society Monthly Reporter* 11, no. 7 (July 1882): 110, BDL, UMCA UX 73.

47. Letter from L. Pennell to E. Steere, September 21, No year, Box List: A1(III)C.

48. Letter from L. Pennell to E. Steere, September 21, No year. *Wajinga* is Swahili for "fools" or "simpletons." There is little evidence of what his and Pennell's working language might have been; likely they communicated in a combination of Swahili and English, and it seems that one of the source texts they used was an Arabic-language Bible. See Letter from L. Pennell to E. Steere, May 22, No year, Box List: A1(III)C.

49. See, for example, Letter from L. Pennell to E. Steere, No date [949–953] and Letter from L. Pennell to E. Steere, May 22, No year, Box List: A1(III)C.

50. "*Rikardo L. Pennelli anampa Sheikh Abdul Assiz salaamu nyingi akamwomba illi kukubali chuo hiki. Ndiye anamshukuru sana kwa ajili amemzayidia kufasiria Anjili, Habari Mema ya Muungu akamomba Muungu sana ampe thawabu ya kuamini na kuokoka kwa Isa atakaporudi siku ya mwisho kuwaamua wazima na wafu. Amin.*" Letter from L. Pennell to E. Steere, No date [955–966], Box List: A1(III)C. The Swahili in this passage is the message that Pennell asked Steere to write out in Arabic script; the translation from Swahili to English is my own.

51. Letter from L. Pennell to E. Steere, No date [949–953]; and Letter from Pennell to Steere, August 20, No year, Box List: A1(III)C.

52. Pennell referenced conversations with both Kassim and Cassim. Given the similarity of the names, it is hard to believe that they were two different people. On the other hand, given Pennell's exactness in spelling and word

choice in so many other facets of his writing, his inconsistency in the spelling of proper names is surprising. For the present I assume that Kassim and Cassim were in fact the same person. For all the interlocutors, as mentioned previously, I use the spelling most commonly used in the mission correspondence.

53. Letter from L. Pennell to E. Steere, October 15, No year, Box List: A1(III)C.
54. Letter from L. Pennell to E. Steere, No date [949–953], Box List: A1(III)C.
55. Steere, *Handbook* (1870), Part II: 127.
56. Letter from L. Pennell to E. Steere, December 14, No year, Box List: A1(III)C. The word can be used with or without a sexual connotation.
57. Letter from L. Pennell to E. Steere, September 21, No year, Box List: A1(III)C.
58. Letter from L. Pennell to E. Steere, September 21, No year.
59. Letter from L. Pennell to E. Steere, November 2, No year; and Letter from L. Pennell to E. Steere, October 15, No year, Box List: A1(III)C.
60. Letter from L. Pennell to E. Steere, No date [955–966], Box List: A1(III)C.
61. Edward Steere, *Swahili Tales, as Told by Natives of Zanzibar* (London: Bell & Daldy, 1870), ix.
62. Steere, *Handbook* (1870), vii.
63. Steere, *Handbook* (1870), v–vi.
64. Steere, *Swahili Tales,* ix. I suspect Masazo was another spelling of Masasa's name.
65. Letter from L. Pennell to E. Steere, No date [949–953], Box List: A1(III)C.
66. Letter from L. Pennell to E. Steere, No date [891–892], Box List: A1(III)C.
67. These two details were noted in a copy of Steere's diary, found in three volumes: Steere Diary v. 2, October 8, 1865; and Steere Diary v. 3, December 30, 1866, Box List: A1(II)A.
68. Letter from L. Pennell to E. Steere, May 9, No year, Box List: A1(III)C.
69. "The Register of the Old Boys of St. Andrew's College, Kiungani and Minaki, Together with Short Notes of History of the College, 1871–1931," BDL, UMCA SF No. 79 I-II. Mission historians sometimes date the official opening of the college to 1871 when the chapel was consecrated.
70. "To the Supporters of the Central African Mission," September 20, 1873, 11, Box List: A1(III)A.
71. Letter from L. Pennell to E. Steere, December 14, No year, Box List: A1(III)C.
72. Letter from L. Pennell to E. Steere, May 9, No year, Box List: A1(III)C.
73. "To the Supporters of the Central African Mission," September 20, 1873, 7, Box List: A1(III)A.
74. Letter from W. Tozer to E. Steere, January 7, 1870, Box List: A1(II)A.
75. Letter from L. Pennell to E. Steere, No date [949–953], Box List: A1(III)C. Note that this letter must have been written before March 1, 1871, the date on which George Farajallah died during a cholera outbreak. He was buried at the cemetery at Kiungani.
76. "The Key to Central Africa: Have We Found It?" (London: Bemrose and Sons, 1880), 19, BDL.

77. "The Register of the Old Boys of St. Andrew's College," BD, UMCA SF No. 79 I-II.

78. "The Key to Central Africa," 14–15; Letter from E. Steere to J. W. Festing, August 1, 1874, Box List: A1(III)A. Swedi also served on the mainland, at Magila and Masasi.

79. Letter from W. Tozer to E. Steere, September 30, 1869, Box List: A1(II)A.

80. This daily schedule was described in Letter from A. C. Madan to R. M. Heanley, February 6, 1881, Box List: A1(VI)A.

81. Letter from L. Pennell to E. Steere, November 2, No year; and Letter from L. Pennell to E. Steere, May 22, No year, Box List: A1(III)C.

82. Letter from L. Pennell to E. Steere, May 22, No year, Box List: A1(III).

83. Letter from Pennell to Steere, July 26, No year, Box List: A1(III)C.

84. Steere, *Handbook* (1870); Edward Steere, *A Handbook of the Swahili Language as Spoken at Zanzibar*, 2nd ed. (London: George Bell and Sons, 1875); Edward Steere, *A Handbook of the Swahili Language as Spoken at Zanzibar*, 3rd ed., revised and enlarged by A. C. Madan (London: Society for Promoting Christian Knowledge, 1884); A. C. Madan, *English-Swahili Dictionary* (Oxford: Clarendon, 1894); A. C. Madan, *Swahili-English Dictionary* (Oxford: Clarendon, 1903); *Kitabu cha Agano Jipya la Bwana na Mkokozi Wetu Isa Masiya* (London: British and Foreign Bible Society, 1883). For a discussion of subsequent versions of the New Testament, see Elizabeth Coldham, *A Bibliography of Scriptures in African Languages*, Vol. 2 (London: British and Foreign Bible Society, 1966), 620–42.

85. Arthur Cornwallis Madan was a lay teacher with the UMCA on Zanzibar, and he took up Steere's linguistic mantle after the bishop's death.

86. Letter from Pennell to Steere, December 14, No year, Box List: A1(III)C.

87. Letter from L. Pennell to E. Steere, November 2, No year, Box List: A1(III)C.

88. Letter from L. Pennell to E. Steere, November 2, No year.

89. Letter from L. Pennell to E. Steere, November 2, No year.

90. Letter from L. Pennell to E. Steere, No date, [949–953], Box List: A1(III)C.

91. Letter from Pennell to Steere, November 2, No year, Box List: A1(III)C.

92. The choice of *padre* alongside *kasisi* is a curious one. Likely the term *padre* had entered Swahili through Portuguese, and it may also have been familiar to Arabic speakers.

93. Letter from L. Pennell to E. Steere, November 2, No year; and Letter from L. Pennell to E. Steere, October 15, No year, Box List: A1(III)C.

94. Letter from E. Steere to "Dear Sir," March 28, 1865, Box List: A1(1)A; Heanley, *A Memoir of Edward Steere*, 11.

95. Steere, *Handbook* (1870).

96. "Central African Mission, Report of Anniversary Services and Meeting, 1882," 31–32, Box List: B5–B6.

97. For a list of UMCA publications through 1884—likely not comprehensive but nonetheless helpful—see "Our Zanzibar Printing Press," *Central Africa* 16 (April 1884): 62–64.

98. Steere, *Handbook* (1870), iv.

99. As Thomas McDow argues, those who, like the first generation of mission students, were enslaved in the interior and sent to labor on coastal plantations "would have been on the lowest rungs of the coastal social hierarchy . . . below slaves of more refined categories, such as those born into slavery at the coast." McDow, *Buying Time,* 146–47.

100. For elaborations on the concept of "social rebirth," see Walter Hawthorne, "'Being Now, as It Were, One Family': Shipmate Bonding on the Slave Vessel Emilia, in Rio de Janeiro and throughout the Atlantic World," *Luso-Brazilian Review* 45, no. 1 (2008): 53–77; and John Mason, *Social Death and Resurrection: Slavery and Emancipation in South Africa* (Charlottesville: University of Virginia Press, 2003).

101. Orlando Patterson, *Slavery and Social Death: A Comparative Study* (Cambridge, MA: Harvard University Press, 1982).

102. See Stephanie Smallwood, *Saltwater Slavery: A Middle Passage from Africa to American Diaspora* (Cambridge, MA: Harvard University Press, 2007); and Elisabeth McMahon, *Slavery and Emancipation in Islamic East Africa: From Honor to Respectability* (New York: Cambridge University Press, 2013).

103. Patterson, *Slavery and Social Death,* 337.

104. For a volume focused on the varieties of "middle passages" beyond the trans-Atlantic slave trade, see Emma Christopher, Cassandra Pybus, and Marcus Rediker, eds., *Many Middle Passages: Forced Migration and the Making of the Modern World* (Berkeley: University of California Press, 2007).

105. I refer to the UMCA student narratives as "conversion narratives" rather than "slave narratives" or "captivity narratives" in order to emphasize my use of them as a theoretical and evidential underpinning with which to study the narrators' experiences of social rebirth. They would also fit comfortably in the genre referred to by Marcia Wright as the "evangelical biographical tradition." Marcia Wright, *Strategies of Slaves and Women: Life-Stories from East/Central Africa* (New York: Lilian Barber Press: 1993), 24. See also Derek Peterson, *Ethnic Patriotism and the East African Revival: A History of Dissent, c. 1935–1972* (New York: Cambridge University Press, 2012); and Morgan Robinson, "Binding Words: Student Biographical Narratives and Religious Conversion," in *The Individual in African History: The Importance of Biography in African Historical Studies,* ed. Klaas van Walraven (Boston: Brill, 2020).

106. A. C. Madan, *Kiungani; or, Story and History from Central Africa* (London: George Bell and Sons, 1887).

107. "Panya," *African Tidings* no. 96 (October 1897): 111, BDL.

108. "Panya," 112.

109. "Panya," 113.

110. "The Story of Fayida," *African Tidings* no. 99 (January 1898): 4, BDL.

111. Nurse and Hinnebusch, *Swahili and Sabaki,* 43, Map 4.

112. In three of the narratives, the enslaved children were brought first to Madagascar, Mozambique, or the Comoros before arriving at Zanzibar.

113. "History of a Nyassa Boy (I)," Madan, *Kiungani,* 24. The volume did not give the names of the students but rather referred to them by ethnic categories.

114. For instances of forgetting, see "Nyassa Boy (I)" and "Yao Boy," in Madan, *Kiungani.* For the latter, see "Zaramo Boy" in Madan, *Kiungani,* 60.

115. See "History of a Nyassa Boy (I)," 25; and "History of a Yao Boy," in Madan, *Kiungani,* 59.

116. Pier Larson, "Horrid Journeying: Narratives of Enslavement and the Global African Diaspora," *Journal of World History* 19, no. 4 (December 2008): 453–54.

117. See, for example, "History of a Nyassa Boy (I)," 25; "History of a Makua Boy" (1), 40; "History of a Ganda Boy," 97; and "History of a Nyoro Boy," 112, in Madan, *Kiungani.*

118. "Fayida," *Stories of Africa* no. 2, 5–6, BDL.

119. "History of a Makua Boy," in Madan, *Kiungani,* 40–41. Note that the narrator described his age with reference to a fellow student, "M."

120. Madan, *Kiungani,* 41.

121. Madan, 43. The redacted names, printed as such in the text, were those who became the narrator's classmates on Zanzibar.

122. Madan, 44–45.

123. "History of a Nyassa Boy," in Madan, *Kiungani,* 25.

124. Smallwood, *Saltwater Slavery,* 119.

125. McMahon, *Slavery and Emancipation,* 194n2.

126. McMahon, 194.

127. McMahon, 201.

128. Larson, "Horrid Journeying," 448.

129. "But They Are in Peace," *African Tidings* no. 98 (December 1897): 137, BDL.

130. "But They Are in Peace," 137.

131. "Among the School Children in Zanzibar," *The Children's Tidings* no. 13 (c. July 1888): 4, BDL.

132. "A Visit to Kiungani College," c. 1880–81, 63–64, Box List: A1(III)C.

133. "Cast Out," *Stories of Africa* no. 9, 3–5, BDL

134. "History of a Zaramo Boy," *The Children's Tidings* no. 11 (c. January 1888): 5–6, BDL.

CHAPTER 2: MSIMULIZI AND THE CULTIVATION OF THE UPELEKWA

Epigraph: *Msimulizi* no. 19, October 1891, 492, BDL.

1. Derek Peterson and Emma Hunter, "Print Culture in Colonial Africa," in *African Print Cultures: Newspapers and Their Publics in the Twentieth Century,* ed. Derek Peterson, Emma Hunter, and Stephanie Newell (Ann Arbor: University of Michigan Press, 2016), 6.

2. Benedict Anderson, *Imagined Communities: Reflections on the Origin and Spread of Nationalism,* rev. ed. (New York: Verso, 2006), 146.

3. Anderson, 145.

4. Deborah Coen, *Climate in Motion: Science, Empire, and the Problem of Scale* (Chicago: University of Chicago Press, 2018), 17.

5. Jonathon Glassman, *War of Words, War of Stones: Racial Thought and Violence in Colonial Zanzibar* (Bloomington: Indiana University Press, 2011), 18.

6. Peterson describes a similar, if perhaps more contentious, process among Gikuyu speakers and writers in central Kenya; Derek Peterson, *Creative Writing: Translation, Bookkeeping, and the Work of Imagination in Colonial Kenya* (Portsmouth, NH: Heinemann, 2004), 8.

7. Peterson and Hunter, "Print Culture in Colonial Africa," 18.

8. Charles Good, *The Steamer Parish: The Rise and Fall of Missionary Medicine on an African Frontier* (Chicago: University of Chicago Press, 2004).

9. Paul Kollman, *The Evangelization of Slaves and Catholic Origins in Eastern Africa* (Maryknoll, NY: Orbis Books, 2005).

10. For overviews of Christian missionary activity in Tanganyika, see Roland Oliver, *The Missionary Factor in East Africa* (New York: Longmans, Green, 1952); Marcia Wright, *German Missions in Tanganyika, 1891–1941: Lutherans and Moravians in the Southern Highlands* (Oxford: Clarendon, 1971); John Iliffe, *A Modern History of Tanganyika* (New York: Cambridge University Press, 1979), 84–87; and Adrian Hastings, *The Church in Africa: 1450–1950* (New York: Oxford University Press, 1994).

11. By the early 1890s, two more printing presses had been established at Magila and Likoma. The Likoma press printed mainly in Chinyanja, or Chewa, but also in the Yao language and the languages of the Lake Nyasa, as well as English. See "Likoma Printing Office," *Central Africa* no. 405 (September 1916): 229–33.

12. Oliver, *Missionary Factor*, 180–81.

13. There were some members of the UMCA who believed that more emphasis should be put on vernacular languages. See, for example, Herbert Woodward's letter in *Central Africa* no. 118 (October 1892): 154.

14. Similar trends held for the UMCA's other schools, but at Kiungani the effects were most pronounced.

15. "The Register of the Old Boys of St. Andrew's College, Kiungani and Minaki, Together with Short Notes on the History of the College. 1871–1931," BDL, UMCA SF Box List, SF No. 79 I-II. In 1889, about 118 students attended Kiungani, 113 attended Mbweni girls' school, 166 attended Magila, and 79 attended Newala. Five years, later, in 1894, Godfrey Dale reported that the number of students at Kiungani was virtually the same, at 120. See "Census of Africans Connected with the Mission, Easter, 1889," *Central Africa* no. 82 (October 1889): 146; and Letter from G. Dale to D. Travers, December 16, 1894, Box List: A1(VII-VIII).

16. Letter from C. Maples to W. Penney, July 28, 1885, Box List: A1(IX-XI); Letter from J. Bartlett to L. H. Frere, July 20, 1888, Box List: A1(VI)B; Letter from Agnes Sapuli to C. Child, October 20, 1898, Box List: A5; and Letter from H. Woodward, Magila, 1899, Box List: A1(VII-VIII).

17. Letter from C. Maples to W. Bishop, March 6, 1877, Box List: A1(IX-XI).

18. Letter from A. C. Madan to W. Penney, January 9, 1884, Box List: A1(VI)A.

19. For a masterful examination of the Bushiri uprising that prompted the blockade, see Jonathon Glassman, *Feasts and Riot: Revelry, Rebellion, and Popular Consciousness on the Swahili Coast, 1856–1888* (Portsmouth, NH: Heinemann, 1995).

20. "St. Andrew's College, Kiungani," *Central Africa* no. 204 (December 1899): 216.

21. "Masasi News," *Central Africa* no. 200 (August 1899): 140; BDL: Letter from W. Johnson to W. Bishop, August 3, 1877, Box List: A1(VI)B; Letter from J. Farler to W. Penney, June 27, 1887, Box List: A1(VI)A; Letter from J. Farler to Allchin, February 23, 1877, Box List: A1(VI)A; and Letter to D. Travers from Magila, March 6, 1891, Box List: A1(VI)B.

22. "Msalabani, 1917–18," *Central Africa* no. 422 (February 1918): 27. For other articulations of the mission's policy on vernacular languages, see "Language Study," *Central Africa* no. 441 (September 1919): 131–34; "Language Study II," *Central Africa* no. 443 (November 1919): 167–70; "Sphinxhaven," *Central Africa* no. 484 (April 1923): 69; "The Diocese of Masasi," *Central Africa* no. 527 (November 1926): 228–29.

23. "Early Days at Unangu, Nyasaland," *Central Africa* no. 135 (March 1894): 36–37. This echoed missionary criticism of the use of Arabic in Qur'anic schools on Zanzibar.

24. Edward Steere, *Collections for a Handbook of the Yao Language* (London: Society for Promoting Christian Knowledge, 1871); "'Pa Nyanja Ndi pa Mtunda,' a Chinyanja School Reader," *Central Africa* no. 440 (August 1919): 111; "Lack of Books," *Central Africa* no. 448 (April 1920): 63–64; "Annual Report," *Central Africa* no. 474 (June 1922): 148; and "Review," *Central Africa* no. 510 (June 1925): 134. I use the names of the languages that the mission itself used.

25. In 1925, for instance, *Central Africa* reported that over the course of his career, Bishop Hine had "held confirmations in five different languages." See "Days Gone By," *Central Africa* no. 508 (April 1925): 74.

26. Letter from C. Maples to R. M. Heanley, August 3, 1877, Box List: A1(IX-XI).

27. "Mambo ya Chuoni na Kawaida za Mafundisho" (Zanzibar: Universities' Mission to Central Africa, 1890), iv, BDL.

28. "Home Jottings," *Central Africa* no. 134 (February 1894): 31.

29. "Women Workers in the UMCA," *Central Africa* no. 193, (January 1899): 5–6; "Home Jottings," *Central Africa* no. 195 (March 1899): 45; Printed Letter from Bishop Hine 1902, 7–8, Box List: A1(XIII); Hine Pastoral Letter (Zanzibar: Universities' Mission Printing Office, 1905), 8, Box List: A1(XIII).

30. "A Step Forward," *Central Africa* no. 73 (January 1889): 4–5.

31. Letter from Y. Abdullah to I. Hall, January 2, 1894, Box List: A5.

32. A. E. M. Anderson-Morshead, *The History of the Universities' Mission to Central Africa, 1859–1896* (London: Universities' Mission to Central Africa, 1897), 338.

33. Letter from F. Weston to D. Travers, July 18, 1906, Box List: A1(XIV); Letter from F. Weston to W. Bishop, July 24, 1906, Box List: A1(XIV); Letter from F. Weston to D. Travers, July 27, 1906, Box List: A1(XIV); and Letter from F.

Weston to H. M., August 3, 1906, Box List: A1(XVII)A. The theological college was eventually moved, in 1925, to Minaki, just outside of Dar es Salaam.

34. Letter from F. Weston to D. Travers, July 18, 1906, Box List: A1(XIV); and Letter from F. Weston to H. M., August 3, 1906, Box List: A1(XVII)A.

35. On Barak, *On Time: Technology and Temporality in Modern Egypt* (Berkeley: University of California Press, 2013). See also Erik Gilbert's argument about the resilience of dhows in the face of steamships: Erik Gilbert, *Dhows and the Colonial Economy in Zanzibar, 1860–1970* (Athens: Ohio University Press, 2005).

36. The British Consul at Zanzibar attempted to create a post office in the late 1860s, to the chagrin of a group of merchants who wrote to the consul Henry Churchill in 1869 that "while we have no objection to pay a fair compensation for the passage of our letters we doubt the justice of paying postage on letters received through one channel, only, as vessels under the French, German, and American flags still carry mail matter free as heretofore." Letter from merchants to H. Churchill, February 16, 1869, ZNA, AA3–12.

37. "The Key to Central Africa," 29, BDL; and J. C. Russell and N. C. Pollock, *News from Masasi* (Vienna: Afro-Pub, 1993), 5.

38. "German Steam Communication with East Africa," *Central Africa* no. 90 (June 1890): 90; and Russell and Pollock, *News from Masasi*, 5.

39. "Postal Improvements," *Central Africa* no. 104 (August 1891).

40. Jeremy Prestholdt, *Domesticating the World: African Consumerism and the Genealogies of Globalization* (Berkeley: University of California Press, 2008), 81; Sujatha Sosale, "Mapping and Modernizing the Indian Ocean Rim: Communication Technologies under Colonial Britain," *Global Media and Communication* 10, no. 2 (2014): 155–176; and Jürgen Osterhammel, *The Transformation of the World: A Global History of the Nineteenth Century,* trans. Patrick Camiller (Princeton, NJ: Princeton University Press, 2015), 425.

41. "Home Jottings," *Central Africa* no. 17 (May 1884): 94.

42. "The Telegraph Office at Blantyre," *Central Africa* (January 1895): 7–8.

43. "The Telegraph Office at Blantyre," 7–8; and "Post Bag," *Central Africa* (February 1895): 29.

44. Letter from E. Steere to P. Steere, January 17, 1865, Box List: A1(III)A; Letter from E. Steere to P. Steere, October 19, 1872, Box List: A1(III)B; Letter from M. Allen to R. M. Heanley, July 18, 1877, Box List: A1(IV)A; Letter from W. Tozer to E. Steere, February 17, 1871, Box List: A1(I)A; Letter from E. Steere to R. M. Heanley, April 3, 1880, Box List: A1(III)A; Letter from E. Steere to P. Steere, November 16, 1881, Box List: A1(III)A; and Letter from Thackeray to Leeke, September 26, 1887, Box List: A1(VI)A.

45. "Home Jottings," *Central Africa* no. 91 (July 1890): 122.

46. See, for instance, Letter from C. Maples to W. Bishop, 1887, Box List: A1(IX-XI).

47. Letter from J. Halliday to C. Euan-Smith, August 31, 1888, ZNA, AA2–47.

48. Letter from W. C. Porter to Child, July 30, 1889, Box List: A1(VI)A.
49. "Correspondence Compilation," March 1862, ZNA, AA12–8.
50. Letter from E. Steere to P. Steere, January 17, 1865, Box List: A1(III)A.
51. Steere Diary, Friday April 28, Box List A-F: D8(2); and Letter from L. Pennell to E. Steere, July 26, No year, Box List: A1(III)C.
52. Annual Report 1871–72, 6, Box List: A1(I)A; and Letter from W. Tozer to E. Steere, March 21, 1871, Box List: A1(I)A.
53. Letter from E. Steere to P. Steere, October 19, 1872, Box List: A1(III)B.
54. Letter from E. Bennett to D. Travers, October 31, 1889, Box List: A1(VI)B.
55. *Msimulizi* was the first periodical printed in eastern Africa in the Latin script; it was not until the twentieth century that other missions began publishing newspapers and/or newsletters in Swahili. The UMCA itself, as we shall see, tried to replicate *Msimulizi* with the publications *Mtenga watu, Maongezi na Maarifa,* and *Habari za Mwezi.* This latter was first published in 1895/96 and lasted until World War I.
56. "A Step Forward," *Central Africa* no. 73 (January 1889): 4–5.
57. "A Step Forward," 4–5.
58. There was a brief revival of the magazine in 1904/05; during this second period, it was under the joint editorial control of Revs. Frank Weston and Samwil Chiponde (his third time at the helm).
59. *Msimulizi* no. 1 (October 1888): 3, BDL. (Hereafter I will forego the note "BDL," but all issues of *Msimulizi* can be found in the Bodleian Library system.)
60. *Msimulizi* no. 1: 2. "*Killa miezi miwili tumepewa ruhusa ya kukusanya habari za hapa Unguja, ndio za Mkunazini na Mbweni na Kiungani, na kupata pia habari za pande za Boonde na za Nyassa na za Newala na miji ya kule, na kuzipiga chapa hapa Kiungani na kuzifanya kuwa kitabu kidogo.*" All translations from the Swahili are my own.
61. Madan's 1903 Swahili-English dictionary defined *pesa*—the Swahili word used in the magazine to measure its price—as "a pice, the Indian quarter anna, or 3-pice piece, a farthing." It also meant, and means, money in general.
62. *Msimulizi* no. 1 (October 1888): 1.
63. For a selection of the use of the word *upelekwa* in *Msimulizi,* see no. 1 (October 1888): 2; no. 6 (August 1889): 79; no. 8 (December 1889): 112; no. 9 (February 1890): 128; no. 10 (April 1890): 171, 175; no. 11 (June 1890): 189; no. 12 (August 1890): 213; no. 13 (October 1890): 229; no. 17 (June 1891): 437; no. 18 (August 1891): 454; no. 19 (October 1891): 485; no. 20 (December 1891): 493; no. 22 (April 1892): 525–26; no. 23 (June 1892): 553; no. 24 (August 1892): 582; no. 26 (December 1892): 619; no. 28 (April 1893): 650; no. 29 (June 1893): 669; no. 30 (August 1893): 678; no. 34 (April 1894): 750; no. 35 (June 1894): 769–70; no. 36 (August 1894): 780; no. 37 (October 1894): 801; no. 38 (December 1894): 823; no. 39 (February 1895): 823; no. 40 (April 1895): 853; no. 41 (June 1895): 887; no. 43 (October 1895): 908; and no. 46 (April 1896): 966.

64. Johann Krapf's 1882 Swahili-English dictionary defined *mpeekua* as "a person sent, a missionary," but included the note that "*mpeekua* is doubtless an erratum, instead of *mpelékua* (from *ku péleka*, to send)." The entry also indicates that Krapf drew this definition from Steere. Johann L. Krapf, *A Dictionary of the Suaheli Language* (London: Trübner, 1882), 242.

65. If the phrase was understood to refer to a sending from God, one could read it as a direct reference to Jesus as "the one sent"; but the literal and the figurative interpretations need not be mutually exclusive. Emma Hunter similarly analyzes the word *uraia* ("citizenship"), noting that when the authors of a Swahili-language primer added "'u' to the word *raia*, they self-consciously created a new abstract noun. In this formulation, citizenship or subjecthood now meant something more active, with an implied moral content." Emma Hunter, *Political Thought and the Public Sphere in Tanzania: Freedom, Democracy and Citizenship in the Era of Decolonization* (Cambridge: Cambridge University Press, 2015), 92.

66. My heartfelt thanks to the anonymous reader who helped clarify my thinking about the word and the concept of the *Upelekwa*. Many thanks, too, to the audience members at a paper presentation at the 2017 Annual Meeting of the African Literature Association for their feedback.

67. "*Kwani hapa Kiungani tukiisha kukaa siku nyingi tunatawanyika huko na huko, killa mtu kwa kazi yake, tukikaa mbalimbali sana, tukijaribu kufanya kazi zile tutakazopata katika Upelekwa wetu. Tena mtu akikaa mbali hapati nafasi marra kwa marra kuwaandikia rafiki zake zote wakaao pangine pangine, ndio maana aweza kupata kidogo tu habari za kwao. Basai shauri la kuleteana habari za watu na za mambo yanayotendekatendeka katika killa mji wa Upelekwa huu wetu litakuwa shauri la kufaa sana.*" *Msimulizi* no. 1 (October 1888): 1–2.

68. *Msimulizi* no. 17 (June 1891): 437; *Msimulizi* no. 18 (August 1891): 454; *Msimulizi* no. 23 (June 1892): 553; and *Msimulizi* no. 20 (December 1891): 493.

69. "*Tumepokea kwa furaha mno tunajivuna sana sisi kwa kupata Kasisi wa kabila letu kuliko ninyi mnaokaa katika miji ya upelekwa mingine yote.*" *Msimulizi* no. 10 (April 1890): 171.

70. Hunter, *Political Thought*, 66.

71. The technique of personification was not unique to *Msimulizi* and would be utilized in future East African newspapers as well. See, for example, Emma Hunter, "'Our Common Humanity': Print, Power, and the Colonial Press in Interwar Tanganyika and French Cameroun," *Journal of Global History* 7, no. 2 (2012): 288–89.

72. *Msimulizi* no. 2 (December 1888): 14; *Msimulizi* no. 8 (December 1889): 112; and *Msimulizi* no. 9 (February 1890): 128.

73. "*Bassi nina furaha kama killa upande rafiki zangu wamenipokea kwa furaha, na kuniambia, njoo, rafiki, njoo tena, killa miezi miwili njoo kwetu utusimulie. Bassi ndio maana nimekuja tena hivi sasa marra ya pili, na safari hii ninakuja burre kama kwanza, unipokee kama zawadi, lakini*

safari ya tatu utataka kulipa pesa moja, urathi, bwana, (ao pesa sita kwa mwaka) kwani safari yangu ina gharama, haina buddi." Msimulizi no. 2 (December 1888): 14.

74. *"Nimefika marra kwa marra kwa killa mji wa Upelekwa wetu nimezungumza na watu sana, wamefurahi kupata habari za ndugu zao pangine pote, kwani ndizo niwapazo sana, hatta huniona sasa kuwa kama rafiki wa kutazamiwa sana. Hatta nilipo huku Unguja—kwani mimi mzalia, ati, wa kisiwa cha Unguja—Waletaji habari hawakosi kuniletea habari za kwao, hawanisahau, illa labda mmoja wawili wamepitiwa mahali."* Msimulizi no. 8 (December 1889): 112.

75. *Msimulizi* no. 8, 113.

76. *Msimulizi* no. 9 (February 1890): 128–29.

77. Glassman, *War of Words, War of Stones,* 150.

78. *Msimulizi* no. 18 (August 1891): 443–44. Charles Good indicated that *Mtenga watu* was established in 1895, but this reference in *Msimulizi* seems to tell us that it was published at least as early as 1891. Good, *The Steamer Parish,* 173n14.

79. *Msimulizi* no. 17 (June 1891): 431–32. An 1897 article in *Central Africa* noted that *Mtenga watu* appeared only irregularly due to "the pressure of work and want of type at Likoma." See "Post Bag," *Central Africa* no. 174 (June 1897): 91.

80. *"Bassi nini? mzee ashindwe na mtoto? kwani mtoto ninaye jina lake 'Mtenga watu,' na yeye apiga fahari kidogo, ajitazamisha, ajitembeza, mmalidadi, hatta mimi mzee nifanyeje? Nampenda. Siye mtoto wangu? Siye mzuri? Lakini akumbuke kumheshimu baba. Na baba asimkasirishe mtoto. Amwonye tu."* Msimulizi no. 18 (August 1891): 443.

81. I was able to find one copy—the second issue—in the UMCA Papers from February 1892. It seems that in 1896 *Maongezi na maarifa* was replaced by a magazine called *Habari za Mwezi* that was printed at the mission press but "utilized by the Government for the circulation of its laws, &c." Printed letter from H. Woodward, Magila, 1896, Box List: A1(VII-VIII).

82. *"Jee Mtengenezaji wa Msimulizi, uhali gani? Lakini umeona yule 'Maongezi na Maarifa'? Na sisi twainuka somo, haifai baba 'Msimulizi' na mtoto 'Mtenga watu' watembee peke yao, sharti wawe na karani, na karani huyo inamfaa avae vizuri kupita bwana na yule mtoto wake wasipate kumtharau. Chapa yetu yaendelea bwana hatta inatupa Maongezi na Maarifa, ebu yasomeni, mtayatambua."* Msimulizi no. 19 (October 1891): 480.

83. Another style of conversation via the magazine was the asking and answering of *vitendawili,* or riddles. See, for example, *Msimulizi* no. 11 (June 1890): 198; *Msimulizi* no. 12 (August 1890): 199; *Msimulizi* no. 22 (April 1892): 546; and *Msimulizi* no. 24 (August 1892): 584.

84. *Msimulizi* no. 46 (April 1895): 965.

85. *Msimulizi* no. 47 (June 1896): 989.

86. *Msimulizi* no. 47, 989.

87. *"Bassi huzuni nyingi sana aliyo nayo mwanamke huyu, kufikiri habari za mumewe na kufikiri habari za mtoto wake, lakini hatujui yatakavyokuwa, kwani tunasikia marra kwa marra huyu mwanawe anataka kujiua lakini watu tu wanamzuia."* *Msimulizi* no. 23 (June 1892): 564.

88. Anne Marie Stoner-Eby, "African Leaders Engage Mission Christianity: Anglicans in Tanzania, 1876–1926" (PhD diss., University of Pennsylvania, 2003), 185–90, ProQuest Dissertations and Theses Global.

89. Stoner-Eby, 190.

90. One cannot but mention here President Juilus Nyerere's later emphasis on *Ujamaa*, meaning "familyhood" and often glossed as "African socialism."

91. *Msimulizi* no. 4 (April 1889): 59.

92. *"Mpenzi mtengenezaji salamu sana. Baada ya salamu nakuurifu habari za siku hizi. Kweli ndugu zetu, kama mjuavyo, katika killa Station ya Upelekwa huu killa mwaka naamu kuna furaha kwa killa Mmasihiya, kwa maana jamaa zetu watakaribishwa katika Ujamaa ulio mkuu. Haitaji niunene, kwani mwajua vema sana maana yake."* *Msimulizi* no. 18 (August 1891): 454.

93. *Msimulizi* no. 34 (August 1894): 755; *Msimulizi* no. 5 (June 1889): 68; *Msimulizi* no. 43 (October 1895): 906; *Msimulizi* no. 32 (August 1894): 708; and *Msimulizi* no. 34 (April 1894): 747.

94. *Msimulizi* no. 48 (August 1896): 1022; and *Msimulizi* no. 29 (June 1893): 669.

95. *Msimulizi* no. 18 (August 1891): 454. A baptism example can be found in *Msimulizi* no. 29 (August 1896): 669.

96. *Msimulizi* no. 9 (February 1890): 153.

97. *Msimulizi* no. 7 (October 1889): 111.

98. *Msimulizi* no. 34 (April 1894): 747.

99. *Msimulizi* no. 28 (April 1893): 660.

100. For just one example, see *Msimulizi* no. 34 (April 1894): 757.

101. *Msimulizi* no. 36 (August 1894): 789.

102. *Msimulizi* no. 20 (December 1891): 497.

103. The shared experiences could also come through historical memory, as with the annual celebration of St. Bartholomew's Day; this marked the day of the mission's very first baptisms on that saint's day in 1865.

104. *Msimulizi* no. 18 (August 1891): 456–57. For more on the UMCA Guilds, see Morgan Robinson, "An Uncommon Standard: A Social and Intellectual History of Swahili, 1864–1925" (PhD diss., Princeton University, 2018), 163–65, ProQuest Dissertation and Theses Global; and Andreana Prichard, *Sisters in Spirit: Christianity, Affect, and Community Building in East Africa, 1860–1970* (East Lansing: Michigan State University Press, 2017), 128–33.

105. *Msimulizi* no. 20 (December 1891): 506–7.

106. For more on the effects of Britain's "documentary regime" on mobility across the Indian Ocean, see Thomas McDow, *Buying Time: Debt and Mobility in the Western Indian Ocean* (Athens: Ohio University Press, 2018), 165–89.

107. For example, the article *"Bandera ya Kwini"* ("Flag of the Queen"), *Msimulizi* no. 17 (June 1891): 440–41; and Madan's contribution to *Msimulizi*

no. 42 (August 1895): 900. Emma Hunter, in her study of newspapers in mid-twentieth-century Tanzania, described a situation that rings true for *Msimulizi* several decades earlier: "[Such periodicals] cannot be understood either as a space in which colonial officials imposed their view of the world of their readers, or as a space in which Africans could debate purely among themselves. Rather . . . we must remember that we are dealing with an intellectual environment shared among colonial officials, missionaries, and the growing number of Africans who could read and write in Swahili." Hunter, *Political Thought*, 41.

108. See Karin Barber, ed., *Africa's Hidden Histories: Everyday Literacy and Making the Self* (Bloomington: Indiana University Press, 2006), 7; Karin Barber, *The Anthropology of Texts, Persona and Publics* (New York: Cambridge University Press, 2007), 139; and Emily Callaci, *Street Archives and City Life: Popular Intellectuals in Postcolonial Tanzania* (Durham, NC: Duke University Press, 2017), 12.

109. Barber, *Anthropology of Texts*, 155.

110. Andreana Prichard has argued much the opposite: that as the female adherents of the mission stayed connected through their "bonds of affective spirituality," they were simultaneously severing other networks. "In forging strong and enduring ties between one another and across space and time," Prichard reflected, "Mbweni graduates and their descendants were at the same time distancing themselves from the other communities to which they had once belonged." Prichard, *Sisters in Spirit*, 148–49. This argument holds truer for the never-enslaved adherents from the mainland; for the formerly enslaved students, their ties to home had been severed long before they dedicated their efforts to community-building within the mission's network. And even for those adherents who did choose to distance themselves from natal ties, such a decision was often made in the hope of returning to one's home community, thereby expanding one's new Christian community into the home one had left behind.

111. See Letter from E. Steere to J. Festing, June 2, 1875, Box List: A1(III)A; and "Missionary Life in Central Africa, by Geo. Wm. Mallender, Seven Years Member of the Universities' Mission to Central Africa, May 1888–1895," Box List: A1(IV)B.

112. *Central Africa* no. 13 (January 1884): 8.

113. Central African Mission: Report of Anniversary Services and Meeting 1882, 32, Box List: B5–6.

114. See, for example, Letter from A. M. Madan to R. M. Heanley, February 6, 1881, Box List: A1(VI)A; and Letter from A. C. Madan to W. Penney, October 26, 1885, Box List: A1(VI)A.

115. By the early 1890s, the Church of Scotland Mission had a printing press at its Blantyre station and the Free Church of Scotland worked a press at Livingstonia, but they printed material in Yao, Nyanja/Chewa, and other vernacular languages of the Lake Nyasa region: Oliver, *Missionary Factor*,

62, 92. Sultan Barghash brought a press to Zanzibar, for printing in the Arabic script, in the late-1870s: Amal Ghazal, "The Other 'Andalus': The Omani Elite in Zanzibar and the Making of an Identity, 1880s–1930s," *MIT Electronic Journal of Middle East Studies* (Fall 2005): 43–58; and Valerie Hoffman, "Muslim-Christian Encounters in Late Nineteenth-Century Zanzibar," *MIT Electronic Journal of Middle East Studies* (Fall 2005): 59–78. Joan Russell has indicated that the Church Missionary Society had a press at Freretown but that Steere's *Handbook* was still "the basic text-book for many European learners along the coast." Joan Russell, *Communicative Competence in a Minority Group: A Sociolinguistic Study of the Swahili-Speaking Community in the Old Town, Mombasa* (Leiden: Brill, 1981), 50–51. The CMS did have a printing press earlier (by 1879) in Uganda, but there it focused on printing in Luganda: Louis Timothy Manarin, "And the Word Became Kigambo: Language, Literacy and Bible Translation in Buganda, 1875–1931" (PhD diss., Indiana University, 2008), 79–81, ProQuest Dissertation and Theses Global. Meanwhile, as late as 1897, according to a report in *Central Africa,* the press at Mkunazini was printing materials in seven languages, besides Swahili, for various parties including the CMS and a German missionary society: "The Printing Press," *Central Africa* no. 172 (April 1897). The UMCA presses also took on government work, as in 1902 when the Magila printing press was working on a Swahili-German grammar for the German administration: *African Tidings* no. 155 (September 1902): 102.

116. Letter from A. C. Madan to W. Penney, April 24, 1884, Box List: A1(VI)A.
117. Letter from W. Bishop to Viner, March 5, 1890, Box List: A1(VI)B.
118. Peterson, *Creative Writing,* 7.
119. Barber, *Anthropology of Texts,* 161.
120. Hunter, *Political Thought,* 233.

CHAPTER 3: GERMAN ZEIT AND SWAHILI TIME

Epigraph: *Kwetu* no. 7 (April 13, 1938): 6, TNA, File No. 23754, Kwetu Vol. 1.

1. Editorial cited in Philip Sadrove, "The Press: Engine of a Mini-Renaissance in Zanzibar (1860–1920)," in *History of Printing and Publishing in the Languages and Countries of the Middle East,* ed. Philip Sadgrove (Oxford: Oxford University Press, 2005), 160.

2. Emma Hunter, "Language, Empire and the World: Karl Roehl and the History of the Swahili Bible in East Africa," *Journal of Imperial and Commonwealth History* 41, no. 4 (2013): 612.

3. See (among many others) James Giblin and Jamie Monson, eds., *Maji Maji: Lifting the Fog of War* (Boston: Brill, 2010); G. C. K. Gwassa and John Iliffe, *Records of the Maji Maji Rising* (Nairobi: East African Publishing House, 1967); and John Iliffe, *Modern History of Tanganyika* (New York: Cambridge University Press, 1979), 168–202. Much of the following discussion relies on Anglophone secondary literature, a consequence of my own linguistic

shortcomings and a testament to the good English-language work that has been done on this period.

4. Marcia Wright's historiographic correction, to uncover local contributions to German colonial policy, reinforces the point that the various levels of administration were not always pulling in the same direction: Marcia Wright, "Local Roots of Policy in German East Africa," *Journal of African History* 9, no. 4 (1968): 621–30.

5. Ann Brumfit, "The Rise and Development of a Language Policy in German East Africa," *Sprache und Geschichte in Afrika* 2 (1980): 236–39, 253–54.

6. See Marcia Wright, "Swahili Language Policy, 1890–1940," *Swahili: Journal of the Institute of Swahili Research / Jarida la Chuo cha Uchunguzi katika Lugha ya Kiswahili* 35, no. 1 (March 1965): 40–48, SOAS; and John Iliffe, *Tanganyika under German Rule, 1905–1912* (New York: Cambridge University Press, 1969), 180–89. For detail on the history of *akidas* in Bagamoyo, see Steven Fabian, *Making Identity on the Swahili Coast: Urban Life, Community, and Belonging in Bagamoyo* (New York: Cambridge University Press, 2019), 211–60.

7. Brumfit, "Rise and Development," 281–306. See also Sara Pugach, "Afrikanistik and Colonial Knowledge: Carl Meinhof, the Missionary Impulse, and African Language and Culture Studies in Germany, 1887–1919" (PhD diss., University of Chicago, 2011), 146, ProQuest Dissertations and Theses Global.

8. Wolfgang Mehnert argues that, initially, East Africa was the exception in German language policy and that in Togo, Cameroon, and Southwest Africa, German was introduced as a medium of instruction in schools as early as possible. Wolfgang Mehnert, "The Language Question in the Colonial Policy of German Imperialism," in *African Studies-Afrika-Studien,* ed. Thea Büttner and Gerhard Brehme (Berlin: Akademie Verlag, 1973), 384–85.

9. Brumfit, "Rise and Development," 247–51.

10. Brumfit, 259. There was also racism in the assumption that Swahili, because of its association with coastal, Arabicized society, was superior to the languages (and peoples) of the interior. See Pugach, "Afrikanistik and Colonial Knowledge," 114–15.

11. Though, as Katrin Bromber notes, "a clear decision was never taken on the German side" and Swahili "remained a controversial issue in German colonial policy." See Katrin Bromber, "German Colonial Administrators, Swahili Lecturers and the Promotion of Swahili at the Seminar für Orientalische Sprachen in Berlin," *Sudanic Africa* 15 (2014): 39.

12. Wright, "Local Roots," 624.

13. Much of the following is based on Fabian Krautwald, "The Bearers of News: Print and Power in German East Africa," *Journal of African History* 62, no. 1 (2021): 5–28.

14. Krautwald, "Bearers of News," 12.

15. See also Jörg Haustein, "Provincializing Representation: East African Islam in the German Colonial Press," in *Religion, Media, and Marginality in*

Modern Africa, ed. Felicitas Becker, Joel Cabrita, and Marie Rodet (Athens: Ohio University Press, 2018), 70–92.

16. For a thorough but racially and politically censurable examination of newspapers in German East Africa, see Hilde Lemke, "Die Suaheli-Zeitungen und-Zeitschriften in Deutsch-Ostafrika" (PhD diss., Universität Leipzig, 1929).

17. Krautwald, "Bearers of News," 15.

18. Krautwald, 21–28.

19. Charles Pike, "History and Imagination: Swahili Literature and Resistance to German Language Imperialism in Tanzania, 1885–1910," *International Journal of African Historical Studies* 19, no. 2 (1986): 229; and Brumfit, "Rise and Development," 275.

20. Derek Peterson, "Language Work and Colonial Politics: The Making of Standard Swahili and 'School Kikuyu,'" in *The Study of Language and the Politics of Community in Global Context,* ed. David Hoyt and Daren Oslund (Lanham, MD: Lexington Books, 2006), 190.

21. Wright, "Local Roots," 624.

22. One of the first such was *Chuo cha kwanza,* written by Christian Gottlieb Barth, a headmaster at Tanga, in 1893. It was revised in 1898 by Paul Blank, the same year that Oswald Rutz compiled a Swahili reading book. See Brumfit, "Rise and Development," 247, 255, 315n59; and Fabian, *Making Identity on the Swahili Coast,* 248–51. After 1906, the German government schools began using a short series of Swahili readers known as the Rechenberg Library, named for Governor Albrecht von Rechenberg (governor from 1906 to 1912). Rechenberg was reportedly quite comfortable in Swahili, and his successor, H. Schnee, attended Swahili language classes at the Seminar for Oriental Languages in Berlin. See Wright, "Swahili Language Policy," 44, 46; Brumfit, "Rise and Development," 315n60; Wilfred Whiteley, *Swahili: The Rise of a National Language* (London: Methuen, 1969), 59; and Iliffe, *Tanganyika Under German Rule,* 49–81.

23. Brumfit, "Rise and Development," 263.

24. Brumfit, 250.

25. Brumfit, 270.

26. See Pugach, "Afrikanistik and Colonial Knowledge," and *Africa in Translation: A History of Colonial Linguistics in Germany and Beyond, 1814–1945* (Ann Arbor: University of Michigan Press, 2012).

27. Bromber, "German Colonial Administrators," 41.

28. Pugach, "Afrikanistik and Colonial Knowledge," 166–68.

29. Pugach, 209–10.

30. Benedict Anderson, *Imagined Communities: Reflections on the Origin and Spread of Nationalism,* rev. ed. (New York: Verso, 2006), 71.

31. I consciously conflate these terms because, in this period, the disciplines themselves were in flux; Sara Pugach notes that "from the beginning of his career, Meinhof had described himself as a linguist, not a philologist."

Pugach, *Africa in Translation*, 134. For an excellent history on comparative philology and linguistics in a colonial context, see Rachael Gilmour, *Grammars of Colonialism: Representing Languages in Colonial South Africa* (New York: Palgrave Macmillan, 2006).

32. Errington, *Linguistics in a Colonial World*, 82.

33. See Judith Irvine, "Mastering African Languages: The Politics of Linguistics in Nineteenth-Century Senegal," *Social Analysis: The International Journal of Anthropology* 33 (September 1993): 36; Joseph Errington, *Linguistics in a Colonial World: A Story of Language, Meaning, and Power* (Malden, MA: Blackwell, 2008), 62–64, 70–91; and Tuska Benes, *In Babel's Shadow: Language, Philology, and the Nation in Nineteenth-Century Germany* (Detroit: Wayne State University Press, 2008), 10.

34. See Errington, *Linguistics in a Colonial World*, 82–83; and Benes, *In Babel's Shadow*, 10–11.

35. Pugach, *Africa in Translation*, 2.

36. Errington, *Linguistics in a Colonial World*, 70–92.

37. Pugach, *Africa in Translation*, 64–65.

38. Madan, *Swahili-English Dictionary*, iii.

39. Meinhof did concede that colonial governments would have to choose an *Einheitssprache*, or a "unifying language," to be used for administrative purposes, but he was less interested in what that standard should look like for specific languages. Pugach, "Afrikanistik and Colonial Knowledge," 114.

40. Pugach, *Africa in Translation*, 82–84.

41. Pugach, "Afrikanistik and Colonial Knowledge," 10–11.

42. See Pugach, *Africa in Translation*, 14; and Errington, *Linguistics in a Colonial World*, 123–47.

43. John Iliffe, "The Effects of the Maji Maji Rebellion of 1905–1906 on German Occupation Policy in East Africa," in *Britain and Germany in Africa: Imperial Rivalry and Colonial Rule*, ed. Prosser Gifford and William Roger Louis (New Haven, CT: Yale University Press, 1967), 557.

44. Referred to interchangeably as the Translation Committee and the Revision Committee—a fact notable in its own right. I default to the former.

45. See "Acts of the Synod, Zanzibar, 1893," 5, Box List: A1(V)A; "Decisions of the Bishop in Regard to Certain Resolutions Drawn Up in Conference at Zanzibar, October 1896," 1–2, Box List: A1(V)A. Chiponde would be ordained a priest in 1903.

46. See Aloo Osotsi Mojola, "The Swahili Bible in East Africa from 1844 to 1996: A Brief Survey with Special Reference to Tanzania," in *The Bible in Africa: Transactions, Trajectories, and Trends*, ed. Gerald West and Musa Dube (Boston: Brill, 2000), 511–23; "List of Swahili Books Published by the Universities' Mission with the Names of the Translators," Box List: D2; and "Pastoral: 1907. J. E. Hine, Bishop," 2–3, Box List: A1(XIII).

47. "Our Thirty-Sixth Anniversary," *Central Africa* no. 175 (July 1897): 103.

48. Madan, *Swahili-English Dictionary*, viii.

49. Madan, v.
50. Madan, vii.
51. Bishop J. E. Hine, Pastoral (Zanzibar: Universities' Mission Press, 1905), 3, Box List: A1(XIII).
52. Letter from G. Dale to D. Travers, June 23, 1907, Box List: A1(XIV).
53. For a handful of other changes, see Bishop J. E. Hine, Pastoral (Zanzibar: Universities' Mission Printing Office, 1907), 2–3, Box List: A1(XIII).
54. Rev. J. E. Hine, Pastoral (Zanzibar: Universities' Mission Printing Office, 1905), 3–4, Box List: A1(XIII).
55. Letter from J. E. Hine to D. Travers, December 13, 1903, Box List: A1(XIII).
56. The CMS, for instance, supported the efforts of first Martin Klamroth of the Berlin Mission and then Karl Roehl of the Bethel Mission to "de-Arabicize" and "re-Bantuize" existing Swahili Bible translations, a project that continued into the 1930s. See Wright, "Swahili Language Policy," 46–47; Hunter, "Language, Empire and the World"; and Farouk Topan, "Swahili as a Religious Language," *Journal of Religion in Africa* 22, no. 4 (1992): 339–42. For a comparative case from West Africa, see Ben Fulford, "An Igbo Esperanto: A History of the Union Ibo Bible, 1900–1950," *Journal of Religion in Africa* 32, no. 4 (November 2002): 457–501.
57. Bishop J. E. Hine, Pastoral (Zanzibar: Universities' Mission Printing Office, 1907), 2, Box List: A1(XIII).
58. Madan, *Swahili-English Dictionary*, 109. *Bin Maryamu* translates to "son of Mary."
59. Rev. J. E. Hine, Pastoral (Zanzibar: Universities' Mission Printing Office, 1905), 5, Box List: A1(XIII).
60. The ordination was heartily celebrated in all mission publications, including *Msimulizi*. See "*Kuamriwa Kasisi Wetu Mweusi wa Kwanza*," *Msimulizi* no. 9 (February 1890): 129–30, BDL.
61. See Letter from A. C. Madan to W. H. Penney, November 19, 1883, Box List: A1(VI)A; "Home Jottings," *Central Africa* no. 14 (February 1884): 36; and "Home Jottings," *Central Africa* no. 25 (January 1885): 16. His travel and school fees in England were paid for by contributions from *Central Africa* readers.
62. For his preaching in Yao, see "A Letter from the Rev. Cecil Majaliwa," *Central Africa* no. 47 (November 1886): 174–75; and "Letter from the Bishop," *Central Africa* no. 113 (May 1892): 67. It is possible that Yao was Majaliwa's mother tongue but that he forgot the language after being enslaved at a very young age; see *Central Africa* no. 83 (November 1889): 159; and Robert Keable, *Darkness or Light: Studies in the History of the Universities' Mission to Central Africa Illustrating the Theory and Practice of Missions*, 2nd ed. (London: Universities' Mission to Central Africa, 1914), 142–43. For reference to Cecil's family, see "A Family Group," *African Tidings* no. 97 (November 1897): 125–26; and Letter from Cecil Majaliwa to "All My Friends," June 9, 1897, Box List: E1.

63. *Msimulizi* no. 25 (October 1892): 600, BDL.

64. "Our Zanzibar Printing Press," *Central Africa* no. 16 (April 1884): 63; and Letter from Madan to W. H. Penney, July 4, 1883, Box List: A1(VI)A.

65. "Wants Column," *Central Africa* no. 128 (August 1893): 128. For samples of Cecil's English writing, see Letter from C. Majaliwa to "All My Friends," May 30, 1896, Box List: A5; Letter from C. Majaliwa to "All My Friends," June 9, 1897, Box List: E1.

66. George Herbert Wilson, *The History of the Universities' Mission to Central Africa* (London: Universities' Mission to Central Africa, 1936), 222; and Keable, *Darkness or Light*, 142–45. For the scandals, see Letter from J. Hine to D. Travers, November 18, 1903; Letter from J. Hine to D. Travers, November 26, 1903; and Letter from J. Hine to D. Travers, January 11, 1907, Box List: A1(XIII); Extract from letter written by Frank Weston, August 21, No Year, Box List: A1(XVII)B; and *Zanzibar Diocesan Gazette* no. 2 (August 1911): 11, Box List: A1(XVIII)A.

67. According to Justin Willis, it is likely that Limo was actually a nonrelated dependent of the leader Semnkai. See Justin Willis, "The Nature of a Mission Community: The Universities' Mission to Central Africa in Bonde," *Past and Present* 140 (August 1993): 148–49; and Michelle Liebst, *Labour and Christianity in the Mission: African Workers in Tanganyika and Zanzibar, 1864–1926* (Rochester, NY: James Currey, 2021), 40.

68. "The Register of the Old Boys of St. Andrew's College, Kiungani and Minaki," BDL, UMCA SF Box List: SF No. 79 I-II.

69. See "Home Jottings," *Central Africa* no. 77 (May 1889): 83; "Home Jottings," *Central Africa* no. 78 (June 1889): 98; "Home Jottings," *Central Africa* no. 80 (August 1889): 130; "Home Jottings," *Central Africa* no. 81 (September 1889): 141; and "Wants Column," *Central Africa* no. 117 (September 1892): 147.

70. See, for example, "Speech at the Annual Meeting, By Peter Limo," *The Children's Tidings* no. 25 (July 1891): 54–55; and "Home Jottings," *Central Africa* no. 121 (January 1893): 12.

71. Small Notebook Title "Calendar of the Universities' Mission," Entry for March 11, 1894, Box List: A1(VI-VIII); Wilson, *History*, 90.

72. BDL: *Msimulizi* no. 34 (April 1894): 743; *Msimulizi* no. 35 (June 1894): 777; and "The Ordination to the Priesthood of the Rev. P. Limo," *Central Africa* no. 137 (May 1894): 71–72.

73. Letter from C. Thackeray to Leeke, October 2, 1894, Box List: A1(VI)A.

74. Letter from C. Thackeray to Leeke, October 2, 1894.

75. Letter from J. Farler to W. H. Penney, July 24, 1887; and Letter from J. Farler to W. H. Penney, February 1888, Box List: A1(VI)A:

76. A. E. M. Anderson-Morshead, *The History of the Universities' Mission to Central Africa, 1859–1909*, 5th ed. (London: Universities' Mission to Central Africa, 1909), 205; and Mojola, "Swahili Bible," 515.

77. Letter from Petro Limo to D. Travers, September 23, 1895, Box List: E1.

78. "The Magila District," *Central Africa* no. 170 (February 1897): 20.

79. Some of the writers integrated English into their correspondence as well, demonstrating mastery or at least exposure to the mission's two most important languages.

80. Several historians have written about Agnes Sapuli using her letters, including Joan Russell and Norman Pollock, *News from Masasi* (Vienna: Afro-Pub, 1993); Anne Marie Stoner-Eby, "African Leaders Engage African Christianity: Anglicans in Tanzania, 1876–1926" (PhD diss., University of Pennsylvania, 2003); and Prichard, *Sisters in Spirit: Christianity, Affect, and Community Building in East Africa, 1860–1970* (East Lansing: Michigan State University Press, 2017). She is also central to an article of my own: Robinson, "La Belle Époque from Eastern Africa: An Individual Experience of the 'Globalizing' World, 1898–1918," *Journal of Eastern African Studies* 13, no. 4 (2019): 584–600.

81. Prichard details the concept of an "affective spiritual community" throughout her book.

82. Prichard, *Sisters in Spirit*, 145. It is unclear who did the translations or where this occurred; Russell and Pollock posit that they were done at the mission's London headquarters by members who could read Swahili.

83. For a collection of the general biographical information available about Ajanjeuli/Agnes, I have found the study written by Russell and Pollock very helpful—it puts Agnes and her life into both political and environmental contexts.

84. Letter from C. Majaliwa to "My dear Friend," August 22, 1895, Box List: A5.

85. Russell and Pollock, *News,* 89–91; and Letter from A. H. Carnon to C. Child, September 13, 1897, Box List: A5.

86. Letter from A. H. Carnon to C. Child, September 13, 1897.

87. Letter from A. H. Carnon to C. Child, September 13, 1897.

88. Letter from A. Achitinao to C. Child, March 15, 1898, Box List: A5.

89. "*Natumaini kama barua hii mtaipata kabla ya Xmas au karibu na Xmas.*" Letter from A. Achitinao to "Wapenzi," November 17, 1899, Box List: A5. Unless otherwise noted, the letters excerpted from this point forward were written in Swahili, and the English translations are my own, checked against the included translations.

90. "*Mwambie Miss Clara Garnett kama salaam nitamwandikia barua mail ya pili leo nina haraka sana kwani kesho ni Post huko Masasi na hapa petu ni mbali kidogo na Masasi.*" Letter from A. Sapuli to C. Child, November 9, 1901, Box List: A5. Russell and Pollock estimated that it would have taken someone four or five hours to walk from the Mwiti station, where Agnes lived from 1900 until 1910, to Masasi. Russell and Pollock, *News from Masasi,* 56.

91. Agnes sent two letters to England in which she apologized for not sending the news to Child prior to their wedding; there had been some difficulty with a family member opposing the marriage, and Rev. Carnon (soon thereafter Archdeacon) had to intervene in order to perform the marriage. See

Letter from A. Sapuli to "Mpenzi," November 18, 1900; and Letter from A. Sapuli to "Mpenzi," January 1901, Box List: A5.

92. Letter from A. Sapuli to C. Child, October 17, 1901, Box List: A5.

93. For reference to three of the children who died, see Letter from Agnes and Francis Sapuli to C. Child, September 20, 1912, Box List: A5. See also Russell and Pollock, *News from Masasi*, 107, 109, 120, 122, 124, 128–30.

94. Letter from A. Sapuli to C. Child, Received December 2, 1911, Box List: A5.

95. "*Sasa anajua kusoma na kuandika na kushona kidogo.*" Letter from Agnes and Francis Sapuli to C. Child, September 20, 1912, Box List: A5.

96. "*Twatumaini akiisha kujua kuandika vema nitamwambia Miss Dutton awandikie watoto wa St. Agnes' barua.*" Letter from Agnes and Francis Sapuli to C. Child, September 20, 1912.

97. "*Nataka kupata barua zenu na mimi barua hii ndio ya kwanza kwenu nimeandika kwa mkono wangu.*" Letter from Rose Annie Sapuli to "Watoto wa St. Agnes," April 13, 1913, Box List: A5.

98. See Letter from A. Sapuli to C. Child, Received December 2, 1911; and Postcard from S. M. Elliott to C. Child, November 28, 1912, Box List: A5.

99. Letter from F. Sapuli to Child, October 16, 1919, Box List: A5.

100. Prichard, *Sisters in Spirit*, 4.

101. See, for example, Letter from A. Achitinao to C. Child, March 15, 1898; Letter from A. Achitinao to C. Child, October 22, 1899; and Letter from A. Sapuli to C. Child, Received December 2, 1911, Box List: A5.

102. "*Habari gani siku hizi huko Ulaya?*" Letter from A. Sapuli to "Mpenzi," November 18, 1900, Box List: A5.

103. "*Yanakumbusha killa siku rafiki zangu wa St. Agnes.*" Letter from A. Sapuli to C. Child, October 17, 1901, Box List: A5.

104. See Letter from A. Sapuli to C. Child, March 6, 1907; and Letter from A. Sapuli to C. Child, April 9, 1908, Box List: A5. Agnes did send a photograph of her family to Child in 1908: see Letter from A. Sapuli to C. Child, August 30, 1908, Box List: A5.

105. Letter from F. Sapuli to "My dear Father," October 16, 1919, Box List: A5. Sapuli wrote in English.

106. For reference to Agnes's mother tongue, see Russell and Pollock, *News from Masasi*, 1.

107. "*Ndio maana leo siandiki barua hii kwa Kiingereza illi niweze kuandika mengi, illi upate kujua hali yangu tangu kutoka Hegongo.*" Letter from F. Sapuli to "Mpenzi Bwana," January 16, 1924. Box List: A5.

108. "*Kwa Wakiungani wote, salaam waama baada ya salaam nakuarifuni ya kuwa nimekuja kukaa!*" *Msimulizi* no. 1 (March 1904): 1, BDL.

109. *Msimulizi* no. 4 (October 1904): 62–64; and *Msimulizi* no. 5 (February 1905): 71–78, BDL.

110. "*Bassi waonaje? Ya kale si ya sasa. Yote ya kale yameisha toweka illa yapo ya sasa tu. Na juu ya inchi ilivyo sasa, yote ni amani, tangu pwani hatta Buganda.*" *Msimulizi* no. 5 (February 1905): 75, BDL.

111. For more on World War I in East Africa, see Michelle Moyd, *Violent Intermediaries: African Soldiers, Conquest, and Everyday Colonialism in German East Africa* (Athens: Ohio University Press, 2014) and "Centring a Sideshow: Local Experiences of the First World War in Africa," *First World War Studies* 7, no. 2 (2016): 111–30.

112. For the plight of porters, see Iliffe, *Modern History of Tanganyika,* 249–50. Bishop Frank Weston organized and led a volunteer carrier corps from Zanzibar to the mainland in 1916. See A. G. Blood, *The History of the Universities' Mission to Central Africa, 1907–1932, Volume 2* (London: Universities' Mission to Central Africa, 1957), 89–91.

113. This was not totally unprecedented—during the Maji Maji war, Rev. Daudi Machina had taken charge of the stations surrounding Masasi. See A. E. M. Anderson-Morshead, *The Universities' Mission to Central Africa, 1859–1909,* 5th ed. (London: Universities' Mission to Central Africa, 1909), 338–40; and Iliffe, *Modern History of Tanganyika,* 233.

114. "Wanted in Nyasaland," *Central Africa* no. 435 (March 1919): 27.

115. See Iliffe, *Modern History of Tanganyika,* 256–57; and Felicitas Becker, *Becoming Muslim in Mainland Tanzania, 1890–2000* (New York: Oxford University Press, 2008).

116. Iliffe, *Modern History of Tanganyika,* 257.

117. According to John Iliffe, following the war the "British expelled German missionaries remorselessly. The last left in 1922. None returned until 1925." Iliffe, *Modern History of Tanganyika,* 256. Article 438 of the Treaty of Versailles stipulated that the property of German missions be placed under the care of a mission of the same denomination but made no mention of nationality. In effect, this meant that British missions generally took over the sites of former German mission stations. See Richard Pierard, "Shaking the Foundations: World War I, the Western Allies, and German Protestant Missions," *International Bulletin of Missionary Research* 22, no. 1 (January 1998): 13–19.

118. Naturally the mission's main fundraising organ was a key place in which to express optimism. It is possible that the home supporters of the UMCA did not share this optimism, for the mission was financially constrained throughout the interwar period.

119. "Post Bag," *Central Africa* no. 423 (March 1918): 69.

120. "Education in Zanzibar Diocese," *Central Africa* no. 429 (September 1918): 165.

121. As Anne Marie Stoner-Eby calculates, "the 59 ordinations after WWI was significantly higher than the 45 ordinations that had occurred in the previous twenty-five years. The great increase in ordinations meant that by 1925 there were 45 African clergy in the UMCA. This was more than double the 23 African clergy in 1915." Stoner-Eby, "African Leaders," 269. John Iliffe notes that most other missionary societies in eastern Africa only began ordaining African priests in the 1910s and later: Iliffe, *Modern History of Tanganyika,* 260.

122. See, for instance, Letter to Travers from Magila, March 6, 1891, Box List: A1(VI)B, in which the letter writer recounted of the Magila school that "most of the teaching is in Swahili, a little is in Bondei but now it is only the very old people who do not understand Swahili."

123. Mission teacher Clara Monro described how she taught Swahili reading at the smaller "village schools" in northeastern Tanganyika: "The beginners use cards, with the syllables printed very largely, and these are arranged on a wooden board with grooves. The teacher, as soon as the children know a set of syllables, makes words with the cards for the children to read, and then the children come up in turn and make words. . . . They love this 'word building,' but they always long for books, and as soon as they know the syllables they are put into the First Reader. There are three Readers, all very well arranged and interesting and illustrated. The children begin to read words from the start, and soon get on to sentences. By the time they have finished the Third Reader they can read anything in Swahili." C. C. Monro, "Village Schools in Tanganyika," *Central Africa* no. 481 (January 1923): 8–9.

124. "Language Study II," *Central Africa* no. 443 (November 1919): 167–70.

125. "News from Milo," *Central Africa* no. 527 (November 1926): 240. In a letter written to Rev. Child in 1903, Agnes Sapuli noted that the lessons at her Mwiti school included "Swahili reading." Letter from A. Sapuli to C. Child, February 25, 1903, Box List: A5.

126. Derek Peterson, *Ethnic Patriotism and the East African Revival: A History of Dissent, c. 1935–1972* (New York: Cambridge University Press, 2012), 215.

CHAPTER 4: INTERLOCUTORS IN INTERTERRITORIAL CODIFICATION

1. Letter from L. C. H. Weekes to the Under Secretary of State, March 21, 1932, CO 822/45/11. Derek Peterson recounted a similar story about a Chigogo examination in "Vernacular Language and Political Imagination," in *Tracing Language Movement in Africa,* ed. Ericka Albaugh and Kathryn de Luna (New York: Oxford University Press, 2018), 169–70.

2. Weekes to Under Secretary of State, March 21, 1932.

3. Draft letter from J. Frederick N. Green to Secretary, Civil Service Commission, April 14, 1932, CO 822/45/11. The resolution was confirmed at the first meeting of the Inter-Territorial Language Committee in 1930: Circular Letter from F. Johnson, October 30, 1930, TNA, File No. 12454, Inter-Territorial Language Committee [Hereafter ILC] Vol. 1.

4. Green to Secretary, Civil Service Commission, April 14, 1932.

5. Copy of letter from L. C. H. Weekes to War Office, April 21, 1932, CO 822/45/11.

6. Inter-Territorial Language (Swahili) Committee *Bulletin* no. 15 (August 1941): 19. (Hereafter ILC *Bulletin.* Copies of it and its successor periodicals can be found in the SOAS library.)

7. As Peterson and Hunter observe, "Profundity is an affect generated by a felicitous organization of words and phrases. Profundity is also an artifice of the printer." Derek Peterson, Emma Hunter, and Stephanie Newell, eds.,

African Print Cultures: Newspapers and Their Publics in the Twentieth Century (Ann Arbor: University of Michigan Press, 2016), 23.

8. Thomas Kuhn, "The Essential Tension: Tradition and Innovation in Scientific Research," in *The Essential Tension: Selected Studies in Scientific Tradition and Change* (Chicago: University of Chicago Press, 1977), 227.

9. ILC *Bulletin* no. 1 (October 1930): 10, SOAS, PP MS 42, Whiteley Collection, Box 10, File S/55.

10. Derek Peterson, "Translating the Word: Dialogism and Debate in Two Gikuyu Dictionaries," *Journal of Religious History* 23, no. 1 (February 1999): 36.

11. See Michael Callahan, *Mandates and Empire: The League of Nations and Africa, 1914–1931* (Portland, OR: Sussex Academic Press, 1999); Peter Dumbuya, *Tanganyika under International Mandate, 1919–1946* (Lanham, MD: University Press of America, 1995); Susan Pedersen, "The Meaning of the Mandates System: An Argument," *Geschichte und Gesellschaft* 32, no. 4 (October 2006): 560–82; and Hans-Georg Wolf, "British and French Language and Educational Policies in the Mandate and Trusteeship Territories," *Language Sciences* 30 (2008): 553–74.

12. "The Covenant of the League of Nations," Article 22, Avalon Project, Yale Law School, accessed September 28, 2021, https://avalon.law.yale.edu/20th _century/leagcov.asp#art22.

13. Thomas Jesse Jones, *Education in East Africa: A Study of East, Central and South Africa* (New York: Phelps-Stokes Fund, 1925); and John Iliffe, *Modern History of Tanganyika* (New York: Cambridge University Press, 1979), 338.

14. "Conference between Government and Missions," 160.

15. "Conference between Government and Missions," 163.

16. "Conference between Government and Missions," 160.

17. "Conference between Government and Missions," 166, 165. No doubt Johnson, a Kiunguja partisan, had a vested interest in describing the differences between the two dialects in this way. I should note here, too, that the term "native" appears often in the sources: recognizing its offensiveness, I use the word only when quoting directly or as a part of the linguistic phrase "native-speaker."

18. In his study of Swahili dialects, Derek Nurse argued that over the course of the nineteenth and twentieth centuries, economic and political power along the East African coast shifted south to Mombasa and Zanzibar. "This was implicitly acknowledged linguistically," he continued, "by basing today's Standard Swahili on the dialects of (primarily) Zanzibar (Unguja) and (very secondarily) Mombasa (Mvita)." See Nurse, "A Tentative Classification of the Primary Dialects of Swahili," *Sprache und Geschichte in Afrika* 4 (1982): 182.

19. R. A. Snoxall, "The East African Interterritorial Language (Swahili) Committee," in *Swahili Language and Society,* ed. Joan Maw and David Parkin (Vienna: Afro-Pub, 1984), 21.

20. Whiteley, *Swahili: The Rise of a National Language* (London: Methuen, 1969), 81.

21. It is not clear why the Kenyan administration did not send any representatives. Andrew Marshall argues that this was because the conference took place during the arrival of Kenya's new governor; see Marshall, "Kiswahili and Decolonization: The Inter-Territorial Language Committee and Successor Organizations, 1930–1970" (master's thesis, American University, 2015), 32, ProQuest Dissertations and Theses Global. Derek Peterson, however, notes that the Kenyan Secretariat claimed to have lost the invitation letter; see Peterson, "Language Work and Colonial Politics in Eastern Africa: The Making of Standard Swahili and 'School Kikuyu,'" in *The Study of Language and the Politics of Community in Global Context*, ed. David Hoyt and Daren Oslund (Lanham, MD: Lexington Books, 2006), 192. Joan Russell, for her part, chalked the absence of representatives of the Church Missionary Society in Mombasa up to "an error in the Government Secretariat in Nairobi"; see Russell, *Communicative Competence in a Minority Group: A Sociolinguistic Study of the Swahili-Speaking Community in the Old Town, Mombasa* (Leiden: Brill, 1981), 55. As for Uganda, the governor preferred that Luganda, and eventually English, be the official lingua franca of that territory.

22. Draft Memo from Rivers-Smith to Chief Secretary, July 1929, TNA, File No. 12454, ILC Vol. 1.

23. Memo from F. J. Durman to Director of Education, August 23, 1929, TNA, File No. 12454, ILC Vol. 1.

24. Letter from F. Johnson to Acting Director of Education, January 6, 1930, TNA, File No. 12454, ILC Vol. 1.

25. Letter from F. Johnson to Chief Secretary, February 5, 1930, TNA, File No. 12454, ILC Vol. 1.

26. Letter from F. Johnson to Chief Secretary, April 8, 1930, TNA, File No. 12454, ILC Vol. 1. Just as Johnson was recruiting him, Watts was helping to establish the African Association. In *Kwetu,* Watts was remembered as "a champion of Africans" both for his skill as "a born organizer of movements" and for his work with the ILC. See Iliffe, *Modern History of Tanganyika,* 407; *Kwetu* no. 20 (December 10, 1938): 9, TNA, File No. 23754, Kwetu Vol. 2; and *Kwetu* no. 1 (January 14, 1939): 13, File No. 23754, Kwetu Vol. 3.

27. "Memorandum on the Functions and Constitution of the Inter-Territorial Language Committee (Kenya, Tanganyika, Uganda, and Zanzibar), By the Secretary, Inter-Territorial Language Committee," 4; and "Inter-Territorial Language Committee Agenda and Unconfirmed Minutes of the Second Meeting, 24 to 27 January 1931: Appendix A. Annual Report of the Inter-Territorial Language Committee, 1930," 1, TNA, File No. 12454, ILC Vol. 2.

28. "Inter-Territorial Language Committee Agenda and Unconfirmed Minutes of the Eighth Meeting 25 and 26 of January 1939," 1–3, CO 822/98/1.

29. "Inter-Territorial Language Committee Agenda and Unconfirmed Minutes of the Second Meeting, 24 to 27 January 1931: Appendix A. Annual Report of the Inter-Territorial Language Committee, 1930," 2, TNA, File No. 12454, ILC Vol. 2.

30. "Inter-Territorial Language Committee Agenda and Unconfirmed Minutes of the Second Meeting, 24 to 27 January 1931: Appendix A. Annual Report of the Inter-Territorial Language Committee, 1930," 5, TNA, File No. 12454, ILC Vol. 2.

31. ILC *Bulletin* no. 1 (October 1930), SOAS, PP MS42, Whiteley Collection, Box 10, File S/55.

32. "Inter-Territorial Language Committee Agenda and Unconfirmed Minutes of the Third Meeting, 20th to 22nd June 1932," 5, TNA, File No. 12454, ILC Vol. 2. See Appendix A for the draft constitution.

33. "Appendix B: Suggested Constitution and Functions of the Inter-Territorial Language (Swahili) Committee for the East African Dependencies," [297 and 306], TNA, File No. 12454, ILC Vol. 2.

34. "Appendix B: Suggested Constitution," [297], File No. 12454, ILC Vol. 2.

35. "Constitution and Functions of the Inter-Territorial Language (Swahili) Committee to the East African Dependencies" (1934), 1, SOAS, Y Swahili B39.

36. "Constitution and Functions," 7n2.

37. ILC *Bulletin* no. 7 (January 1934): 3.

38. ILC *Bulletin* no. 7: 4.

39. ILC *Bulletin* no. 7: 5.

40. ILC *Bulletin* no. 7: 6.

41. Nathaniel Mathews, "Imagining Arab Communities: Colonialism, Islamic Reform, and Arab Identity in Mombasa, Kenya, 1897–1933," *Islamic Africa* 4, no. 2 (2013): 135–63. For more detail on the life and ideas of Sheikh al-Amin Mazrui, see Kai Kresse and Hassan Mwakimako, trans., *Guidance (Uwongozi), by Sheikh al-Amin Mazrui: Selections from the First Swahili Islamic Newspaper* (Boston: Brill, 2017); and Alamin Mazrui and Ibrahim Noor Shariff, *The Swahili: Idiom and Identity of an African People* (Trenton, NJ: Africa World Press, 1994), 73.

42. ILC *Bulletin* no. 7 (January 1934): 9. Thanks to Meg Arenberg for pointing me to Sheikh al-Amin's insistence that *harufu* is improperly spelled by the ILC as *herufi*.

43. ILC *Bulletin* no. 7 (January 1934): 10.

44. Broomfield was also the author of *Sarufi ya Kiswahili: A Grammar of Swahili in Swahili for Swahili-Speaking People* (London: Sheldon Press, 1931).

45. "An Answer by Canon Broomfield to the Memorandum Entitled *Modern Swahili*," ILC *Bulletin* no. 7 (January 1934): 17.

46. ILC *Bulletin* no. 7: 14.

47. ILC *Bulletin* no. 7: 18.

48. ILC *Bulletin* no. 7: 19.

49. Broomfield had elaborated on his belief in the benefit of Europeans' "more scientific knowledge of languages," in a 1930 article: G. W. Broomfield, "The Development of the Swahili Language," *Africa: Journal of the International African Institute* 3, no. 4 (October 1930): 521.

50. ILC *Bulletin* no. 7 (January 1934): 21.

51. "Inter-Territorial Language Committee Agenda and Unconfirmed Minutes of the Second Meeting, 24th to 27th January 1931: Appendix A. Annual Report of the Inter-Territorial Language Committee, 1930," 2, TNA, File No. 12454, ILC Vol. 2.
52. "Note on Madan's Dictionaries," 1, CO 822/36/15
53. "Inter-Territorial Language Committee, Agenda and Unconfirmed Minutes of the Second Meeting, 24th to 27th January 1931," 6–7, TNA, File No. 12454, ILC Vol. 2.
54. J. B. Williams, Handwritten Memo, April 9, 1931 [2], CO 822/36/15.
55. Madan's Swahili-English Dictionary: J. B. Williams, Handwritten Memo, April 9, 1931 [2], CO 822/36/15.
56. Madan's Swahili-English Dictionary: J. B. Williams, Handwritten Memo, April 9, 1931 [2–3], CO 822/36/15.
57. A. Russell, Handwritten Memo, April 17, 1931 [5], CO 822/36/15.
58. "Inter-Territorial Language Committee Agenda and Unconfirmed Minutes of the Fifth Meeting 12th to 14th January 1935: Appendix No. 4 Report of the Inter-Territorial Language Committee, July 1933 to December 1934," 25, CO 822/67/12.
59. "Note on Madan's Dictionaries," 4, CO 822/36/15.
60. Circular letter from Frederick Johnson, November 10, 1930, TNA, File No. 19637, Swahili Dictionary.
61. This, it must be noted, opened Standard Swahili at least theoretically to various dialects from around the region.
62. See, for instance, Geoffrey Lewis, *Turkish Language Reform: A Catastrophic Success* (New York: Oxford University Press, 1999); and Christian Flow, "Writing the Thesaurus of Latinity: A Study in the History of Philological Practice" (PhD diss., Princeton University, 2019), 229–92, ProQuest Dissertations and Theses Global.
63. Circular letter from Frederick Johnson, November 10, 1930, TNA, File No. 19637, Swahili Dictionary.
64. Circular letter from Frederick Johnson, November 10, 1930.
65. Circular letter from Frederick Johnson, November 10, 1930.
66. "Inter-Territorial Language Committee Agenda and Unconfirmed Minutes of the Third Meeting 20th to 22nd June 1932: Appendix C, Report of the Inter-Territorial Language Committee, January 1931 to June 1932," 8, TNA, File No. 12454, ILC Vol. 2.
67. "Inter-Territorial Language Committee Agenda," TNA, File No. 12454, ILC Vol. 2.
68. "Inter-Territorial Language Committee Agenda and Unconfirmed Minutes of the Fifth Meeting 12th to 14th January 1935: Appendix No. 4, Report of the Inter-Territorial Language Committee, July 1933 to December 1934," 4, CO 822/67/12.
69. ILC *Bulletin* no. 8 (May 1935): 7.
70. "Inter-Territorial Language Committee Agenda and Unconfirmed Minutes of the Third Meeting 20th to 22nd June 1932: Appendix C. Report of the

Inter-Territorial Language Committee, January 1931 to June 1932," 8, TNA, File No. 12454, ILC Vol. 2.

71. ILC *Bulletin* no. 10 (April 1936): 6; Circular letter from C. J. T. Biscoe, March 4, 1935, TNA, File No. 19637, Swahili Dictionary.

72. Letter from Manager of Dar es Salaam Bookshop, November 18, 1935, TNA, File No. 19637, Swahili Dictionary.

73. Circular letter from C. J. T. Biscoe, March 4, 1935, TNA, File No. 19637, Swahili Dictionary.

74. "*Nitafurahi sana kama mtu ye yote aonaye makosa humo atanipelekea habari ili makosa yaondolewe, na wajuao maneno ya Kiswahili yasiyomo humo watanipelekea habari ili yatiwe baadaye kitabu kipigwapo chapa mara ya pili, maana ndivyo tutakavyoweza kutunga 'Kamusi' iliyostahili lugha ya Kiswahili.*" Frederick Johnson, *Kamusi ya Kiswahili yaani Kitabu cha Maneno ya Kiswahili* (London: Sheldon Press, 1935), iv.

75. "Inter-Territorial Language (Swahili) Committee to the East African Dependencies, Report for the Year 1936," 4, CO 822/80/8.

76. "Inter-Territorial Language (Swahili) Committee to the East African Dependencies, Report for the Year 1936," 5.

77. "Rev. B. J. Ratcliffe," [20], TNA, File No. 25005, Secretary ILC, Vol. 1. Ratcliffe was also co-author, with Howard Elphinstone, of the *Modern Swahili* grammar and subject of the infamous ditty: "But 'safi' stuff is heard alone/When Ratcliffe talks to Elphinstone."

78. Letter from B. J. Ratcliffe to Bailey, December 8, 1937, TNA, File No. 25005, Secretary ILC Vol. 1.

79. Copy of letter from W. Hendry to Secretary, Governors' Conference, April 9, 1937, TNA, File No. 25005, Secretary ILC Vol. 1.

80. Hendry to Secretary, Governors' Conference, April 9, 1937.

81. Copy of Letter from P. Msaba to the Secretary to the Delegates, Clarendon Press [29], TNA, File No. 25005, Secretary ILC Vol. 1.

82. Handwritten Memo, May 21, 1941 [3], CO 822/108/24.

83. "Conference of Governors of British East African Territories, Inter-Territorial Language Committee, Note by Secretary" [13], CO 822/74/4.

84. "Conference of Governors," CO 822/74/4.

85. "Conference of Governors" [15], CO 822/74/4.

86. "Conference of Governors of British East African Territories, Inter-Territorial Language Committee, Memorandum by the Government of Tanganyika Territory" [17], CO 822/74/4.

87. "Conference of Governors, Memorandum" [18], CO 822/74/4.

88. "Conference of Governors of British East African Territories, Inter-Territorial Language Committee, Note by Secretary" [15–16]; and "Conference of Governors of British East African Territories, June 1936, Inter-Territorial Language Committee, Note by Secretary" [19], CO 822/74/4.

89. "Conference of Governors, Note by Secretary, June 1936" [19], CO 822/74/4.

90. "Extract from Proceedings of E. A. Governors Conference, June 1936," [20], CO 822/74/4.

91. "Inter-Territorial Language (Swahili) Committee, Agenda and Unconfirmed Minutes of the Fifth Meeting, 12th to 14th January 1935," 9, CO 822/67/12.

92. "Inter-Territorial Language Committee, Agenda and Unconfirmed Minutes of the Seventh Meeting, 2nd and 3rd May 1938," 4, CO 822/86/14.

93. Frederick Johnson, *A Standard English-Swahili Dictionary* and *A Standard Swahili-English Dictionary* (London: Oxford University Press, 1939).

94. "Inter-Territorial Language (Swahili) Committee, Report for the Year 1936," 4, CO 822/80/8.

95. "Inter-Territorial Language (Swahili) Committee, Report for the Year 1939," 12, CO 822/104/2.

96. "Inter-Territorial Language (Swahili) Committee, Report for the Year 1939," 13.

97. ILC *Bulletin* no. 14 (September 1940): 17.

98. "Agenda and Minutes of the Second Meeting of the Inter-Territorial Language (Swahili) Committee Readers and Assistant Readers, 26th and 27th January 1942: Appendix V. Further comments received upon recommendations made at the 1941 Meeting of Readers regarding word-equivalents," 19–20, CO 822/108/25.

99. "Agenda and Minutes of the Second Meeting of the Inter-Territorial Language (Swahili) Committee Readers and Assistant Readers, 26th and 27th January 1942: Appendix VIII. Memorandum on 'Arithmetical Terminology' by the Rev. Fr. A. Loogman," 26.

100. "Inter-Territorial Language Committee, Agenda and Unconfirmed Minutes of the Eighth Meeting, 25th and 26th of January 1939: Appendix B," 6, CO 822/98/1.

101. ILC *Bulletin* 13 (April 1939): 10.

102. ILC *Bulletin* 15 (August 1941): 12.

103. ILC *Bulletin* 15: 12.

104. ILC *Bulletin* 15: 18.

105. ILC *Bulletin* 15: 18.

106. ILC *Bulletin* 15: 12.

107. Abdulla Mohamed el Hathramy was listed as being a member of the standardization subcommittee, though he was not included on the master list of attendees. M. O. Abbasi, of the Indian Association, was also present.

108. John Iliffe notes that the two were brothers. Iliffe, *Modern History of Tanganyika,* 265–66.

109. "Conference between Government and Missions," 102.

110. "Conference between Government and Missions," 102.

111. "Conference between Government and Missions," 103.

112. Circular letter from F. Johnson, November 10, 1930, TNA, File No. 19637, Swahili Dictionary.

113. "Inter-Territorial Language Committee Agenda and Unconfirmed Minutes of the Third Meeting, 20th to 22nd June 1932," 8, TNA, File No. 12454, ILC Vol. 2.

114. "*Hao walisoma nakili ya kitabu tangu mwanzo hata mwisho wakanipa maelezo na mashauri mengi ya kufaa.*" Johnson, *Kamusi ya Kiswahili,* iii.

115. See, for instance, ILC *Bulletin* no. 7 (January 1934): 15–17; *Bulletin* no. 10 (April 1936): 9–10; and *Bulletin* no. 14 (September 1940): 18.

116. ILC *Bulletin* no. 13 (April 1939): 17–18.

117. ILC *Bulletin* no. 19 (November 1945): 8–9, 15–20.

118. ILC *Bulletin* no. 20 (July 1947): 14. A marginal note in one copy of this issue corrects the second name to read "M. B. Nsimbi."

119. See Ryan Ronnenberg, "'House of Believers': Irony and Commensurability in Tanganyikan Colonial Discourse," *African Identities* 10, no. 1 (February 2012): 37; and Fabian Krautwald, "Bearers of News: Print and Power in German East Africa," *Journal of African History* 62, no. 1 (2021): 27.

120. Krautwald, 27.

121. Katrin Bromber, "*Ustaarabu:* A Conceptual Change in Tanganyika Newspaper Discourse in the 1920s," in *Global Conceptual History: A Reader,* ed. Margrit Pernau and Dominic Sachsenmaier (New York: Bloomsbury, 2016), 291; and Emma Hunter, "'Our Common Humanity': Print, Power, and the Colonial Press in Interwar Tanganyika and French Cameroun," *Journal of Global History* 7, no. 2 (2012): 285. For more on *Mambo Leo* and the newspaper landscape in Tanzania, see James Scotton, "Tanganyika's African Press, 1937–1960: A Nearly Forgotten Pre-Independence Forum," *African Studies Review* 21, no. 1 (April 1978): 1–18; James Brennan, "Politics and Business in the Indian Newspapers of Colonial Tanganyika," *Africa* 81, no. 1 (2011): 42–67; Hunter, "Dutiful Subjects, Patriotic Citizens, and the Concept of 'Good Citizenship' in Twentieth-Century Tanzania," *The Historical Journal* 56, no. 1 (March 2013): 257–77; Hunter, "Print Media, the Swahili Language, and Textual Cultures in Twentieth-Century Tanzania, ca. 1923–1939," in *Indigenous Textual Cultures: Reading and Writing in the Age of Global Empire,* ed. Tony Ballantyne, Lachy Paterson, and Angela Wanhalla (Durham, NC: Duke University Press, 2020), 175–94; and Ronneberg, "'House of Believers.'" For a broad overview of the print media and radio in Tanzania, see Martin Sturmer, *The Media History of Tanzania* (Ndanda, Tanzania: Ndanda Mission Press, 1998).

122. James Brennan, *Taifa: Making Nation and Race in Urban Tanzania* (Athens: Ohio University Press, 2012); Hunter, *Political Thought;* Bromber, "*Ustaarabu*"; and Jonathon Glassman, *War of Words, War of Stones: Revelry, Rebellion, and Popular Consciousness on the Swahilil Coast, 1856–1888* (Portsmouth, NH: Heinemann, 1995).

123. Bromber, "*Ustaarabu,*" 292–300.

124. Hunter, "Print Media," 184.

125. "*Kutengeneza namna moja ya kuandika Kiswahili katika nchii hii,*" *Mambo Leo* 36 (December 1925): 259–60.

126. East African readers and contributors to *Mambo Leo,* for their part, opposed rigid linguistic exactitude, and strict adherence to official spelling reforms never took hold in the paper: Hunter, "Print Media," 185.

127. For more on the rivalry between the TAWCA and the African Association, see N. J. Westcott, "An East African Radical: The Life of Erica Fiah," *Journal of African History* 22, no. 1 (1981): 90–92.

128. *Kwetu* no. 1 (November 18, 1937), TNA, File No. 23754, Kwetu Vol. 1.

129. See Westcott, "East African Radical," 93; and, for example, "Let Sleeping Dogs Lie," *Kwetu* no. 1 (January 14, 1939): 5, TNA, File No. 23754, Kwetu Vol. 3.

130. Westcott, "East African Radical," 93.

131. Westcott, 100.

132. "*Ustaarabu*," *Kwetu* no. 19 (November 22, 1938): 12, TNA, File No. 23754, Kwetu Vol. 1.

133. By early 1939, Fiah had added to the motto, describing the paper as: "The only Native Journal in Tanganyika that keeps thinking people well informed." *Kwetu* no. 3 (February 21, 1939), TNA, File No. 23754, Kwetu Vol. 1.

134. Indeed, there would not even be any African representatives appointed to the territory's Legislative Council until 1945, and no elections for the same until 1958. Hunter, *Political Thought*, 98.

135. "*Chapa au vyapa katika nchi ni kama njia, kwa mfano: kama hakuna njia ya kuendea Dodoma na Tabora kununua ng'ombe, hatutapata nyama Dar es Salaam. Mtu akijaribu kupita porini atashambuliwa na kina Simba, nk. Kama watu wa nchi yo yote hawana gazeti lao wenyewe, ni sawa sawa na nchi isiyokuwa na njia.*" "*Kwetu Katika Mji wa Dar es Salaam,*" *Kwetu* no. 1 (January 16, 1940): 3, TNA, File No. 23754, Kwetu Vol. 3.

136. "*Ustaarabu Kwetu,*" *Kwetu* no. 17 (October 16, 1938): 4, TNA, File No. 23754, Kwetu Vol. 1.

137. *Kwetu* no. 13 (August 2, 1938): 11, TNA, File No. 23754, Kwetu Vol. 1.

138. Fiah actually used the phrase twice: "*Makosa Gazetini,*" *Kwetu* no. 3 (February 23, 1941): 3; and "*Mtu si Mashini,*" *Kwetu* no. 13 (August 19, 1941): 7, TNA, File No. 23754, Kwetu Vol. 3.

139. Most every issue included a disclaimer such as: "*Mtengenezaji hana lawama katika barua hizo zifuatazo.*" ("The Mtengenezaji is not responsible for the letters that follow.")

140. See, for instance, Fiah's note following a letter to the editor: *Kwetu* no. 13 (August 2, 1938): 15, TNA, File No. 23754, Kwetu Vol. 1.

141. "*Viongozi wa Kwetu,*" *Kwetu* no. 7 (April 13, 1938): 5, TNA, File No. 23754, Kwetu Vol. 1.

142. "Maandishi ya Barua," *Kwetu* no. 16 (September 27, 1938): 14, TNA, File No. 23754, Kwetu Vol. 1.

143. "*Kama ujuavyo kwamba elimu haina mwisho, imempasa kila mtu apendaye kuongeza elimu yake ajitahidi kuvipata.*" "*Vitabu Vipya,*" *Kwetu* no. 1 (January 16, 1940): 6, TNA, File No. 23754, Kwetu Vol. 3.

144. "Maandishi ya Barua," *Kwetu* no. 16 (September 27, 1938): 14, TNA, File No. 23754, Kwetu Vol. 1.

145. "*Tumeandika barua kwa Mkubwa wa Lugha atufahamishe tofauti ya maneno hayo.*" Kwetu no. 16 (September 27, 1938): 14.

146. *"Viongozi wa Kwetu,"* *Kwetu* no. 11 (August 4, 1940): 6, TNA, File No. 23754, *Kwetu* Vol. 2.

147. *"Wandikaji,"* *Kwetu* no. 8 (May 21, 1939): 2, TNA, File No. 23754, *Kwetu* Vol. 2.

148. "Maandishi ya Barua," *Kwetu* no. 16 (September 27, 1938): 14–15, TNA, File No. 23754, *Kwetu* Vol. 1. See also *"Hali ya Kiswahili,"* *Kwetu* no. 10 (July 17, 1940): 6, TNA, File No. 23754, *Kwetu* Vol. 1, and TNA, File No. 23754, *Kwetu* Vol. 2.

149. *"Wandikaji,"* *Kwetu* no. 8 (May 21, 1939): 2, TNA, File No. 23754, *Kwetu* Vol. 2.

150. "Maandishi ya Barua," *Kwetu* no. 16 (September 27, 1938): 15, TNA, File No. 23754, *Kwetu* Vol. 1.

151. Johnson, *Kamusi ya Kiswahili,* iv.

152. See, for instance, W. C. Gondwe, *"Kutaja Saa,"* *Kwetu* no. 21 (December 27, 1938): 13, 15, TNA, File No. 23754, *Kwetu* Vol. 2.; and Gondwe, *"Kutaja Saa,"* *Kwetu* no. 1 (January 14, 1939): 27, 29, TNA, File No. 23754, *Kwetu* Vol. 3.

153. *"Aidha, watu tumechanganyikana, tunaonaje ajabu kwa kuchanganya lugha?"* Gondwe, *"Kutaja Saa,"* *Kwetu* no. 1 (January 14, 1939): 29, TNA, File No. 23754, *Kwetu* Vol. 3.

154. B. Salim, "Good English," *Kwetu* no. 10 (June 25, 1942): 3, TNA, File No. 23754, *Kwetu* Vol. 3.

155. "Good English, ya Mwandishi wa Rufiji," *Kwetu* no. 12 (July 31, 1942): 6, TNA, File No. 23754, *Kwetu* Vol. 3.

156. *"Na kukichanganya na lugha zetu haikosi: ni mazoea."* A. Amon, "Good English," *Kwetu* no. 12 (July 31, 1942): 3, TNA, File No. 23754, *Kwetu* Vol. 3. I believe that the date printed at the top of the page is a misprint and that this article appeared in the July 31 edition.

157. ILC *Bulletin* no. 22 (August 1952): 1.

158. ILC *Bulletin* no. 15 (August 1941): 18. Whiteley echoed these sentiments in *Swahili,* 87.

159. ILC *Bulletin* no. 22 (August 1952): 2.

160. *"Kutengeneza Kiswahili ni kazi ya wenyeji ambao ni lugha yao wenyewe."* *"Hali ya Kiswahili,"* *Kwetu* no. 10 (July 17, 1940): 6, TNA, File No. 23754, *Kwetu* Vol. 2.

161. Abdallah Khalid, *The Liberation of Swahili from European Appropriation* (Nairobi: East African Literature Bureau, 1977). Khalid proposed a complete overhaul of Standard Swahili, using the Kimvita dialect. For an overview of contemporary and retrospective criticism, see Mazrui and Noor Shariff, *The Swahili,* 73–78.

162. *"Madhumuni yake yalikuwa ni kuirahisisha kazi ya utawala kuliko kuleta manufaa kwa wenyeji wa nchi hizi."* Chiraghdin and Mnyampala, *Historia ya Kiswahili,* 58.

163. Chiraghdin and Mnyampala, 61.

164. Mugane, *Story of Swahili,* 213.

165. *"Lugha hizi ndizo ndisha za lugha sanifu; samadi yake yatoka humo."* Shihabuddin Chiraghdin and Mathias Mnyampala, *Historia ya Kiswahili*

(Nairobi: Oxford University Press, 1977), 64. I thank one of the anonymous reviewers of the manuscript as well as Meg Arenberg and Abdilatif Abdalla for their help with this interpretation.

166. Ireri Mbaabu, *New Horizons in Kiswahili: A Synthesis in Developments, Research and Literature* (Nairobi: Kenya Literature Bureau, 1985).

167. Mbaabu, *New Horizons,* 207.

168. Mahmood Mamdani, *Citizen and Subject: Contemporary Africa and the Legacy of Late Colonialism* (Princeton, NJ: Princeton University Press, 1996).

169. Ngũgĩ wa Thiong'o, *Decolonising the Mind: The Politics of Language in African Literature* (Portsmouth, NH: Heinemann, 1986).

170. Thiong'o, 66–67.

171. Thiong'o, 68.

172. Thiong'o, 16–17.

173. The Gikuyu word used to gloss "missile"—*ngurukuhĩ*—can be a noun meaning "[a] short piece of stick used as missile" or a verb meaning "cutting put into earth to take root, slip." See Monica Popescu, "Aesthetic Solidarities: Ngũgĩ wa Thiong'o and the Cold War," *Journal of Postcolonial Writing* 50, no. 4 (2014): 386, 395n2. As Derek Peterson argues, in *Decolonising the Mind* Ngũgĩ overstates the seamless connection between the Gikuyu language and the Gikuyu people; long before attempts at standardization, that language was used to conduct debates about central sociopolitical questions, underscoring divisions within the community. Peterson, *Creative Writing: Translation, Bookkeeping, and the Work of Imagination in Colonial Kenya* (Portsmouth, NH: Heinemann, 2004), 222.

174. Emma Hunter likewise points to the "awkward fit" of Swahili for champions of vernacular languages; see Hunter, "Print Media," 176.

175. Thiong'o, *Decolonising the Mind,* 84–85. He celebrated, too, translation in the opposite direction (from Swahili, in this case Kimvita, to Gikuyu) in a 2016 essay honoring the Kenyan poet Abdilatif Abdalla: Ngũgĩ wa Thiong'o, "Abdilatif Abdalla and the Voice of Prophecy," in *Abdilatif Abdalla: Poet in Politics,* ed. Rose Marie Beck and Kai Kresse (Dar es Salaam: Mkuki na Nyota, 2016), 15–17.

CHAPTER 5: THE EAST AFRICAN LITERATURE BUREAU

1. Letter from Ali Ahmed Jahadhmy to J. W. T. Allen, August 30, 1972, SOAS, PP MS20, J. W. T. Allen Papers, Box 1, File 6.

2. Jahadhmy, perhaps inadvertently, put a point on his disdain for the standardizers by using an anglicized plural, *fundis,* rather than the standard *mafundi.*

3. The phrase is taken from a series of files in the Tanganyika National Archives: File. No. 32525: Production of Literature and Text-Books for the African and Asian Communities, Vol. 1, 2, 4 & 5. (Hereafter "Production of Literature.")

4. Barak, *On Time: Technology and Temporality in Modern Egypt* (Berkeley: University of California Press, 2013), 242.

5. Barak, 242.

6. "Constitution and Functions of the Inter-Territorial Language (Swahili) Committee to the East African Dependencies" (1934), 1, SOAS, Y Swahili B39.

7. "Inter-Territorial Language (Swahili) Committee, Agenda and Unconfirmed Minutes of the Fifth Meeting, 12th to 14th January 1935: Appendix No. 2: Sub-Committee for the Swahili Essay Competition" [14–15], CO 822/67/12.

8. In 1938 alone, over three hundred essays were submitted. See "Inter-Territorial Language (Swahili) Committee, Agenda and Unconfirmed Minutes of the Eighth Meeting, 25th and 26th of January 1939: Appendix D, Report by the Secretary for the Year 1938," 13, CO 822/98/1.

9. The competition was advertised in various places including *Kwetu*, where an announcement was printed in 1939 in both Swahili and English. See *Kwetu* no. 13 (August 21, 1939): 4–5, TNA, File No. 23754, Kwetu, Vol. 3.

10. ILC *Bulletin* no. 16 (October 1942): 5.

11. "Inter-Territorial Language (Swahili) Committee, Report for the Year 1939," 16, CO 822/104/2.

12. "Swahili Authorship Competition, 1939," 1, CO 822/104/2.

13. It is possible that this was the same Thomas Mbotela who would go on to become a moderate leader within the Kenya African Union, resign from the party, become a city councilor, and be killed by Mau Mau militants in November 1952.

14. "Swahili Authorship Competition, 1939," 2, CO 822/104/2.

15. "Swahili Authorship Competition, 1939," 2.

16. "Swahili Authorship Competition, 1939," 3.

17. "Swahili Authorship Competition, 1939," 3.

18. "Inter-Territorial Language (Swahili) Committee Swahili Authorship Competition—1941," [5], CO 822/108/25.

19. "Inter-Territorial Language (Swahili) Committee Swahili Authorship Competition—1941," [5].

20. "Inter-Territorial Language (Swahili) Committee Swahili Authorship Competition—1941," [6].

21. Andrew Ivaska, *Cultured States: Youth, Gender, and Modern Style in 1960s Dar es Salaam* (Durham, NC: Duke University Press, 2011), 46–48.

22. Salum Kombo, *Ustaarabu na Maendeleo ya Mwafrika* (Nairobi: East African Literature Bureau, 1950).

23. "*Mwafrika wa juzi hakujua thamani ya kabila na kwa hiyo hakujali lo lote zaidi ya ukoo wake. Mwafrika wa jana aliendelea mbele kidogo akapata kujua thamani ya kabila badala ya ukoo, na katika kuvuta hatua mbele zaidi, Mwafrika wa leo anajali sana taifa kuliko kabila au ukoo, na hii ni ishara njema kuwa yeye amevuta hatua kubwa zaidi mbele katika ustaarabu kwa kuhusiana na mambo ya ulimwengu.*" Kombo, *Ustaarabu na Maendeleo*, 2. Also translated and quoted in James Brennan, *Taifa: Making Nation and Race in Urban Tanzania* (Athens: Ohio University Press, 2021), 127–28.

24. Kombo, *Ustaarabu na Maendeleo*, 49–51.

25. "*Na sasa, paelezwe kuwa hasara hizi mbili—za kunyang'anywa fedha na kupoteza maisha ghafla—zisingalipatikana ila ni kwa sababu ya kutojua kusoma.*" Kombo, 51,

26. Kombo, 51.

27. V. Y. Mudimbe, *The Invention of Africa: Gnosis, Philosophy, and the Order of Knowledge* (Bloomington: Indiana University Press, 1988), 77.

28. Mudimbe, 77.

29. Mudimbe, 77.

30. ILC *Bulletin* no. 20 (July 1947): 1.

31. The idea had been floated a decade earlier by the four directors of education; see "Extract from the Proceedings of Conference of Directors of Education of Kenya, Tanganyika, Uganda and Zanzibar, February–March 1936," TNA, File No. 22997, Supply of Native Literature.

32. Huxley's biography is not entirely pertinent here, except to say that she was an occasionally critical but undying supporter of the British empire, and her recommendations for the bureau reflected that support. Ngũgĩ wa Thiong'o classified Huxley's writing as being among the "downright racist literature" of the colonial period: Thiong'o, *Decolonising the Mind: The Politics of Language in African Literature* (Portsmouth, NH: Heinemann, 1986), 92.

33. "Literature for Africans, Report [127A]," 1–2, TNA, File No. 32525, Production of Literature Vol. 1.

34. See Emma Hunter, "Dutiful Subjects, Patriotic Citizens, and the Concept of 'Good Citizenship' in Twentieth-Century Tanzania," *Historical Journal* 56, no. 1 (March 2013): 257–77, and *Political Thought and the Public Sphere in Tanzania: Freedom, Democracy and Citizenship in the Era of Decolonization* (Cambridge: Cambridge University Press, 2015).

35. "Literature for Africans, Report [127A]," 17–18, TNA, File No. 3 2525, Production of Literature Vol. 1.

36. "Literature for Africans, Report [127A]," 18.

37. The EALB was overseen by the East African High Commission, which had superseded the Governors' Conference that same year.

38. "A Proposed Literature Organization for East Africa: The Preliminary Scheme [225B]," 17, TNA, File No. 32525, Production of Literature Vol. 2.

39. "A Proposed Literature Organization for East Africa: The Preliminary Scheme [225B]," 17.

40. East African Inter-Territorial Language (Swahili) Committee *Bulletin* no. 21 (May 1951): 1–2. [Hereafter EASC *Bulletin*.]

41. EASC *Bulletin* no. 21 (May 1951): 2–3.

42. EASC *Bulletin* no. 22 (August 1952): 2.

43. EASC *Bulletin* no. 22: 3.

44. EASC *Bulletin* no. 23 (June 1953): 5.

45. *Journal of the East African Swahili Committee* no. 24 (June 1954): 5.

46. "A Proposed Literature Organization for East Africa: The Preliminary Scheme [225B]," 4, TNA, File No. 32525, Production of Literature Vol. 2.

47. "The East African Literature Bureau," extract from *Year Book of Education* (1960), 537, PP MS12, C. G. Richards Papers 4/60. (The Richards collection is housed at SOAS; the first numeral refers to the box, the second to the file.)

48. East African Literature Bureau [Hereafter EALB] Annual Report 1954–5: 1; EALB Annual Report 1955–6: 1, PP MS12, C. G. Richards Papers 2/22 and 2/23.

49. EALB Annual Report 1950: 5, PP MS12, C. G. Richards Papers 2/18.

50. "A Proposed Literature Organization for East Africa: The Preliminary Scheme [225B]," 8, TNA, File No. 32525, Production of Literature Vol. 2.

51. "East African Literature Bureau General Circular No. 2, August 1949," CO 822/147/7.

52. Ahmad Rahman, *The Regime Change of Kwame Nkrumah: Epic Heroism in Africa and the Diaspora* (New York: Palgrave MacMillan, 2007), 33–34.

53. EALB Annual Report 1952: 4, PP MS12, C. G. Richards Papers 2/20.

54. EALB Annual Report 1955–56: 13, PP MS12, C. G. Richards Papers 2/23.

55. EALB Annual Report 1951: 4, PP MS12, C. G. Richards Papers 2/19.

56. "Minutes of the Sixth Meeting of the Advisory Council, 9th October 1953," 4, TNA, File No. 32525, Production of Literature Vol. 5.

57. "A Proposed Literature Organization for East Africa: The Preliminary Scheme [225B]," 11, TNA, File No. 32525, Production of Literature Vol. 2.

58. "The East African Literature Bureau," extract from *Year Book of Education* (1960), 537, PP MS12, C. G. Richards Papers 4/60.

59. EALB Annual Report 1960–61: 2, PP MS12, C. G. Richards Papers 2/27.

60. EALB Annual Report 1953: 18, PP MS12, C. G. Richards Papers 2/21.

61. "Literature for Africans, Report [127A]," 11, TNA, File No. 32525, Production of Literature Vol. 1.

62. "Publishing: Paper for All-African Literature Conference, Mindolo, June 1961," 6, PP MS12, C. G. Richards Papers 4/58.

63. EALB Annual Report 1950: 2, PP MS12, C. G. Richards Papers 2/18.

64. "A Proposed Literature Organization for East Africa: The Preliminary Scheme [225B]," 11, TNA, File No. 32525, Production of Literature Vol. 2.

65. EALB Annual Report 1955–6: 18, PP MS12, C. G. Richards Papers 2/23.

66. EALB Annual Report 1955–6: 18.

67. EALB Annual Report 1955–6: 14.

68. EALB Annual Report 1953: 8, PP MS1, C. G. Richards Papers 2/21. According to the same table, 1 percent of the total volumes printed were language studies.

69. EALB Annual Report 1953: 8.

70. EALB Annual Report 1956–7: 10, PP MS12, C. G. Richards Papers 2/24.

71. EALB Annual Report 1955–6: 13, PP MS12, C. G. Richards Papers, Box 2/23.

72. EALB Annual Report 1955–6: 13.

73. Emily Callaci, *Street Archives and City Life: Popular Intellectuals in Postcolonial Tanzania* (Durham, NC: Duke University Press, 2017), 147. See also Jan Blommaert, *State Ideology and Language in Tanzania*, 2nd ed. (Edinburgh:

Edinburgh University Press, 2014), 91–106. These ambitions followed the EALB into the postcolonial period as Julius Nyerere made not just literacy but also the habit of reading a part of his *Ujamaa* policies. The East African Literature Bureau continued operations until the collapse of the East African Community in 1977.

74. "Interview with Charles Richards for African Book Publishing Record, Second Draft, April 1976," 9, PP MS12, C. G. Richards Papers 11/111a.

75. "Interview with Charles Richards for African Book Publishing Record, Second Draft, April 1976," 9.

76. "The Development of African Literature: Lecture for Makerere College Faculty of Education African Studies Centre, 29 November 1962," 5, PP MS12, C. G. Richards Papers, 4/58.

77. See, for instance, Copy of Letter from Mark Young to Malcolm MacDonald, December 9, 1939, TNA, File No. 23775, Books Used in Govt. Schools.

78. "Libraries Service for Africans, East African Literature Bureau, Notes circulated as a Preliminary to a Conference on beginning the Service, 1 December 1950," 3, TNA, File No. 41415, Libraries Scheme of the EALB.

79. Handwritten memo No. 29 from E. C. Baker, April 12, 1949 [11], TNA, File No. 23775, Books Used in Govt. Schools.

80. "Literature for Africans, Report [127A]," 8, TNA, File No. 32525, Production of Literature Vol. 1.

81. "Literature for Africans, Report [127A]," 8.

82. "Literature for Africans, Report [127A]," 8.

83. "Literature for Africans, Report [127A]," 8.

84. EALB Annual Report 1956–57: 29–33, PP MS12, C. G. Richards Papers 2/23.

85. "A Proposed Literature Organization for East Africa: The Preliminary Scheme [225B]," 25, TNA, File No. 32525, Production of Literature Vol. 2.

86. "Scheme for the Periodicals Section of the East African Literature Bureau, Introductory Note," 14, TNA, File No. 41416, Periodicals Scheme of the EALB.

87. Letter from Acting Administrator to Under-Secretary of State for the Colonies, June 8, 1950, TNA, File No. 41416, Periodicals Scheme of the EALB.

88. See "Minutes of the Sixth Meeting of the Advisory Council, 9 October 1953," 5, TNA, File No. 32525: Production of Literature Vol. 5; and EALB Annual Report 1954–5: 13, PP MS12, C. G. Richards Papers 2/22.

89. EALB Annual Report 1954–5: 13, PP MS12, C. G. Richards Papers 2/22.

90. *Tazama,* September 15, 1954 [176–191], CO 822/1061.

91. Handwritten memo [6–7], CO 822/1061.

92. Ratcliffe retired in 1949 and was replaced by Wilfred Whiteley in 1952, followed by J. W. T. Allen in 1959 and Jan Knappert in 1964. For ILC/EASC engagement with non-Standard dialects, see, for instance, EASC *Bulletin* no. 23 (June 1953): 4; *Journal of the East African Swahili Committee* no. 24 (June 1954): 15; and "Agenda and Minutes of the Second Meeting of the Inter-Territorial Language (Swahili) Committee Readers and Assistant Readers, 26 and 27 January 1942," 2, CO 822/108/25.

93. EASC *Bulletin* no. 23 (June 1953): 6. Textbooks were still the exception; the ILC imprimatur was required for books adopted in schools.

94. EASC *Bulletin* no. 23 (June 1953): 6.

95. EASC *Bulletin* no. 23: 6.

96. EASC *Bulletin* no. 21 (May 1951): 7.

97. "A Proposed Literature Organization for East Africa: The Preliminary Scheme [225B]," 5, TNA, File No. 32525, Production of Literature Vol. 2.

98. See "Recent Developments in African Literature, Public Lecture in the Hall of the College of Further Education, Lusaka, 26 September 1963, C. G. Richards," 2; and "The Development of African Literature: Lecture for Makerere College Faculty of Education African Studies Course, 29 November 1962," 3, PP MS12, C. G. Richards Papers 4/58.

99. "Recent Developments in African Literature, Public Lecture in the Hall of the College of Further Education, Lusaka, 26 September 1963, C. G. Richards," 2, PP MS12, C. G. Richards Papers 4/58.

100. EALB Annual Report 1951: 4, PP MS 12, C. G. Richards Papers 2/19; and 2/21: EALB Annual Report 1953: 18. Wilfred Whiteley criticized the EALB for *not* doing a good enough job shepherding "original" material to publication: Letter from W. Whiteley to M. Guthrie, 6. November 1959, SOAS, PP MS42, Whiteley Collection, Box 10, File S/52.

101. "Literature for Africans, Report [127A]," 14, TNA, File No. 32525, Production of Literature Vol. 1; "Record of a Meeting held in the Education Department Dar es Salaam on Tuesday, 15th April, 1947, to discuss the proposals of the East African Governors' Conference for a Literature Organisation for East Africa," 5, TNA, File No. 32525, Production of Literature Vol. 2; and EALB Annual Report 1950: 5, PP MS 12, C. G. Richards Papers 2/18.

102. EALB Annual Report 1953: 18, PP MS 12: C. G. Richards Papers 2/21.

103. ILC *Bulletin* no. 19 (November 1945): 29.

104. ILC *Bulletin* no. 19: 29.

105. "East African Literature Bureau General Circular No. 2, August 1949," 5, CO 822/147/7.

106. EALB Annual Report 1950: 5, PP MS12, C.G. Richards Papers 2/18.

107. "East African Literature Bureau General Circular No. 2, August 1949," 4, CO 822/147/7.

108. "East African Literature Bureau General Circular No. 2, August 1949," 4.

109. EALB Annual Report 1950: 5, PP MS12, C. G. Richards Papers 2/18.

110. "Helps and Explanations for Authors No. 1, How a Book is Published" (1956), PP MS12, C. G. Richards Papers 3/43a.

111. "Helps and Explanations for African Authors No. 2, Some Forms of Writing" (1965): 1, PP MS12, C. G. Richards Papers 3/43b. I am not sure whether No. 2 was only printed ten years after No. 1 or if this happened to be the copy placed in the file.

112. "Helps and Explanations for African Authors No. 2" (1965): 3.

113. "Helps and Explanations for African Authors No. 2," 2.

114. "Helps and Explanations for African Authors No. 2," 13.

115. "Helps and Explanations for African Authors No. 2," 4.

116. "Helps and Explanations for African Authors No. 2," 7.

117. "Helps and Explanations for African Authors No. 2," 9.

118. "Helps and Explanations to African Authors No. 5, Short Story Writing, by Donald Stuart" (1963): 3, PP MS12, C. G. Richards Papers 3/43e.

119. "Helps and Explanations for African Authors No. 2, Some Forms of Writing" (1965): 9, PP MS12, C. G. Richards Papers 3/43b.

120. "Helps and Explanations for African Authors No. 2," 11.

121. "Helps and Explanations to East African Authors No. 4, Novels and Novel Writing, Edgar Wright" (1964): 2, PP MS12, C. G. Richards Papers 3/43d.

122. "Helps and Explanations to East African Authors No. 4" (1964): 3.

123. "Helps and Explanations to East African Authors No. 4," 2.

124. EALB Annual Report 1960–61: 12, PP MS12, C. G. Richard Papers 2/27. In a typewritten note in his papers, Richards wrote that the Rockefeller competition began in 1957/58, and that Muhammed Said Abdulla's *Mzimu wa Watu wa Kale* was the first winner. The frontispiece of the novel concurs with the earlier prizewinning date but makes no mention of the Rockefeller Foundation. For Richards' copy of Abdulla, see PP MS12, C. G. Richards Papers 3/51.

125. Thiong'o, *Birth of a Dream Weaver: A Writer's Awakening* (New York: New Press, 2016), 83. Ngũgĩ's submission won the 1961 competition and was later published as *The River Between*. See "No Carpet on the Floor: Recollections and Reflections, by Charles Granston Richards, on the Work of Forty Years 1935 to 1975 in the Development of Literature and Publishing," 37, PP MS 12, C. G. Richards Papers 1/o; and Thiong'o, *Birth of a Dream Weaver,* 168–69.

126. Muhammed Said Abdulla, *Mzimu wa Watu wa Kale* (Nairobi: East African Literature Bureau, 1960).

127. See, for instance, Elena Bertoncini, "Two Contemporary Swahili Writers—Muhammed Said Abdulla and Euphrase Kezilahabi," in *The East African Experience: Essays on English and Swahili Literature,* ed. Ulla Schild (Berlin: Dietrich Reimer, 1980), 85–90; and Xavier Garnier, *Swahili Novel: Challenging the Idea of a "Minor Literature"* (Suffolk, UK: James Currey, 2013), 142–62.

128. Abdulla, *Mzimu,* 41.

129. Bertoncini, "Two Contemporary"; and Garnier, *Swahili Novel,* 142–62.

130. Callaci, *Street Archives and City Life,* 145.

131. Abdulla, *Mzimu,* 67.

132. Garnier, *Swahili Novel,* 17.

133. "Helps and Explanations for African Authors No. 6, Notes on the Writing of Poetry in English, By Gerald Moore" (1964): 1, PP MS12, C. G. Richards Papers 3/43f.

134. "Helps and Explanations for African Authors No. 6" (1964): 5.

135. For a beautiful exploration of art students in apartheid-era South Africa finding creativity under even more constrained circumstances, see Daniel

Magaziner, *The Art of Life in South Africa* (Athens: Ohio University Press, 2016).

136. See John Mugane, *The Story of Swahili* (Athens: Ohio University Press, 2015), 220; and "In Memoriam," *Swahili: Journal of the East African Swahili Committee* 33, no. 1 (1962/3): x. Despite others' Shakespeare comparisons, Mugane argued that Robert "produced nothing written that approached the Ajami literature of old."

137. "Swahili: The National Language of Kenya, by Ali Abdallah Beck," 35, PP MS 20, J. W. T. Allen Papers 3/12.

138. Xavier Garnier, "Talking about Oneself to Act in the World: A Swahili Autobiography," *Swahili Forum* 19 (2012): 114.

139. Ann Biersteker, *Kujibizana: Questions of Language and Power in Nineteenth- and Twentieth-Century Poetry in Kiswahili* (East Lansing: Michigan State University Press, 1996), 40, 68.

140. Biersteker, *Kujibizana*, 76–80, 204–205. Biersteker also mentions the writing of Saadan Kandoro, Mathias Mnyampala, and Amri Abedi.

141. Garnier, "Talking about Oneself," 109.

142. See Kelly Askew, *Performing the Nation: Swahili Music and Cultural Politics in Tanzania* (Chicago: University of Chicago Press, 2002), 95–96; Biersteker, *Kujibizana*, 29–30; Iliffe, *Modern History of Tanganyika*, 379–80.

143. "Inter-Territorial Language (Swahili) Committee to the East African Dependencies, Report for the Year 1936," 5, CO 822/80/8.

144. See "Inter-Territorial Language Committee, Agenda and Unconfirmed Minutes of the Seventh Meeting, 2nd and 3rd May 1938: Appendix B. Report for the Year 1937," 9, CO 822/86/14; and "Agenda and Minutes of the Second Meeting of the Inter-Territorial Language (Swahili) Committee Readers and Assistant Readers, 26th and 27th of January 1942: Appendix II: The Sub-Committee's Report on the Swahili Essay Competition 1941," 11, CO 822/108/25.

145. "The Inter-Territorial Language (Swahili) Committee to the East African Dependencies, Report for the Year 1939," 4–6, CO 822/104/2.

146. "In Memoriam," *Swahili: Journal of the East African Swahili Committee* 33, no. 1 (1962/3).

147. See "East African Literature Bureau Advisory Council," *High Commission Gazette,* August 30, 1952, TNA, File No. 32525, Production of Literature Vol. 5; and EALB Annual Reports, 1958–1962, PP MS 12, C. G. Richards Papers, Box 2.

148. See "Book News Sheet, March 1951," TNA, File No. 41415, Libraries Scheme of the EALB; and EALB Annual Report 1958–9: 30, PP MS 12, C. G. Richards Papers 2/25.

149. "Book News Sheet, March 1951," TNA, File No. 41415, Libraries Scheme of the EALB.

150. Mbaabu, *New Horizons in Kiswahili: A Synthesis in Developments, Research and Literature* (Nairobi: Kenya Literature Bureau, 1985), 108. See too: Farouk

Topan, "Why Does a Swahili Writer Write? Euphoria, Pain, and Popular Aspirations in Swahili Literature," *Research in African Literatures* 37, no. 3 (Fall 2006): 108–10; and Said Khamis, "Classicism in Shaaban Robert's Utopian novel, 'Kusadikika,'" *Research in African Literature* 32, no. 1 (Spring 2001): 47–65.

151. K. Inyani Simala, "Swahili Poetic Text and African Historiography," *Sudanic Africa* 15 (2004): 27.

152. Biersteker, *Kujibizana,* 40.

153. Biersteker, 47–48.

154. Thiong'o, *Decolonising the Mind,* xii.

155. See M. M. Mulokozi, ed., *Barua za Shaaban Robert 1931–1958* (Dar es Salaam: Taasisi ya Uchunguzi wa Kiswahili, 2002), 192.

156. *"Moyo wangu uliyeyuka tamthili ya theluji chini ya jua juu ya mambo mengi ya nchi, nikaona ilikuwa wajibu na heshima kwangu kusaidia kuratibu na kujenga usitawi kama walivyotenda wengine."* Shaaban Robert, *Maisha Yangu na Baada ya Miaka Hamsini* (London: Thomas Nelson and Sons, 1966), 76–77.

157. *"Mpaka serikali ilipozuia watumishi wake kuwa wanachama na kushiriki katika siasa."* Robert, *Maisha Yangu,* 77.

158. Robert, 111. This concern was also raised at the 1963 annual meeting of the EASC, where it was decided to apply for a special permit to import Robert's works. See *Swahili: Journal of the East African Swahili Committee* 34, no. 1 (1964): 3.

159. *"Walakini, ikiwa chango ndogo kama ilivyokuwa yangu mimi ya sadaka, ilisaidia kupatikana kwa ufanifu wa uhuru na amani kwa watu katika Afrika Kusini, hasara hii ilikuwa si kubwa ilinganishwapo na furaha ya ushindi uliotazamiwa kuja kwa watu mwisho."* Robert, *Maisha Yangu,* 111.

160. *"Nilikuwa ninasaidia kununua au kukomboa utukufu wa mwanadamu kwa chango ndogo sana ya sadaka."* Robert, 111.

161. Garnier, "Talking about Oneself," 115.

162. *"Kazi ya hiari hushinda utumwa. Uandishi ulikuwa kazi ya hiari kwangu."* Robert, *Maisha Yangu,* 78.

163. Robert, 78.

164. *"Mwandishi si mtu wa ajabu awezaye kuishi kwa kula hewa na kunywa ukungu."* Robert, 82.

165. Shaaban Robert, *Kielezo cha Insha* (Johannesburg: Witwatersrand University Press, 1954).

166. *"Kutunga na kuandika kuna mashaka mengi. Pasipo mwongozo wa namna fulani watu wengi, ambao labda wengekuwa waandishi bora, hukata tamaa wakasema kwamba elimu hii imejaliwa watu wachache tu."* Robert, vi.

167. *"Lazima mtu aandike insha nyingi kabla ya kuwa mwandishi mwema."* Robert, 2.

168. *"Mwanafunzi habanwi katika pembe moja ya maandiko. Apewa nafasi maridhawa. Ana hiari ya kuchagua namna apendayo katika kazi yake."* Robert, 3.

169. Robert, 4–8.
170. Robert, 101–2.
171. Robert, 102.

CHAPTER 6: RUMBLINGS OF UNANTICIPATED DEMAND

1. Papers related to this case located in TNA, File No. 26949: Education of the Sons of Ex-African Teacher, Kihama Sangiwa.
2. Letter from S. M. Mtengeti to the Chief Secretary, June 21, 1943.
3. Letter from S. M. Mtengeti to R. J. Mason, Director of Education, June 2, 1943.
4. Typewritten memorandum by R. J. Mason, June 28, 1943.
5. Letter from Chief Secretary to Director of Education, July 6, 1943.
6. See Frederick Cooper, "Possibility and Constraint: African Independence in Historical Perspective," *Journal of African History* 49, no. 2 (2008): 167–96, and *Africa Since 1940: The Past of the Present,* 2nd ed. (New York: Cambridge University Press, 2019), 51–86, 116–95; and James Scott, *Seeing Like a State: How Certain Schemes to Improve the Human Condition Have Failed* (New Haven, CT: Yale University Press: 1998), 223–29. This period is sometimes also referred to as a "second colonial occupation."
7. See, for instance, Frederick Cooper, *Citizenship between Empire and Nation: Remaking France and French Africa, 1945–1960* (Princeton, NJ: Princeton University Press, 2014), and *Decolonization and African Society: The Labor Question in French and British Africa* (New York: Cambridge University Press, 1996); and Andrew Burton, "Townsmen in the Making: Social Engineering and Citizenship in Dar es Salaam, c. 1945–1960," *International Journal of African Historical Studies* 36, no. 2 (2003): 331–65.
8. Letter from S. M. Mtengeti to Headmaster, Government Central School, Old Moshi, July 23, 1945.
9. Here I borrow from Jan Blommaert's formulation: "There was not only a growing tradition of political talk *in* Swahili, but also an amount of political talk *about* Swahili." Blommaert, *State Ideology and Language in Tanzania,* 2nd ed. (Edinburgh: Edinburgh University Press, 2014), 41.
10. "A Proposed Literature Organization for East Africa: The Preliminary Scheme [225B]," 13, TNA, File No. 32525, Production of Literature Vol. 2.
11. Copy of Letter from W. F. Dawson to G. Annesley, October 2, 1950; and Copy of Letter from Acting Administrator of the East Africa High Commission to the Chief Secretaries, February 10, 1950, 2 and 5, CO 822/147/7.
12. "Report on the East African Library Service for the Year 1952," CO 822/596.
13. "Libraries Service for Africans, East African Literature Bureau, Notes circulated as a Preliminary to a Conference on beginning the Service," 2, TNA, File No. 41415, Libraries Scheme of the EALB.
14. "Report on the East African Library Service to December 1951," 5, CO 822/596.
15. "Report on the East African Library Service to December 1951," 1.
16. Handwritten Memo from K. G. Fry, July 21, 1953, CO 822/596.

17. Member's Circular Letter No. 21 of 1951: East African Literature Bureau Libraries, October 6, 1951, TNA, File No. 41415, Libraries Scheme of the EALB.

18. "Minutes of the Sixth Meeting of the Advisory Council, 9 October, 1953: Libraries Service-East African Literature Bureau," 2, TNA, File No. 32525, Production of Literature Vol. 5.

19. "Report on the East African Library Service for the Year 1952," 3–4, CO 822/596.

20. "Minutes of the Sixth Meeting of the Advisory Council, 9 October, 1953: Libraries Service-East African Literature Bureau," 1, TNA, File No. 32525, Production of Literature Vol. 5.

21. "Minutes of the Sixth Meeting of the Advisory Council, 9 October, 1953: Libraries Service-East African Literature Bureau," 2.

22. "Minutes of the Sixth Meeting of the Advisory Council, 9 October, 1953: Libraries Service-East African Literature Bureau," 3; and "Report on the East African Library Service for the Year 1952," 3, CO 822/596.

23. EALB Annual Report 1952, 8, PP MS12, C. G. Richards Papers 2/20.

24. EALB Annual Report 1955–6, 3. See also Table C on page 7, PP MS12, C. G. Richards Papers 2/23.

25. EALB Annual Report 1956–7, 5, PP MS12, C. G. Richards Papers 2/24.

26. EALB Annual Report 1958–9, 1 and 4, PP MS12, C. G. Richards Papers 2/25.

27. EALB Annual Report 1952, 10, PP MS12, C. G. Richards Papers 2/20.

28. "Report on the East African Library Service for the Year 1952—Analysis by Subject Matter of the Books Issued by the Kenya Branch Postal Library Service, May to December 1952," CO 822/596.

29. See EALB Annual Report 1954–5, 9, PP MS12, C. G. Richards Papers 2/22; and 2/25: EALB Annual Report 1958–9, 5.

30. "Colonial Office Committee on Mass Education (Community Development), Minutes of Meeting on 6 June 1952," 5, CO 822/596.

31. EALB Annual Report 1954–5, 11, PP MS12, C. G. Richards Papers 2/22. By 1956, Zanzibar and Pemba, with twenty-two centers, reportedly had the greatest number of book boxes in proportion to their size and population; see C. G. Richards Papers 2/23: EALB Annual Report 1955–6, 5.

32. "Libraries Service for Africans, East African Literature Bureau, Notes circulated as a Preliminary to a Conference on beginning the Service," 4, TNA, File No. 41415, Libraries Scheme of the EALB.

33. Copy of Letter from E. N. Fitzgerald to R. L. Sharp, September 30, 1952; and "Report on the East African Library Service to December 1951," 10, CO 822/596.

34. "Minutes of the Sixth Meeting of the Advisory Council, 9 October 1953: Libraries Service-East Africa Literature Bureau," 2, TNA, File No. 32525, Production of Literature Vol. 5.

35. "Report on the Libraries Section," 2, TNA, File No. 32525, Production of Literature Vol. 5.

36. "Report on the East African Library Service for the Year 1952," 9, CO 822/596.

37. "Report on the East African Library Service to December 1951," 3–4, CO 822/596.

38. "Report on the East African Library Service to December 1951," 10.

39. "Report on the Libraries Section," 1, TNA, File No. 32525, Production of Literature Vol. 5.

40. "Report on the Libraries Section," 1.

41. "Report on the Libraries Section," 1.

42. "East African Literature Bureau: Notes of meeting held in the Office of the Commissioner of Social Development, 4 February 1954," 1, TNA, File No. 41415, Libraries Scheme of the EALB.

43. EALB Annual Report 1954–5, 11, SOAS, PP MS12, C. G. Richards Papers 2/22.

44. See, for instance, "Report on the Libraries Section," 1, TNA, File No. 32525, Production of Literature Vol. 5; "Report on the East African Library Service for the Year 1952," 1, CO 822/596; EALB Annual Report 1952, 8, PP MS12, C. G. Richards Papers 2/20; and 2/23: EALB Annual Report 1955–6, 4.

45. Letter from G. Annesley to Director of Education, Dar es Salaam, February 21, 1952, TNA, File No. 32525, Production of Literature Vol. 4.

46. See Letter from G. Annesley to Director of Education, Dar es Salaam, February 21, 1952; and "Libraries Service for Africans, East African Literature Bureau, Notes circulated as a Preliminary to a Conference on beginning the Service," 3–4, TNA, File No. 41415, Libraries Scheme of the EALB.

47. See "Training of African Librarians" [14], CO 822/596; "Minutes of the Seventh Meeting of the Advisory Council, 2 November 1954: Appendix A. Director's Report to the Advisory Council," [22], CO 822/1062; EALB Annual Report 1954–5, 8, PP MS12, C. G. Richards Papers 2/22; 2/24: EALB Annual Report 1956–7, 4; and Letter from S. W. Hockey to C. G. Richards, June 6, 1966, PP MS12, C. G. Richards Papers 15/146.

48. "Memorandum on the East African Literature Bureau," 6 [57], CO 822/1062. See also EALB Annual Report 1955–6, 5, PP MS12, C. G. Richards Papers 2/23.

49. Letter from G. Annesley to Director of Education, Dar es Salaam, February 21, 1952, TNA, File No. 32525, Production of Literature Vol. 4.

50. Letter from G. Annesley to Director of Education, Dar es Salaam, February 21, 1952.

51. Letter from G. W. Baker to Director of Education, Dar es Salaam, August 22, 1951, TNA, File No. 41415, Libraries Scheme of the EALB.

52. Letter from Provincial Commissioner, Morogoro, Eastern Province to Member for Local Government, Dar es Salaam, February 28, 1953, TNA, File No. 41415, Libraries Scheme of the EALB.

53. "Literature for Africans, Report [127A]," 15, TNA, File No. 32525, Production of Literature Vol. 1.

54. Handwritten Memo [19–20], TNA, File No. 22997, Supply of Native Literature.

55. "A Proposed Literature Organization for East Africa: The Preliminary Scheme [225B]," 13, TNA, File No. 32525, Production of Literature Vol. 2.

56. Letter from Provincial Commissioner, Tanga to Member for Local Government, Dar es Salaam, November 27, 1951, TNA, File No. 41415, Libraries Scheme of the EALB.

57. Letter from Senior Provincial Commissioner, Arusha, Northern Province to Member for Local Government, Dar es Salaam, December 1, 1951, TNA, File No. 41415, Libraries Scheme of the EALB.

58. "Memo from Office of the East Africa High Commission Containing Minutes of Advisory Council Meeting," February 10, 1950, 2, CO 822/147/7.

59. "Memo from Office of the East Africa High Commission Containing Minutes of Advisory Council Meeting," February 10, 1950, 2.

60. See, for instance, EALB Annual Report 1953, 13, PP MS12, C. G. Richards Papers 2/21; 2/22: EALB Annual Report 1954–5, 7; 2/23: East African Literature Bureau 1955–6, 3–4; 2/25: EALB Annual Report 1958–9, 3, 6.

61. EALB Annual Report 1959–60, 1–2, PP MS12, C. G. Richards Papers, 2/26.

62. Handwritten Memo from J. H. Harris, June 28, 1950, CO 822/147/7.

63. For an in-depth examination of the poetry of Kandoro and Shaaban Robert in terms of nationalist and anticolonial politics, see Ann Biersteker, *Kujibizana: Questions of Language and Power in Nineteenth- and Twentieth-Century Poetry in Kiswahili* (East Lansing: Michigan State University Press, 1996), 23–94.

64. Biersteker, 32–39.

65. John Iliffe, *Modern History of Tanganyika* (New York: Cambridge University Press, 1979), 475–76.

66. Kandoro's poem did express an early anticolonial agenda, as in the second verse which calls for Africans to lead government; see Biersteker, *Kujibizana,* 33.

67. Biersteker, 34.

68. "Extract of Memorandum submitted to H. E. by the Meru Coffee Growers Association dated 15.10.1933, at Arusha," TNA, File No. 19191, Language to be used as medium of instruction in Schools Vol. 1.

69. Copy of letter from E. G. Rowe to Treasurer, Dar es Salaam, January 5, 1934, TNA, File No. 19191, Language to be used as medium of instruction in Schools Vol. 1.

70. Letter from Official Translator of German Documents to K. S. Bajwa, June 14, 1934, TNA, File No. 21821, Translation of Official Documents.

71. Typewritten Memo, April 24, 1930 [5], CO 822/29/4.

72. "Extract from Minutes of the Conference of Senior Administrative Officers, Held at the Secretariat, Dar es Salaam, 21st to 24th October 1929," CO 822/29/4.

73. See "Yanayosemwa na Watu Barabarani," *Kwetu* no. 10 (June 27, 1939): 8, TNA, File No. 23754, Kwetu Vol. 2; and "Kusema Kiswahili Katika Mikutano Ya Wazungu," *Kwetu* Special Number (July 1944): 6, File No. 23754, Kwetu Vol. 3.

74. "Sema Kweli Ufanikiwe," *Kwetu* no. 13 (August 21, 1939): 9, TNA, File No. 23754, Kwetu Vol. 3.

75. "Extract from Minutes of the Conference of Senior Administrative Officers, Held at the Secretariat, Dar es Salaam, 21st to 24th October 1929," CO 822/29/4.

76. "Translation into Kiswahili of legislation affecting the African," Circular Letter from Chief Secretary to All Provincial Commissioners, March 26, 1949, TNA, File No. 13410, Translation and Printing.

77. Letter from Provincial Commissioner, Morogoro, Eastern Province to Member for Lands and Mines, September 3, 1951, TNA, File No. 13410, Translation and Printing.

78. Copy of Letter from C. Caidz to Provincial Commissioner, Dar es Salaam, July 6, 1951, TNA, File No. 13410, Translation and Printing.

79. "Native Subordinate Courts," May 18, 1939, TNA, File No. 13410, Translation and Printing.

80. "Native Subordinate Courts," May 18, 1939.

81. Circular Letter from Member for Local Government, Dar es Salaam to all Provincial Commissioners and District Commissioners, October 16, 1950, TNA, File No. 13410, Translation and Printing.

82. See "Saving Telegram from Education, Dar es Salaam to Secretary, Civil Service Board, Dar es Salaam, 29 July 1946"; "Extract of Minutes of P. C. S.'s Conference, June 1948"; "Copy of Saving Telegram from Education, Dar es Salaam to Humanities, Dar es Salaam, 12 May 1948"; Copy of Letter from R. Craufurd-Benson to Director of Education, August 18, 1953, TNA, File No. 13410, Translation and Printing.

83. *Journal of the East African Swahili Committee* 28, no.1 (January 1958): 8.

84. Handwritten Memo [189], TNA, File No. 13410, Translation and Printing.

85. Letter from A de V. Wade to A. C. C. Parkinson, July 21, 1930, CO 822/29/4. This phrase, "culpable homicide not amounting to murder," seems to have been a touchstone for the colonial courts—Samuel Chiponde used the same example at the 1925 Education Conference, though he deployed it to argue in favor of Swahili translation. See *Conference between Government and Missions. Convened by His Excellency the Governor, Sir Donald Cameron. Report of proceedings. Held at Dar es Salaam, 5th to 12th October 1925* (Dar es Salaam: Government Printer, c. 1926), 102.

86. Handwritten Memorandum [171], August 5, 1953, TNA, File No. 13410, Translation and Printing.

87. See, for instance, CO 822/29/4: Handwritten Memo from A. C. C. Parkinson, April 23, 1930; Copy of Confidential Report from Lord Passfield, Secretary of State for the Colonies to Governor Symes, July 2, 1931; Letter from H. M. M. Moore to A. C. C. Parkinson, March 24, 1930; "Native Affairs Department Circular No. 35, Publication of Laws in Ki-Swahili," October 27, 1927.

88. "Extract from Minutes of the Conference of Senior Administrative Officers, Held at the Secretariat, Dar es Salaam, 21st to 24th October 1929," CO 822/29/4.

89. Letter from A de V. Wade to A. C. C. Parkinson, July 21, 1930, CO 822/29/4.

90. "Supervision of Native Courts by the High Court," *Kwetu* Special Number (November 1941): 9, TNA, File No. 23754, Kwetu Vol. 3.

91. "Extract from minutes of meeting of the Standing Finance Committee held on 29 May 1946," TNA, File No. 13410, Translation and Printing.
92. "Extract from minutes of meeting of the Legislative Council held on 25 July 1946," TNA, File No. 13410, Translation and Printing.
93. Letter from Information Department to F. A. Montague, July 1, 1946, TNA, File No. 13410, Translation and Printing.
94. "Extract from the Minutes of the 1947 Zanzibar Conference of the Tanganyika African Association, Copy of Letter from the Honorary Secretary of African Association," December 18, 1948, TNA, File No. 13410, Translation and Printing.
95. Letter from Social Welfare Organizer to Chief Secretary, March 1, 1949, TNA, File No. 13410, Translation and Printing.
96. Letter from Social Welfare Organizer to Chief Secretary, March 1, 1949.
97. Copy of Note from F. A. Montague to Honorary Secretary General, Tanganyika African Association, May 9, 1949, TNA, File No. 13410, Translation and Printing.
98. "Translating into Kiswahili of legislation affecting the African," From J. P. Moffett, Dar es Salaam, To All Provincial Commissioners and Public Relations Officer, March 26, 1949, TNA, File No. 13410, Translation and Printing.
99. "Translating into Kiswahili," March 26, 1949.
100. Note from Member for Local Government to District Commissioner, Ruponda, Southern Province, November 27, 1950, TNA, File No. 13410, Translation and Printing.
101. See Copy of Note from A. H. Maddocks, Municipal African Affairs Officer to District Commissioner, Dar es Salaam, June 28, 1951; Letter from Provincial Commissioner, Tanga to Member for Local Government, Dar es Salaam, January 7, 1954; Copy of Letter from Librarian, K.N.C.U Ltd. to Assistant Provincial Education Officer, Moshi, TNA, File No. 13410: Translation and Printing.
102. "Committee on Constitutional Development, Minutes of the third meeting, held in Dar es Salaam, August 25," TNA, File No. 32529, Hansard, Translation into Swahili.
103. "Committee on Constitutional Development," August 25.
104. "Cutting from the Tanganyika Standard, Dated 10 August 1950: Reports in Kiswahili," TNA, File No. 32529, Hansard, Translation into Swahili.
105. Copy of Letter from T. Griffith-Jones, Clerk of Legislative Council to All Provincial Commissioners, August 14, 1950, TNA, File No. 32529, Hansard, Translation into Swahili.
106. Copy of Letter from T. Griffith-Jones, Clerk of Legislative Council to All Provincial Commissioners, August 14, 1950.
107. Handwritten Memo, February 12 [187], TNA, File No. 13410, Translation and Printing.
108. *Swahili: The Journal of the East African Swahili Committee* 29, no.1 (January 1959): 88. This issue of the *Journal* was the first to include both the English and Swahili title on its cover page.

109. *Swahili: The Journal,* 88.
110. *Swahili: The Journal,* 91.
111. *Swahili: The Journal,* 92.
112. *Swahili: The Journal,* 93.
113. *Swahili: Journal of the East African Swahili Committee* 33/2 (1963): 1.
114. *Swahili: Journal of the East African Swahili Committee* 34/1 (1964): 8.
115. For a taste of the debate within missionary circles, see Karl Roehl, "The Linguistic Situation in East Africa," *Africa* 3, no. 2 (April 1930): 191–202; and Gerald Broomfield, "The Re-Bantuization of the Swahili Language," *Africa* 4, no. 1 (January 1931): 77–85. See also Emma Hunter, "Language, Empire and the World: Karl Roehl and the History of the Swahili Bible in East Africa," *Journal of Imperial and Commonwealth History* 41, no. 4 (2013): 600–616.
116. For more on 'Ajamī scripts in East Africa and beyond, see John Mugane, "The Odyssey of 'Ajamī and the Swahili People," *Islamic Africa* 8, nos. 1–2 (2017): 193–216, and "Writing Swahili in Arabic Characters," chap. 8 in *The Story of Swahili* (Athens: Ohio University Press, 2015); and Fallou Ngom, *Muslims beyond the Arab World: The Odyssey of Ajami and the Muridiyya* (New York: Oxford University Press, 2016).
117. "Arabic Script," Memorandum from A. E. Kitching, July 15, 1936, TNA, File No. 24771, Manual on Swahili in Arabic Script Vol. 1.
118. Typewritten Memorandum, July 31, 1936, TNA, File No. 24771, Manual on Swahili in Arabic Script Vol. 1.
119. See Roman Loimeier, *Between Social Skills and Marketable Skills: The Politics of Islamic Education in 20th Century Zanzibar* (Boston: Brill, 2009), 289–338; and Anne Bang, *Sufis and Scholars of the Sea: Family Networks in East Africa, 1860–1925* (New York: Routledge, 2003), 173–87.
120. Letter from J. D. Rankine to E. B. David, August 14, 1953, CO 822/208, Instruction of Languages in Zanzibar.
121. Letter from J. D. Rankine to E. B. David, August 14, 1953. Rankine also noted that the Zanzibar administration was setting up a "Muslim Academy" for "higher Arabic and Islamic study," as well as one Arabic-language primary school.
122. Letter from J. D. Rankine to E. B. David, August 14, 1953.
123. "Report on the East African Library Service for the Year 1952," 7–8, CO 822/596, East African Literature Bureau Libraries Scheme; and EALB Annual Report 1952, 9; EALB Annual Report 1960–61, 12; EALB Annual Report 1961–62, 12; and EALB Annual Report 1962–63, 11, PP MS12, C. G. Richards Papers 2/20, 2/27, 2/28, 2/29.
124. ILC *Bulletin* no. 7 (January 1934): 9–10.
125. Mazrui would handwrite the text on a single, double-sided page before it was cyclostyled; see Kai Kresse and Hassan Mwakimako, trans., *Guidance (Uwongozi), by Sheikh al-Amin Mazrui: Selections from the First Swahili Islamic Newspaper* (Boston: Brill, 2017), 2. For more on Sheikh Al-Amin Mazrui and his publications, see Nathaniel Mathews, "Imagining Arab Communities: Colonialism, Islamic Reform, and Arab Identity in Mombasa, Kenya,

1897–1933," *Islamic Africa* 4, no. 2 (Fall 2013): 135–63; and Randall Pouwels, "Sh. al-Amin B. Ali Mazrui and Islamic Modernism in East Africa, 1875–1947," *International Journal of Middle East Studies* 13, no. 3 (August 1981): 329–45.

126. Alamin Mazrui, *Swahili beyond the Boundaries: Literature, Language, and Identity* (Athens: Ohio University Press, 2007), 112. See also Kresse and Mwakimako, *Guidance (Uwongozi)*, xi.

127. Kresse and Mwakimako, xi.

128. Gudrun Miehe and Clarissa Vierke, eds., *Muhamadi Kijuma: Texts from the Dammann Papers and Other Collections* (Cologne, Germany: Rüdiger Köppe Verlag, 2010), 167.

129. See Gudrun Miehe and Clarissa Vierke, *Muhamadi Kijuma: Texts from the Dammann Papers and Other Collections* (Cologne, Germany: Rüdiger Köppe Verlag, 2010), 169; and Yahya Ali Omar and P. J. L. Frankl, "An Historical Review of the Arabic Rendering of Swahili Together with Proposals for the Development of a Swahili Writing System in Arabic Script (Based on the Swahili of Mombasa)," *Journal of the Royal Asiatic Society,* 3rd ser., vol. 7, no. 1 (April 1997): 60. The gathering was ultimately not held.

130. Miehe and Vierke, *Muhamadi Kijuma*, 55.

131. Miehe and Vierke, 55.

132. Fallou Ngom, "Ajami Literacies of West Africa," in *Tracing Language Movement in Africa,* ed. Ericka Albaugh and Kathryn de Luna (New York: Oxford University Press, 2018), 144.

133. Ngom, 157n13.

134. See Clarissa Vierke, "*Akhi Patia Kalamu:* Writing Swahili Poetry in Arabic Script," in *The Arabic Script in Africa: Studies in the Use of a Writing System,* ed. Meikal Mumin and Kees Versteegh (Boston: Brill, 2014), 326n16; and Kai Kresse, "Reading Mudimbe, Applying 'Mudimbe,' Turning an Insider Out: Problems with the Presentation of a Swahili Poet," *Journal of African Cultural Studies* 17, no. 1 (June 2005): 110, 114.

135. Kresse, "Reading Mudimbe," 114–15.

136. See Kresse, *Philosophising in Mombasa: Knowledge, Islam and Intellectual Practice on the Swahili Coast* (Edinburgh: Edinburgh University Press, 2007), 105–38; Thomas Geider, "Lehnwort- und Neologismenforschung," in *Swahili-Handbuch,* ed. Gudrun Miehe and Wilhelm Möhlig (Cologne, Germany: Rüdiger Köppe Verlag, 1995), 334; and Geider, "The Paper Memory of East Africa: Ethnohistories and Biographies Written in Swahili," in *A Place in the World: New Local Historiographies from Africa and South Asia,* ed. Axel Harneit-Sievers (Boston: Brill, 2002), 275–76.

137. Kresse, "Reading Mudimbe," 118; and Kresse, *Philosophising,* 128–29.

138. Meikal Mumin, "The Arabic Script in Africa: Understudied Literacy," in *The Arabic Script in Africa,* ed. Meikal Mumin and Kees Versteegh (Boston: Brill, 2014), 44.

139. Mumin, 44. Emphasis mine. See also Ngom, "Ajami Literacies of West Africa," 159–60.

140. Helmi Sharawy, "The Heritage of African Language Manuscripts Written in Arabic Characters (Ajami)," in *Political and Social Thought in Africa* (Dakar: CODESRIA, 2014), 77–89.

141. Mumin, "The Arabic Script in Africa," 54.

142. Mugane, "The Odyssey of ʿAjamī," 212. See too: Coleman Donaldson, "The Role of Islam, Ajami Writings, and Educational Reform in Sulemaana Kantèʼs NʼKo," *African Studies Review* 63, no. 3 (September 2020): 462–86; Ngom, *Muslims beyond the Arab World;* and Vierke, "*Akhi Patia Kalamu.*" Both Mugane and Vierke have pointed to the cruel irony that, by the mid-twentieth century, there was more interest in the preservation of ʿAjamī Swahili manuscripts in Europe than in East Africa itself.

143. Clarissa Vierke and Chapane Mutiua, "The Poem about the Prophetʼs Death in Mozambique—Swahili as a Transregional Language of Islamic Poetry," *Journal for Islamic Studies* 38, no. 2 (December 2020): 44–74.

144. "*Hivyo leo katika Afrika ya Mashariki yuko mtu anayeweza kujitokeza na kusema kuwa Kiswahili cha leo ni mali yake? Na hata akisema hivyo ina maana gani!*" Abdu Mtajuka Khamisi, "Kiswahili ikiwa ni Lugha ya Kimataifa," in *Lugha ya Kiswahili: Makala za Semina ya Kimataifa ya Waandishi wa Kiswahili I,* 2nd ed. (Dar es Salaam: Taasisi ya Uchunguzi wa Kiswahili, 2005), 17.

145. "No Carpet on the Floor: Recollections and Reflections, by Charles Granston Richards, on the Work of Forty Years 1935 to 1975 in the Development of Literature and Publishing," 28, PP MS 12, C. G. Richards Papers 1/0.

146. "East African Literature Bureau: Minutes of the Seventh Meeting of the Advisory Council, 2 November 1954: Appendix B. Outline for Discussion Regarding the Development of the E.A. Literature Bureau Libraries Service," 7, CO 822/1062.

147. "*Basi ilikuwa bora taasisi hiyo iwe katika nchi kama Tanzania ambamo Kiswahili kilikuwa kinaungwa mkono na serikali badala ya kuwa Uganda ambamo kingeshindana na Kiluganda.*" See Mbaabu, *Historia ya Usanifishaji wa Kiswahili,* 117.

148. *Swahili: Journal of the Institute of Swahili Research* 35, no. 1 (March 1965). The University College was a branch of the interterritorial University of East Africa until 1970 when the constituent parts broke off into Makerere University, University of Nairobi, and University of Dar es Salaam. Around the same time, the name of the organization would change once again, to *Taasisi ya Uchunguzi wa Kiswahili.*

149. "*Taasisi ya Uchunguzi wa Kiswahili, Chuo Kikuu Dar es Salaam inaendesha shughuli zake kama Taasisi ya kitaifa wala si ya Afrika Mashariki.*" Mbaabu, *Historia ya Usanifishaji wa Kiswahili* (Dar es Salaam: Taasisi ya Uchunguzi wa Kiswahili, 2007), 127. Kenya did continue contributing financially to the institute until 1974. See Mbaabu, *Language Policy in East Africa: A Dependency Theory Perspective* (Nairobi: Educational Research and Publications, 1996), 221.

1. *Swahili: Journal of the East African Swahili Committee* 33, no. 1 (1962/3): 142.
2. See Frederick Johnson, *A Standard Swahili-English Dictionary* (Oxford: Oxford University Press, 1939), 138; and *A Standard English-Swahili Dictionary* (Oxford: Oxford University Press, 1939), 286. For an invaluable discussion of the word *uhuru,* including the EASC's reaction, see Emma Hunter, *Political Thought and the Public Sphere in Tanzania: Freedom, Democracy and Citizenship in the Era of Decolonization* (Cambridge: Cambridge University Press, 2015), 135–57.
3. Hunter, *Political Thought,* 136.
4. Judith Listowel, *The Making of Tanganyika* (London: Chatto and Windus, 1965), 268.
5. See Wilfred H. Whiteley, *Swahili: The Rise of a National Language* (London: Methuen, 1969), 65; and John Iliffe, *A Modern History of Tanganyika* (New York: Cambridge University Press, 1979), 530.
6. See, for instance, Hunter, *Political Thought,* 210–30; Priya Lal, *African Socialism in Postcolonial Tanzania: Between the Village and the World* (New York: Cambridge University Press, 2015); and James Scott, *Seeing Like a State: How Certain Schemes to Improve the Human Condition Have Failed* (New Haven, CT: Yale University Press, 1998), 223–61.
7. S. S. Mushi, "The Role of Swahili Books in Nation-Building Endeavours," *Swahili: Journal of the Institute of Swahili Research* 38, no. 1 (March 1968): 3.
8. Mushi, 3.
9. See Kelly Askew, *Performing the Nation: Swahili Music and Cultural Politics in Tanzania* (Chicago: University of Chicago Press, 2002), 182–84; Jan Blommaert, *State Ideology and Language in Tanzania,* 2nd ed. (Edinburgh: Edinburgh University Press, 2014), 52–57, 92–93; and Karsten Legère, "Formal and Informal Development of the Swahili Language: Focus on Tanzania," in *Selected Proceedings of the 36th Annual Conference on African Linguistics,* ed. Olaoba Arasanyin and Michael Pemberton (Somerville, MA: Cascadilla Proceedings Project, 2006): 176–84.
10. Blommaert, *State Ideology,* 41.
11. Susan Geiger, *TANU Women: Gender and Culture in the Making of Tanganyikan Nationalism, 1955–1965* (Portsmouth, NH: Heinemann, 1997), 56.
12. Susan Geiger, "Tanganyikan Nationalism as 'Women's Work': Life Histories, Collective Biography and Changing Historiography," *Journal of African History* 37, no. 3 (1996): 471.
13. Hunter, *Political Thought,* 29n96.
14. Hunter, 29n93, citing Iliffe, *Modern History of Tanganyika,* 574.
15. Derek Peterson, Emma Hunter, and Stephanie Newell, eds., *African Print Cultures: Newspapers and Their Publics in the Twentieth Century* (Ann Arbor: University of Michigan Press, 2016), 31.
16. Blommaert, *State Ideology,* 33. For an examination of TANU's literacy campaigns and associated literary production, including TANU's desire to

create readers with "the right kinds of communal attitudes, national consciousness, and material aspirations," see Emily Callaci, *Street Archives and City Life: Popular Intellectuals in Postcolonial Tanzania* (Durham, NC: Duke University Press, 2017), 42–49, 146–52.

17. One type of "Swahili identity" according to Alamin Mazrui's typology in *Swahili beyond the Boundaries: Literature, Language, and Identity* (Athens: Ohio University Press, 2007), 3–5.

18. Ireri Mbaabu, *Language Policy in East Africa: A Dependency Theory Perspective* (Nairobi: Educational Research and Publications, 1996), 95–114.

19. Chege Githiora, *Sheng: Rise of a Kenyan Swahili Vernacular* (Rochester, NY: James Currey, 2018), 46–47.

20. Githiora, 48.

21. Alamin Mazrui and Ibrahim Noor Shariff, *The Swahili: Idiom and Identity of an African People* (Trenton, NJ: Africa World Press, 1994), 75.

22. See Githiora, *Sheng;* and Lillian Kaviti, "From Stigma to Status: Sheng and Engsh in Kenya's Linguistic and Literary Space," in Lutz Diegner and Frank Schulze-Engler, eds., "Habari ya English? What About Kiswahili? East Africa as a Literary and Linguistic Contact Zone," *Matatu* 46 (Leiden: Brill, 2015): 223–53.

23. Mazrui and Noor Shariff describe an expansion of Swahili "ethnicity" in Tanzania through that country's language policies, and its corresponding erasure in Kenya: Mazrui and Noor Shariff, *The Swahili,* 45.

24. Binyavanga Wainaina, *One Day I Will Write about This Place: A Memoir* (Minneapolis, MN: Graywolf, 2011), 125.

25. Abdulrazak Gurnah, "Leaning to Read," in *Habari ya English? What about Swahili? East Africa as a Literary and Linguistic Contact Zone,* ed. Lutz Diegner and Frank Schulze-Engler, *Matatu* 46 (Leiden: Brill, 2015), 31; and Salikoko Mufwene, *The Ecology of Language Evolution* (New York: Cambridge University Press, 2001), 12.

26. *Swahili: Journal of the Institute of Kiswahili Research* 35, no. 1 (March 1965): 1.

27. *Swahili: Journal of the East African Swahili Committee* 34, no. 1 (1964): 9, 3.

28. *Swahili: Journal of the Institute of Swahili Research* 36, no. 1 (March 1966): 7. The announcement was also published in Swahili, 9–10.

29. See *Swahili: Journal of the Institute of Swahili Research* 36, no. 1 (March 1966): 8; and *Swahili: Journal of the Institute of Swahili Research* 36, no. 2 (September 1966): 5.

30. *Swahili: Journal of the Institute of Swahili Research* 38, no. 2 (September 1968): 108. Mhina had taken over for J. A. Tejani, who had replaced Whiteley as director in 1967; M. H. Abdulaziz edited the journal.

31. "Dibaji," *Kamusi ya Kiswahili-Kiingereza* (Dar es Salaam: Taasisi ya Uchunguzi wa Kiswahili, 2001).

32. See, for instance, Karsten Legère, "JK Nyerere of Tanzania and the Empowerment of Swahili," in *"Along the Routes to Power": Explorations of Empowerment through Language,* ed. Martin Pütz, Joshua Fishman, and JoAnne Neff

van Aertselaer (Berlin: de Gruyter, 2006), 373–403; and Blommaert, *State Ideology,* 52–90.

33. Benedict Anderson, *Imagined Communities: Reflections on the Origin and Spread of Nationalism,* rev. ed. (New York: Verso, 2006), 80–81. See also Nancy Jacobs, *Birders of Africa: History of a Network* (New Haven, CT: Yale University Press, 2016), 101–5; and Bruno Latour, *Science in Action: How to Follow Scientists and Engineers through Society* (Cambridge, MA: Harvard University Press, 1987) for "soft" facts, and the role of networks and citations in creating "science."

34. See, for instance, Renee Romano, "No Diplomatic Immunity: African Diplomats, the State Department, and Civil Rights, 1961–1964," *Journal of American History* 87, no. 2 (September 2000): 546–79; James Meriwether, "'Worth a Lot of Negro Votes': Black Voters, Africa, and the 1960 Presidential Campaign," *Journal of American History* 95, no. 3 (December 2008): 737–63; Jim Harper, "Tom Mboya and the African Student Airlifts: Inclusion, Equity and Higher Education among Kenyan Women and Men," *Africology: The Journal of Pan African Studies* 10, no. 9 (October 2017): 82–105; and Eric Burton, "Decolonization, the Cold War, and Africans' Routes to Higher Education Overseas, 1957–65," *Journal of Global History* 15, no. 1 (2020): 169–91. Burton notes, too, that the enrollment and sponsorship of students required, besides high-level political support, mobilization at the local level in both the United States and East Africa.

35. Eyamba Bokamba, *African Language Program Development and Administration: A History and Guidelines for Future Programs* (Madison, WI: NALRC Press, 2002), 1–34.

36. See M. L. Nambuo Temu, "African American Students' Self-Awareness through Kiswahili Language," *Journal of Black Studies* 22, no. 4 (June 1992): 534; and John Mugane, "Learning How to Learn Languages: The Teaching and Learning of African Languages," *Languages and Linguistics Compass* 4, no. 2 (2010): 71.

37. For a critique of Swahili studies as taught in Euro-American universities, see John Mugane, *Story of Swahili* (Athens: Ohio University Press, 2015), 189–91.

38. "Freedom Annex Opens," *Washington Post,* November 22, 1968. My eternal gratitude to Emily Kern for bringing this story to my attention and sharing her documents with me.

39. Mamadou Lumumba, "Shule Ya Uhuru: Freedom and Manhood," in *High School,* ed. Ronald Gross and Paul Osterman (New York: Simon and Schuster, 1971), 288.

40. Lumumba, 293.

41. Keith Mayes, *Kwanzaa: Black Power and the Making of the African-American Holiday Tradition* (New York: Routledge, 2009), 50. There were several other "Shule" and institutions with Swahili-inspired names around the country, including Karamu House in Cleveland, Shule ya Watoto in Chicago, Uhuru

Sasa Shule in Brooklyn, and Kazi Shule in Houston. See Steven Almquist, "From the Streets to the Ivory Tower: Kiswahili in African-American Cultural Discourse," *Journal of African American Studies* 23, nos. 1–2 (2019): 92–110; and Russell Rickford, "'Kazi Is the Blackest of All': Pan-African Nationalism and the Making of the 'New Man,' 1969–1975," *Journal of African American History* 101, nos. 1–2 (2016): 97–125.

42. Ali Mazrui and Alamin Mazrui, *The Power of Babel: Language and Governance in the African Experience* (Chicago: University of Chicago Press, 1998), 35.

43. Much of the following background information is drawn from Scot Brown, *Fighting for US: Maulana Karenga, the US Organization, and Black Cultural Nationalism* (New York: New York University Press, 2003).

44. Brown, 7.

45. Mayes, *Kwanzaa: Black Power and the Making of the African-American Holiday Tradition* (New York: Routledge, 2009), 83.

46. As quoted in Mayes, *Kwanzaa*, 83.

47. Mazrui and Mazrui, *The Power of Babel*, 31.

48. Ali Mazrui, "Tanzaphilia," *Transition* 31 (June–July 1967): 20–26. My thanks to Allen Isaacman for pointing to the fact that FRELIMO cadres from Mozambique often learned Swahili while based in Dar es Salaam during the 1960s and 1970s.

49. See Lessie Tate, "The Power of Pan Africanism: Tanzanian/African American Linkages, 1947–1997" (PhD diss., University of Illinois at Urbana-Champaign, 2015), ProQuest Dissertations and Theses Global; and James Karioki, "Tanzania and the Resurrection of Pan-Africanism," *Review of Black Political Economy* 4, no. 4 (1974): 1–26.

50. Mayes, *Kwanzaa*, xix–xxi.

51. Mayes, 228n79. Karenga was also particularly inspired by the Umkhosi festival celebrated in southern Africa.

52. Mayes, 83.

53. Mugane, *Story of Swahili*, 255–59.

54. Brown, *Fighting for US*, 134.

55. Almquist, "From the Streets," 98.

56. Lumumba, "Shule," 300.

57. Almquist, "From the Streets," 97; and Tate, "The Power of Pan Africanism," 148.

58. Almquist, "From the Streets," 103.

59. Bokamba, *African Language Program Development*, 33.

60. "Swahili Lessons: Lesson One," *Black Collegian* 3, no. 4 (March 1973): 10. The lessons, prepared by the Swahili Department of Malcolm X Liberation University, abruptly came to an end with the institution's closure in September 1973.

61. Mayes, *Kwanzaa*, 82.

62. Ngũgĩ wa Thiong'o, "Kiswahili: Urithi Wetu Afrika," Udadisi, published July 8, 2021, https://udadisi.com/kiswahili-urithi-wetu-afrika/.

63. "*Nawaomba mashabiki wote wa Kiswahili: tafadhalini tusifanye Kiswahili ki-kalie kile kiti kilichokuwa kinakaliwa na Kiingereza; kiti cha kujiona kama ni cha cheo cha juu, na kwamba lazima lugha nyingine zikipigie magoti. Tutupi-lie mbali ule wa viwango.*" Thiong'o, "Kiswahili: Urithi Wetu Afrika."
64. "*Kwa hivyo, tujivunie lugha za mama; tujivunie Kiswahili kama lugha ya taifa; na juu yake tukiongeza ujuzi wa Kiingereza au Kimandarin, au Ki-faransa, au Kiyoruba, na kadhalika. Hizi zote zitatuongezea nguvu ya ujuzi na mawasiliano. Lakini msingi wetu ni lugha za mama na Lugha ya Taifa zima, yaani Kiswahili. . . . Kiswahili kinaweza kuwa lugha ya Umoja wa Af-rika!*" Thiong'o, "Kiswahili: Urithi Wetu Afrika."
65. Mazrui and Mazrui, *The Power of Babel*, 126.
66. Mugane, *Story of Swahili*, 273.

Bibliography

PERIODICALS

African Tidings / The Children's Tidings
Central Africa
Bulletin of the Inter-Territorial Language (Swahili) Committee / East African Inter-Territorial (Swahili) Committee
Swahili: Journal of the East African Swahili Committee
Kwetu
Msimulizi
Stories of Africa

BOOKS AND ARTICLES

Abdulla, Muhammed Said. *Mzimu wa Watu wa Kale.* Nairobi: East African Literature Bureau, 1960.

Almquist, Steven. "From the Streets to the Ivory Tower: Kiswahili in African-American Cultural Discourse." *Journal of African American Studies* 23, nos. 1–2 (2019): 92–110.

Alpers, Edward. *Ivory and Slaves: Changing Patterns of International Trade in East Central Africa to the Later Nineteenth Century.* Berkeley: University of California Press, 1975.

Anderson, Benedict. *Imagined Communities: Reflections on the Origin and Spread of Nationalism.* Rev. ed. New York: Verso, 2006.

Anderson-Morshead, A. E. M. *The History of the Universities' Mission to Central Africa, 1859–1896.* London: Universities' Mission to Central Africa, 1897.

———. *The History of the Universities' Mission to Central Africa, 1859–1909.* 5th ed. London: Universities' Mission to Central Africa, 1909.

———. *The History of the Universities' Mission to Central Africa, 1859–1909, Volume 1.* London: Universities' Mission to Central Africa, 1955.

Askew, Kelly. *Performing the Nation: Swahili Music and Cultural Politics in Tanzania.* Chicago: University of Chicago Press, 2002.

Aytürk, Ilker. "Revisiting the Language Factor in Zionism: The Hebrew Language Council from 1904 to 1914." *Bulletin of the School of Oriental and African Studies* 73, no. 1 (2010): 45–64.

Bang, Anne. *Sufis and Scholars of the Sea: Family Networks in East Africa, 1860–1925.* New York: Routledge, 2003.

Barak, On. *On Time: Technology and Temporality in Modern Egypt.* Berkeley: University of California Press, 2013.

Barber, Karin, ed. *Africa's Hidden Histories: Everyday Literacy and Making the Self.* Bloomington: Indiana University Press, 2006.

———. *The Anthropology of Texts, Persons and Publics.* New York: Cambridge University Press, 2007.

Beck, Rose Marie, and Kai Kresse, eds. *Abdilatif Abdalla: Poet in Politics.* Dar es Salaam: Mkuki na Nyota, 2016.

Becker, Felicitas. *Becoming Muslim in Mainland Tanzania, 1890–2000.* New York: Oxford University Press, 2008.

Beinart, William, and Karen Brown. *African Local Knowledge and Livestock Health: Diseases and Treatments in South Africa.* Rochester, NY: James Currey, 2013.

Benes, Tuska. *In Babel's Shadow: Language, Philology, and the Nation in Nineteenth-Century Germany.* Detroit: Wayne State University Press, 2008.

Bertoncini, Elena. "Two Contemporary Swahili Writers—Muhammed Said Abdulla and Euphrase Kezilahabi." In *The East African Experience: Essays on English and Swahili Literature,* edited by Ulla Schild, 85–90. Berlin: Dietrich Reimer, 1980.

Biersteker, Ann. *Kujibizana: Questions of Language and Power in Nineteenth- and Twentieth-Century Poetry in Kiswahili.* East Lansing: Michigan State University Press, 1996.

Blommaert, Jan. *State Ideology and Language in Tanzania.* 2nd ed. Edinburgh: Edinburgh University Press, 2014.

Blood, A. G. *The History of the Universities' Mission to Central Africa, 1907–1932, Volume 2.* London: Universities' Mission to Central Africa, 1957.

———. *The History of the Universities' Mission to Central Africa, 1933–1957, Volume 3.* London: Universities' Mission to Central Africa, 1962.

Bokamba, Eyamba. *African Language Program Development and Administration: A History and Guidelines for Future Programs.* Madison, WI: NALRC Press, 2002.

Bolton, Caitlyn. "Making Africa Legible: Kiswahili Arabic and Orthographic Romanization in Colonial Zanzibar." *American Journal of Islamic Social Sciences* 33, no. 3 (2016): 61–78.

Bremner, G. Alex. "The Architecture of the Universities' Mission to Central Africa: Developing a Vernacular Tradition in the Anglican Mission Field, 1861–1909." *Journal of the Society of Architectural Historians* 68, no. 4 (December 2009): 514–39.

Brennan, James. "Politics and Business in the Indian Newspapers of Colonial Tanganyika." *Africa* 81, no. 1 (2011): 42–67.

———. *Taifa: Making Nation and Race in Urban Tanzania.* Athens: Ohio University Press, 2021.

Bromber, Katrin. "German Colonial Administrators, Swahili Lecturers and the Promotion of Swahili at the Seminar für Orientalische Sprachen in Berlin." *Sudanic Africa* 15 (2014): 39–54.

———. "*Ustaarabu:* A Conceptual Change in Tanganyikan Newspaper Discourse in the 1920s." In *Global Conceptual History: A Reader,* edited by Margrit Pernau and Dominic Sachsenmaier, 289–304. New York: Bloomsbury, 2016.

Broomfield, Gerald. "The Development of the Swahili Language." *Africa: Journal of the International African Institute* 3, no. 4 (October 1930): 516–22.

———. "The Re-Bantuizatation of the Swahili Language." *Africa* 4, no. 1 (January 1931): 77–85.

———. *Sarufi ya Kiswahili: A Grammar of Swahili in Swahili for Swahili-Speaking People.* London: Sheldon, 1931.

Brown, Scot. *Fighting for US: Maulana Karenga, the US Organization, and Black Cultural Nationalism.* New York: New York University Press, 2003.

Brumfit, Ann. "The Rise and Development of a Language Policy in German East Africa." *Sprache und Geschichte in Afrika* 2 (1980): 219–331.

Burton, Andrew. "Townsmen in the Making: Social Engineering and Citizenship in Dar es Salaam, c. 1945–1960." *International Journal of African Historical Studies* 36, no. 2 (2003): 331–65.

Burton, Eric. "Decolonization, the Cold War, and Africans' Routes to Higher Education Overseas, 1957–65." *Journal of Global History* 15, no. 1 (2020): 169–91.

Callaci, Emily. *Street Archives and City Life: Popular Intellectuals in Postcolonial Tanzania.* Durham, NC: Duke University Press, 2017.

Callahan, Michael. *Mandates and Empire: The League of Nations and Africa, 1914–1931.* Portland, OR: Sussex Academic Press, 1999.

Chimerah, Rocha. *Kiswahili: Past, Present and Future Horizons.* Nairobi: Nairobi University Press, 1998.

Chiraghdin, Shihabuddin, and Mathias Mnyampala. *Historia ya Kiswahili.* Nairobi: Oxford University Press, 1977.

Christopher, Emma, Cassandra Pybus, and Marcus Rediker, eds. *Many Middle Passages: Forced Migration and the Making of the Modern World.* Berkeley: University of California Press, 2007.

Coen, Deborah. *Climate in Motion: Science, Empire, and the Problem of Scale.* Chicago: University of Chicago Press, 2018.

Coldham, Elizabeth. *A Bibliography of Scriptures in African Languages.* Vol. 2. London: British and Foreign Bible Society, 1966.

"Conference between Government and Missions. Convened by His Excellency the Governor, Sir Donald Cameron. Report of proceedings. Held at Dar es Salaam, 5th to 12th October 1925." Dar es Salaam: Government Printer, c. 1926.

Cooper, Frederick. *Africa since 1940: The Past of the Present.* 2nd ed. New York: Cambridge University Press, 2019.

———. *Citizenship between Empire and Nation: Remaking France and French Africa, 1945–1960.* Princeton, NJ: Princeton University Press, 2014.

———. *Decolonization and African Society: The Labor Question in French and British Africa*. New York: Cambridge University Press, 1996.

———. "Possibility and Constraint: African Independence in Historical Perspective." *Journal of African History* 49, no. 2 (2008): 167–96.

Crystal, David. *The Stories of English*. New York: Overlook Press, 2004.

Donaldson, Coleman. "The Role of Islam, Ajami Writings, and Educational Reform in Sulemaana Kantè's N'Ko." *African Studies Review* 63, no. 3 (September 2020): 462–86.

Dumbuya, Peter. *Tanganyika under International Mandate, 1919–1946*. Lanham, MD: University Press of America, 1995.

Errington, Joseph. *Linguistics in a Colonial World: A Story of Language, Meaning, and Power*. Malden, MA: Blackwell, 2008.

Fabian, Johannes. *Language and Colonial Power: The Appropriation of Swahili in the Former Belgian Congo, 1880–1938*. New York: Cambridge University Press, 1986.

———. *Language on the Road: Notes on Swahili in Two Nineteenth Century Travelogues*. Hamburg: H. Buske, 1984.

Fabian, Steven. *Making Identity on the Swahili Coast: Urban Life, Community, and Belonging in Bagamoyo*. New York: Cambridge University Press, 2019.

Farsy, Abdallah Salih. *The Shafi'i Ulama of East Africa, c.1830–1970: A Hagiographic Account*. Translated by Randall L. Pouwels. Madison: African Studies Program, University of Wisconsin–Madison, 1989.

Flow, Christian. "Writing the Thesaurus of Latinity: A Study in the History of Philological Practice." PhD diss., Princeton University, 2019. ProQuest Dissertations and Theses Global.

Frankl, P. J. L. "Johann Ludwig Krapf and the Birth of Swahili Studies." *Zeitschrift der Deutschen Morgenländischen Gesellschaft* 142, no. 1 (1992): 12–20.

Fulford, Ben. "An Igbo Esperanto: A History of the Union Ibo Bible 1900–1950." *Journal of Religion in Africa* 32, no. 4 (November 2002): 457–501.

Garnier, Xavier. *The Swahili Novel: Challenging the Idea of a "Minor Literature."* Suffolk, UK: James Currey, 2013.

———. "Talking about Oneself to Act in the World: A Swahili Autobiography." *Swahili Forum* 19 (2012): 106–16.

Geider, Thomas. "Lehnwort- und Neologismenforschung." In *Swahili-Handbuch*, edited by Gudrun Miehe and Wilhelm Möhlig, 323–37. Cologne, Germany: Rüdiger Köppe Verlag, 1995.

———. "The Paper Memory of East Africa: Ethnohistories and Biographies Written in Swahili." In *A Place in the World: New Local Historiographies from Africa and South Africa*, edited by Axel Harneit-Sievers, 255–88. Boston: Brill, 2002.

Geiger, Susan. "Tanganyikan Nationalism as 'Women's Work': Life Histories, Collective Biography and Changing Historiography." *Journal of African History* 37, no. 3 (1996): 465–78.

———. *TANU Women: Gender and Culture in the Making of Tanganyikan Nationalism, 1955–1965*. Portsmouth, NH: Heinemann, 1997.

Ghazal, Amal. "The Other 'Andalus': The Omani Elite in Zanzibar and the Making of an Identity, 1880s–1930s." *MIT Electronic Journal of Middle East Studies* (Fall 2005): 43–58.

Giblin, James, and Jamie Monson, eds. *Maji Maji: Lifting the Fog of War.* Boston: Brill, 2010.

Gilbert, Erik. *Dhows and the Colonial Economy of Zanzibar, 1860–1970.* Athens: Ohio University Press, 2005.

Gilmour, Rachael. *Grammars of Colonialism: Representing Language in Colonial South Africa.* New York: Palgrave Macmillan, 2006.

Githiora, Chege. *Sheng: Rise of a Kenyan Swahili Vernacular.* Rochester, NY: James Currey, 2018.

Glassman, Jonathon. *Feasts and Riot: Revelry, Rebellion, and Popular Consciousness on the Swahili Coast, 1856–1888.* Portsmouth, NH: Heinemann, 1995.

———. *War of Words, War of Stones: Racial Thought and Violence in Colonial Zanzibar.* Bloomington: Indiana University Press, 2011.

Good, Charles. *The Steamer Parish: The Rise and Fall of Missionary Medicine on an African Frontier.* Chicago: University of Chicago Press, 2004.

Gordin, Michael. *Scientific Babel: How Science Was Done Before and After Global English.* Chicago: University of Chicago Press, 2015.

Gurnah, Abdulrazak. "Learning to Read." In *Habari ya English? What about Swahili? East Africa as a Literary and Linguistic Contact Zone,* edited by Lutz Diegner and Frank Schulze-Engler, 23–32. *Matatu* 46. Leiden: Brill, 2015.

Gwassa, G. C. K., and John Iliffe. *Records of the Maji Maji Rising.* Nairobi: East African Publishing House, 1967.

Hamilton, Carolyn. *Terrific Majesty: The Powers of Shaka Zulu and the Limits of Historical Invention.* Cambridge, MA: Harvard University Press, 1998.

Harper, Jim. "Tom Mboya and the African Student Airlifts: Inclusion, Equity and Higher Education among Kenyan Women and Men." *Africology: The Journal of Pan African Studies* 10, no. 9 (October 2017): 82–105.

Harries, Patrick. *Butterflies and Barbarians: Swiss Missionaries and Systems of Knowledge in South-East Africa.* Athens: Ohio University Press, 2007.

Hastings, Adrian. *The Church in Africa: 1450–1950.* New York: Oxford University Press, 1994.

Haustein, Jörg. "Provincializing Representation: East African Islam in the German Colonial Press." In *Religion, Media, and Marginality in Modern Africa,* edited by Felicitas Becker, Joel Cabrita, and Marie Rodet, 70–92. Athens: Ohio University Press, 2018.

Hawthorne, Walter. "'Being Now, as It Were, One Family': Shipmate Bonding on the Slave Vessel Emilia, in Rio de Janeiro and throughout the Atlantic World." *Luso-Brazilian Review* 45, no. 1 (2008): 53–77.

Heanley, R. M. *A Memoir of Edward Steere, D.D., L.L.D., Third Missionary Bishop in Central Africa.* 3rd ed. London: Universities' Mission to Central Africa, 1989.

Hoffman, Valerie. "In His (Arab) Majesty's Service: The Career of a Somali Scholar and Diplomat in Nineteenth-Century Zanzibar." In *The Global Worlds of the*

Swahili: Interfaces of Islam, Identity and Space in 19th and 20th-Century East Africa, edited by Roman Loimeier and Rüdiger Seesemann, 59–78. New Brunswick, NJ: Transaction Publishers, 2006.

———. "Muslim-Christian Encounters in Late Nineteenth-Century Zanzibar." *MIT Electronic Journal of Middle East Studies* (Fall 2005): 59–78.

Hofmeyr, Isabel. *The Portable Bunyan: A Transnational History of "The Pilgrim's Progress."* Princeton, NJ: Princeton University Press, 2003.

Hopper, Matthew. *Slaves of One Master: Globalization and Slavery in Arabia in the Age of Empire.* New Haven, CT: Yale University Press, 2015.

Hunter, Emma. "Dutiful Subjects, Patriotic Citizens, and the Concept of 'Good Citizenship' in Twentieth-Century Tanzania." *Historical Journal* 56, no. 1 (March 2013): 257–77.

———. "Language, Empire and the World: Karl Roehl and the History of the Swahili Bible in East Africa." *Journal of Imperial and Commonwealth History* 41, no. 4 (2013): 600–616.

———. "'Our Common Humanity': Print, Power, and the Colonial Press in Interwar Tanganyika and French Cameroun." *Journal of Global History* 7, no. 2 (2012): 279–301.

———. *Political Thought and the Public Sphere in Tanzania: Freedom, Democracy and Citizenship in the Era of Decolonization.* Cambridge: Cambridge University Press, 2015.

———. "Print Media, the Swahili Language, and Textual Cultures in Twentieth-Century Tanzania, ca. 1923–1939." In *Indigenous Textual Cultures: Reading and Writing in the Age of Global Empire*, edited by Tony Ballantyne, Lachy Paterson, and Angela Wanhalla, 175–94. Durham, NC: Duke University Press, 2020.

Iliffe, John. "The Effects of the Maji Maji Rebellion of 1905–1906 on German Occupation Policy in East Africa." In *Britain and Germany in Africa: Imperial Rivalry and Colonial Rule*, edited by Prosser Gifford and William Roger Louis, 557–75. New Haven, CT: Yale University Press, 1967.

———. *A Modern History of Tanganyika.* New York: Cambridge University Press, 1979.

———. *Tanganyika under German Rule, 1905–1912.* New York: Cambridge University Press, 1969.

Irvine, Judith. "Mastering African Languages: The Politics of Linguistics in Nineteenth-Century Senegal." *Social Analysis: The International Journal of Anthropology* 33 (September 1993): 27–46.

Ivaska, Andrew. *Cultured States: Youth, Gender, and Modern Style in 1960s Dar es Salaam.* Durham, NC: Duke University Press, 2011.

Jacobs, Nancy. *Birders of Africa: History of a Network.* New Haven, CT: Yale University Press, 2016.

Johnson, Frederick. *Kamusi ya Kiswahili yaani Kitabu cha Maneno ya Kiswahili.* London: Sheldon, 1935.

———. *A Standard Swahili-English Dictionary.* Oxford: Oxford University Press, 1939.

Jones, Thomas Jesse. *Education in East Africa: A Study of East, Central and South Africa.* New York: Phelps-Stokes Fund, 1925.

Kamusi ya Kiswahili-Kiingereza. Dar es Salaam: Taasisi ya Uchunguzi wa Kiswahili, 2001.

Karioki, James. "Tanzania and the Resurrection of Pan-Africanism." *Review of Black Political Economy* 4, no. 4 (1974): 1–26.

Kaske, Elisabeth. "Mandarin, Vernacular and National Language—China's Emerging Concept of a National Language in the Early Twentieth Century." In *Mapping Meanings: The Field of New Learning in Late Qing China,* edited by Michael Lackner and Natascha Vittinghoff, 265–304. Boston: Brill, 2004.

Kaviti, Lillian. "From Stigma to Status: Sheng and Engsh in Kenya's Linguistic and Literary Space." In *Habari ya English? What about Swahili? East Africa as a Literary and Linguistic Contact Zone,* edited by Lutz Diegner and Frank Schulze-Engler, 223–53. *Matatu* 46. Leiden: Brill, 2015.

Keable, Robert. *Darkness or Light: Studies in the History of the Universities' Mission to Central Africa Illustrating the Theory and Practice of Missions.* 2nd ed. London: Universities' Mission to Central Africa, 1914.

Khalid, Abdallah. *The Liberation of Swahili from European Appropriation.* Nairobi: East African Literature Bureau, 1977.

Khamis, Said. "Classicism in Shaaban Robert's Utopian Novel 'Kusadikika.'" *Research in African Literatures* 32, no. 1 (Spring 2001): 47–65.

Khamisi, Abdu Mtajuka. "Kiswahili ikiwa ni Lugha ya Kimataifa." In *Lugha ya Kiswahili: Makala za Semina ya Kimataifa ya Waandishi wa Kiswahili I,* 1–18. Dar es Salaam: Taasisi ya Uchunguzi wa Kiswahili, 2005.

Kitabu cha Agano Jipya la Bwana na Mkokozi Wetu Isa Masiya. London: British and Foreign Bible Society, 1883.

Kollman, Paul. *The Evangelization of Slaves and Catholic Origins in Eastern Africa.* Maryknoll, NY: Orbis Books, 2005.

Kombo, Salum. *Ustaarabu na Maendeleo ya Mwafrika.* Nairobi: East African Literature Bureau, 1950.

Krapf, Johann L. *A Dictionary of the Suaheli Language.* London: Trübner, 1882.

———. *Outline of the Elements of the Kisuaheli Language, with Special Reference to the Kinika Dialect.* Tübingen: L. F. Fues, 1850.

———. *Travels, Researches, and Missionary Labors, during an Eighteen Years' Residence in Eastern Africa.* London: Trübner, 1860.

———. *Vocabulary of Six East-African Languages (Kisuaheli, Kinika, Kikamba, Kipokomo, Kihiau, Kigalla).* Tübingen, Germany: L. F. Fues, 1850.

Krautwald, Fabian. "The Bearers of News: Print and Power in German East Africa." *Journal of African History* 62, no. 1 (2021): 5–28.

Kresse, Kai. "Reading Mudimbe, Applying 'Mudimbe,' Turning an Insider Out: Problems with the Presentation of a Swahili Poet." *Journal of African Cultural Studies* 17, no. 1 (June 2005): 103–29.

———. *Philosophising in Mombasa: Knowledge, Islam and Intellectual Practice on the Swahili Coast.* Edinburgh: Edinburgh University Press, 2007.

Kresse, Kai, and Hassan Mwakimako, trans. *Guidance (Uwongozi), by Sheikh al-Amin Mazrui: Selections from the First Swahili Islamic Newspaper.* Boston: Brill, 2017.

Kuhn, Thomas. "The Essential Tension: Tradition and Innovation in Scientific Research." In *The Essential Tension: Selected Studies in Scientific Tradition and Change*, 225–39. Chicago: University of Chicago Press, 1977.

———. *The Structure of Scientific Revolutions.* 4th ed. Chicago: University of Chicago Press, 2012.

Lacunza-Balda, Justo. "Translations of the Quran into Swahili, and Contemporary Islamic Revival in East Africa." In *African Islam and Islam in Africa: Encounters Between Sufis and Islamists*, edited by Eva Evers Rosander and David Westerlund, 95–126. Athens: Ohio University Press, 1997.

Lampland, Martha, and Susan Leigh Star, eds. *Standards and Their Stories: How Quantifying, Classifying, and Formalizing Practices Shape Everyday Life.* Ithaca, NY: Cornell University Press, 2008.

Larson, Pier. "Horrid Journeying: Narratives of Enslavement and the Global African Diaspora." *Journal of World History* 19, no. 4 (December 2008): 431–64.

———. *Ocean of Letters: Language and Creolization in an Indian Ocean Diaspora.* New York: Cambridge University Press, 2009.

Latour, Bruno. *Science in Action: How to Follow Scientists and Engineers through Society.* Cambridge, MA: Harvard University Press, 1987.

Legère, Karsten. "Formal and Informal Development of the Swahili Language: Focus on Tanzania." In *Selected Proceedings of the 36th Annual Conference on African Linguistics*, edited by Olaoba Arasanyin and Michael Pemberton, 176–84. Somerville, MA: Cascadilla Proceedings Project, 2006.

———. "JK Nyerere of Tanzania and the Empowerment of Swahili." In *"Along the Routes to Power": Explorations of Empowerment through Language*, edited by Martin Pütz, Joshua Fishman, and JoAnne Neff van Aertselaer, 373–403. Berlin: de Gruyter, 2006.

Lemke, Hilde. "Die Suaheli-Zeitungen und-Zeitschriften in Deutsch-Ostafrika." PhD diss., Universität Leipzig, 1929.

Lewis, Geoffrey. *Turkish Language Reform: A Catastrophic Success.* New York: Oxford University Press, 1999.

Liebst, Michelle. *Labour and Christianity in the Mission: African Workers in Tanganyika and Zanzibar, 1864–1926.* Rochester, NY: James Currey, 2021.

Listowel, Judith. *The Making of Tanganyika.* London: Chatto and Windus, 1965.

Loimeier, Roman. *Between Social Skills and Marketable Skills: The Politics of Islamic Education in 20th Century Zanzibar.* Boston: Brill, 2009.

Lumumba, Mamadou. "Shule Ya Uhuru: Freedom and Manhood." In *High School*, edited by Ronald Gross and Paul Osterman, 285–300. New York: Simon and Schuster, 1971.

Madan, Arthur C. *English-Swahili Dictionary, Compiled for the Use of the Universities' Mission to Central Africa.* Oxford: Clarendon, 1894.

———. *Kiungani; or, Story and History from Central Africa.* London: George Bell and Sons, 1887.

———. *Swahili-English Dictionary.* Oxford: Clarendon, 1903.

Magaziner, Daniel. *The Art of Life in South Africa.* Athens: Ohio University Press, 2016.

Mamdani, Mahmood. *Citizen and Subject: Contemporary Africa and the Legacy of Late Colonialism.* Princeton, NJ: Princeton University Press, 1996.

Manarin, Louis Timothy. "And the Word Became Kigambo: Language, Literacy and Bible Translation in Buganda, 1875–1931." PhD diss., Indiana University, 2008. ProQuest Dissertations and Theses Global.

Marshall, Andrew. "Kiswahili and Decolonization: The Inter-Territorial Language Committee and Successor Organizations, 1930–1970." Master's thesis, American University, 2015. ProQuest Dissertations and Theses Global.

Mason, John. *Social Death and Resurrection: Slavery and Emancipation in South Africa.* Charlottesville: University of Virginia Press, 2003.

Massamba, David. *Historia ya Kiswahili: 50 BK hadi 1500 BK.* Nairobi: Jomo Kenyatta Foundation, 2002.

Masury, Samuel. "A Vocabulary of the Soahili Language, on the Eastern Coast of Africa." *Memoirs of the American Academy of Arts and Sciences.* New Series, vol. 2 (1846): 248–52.

Mathews, Nathaniel. "Imagining Arab Communities: Colonialism, Islamic Reform, and Arab Identity in Mombasa, Kenya, 1897–1933." *Islamic Africa* 4, no. 2 (Fall 2013): 135–63.

Mavhunga, Clapperton. *The Mobile Workshop: The Tsetse Fly and African Knowledge Production.* Cambridge, MA: MIT Press, 2018.

Mayes, Keith. *Kwanzaa: Black Power and the Making of the African-American Holiday Tradition.* New York: Routledge, 2009.

Mazrui, Ali. "Tanzaphilia." *Transition* 31 (June–July 1967): 20–26.

Mazrui, Ali, and Alamin Mazrui. *The Power of Babel: Language and Governance in the African Experience.* Chicago: University of Chicago Press, 1998.

Mazrui, Alamin. *Swahili beyond the Boundaries: Literature, Language, and Identity.* Athens: Ohio University Press, 2007.

Mazrui, Alamin, and Ibrahim Noor Shariff. *The Swahili: Idiom and Identity of an African People.* Trenton, NJ: Africa World Press, 1994.

Mbaabu, Ireri. *Historia ya Usanifishaji wa Kiswahili.* Dar es Salaam: Taasisi ya Uchunguzi wa Kiswahili, 2007.

———. *Language Policy in East Africa: A Dependency Theory Perspective.* Nairobi: Educational Research and Publications, 1996.

———. *New Horizons in Kiswahili: A Synthesis in Developments, Research and Literature.* Nairobi: Kenya Literature Bureau, 1985.

McDow, Thomas. *Buying Time: Debt and Mobility in the Western Indian Ocean.* Athens: Ohio University Press, 2018.

McMahon, Elisabeth. *Slavery and Emancipation in Islamic East Africa: From Honor to Respectability.* New York: Cambridge University Press, 2013.

Mehnert, Wolfgang. "The Language Questions in the Colonial Policy of German Imperialism." In *African Studies-Afrika-Studien,* edited by Thea Büttner and Gerhard Brehme, 383–97. Berlin: Akademie Verlag, 1973.

Meriwether, James. "'Worth a Lot of Negro Votes': Black Voters, Africa, and the 1960 Presidential Campaign." *Journal of American History* 95, no. 3 (December 2008): 737–63.

Middleton, John. *The World of the Swahili: An African Mercantile Civilization.* New Haven, CT: Yale University Press, 1992.

Miehe, Gudrun, and Clarissa Vierke. *Muhamadi Kijuma: Texts from the Dammann Papers and Other Collections.* Cologne, Germany: Rüdiger Köppe Verlag, 2010.

Mojola, Aloo Osotsi. "The Swahili Bible in East Africa from 1844 to 1996: A Brief Survey with Special Reference to Tanzania." In *The Bible in Africa: Transactions, Trajectories, and Trends,* edited by Gerald West and Musa Dube, 511–23. Boston: Brill, 2000.

Moyd, Michelle. "Centring a Sideshow: Local Experiences of the First World War in Africa." *First World War Studies* 7, no. 2 (2016): 111–30.

———. *Violent Intermediaries: African Soldiers, Conquest, and Everyday Colonialism German East Africa.* Athens: Ohio University Press, 2014.

Mudimbe, V. Y. *The Invention of Africa: Gnosis, Philosophy, and the Order of Knowledge.* Bloomington: Indiana University Press, 1988.

Mufwene, Salikoko. *The Ecology of Language Evolution.* New York: Cambridge University Press, 2001.

Mugane, John. "Learning How to Learn Languages: The Teaching and Learning of African Languages." *Language and Linguistics Compass* 4, no. 2 (2010): 64–79.

———. "The Odyssey of 'Ajamī and the Swahili People." *Islamic Africa* 8, nos. 1–2 (2017): 193–216.

———. *The Story of Swahili.* Athens: Ohio University Press, 2015.

Mulokozi, M. M. *Barua za Shaaban Robert 1931–1958.* Dar es Salaam: Taasisi ya Uchunguzi wa Kiswahili, 2002.

Mumin, Meikal. "The Arabic Script in Africa: Understudied Literacy." In *The Arabic Script in Africa: Studies in the Use of a Writing System,* edited by Meikal Mumin and Kees Versteegh, 41–76. Boston: Brill, 2014.

Nadeau, Jean-Benoît, and Julie Barlow. *The Story of French.* New York: St. Martin's, 2006.

Ngom, Fallou. "Ajami Literacies of West Africa." In *Tracing Language Movement in Africa,* edited by Ericka Albaugh and Kathryn de Luna, 143–64. New York: Oxford University Press, 2018.

———. *Muslims beyond the Arab World: The Odyssey of Ajami and the Muridiyya.* New York: Oxford University Press, 2016.

Nurse, Derek. "A Tentative Classification of the Primary Dialects of Swahili." *Sprache und Geschichte in Afrika* 4 (1982): 165–205.

Nurse, Derek, and Gérard Philippson, eds. *The Bantu Languages.* New York: Routledge, 2003.

Nurse, Derek, and Thomas Hinnebusch. *Swahili and Sabaki: A Linguistic History.* Berkeley: University of California Press, 1993.

Nurse, Derek, and Thomas Spear. *The Swahili: Reconstructing the History and Language of an African Society.* Philadelphia: University of Pennsylvania Press, 1985.

Ogunbiyi, Isaac Adejoju. "The Search for a Yoruba Orthography since the 1840s: Obstacles to the Choice of Arabic Script." *Sudanic Africa* 14 (2003): 77–102.

Ólden, Anthony. "'For Poor Nations a Library Service Is Vital': Establishing a National Public Library Service in Tanzania in the 1960s." *Library Quarterly* 75, no. 4 (October 2005): 421–45.

Oliver, Roland. *The Missionary Factor in East Africa.* New York: Longmans, Green, 1952.

Omar, Yahya Ali, and P. J. L. Frankl. "An Historical Review of the Arabic Rendering of Swahili Together with Proposals for the Development of a Swahili Writing System in Arabic Script." *Journal of the Royal Asiatic Society,* 3rd ser., vol. 7, no. 1 (April 1997): 55–71.

Osseo-Asare, Abena Dove. *Bitter Roots: The Search for Healing Plants in Africa.* Chicago: University of Chicago Press, 2014.

Osterhammel, Jürgen. *The Transformation of the World: A Global History of the Nineteenth Century.* Translated by Patrick Camiller. Princeton, NJ: Princeton University Press, 2015.

Patterson, Orlando. *Slavery and Social Death: A Comparative Study.* Cambridge, MA: Harvard University Press, 1982.

Pedersen, Susan. "The Meaning of the Mandate System: An Argument." *Geschichte und Gesellschaft* 32, no. 4 (October 2006): 560–82.

Peel, John D. Y. *Religious Encounter and the Making of the Yoruba.* Bloomington: Indiana University Press, 2000.

Pellin, Tommaso. "The Sweet Revolutionaries: The Chinese Revolution in Grammar Studies and Henry Sweet." *Language and History* 54, no. 1 (May 2011): 35–57.

Peterson, Derek. *Creative Writing: Translation, Bookkeeping, and the Work of Imagination in Colonial Kenya.* Portsmouth, NH: Heinemann, 2004.

———. *Ethnic Patriotism and the East African Revival: A History of Dissent, c. 1935–1972.* New York: Cambridge University Press, 2012.

———. "Language Work and Colonial Politics in Eastern Africa: The Making of Standard Swahili and 'School Kikuyu.'" In *The Study of Language and the Politics of Community in Global Context,* edited by David Hoyt and Daren Oslund, 185–214. Lanham, MD: Lexington Books, 2006.

———. "Translating the Word: Dialogism and Debate in Two Gikuyu Dictionaries." *Journal of Religious History* 23, no. 1 (February 1999): 31–50.

———. "Vernacular." In *Critical Terms for the Study of Africa,* edited by Guarav Desai and Adeline Masquelier, 331–45. Chicago: University of Chicago Press, 2018.

———. "Vernacular Language and Political Imagination." In *Tracing Language Movement in Africa,* edited by Ericka Albaugh and Kathryn de Luna, 165–86. New York: Oxford University Press, 2018.

Peterson, Derek, Emma Hunter, and Stephanie Newell, eds. *African Print Cultures: Newspapers and Their Publics in the Twentieth Century*. Ann Arbor: University of Michigan Press, 2016.

Pierard, Richard. "Shaking the Foundations: World War I, the Western Allies, and German Protestant Missions." *International Bulletin of Missionary Research* 22, no. 1 (January 1998): 13–19.

Pike, Charles. "History and Imagination: Swahili Literature and Resistance to German Language Imperialism in Tanzania, 1885–1919." *International Journal of African Historical Studies* 19, no. 2 (1986): 201–33.

Pirouet, M. Louise. "The Legacy of Johann Ludwig Krapf." *International Bulletin of Missionary Research* 23, no. 2 (April 1999): 69–74.

Popescu, Monica. "Aesthetic Solidarities: Ngũgĩ wa Thiong'o and the Cold War." *Journal of Postcolonial Writing* 50, no. 4 (2014): 384–97.

Pouwels, Randall. "Sh. al-Amin B. Ali Mazrui and Islamic Modernism in East Africa, 1875–1947." *International Journal of Middle East Studies* 13, no. 3 (August 1981): 329–45.

Prestholdt, Jeremy. *Domesticating the World: African Consumerism and the Genealogies of Globalization*. Berkeley: University of California Press, 2008.

Prichard, Andreana. *Sisters in Spirit: Christianity, Affect, and Community Building in East Africa, 1860–1970*. East Lansing: Michigan State University Press, 2017.

Pugach, Sara. *Africa in Translation: A History of Colonial Linguistics in Germany and Beyond, 1814–1945*. Ann Arbor: University of Michigan Press, 2012.

———. "Afrikanistik and Colonial Knowledge: Carl Meinhof, the Missionary Impulse, and African Language and Culture Studies in Germany, 1887–1919." PhD diss., University of Chicago, 2011. ProQuest Dissertations and Theses Global.

Rahman, Ahmad. *The Regime Change of Kwame Nkrumah: Epic Heroism in Africa and the Diaspora*. New York: Palgrave MacMillan, 2007.

Ranger, Terence. "Missionaries, Migrants and the Manyika: The Invention of Ethnicity in Zimbabwe." In *The Creation of Tribalism in Southern Africa*, edited by Leroy Vail, 118–50. Oxford: James Currey, 1989.

Ratcliffe, B. J., and Howard Elphinstone. *Modern Swahili*. London: Sheldon, 1932.

Rickford, Russell. "'Kazi Is the Blackest of All': Pan-African Nationalism and the Making of the 'New Man,' 1969–1975." *Journal of African American History* 101, nos. 1–2 (2016): 97–125.

Robert, Shaaban. *Kielezo cha Insha*. Johannesburg: Witwatersrand University Press, 1954.

———. *Maisha Yangu na Baada ya Miaka Hamsini*. London: Thomas Nelson and Sons, 1966.

Robinson, Morgan. "Binding Words: Student Biographical Narratives and Religious Conversion." In *The Individual in African History: The Importance of Biography in African Historical Studies*, edited by Klaas van Walraven, 197–218. Boston: Brill, 2020.

———. "Cutting Pice and Running Away: Discipline, Education and Choice at the UMCA Boys' Industrial House, Zanzibar, 1901–1905." *Southern African Review of Education* 19, no. 2 (2013): 9–24.

———. "The Idea of the *Upelekwa:* Constructing a Transcontinental Community in Eastern Africa, 1888–96." *Journal of the History of Ideas* 81, no. 1 (January 2020): 85–106.

———. "La Belle Époque from Eastern Africa: An Individual Experience of the 'Globalizing' World, 1898–1918." *Journal of Eastern African Studies* 13, no. 4 (2019): 584–600.

———. "An Uncommon Standard: A Social and Intellectual History of Swahili, 1864–1925." PhD diss., Princeton University, 2018. ProQuest Dissertations and Theses Global.

Rockel, Stephen. *Carriers of Culture: Labor on the Road in Nineteenth-Century East Africa.* Portsmouth, NH: Heinemann, 2006.

Roehl, Karl. "The Linguistic Situation in East Africa." *Africa* 3, no. 2 (April 1930): 191–202.

Romano, Renee. "No Diplomatic Immunity: African Diplomats, the State Department, and Civil Rights, 1961–1964." *Journal of American History* 87, no. 2 (September 2000): 546–79.

Ronnenberg, Ryan. "'House of Believers': Irony and Commensurability in Tanagnyikan Colonial Discourse." *African Identities* 10, no. 1 (February 2021): 33–54.

Russell, Joan. *Communicative Competence in a Minority Group: A Sociolinguistic Study of the Swahili-Speaking Community in the Old Town, Mombasa.* Leiden: Brill, 1981.

Russell, Joan, and Norman Pollock. *News from Masasi.* Vienna: Afro-Pub, 1993.

Sadgrove, Philip. "The Press: Engine of a Mini-Renaissance in Zanzibar (1860–1920)." In *History of Printing and Publishing in the Languages and Countries of the Middle East,* edited by Philip Sadgrove, 151–78. Oxford: Oxford University Press, 2005.

Scanlon, Padraic. *Freedom's Debtors: British Antislavery in Sierra Leone in the Age of Revolution.* New Haven, CT: Yale University Press, 2017.

Schor, Esther. *Bridge of Words: Esperanto and the Dreams of a Universal Language.* New York: Metropolitan Books, 2016.

Scott, James. *Seeing Like a State: How Certain Schemes to Improve the Human Condition Have Failed.* New Haven, CT: Yale University Press, 1998.

Scotton, James. "Tanganyika's African Press, 1937–1960: A Nearly Forgotten Pre-Independence Forum." *African Studies Review* 21, no. 1 (April 1978): 1–18.

Sharawy, Helmi. "The Heritage of African Language Manuscripts Written in Arabic Characters (Ajami)." In *Political and Social Thought in Africa,* 77–89. Dakar: CODESRIA, 2014.

Sheriff, Abdul. *Dhow Cultures of the Indian Ocean: Cosmopolitanism, Commerce and Islam.* New York: Columbia University Press, 2010.

Simala, K. Inyani. "Swahili Poetic Text and African Historiography." *Sudanic Africa* 15 (2004): 17–38.

Smallwood, Stephanie. *Saltwater Slavery: A Middle Passage from Africa to American Diaspora*. Cambridge, MA: Harvard University Press, 2007.

Snoxall, Ronald A. "The East African Interterritorial Language (Swahili) Committee." In *Swahili Language and Society*, edited by Joan Maw and David Parkin, 15–24. Vienna: Afro-Pub, 1984.

Sosale, Sujatha. "Mapping and Modernizing the Indian Ocean Rim: Communication Technologies under Colonial Britain." *Global Media and Communication* 10, no. 2 (2014): 155–76.

Spear, Thomas. "Neo-Traditionalism and the Limits of Invention in British Colonial Africa." *Journal of African History* 44, no. 1 (2003): 3–27.

Star, Susan Leigh, and James Griesemer. "Institutional Ecology, 'Translations' and Boundary Objects: Amateurs and Professionals in Berkeley's Museum of Vertebrate Zoology, 1907–39." *Social Studies of Science* 10, no. 3 (August 1989): 387–420.

Steere, Edward. *A Handbook of the Swahili Language, as Spoken at Zanzibar*. London: Bell & Daldy, 1870.

———. *A Handbook of the Swahili Language as Spoken at Zanzibar*. 2nd ed. London: George Bell and Sons, 1875.

———. *A Handbook of the Swahili Language as Spoken at Zanzibar*. 3rd ed. Revised and enlarged by Arthur C. Madan. London: Society for Promoting Christian Knowledge, 1884.

———. *Swahili Tales, as Told by Natives of Zanzibar*. London: Bell & Daldy, 1870.

Stoner-Eby, Anne Marie. "African Clergy, Bishop Lucas and the Christianizing of Local Initiation Rites: Revisiting 'The Masasi Case.'" *Journal of Religion in Africa* 38, no. 2 (2008): 171–208.

———. "African Leaders Engage Mission Christianity: Anglicans in Tanzania, 1876–1926." PhD diss., University of Pennsylvania, 2003. ProQuest Dissertations and Theses Global.

Sturmer, Martin. *The Media History of Tanzania*. Ndanda, Tanzania: Ndanda Mission Press, 1998.

"Swahili Lessons: Lesson One." *Black Collegian* 3, no. 4 (March 1973): 10.

Tate, Lessie. "The Power of Black Africanism: Tanzanian/African American Linkages, 1947–1997." PhD diss., University of Illinois at Urbana-Champaign, 2015. ProQuest Dissertations and Theses Global.

Temu, M. L. Nambuo. "African American Students' Self-Awareness through Kiswahili Language." *Journal of Black Studies* 22, no. 4 (June 1992): 532–45.

Thiong'o, Ngũgĩ wa. "Abdilatif Abdalla and the Voice of Prophecy." In *Abdilatif Abdalla: Poet in Politics*, edited by Rose Marie Beck and Kai Kresse, 11–18. Dar es Salaam: Mkuki na Nyota, 2016.

———. *Birth of a Dream Weaver: A Writer's Awakening*. New York: New Press, 2016.

———. *Decolonising the Mind: The Politics of Language in African Literature*. Portsmouth, NH: Heinemann, 1986.

———. "*Kiswahili: Urithi Wetu Afrika.*" Udadisi, July 8, 2021. https://udadisi.com/kiswahili-urithi-wetu-afrika/.

Tilley, Helen. *Africa as Living Laboratory: Empire, Development, and the Problem of Scientific Knowledge, 1870–1950.* Chicago: University of Chicago Press, 2011.

———. "Global Histories, Vernacular Science, and African Genealogies; Or, Is the History of Science Ready for the World?" *Isis: A Journal of the History of Science* 101, no. 1 (March 2010): 110–19.

Topan, Farouk. "Swahili as a Religious Language." *Journal of Religion in Africa* 22, no. 4 (1992): 331–49.

———. "Why Does a Swahili Writer Write? Euphoria, Pain, and Popular Aspirations in Swahili Literature." *Research in African Literatures* 37, no. 3 (Fall 2006): 103–19.

Vierke, Clarissa. "*Akhi Patia Kalamu:* Writing Swahili Poetry in Arabic Script." In *The Arabic Script in Africa: Studies in the Use of a Writing System,* edited by Meikal Mumin and Kees Versteegh, 319–39. Boston: Brill, 2014.

———. *On the Poetics of the Utendi: A Critical Edition of the Nineteenth-Century Swahili Poem 'Utendi wa Haudaji' together with a Stylistic Analysis.* Zurich: Lit Verlag, 2011.

Vierke, Clarissa, and Chapane Mutiua. "The Poem about the Prophet's Death in Mozambique—Swahili as a Transregional Language of Islamic Poetry." *Journal for Islamic Studies* 38, no. 2 (2020): 44–74.

Wainaina, Binyavanga. *One Day I Will Write about This Place: A Memoir.* Minneapolis, MN: Graywolf Press, 2011.

Westcott, N. J. "An East African Radical: The Life of Erica Fiah." *Journal of African History* 22, no. 1 (1981): 85–101.

White, Landeg. *Magomero: Portrait of an African Village.* New York: Cambridge University Press, 1987.

Whiteley, Wilfred H. "Ideal and Reality in National Language Policy: A Case Study from Tanzania." In *Language Problems of Developing Nations,* edited by Joshua Fishman, Charles Ferguson, and Jyotirindra das Gupta, 327–44. New York: Wiley, 1968.

———. *Swahili: The Rise of a National Language.* London: Methuen, 1969.

Willis, Justin. "The Nature of a Mission Community: The Universities' Mission to Central Africa in Bonde." *Past and Present* 140 (August 1993): 127–54.

Wilson, George Herbert. *The History of the Universities' Mission to Central Africa.* London: Universities' Mission to Central Africa, 1936.

Wolf, Hans-Georg. "British and French Language and Educational Policies in the Mandate and Trusteeship Territories." *Language Sciences* 30, no. 5 (September 2008): 553–74.

Wright, Marcia. *German Missions in Tanganyika, 1891–1941: Lutherans and Moravians in the Southern Highlands.* Oxford: Clarendon, 1971.

———. "Local Roots of Policy in German East Africa." *Journal of African History* 9, no. 4 (1968): 621–30.

———. *Strategies of Slaves and Women: Life-Stories from East/Central Africa.* New York: Lilian Barber, 1993.

Index

Abdallah, Yohanna, 53
Abdulla, Muhammad Said, 125, 142–43;
   Mzimu wa Watu wa Kale, 142–43
Abedi, Sheikh Amri, 167–68
abolitionism, 25–26
Achitinao, Ajanjeuli. *See* Sapuli, Agnes
adapted education, 96. *See also* industrial
   education
African Tidings (periodical), 40–46, 57, 83
Afrikanistik, 75–78
'Ajamī, 15, 168, 170–72, 243n142
akida system, 73–74
Ali, 30, 31–33
Al-Islah, 101–2, 169–70
Allen, J. W. T., 123–24
Ambali, Augustine, 63
Ameir, Amour Ali, 115
Anderson, Benedict, 7, 49, 76, 179
Anderson-Morshead, A. E. M., 53
Anglicanism, 1, 15, 25, 27, 28, 39, 69
Annesley, George, 152, 156
Arabic: language, 30–31, 37–38, 42, 96, 169,
   180; script, 13, 15, 24, 28, 31, 75, 83, 101,
   151, 168–72
Arusha, 119, 157, 160
Arusha Declaration, 175
Aziz, Abdul, 30–33, 37

Barak, On, 12–13, 53–54, 125
baraza (verandah / receiving room / as-
   sembly), 117, 159, 163, 175–76; Kenyan
   publication (*Baraza*), 136
Barber, Karin, 66, 70
Barghash (Sultan of Zanzibar), 26, 192n22,
   206n115
Barth, Christian Gottlieb, 209n22
Bennett, Eleanor, 55
Biersteker, Ann, 145

bin Khamis, Muhammed, 30, 31–33
Birley, Thomas, 111
Bishop, William, 67
Black American community, 179–82
Black Collegian (magazine), 182
Black Power movement, 180, 181
Blank, Paul, 74, 209n22
Blommaert, Jan, 176
Bokamba, Eyamba, 182
Bondei language, 9, 28, 41–42, 61, 83
Brennan, James, 116
Britain: colonial administrations of, 5,
   10, 11, 95–96, 112–13, 125, 133, 135, 151,
   160–69
Bromber, Katrin, 116
Broomfield, Gerald, 101–2, 103, 108, 118
Brumfit, Ann, 75
Bububu, 27
Buchanan, L. A. C., 106
Büttner, Carl, 76

Callaci, Emily, 66, 135, 143
Cameron, Donald, 96
caravan trade, 5, 23–24, 25, 40–46, 69
Central Africa (periodical), 40–46, 51, 54,
   56, 57, 67, 79, 82, 90, 91
Child, Cyril, 84–88
Children's Tidings. See African Tidings
Chimerah, Rocha, 9
Chiponde, Samuel, 9–12, 65, 78, 82, 88,
   113–14
Chiraghdin, Shihabuddin, 120–21
Chitangali, 59, 84, 85
Chiwata, 84, 85, 86
Church Missionary Society (CMS), 24, 50,
   67, 80–81, 129
civil rights movement, 179–80
CMS. *See* Church Missionary Society

265

codification. *See* standardization
Coen, Deborah, 12, 49
Colonial Development and Welfare Act, 131, 134, 137, 152, 157
Colonial Institute (Hamburg), 76
commensurability, 12–14, 179, 184; linguistic, 10, 20, 103, 122
community building. *See* community-construction
community-construction, 2, 8, 17–18, 22–23, 25, 40, 48, 184; Swahili as a factor in, 46, 56–58, 66, 72, 83–84; *Upelekwa* as a concept of, 58–60, 69–70
comparative philology, 29, 105. *See also* Afrikanistik
conversion narratives, 40–46, 197n105
Cooper, J. B., 93–94
countertempo, 13, 14, 116
countertemporality. *See* countertempo
creativity, 126–27, 139–44, 148

Dale, Godfrey, 9, 30, 78, 80, 106
Dammann, Ernst, 170
Dar es Salaam, 10, 11, 66, 74, 77, 96, 107, 113, 116, 132, 149, 152, 165, 173, 176, 178
developmentalism, 19, 135–39, 150
dialects, 2, 8, 13–14, 24, 30, 33, 34, 39, 77, 93–94, 97–98, 102, 120–21, 139, 177, 180, 188nn47–48, 191n12, 217nn17–18, 230n92. *See also* Kiamu; Kimvita; Kiunguja
diaspora, 14, 173, 179–82
dictionaries, 6, 7, 18, 24–25; of A. C. Madan, 36–38, 58, 77, 79, 81, 97, 99, 103–4; of the ILC, 95, 99, 103–13, 114–15, 118–19, 174, 178
Dictionary of the Suaheli-Language, A (Krapf), 24
Donaldson, Coleman, 172
duck-rabbit, 3–5, 175, 184; directional duck-rabbit, 8–12; temporal duck-rabbit, 5–8

Eagle Press, 132, 145
EALB. *See* East African Literature Bureau
EASC. *See* East African Swahili Committee
East African Community, ix, 178, 230n73
East African Literature Bureau (EALB), 19, 120, 124–25, 129–35, 140–48, 169, 173, 175; authorship leaflets, 140–42; essay contests, 19, 125–28, 131–32, 145; library system of, 19, 135, 136, 152–59;

and propaganda, 135–39, 158
East African Swahili Committee (EASC), 5, 123, 131, 139, 162, 167–68, 173, 178
Education Conference of 1925, 10–11, 96–98, 99, 113, 114
Engsh, 177
Errington, Joseph, 76, 193n30

Farajallah, George, 34–35, 195n75
Farler, John, 21, 83
Farsy, Abdullah Saleh, 30
Fayida, 41, 42
Fiah, Erica, 116–19, 160, 163
fictive kinship. *See* networked kinship
Fisher, Cathrew, 90
Foxley, Alice, 40–41
Freedom School. *See* Shule ya Uhuru
friendship, 44

Garnier, Xavier, 146
Geiger, Susan, 176
German colonial administration, 5, 17–18, 71–75, 78, 85, 91–92, 159–60
German East Africa. *See* German colonial administration
Gikuyu language, 6, 122, 131, 226n173
Glassman, Jonathon, 61, 116
Guild of the Good Shepherd, 65
Gurnah, Abdulrazak, 177

Hadhramy, Sheikh Abdulla Muhammad el-, 99, 115
Halil, Muhamad Salim, 114
Halliday, Michael, 9
Handbook of the Swahili Language, A (Steere), 36, 37, 38, 67, 97; published in 1870, 33, 39, 44, 58; published in 1875, 58; published in 1884, 23
Harries, Patrick, 22
Hellier, A. B., 95, 113, 120
Hendry, W., 108
Hinawy, Sheikh Mbarak Ali, 99
Hine, John, 80–81
Hofmeyer, Isabel, 29
Hollingsworth, L. W., 106
Holmes, Sherlock, 143
Hunter, Emma, 48, 70, 72, 116, 176, 203n65
Huxley, Elspeth, 129, 133, 134, 136–37, 156, 228n32

ILC. *See* Inter-Territorial Language Committee
Iliffe, John, 78

industrial education, 26–27, 53, 67
Institute of Kiswahili Research, 123, 172, 173, 178
Institute of Kiswahili Studies, 131
International Institute of African Languages and Cultures, 189n57
Inter-Territorial Language Committee (ILC), 6, 18, 93, 94–95, 118, 124–31, 139–40, 145, 161; *Bulletin*, 100–101, 106, 112, 113, 115, 130, 140, 145, 169; constitution of, 100; imprimatur of, 99, 103, 130, 137; initial organization of, 98–100
Islam, 28, 70, 73–74, 82, 90; debates with Christian missionaries, 30

Jahadhmy, Ali Ahmed, 123–24, 140
Johnson, Frederick, 97–98, 99, 105, 106, 107–8, 109, 111, 114, 119
Johnson, William Percival, 90
Journal of the East African Swahili Committee, 131, 162, 167, 178

Kabyemera, C. P., 167
Kampala, 131, 132, 152, 155
Kandoro, Saadan, 159
Kaninchen und Ente. See duck-rabbit
Karenga, Maulana, 180–82
Kasaja, J., 115
Kasese, Paul, 63–64
Kassim, 30, 31–33, 37
Kathibeni, Clement, 62
Kenya, 6, 15, 94, 95–96, 98, 100, 109–10, 126, 134, 152–59, 162, 163, 177
Khalid, Abdallah, 120
Khalid, Sayyid Majid, 114
Khamisi, Abdu Mtajuka, 172
Kiamu, 171
Kibwebwe, W., 156
Kielezo cha Insha, 147–48
Kihama, Rajabu, 149–51
Kijuma, Muhamadi, 170, 171
Kilimani, 27
Kilimanjaro Native Co-operative Union (KNCU), 157, 162–63, 165
Kimvita, 24, 31, 97–98, 101, 113, 170, 225n161
King, R. S., 167
King, Walter, 78
King's African Rifles, 93
Kiongozi (newspaper), 74–75, 115, 117
Kisenge, Elias, 175
Kitching, A. E., 168
Kiungani, 1–2, 26, 29, 43, 51, 52–53, 56–57, 59, 67, 82, 88; *Kiungani; or, Story and*

History from Central Africa, 40–46; students as linguistic interlocutors, 30, 33–36
Kiunguja, 16, 23, 24, 28, 66, 78, 92, 97, 98, 102, 119–20, 188n47
KNCU. *See* Kilimanjaro Native Cooperative Union
Kombo, Salum, 127–28
Korogwe, 83
Krapf, Johann Ludwig, 16, 24–25, 76, 77, 111; *Dictionary of the Suaheli-Language, A*, 24
Krautwald, Fabian, 74–75
Kwa Kibai, 83
Kwa Magome, 83
Kwanzaa, 181–82
Kwetu (newspaper), 116–19, 120, 160

Lake Nyasa (Malawi), 17, 22, 25, 42, 49, 50, 54, 55, 62–63, 66, 84, 89, 90
Lambert, Harold, 170
Lampland, Martha, 24
Larson, Pier, 14, 42, 45
League of Nations, 95–96
LegCo. *See* Legislative Council of Tanganyika
Legislative Council of Tanganyika, 159, 163–66
Likoma, 49, 50, 54, 56, 62, 66
Limo, Peter, 46, 64–65, 78, 82–83
Lindi, 85
lingua franca, 5, 22, 23, 28, 29, 73, 75, 91, 128, 166, 169, 171, 173, 177, 181
linguistic landscape of East Africa, 28, 41–42, 88
Livingstone, David, 25
Lubwama, A. S., 115
Luganda, 67, 131, 134, 137, 140, 173
Luo language, 7–8, 131

Maasai language, 28, 42
Mabruki, Francis, 34–35
Machaku, Ackworth, 78, 81
Madagascar, 7, 14, 28, 42
Madan, Arthur Cornwallis, 36–37, 40, 67, 77, 78, 79, 111
Magila, 35, 49, 51, 56, 62, 65, 66, 82, 83
Majaliwa, Cecil, 27, 46, 59, 78, 82, 84
Majaliwa, Lucy, 84
Maji Maji war, 70, 72, 91
Makanyassa, Owen, 1–5, 10, 47, 56, 67
Makerere University, 131, 139, 142, 145, 173, 174

Townshend, Mary, 65
Tozer, Helen, 55
Tozer, William, 25, 29, 30, 34, 35, 38
translation: biblical, 2, 24, 28, 30–31, 34–
35, 39, 46, 67, 78–79; into languages
other than Swahili, 52; of laws into
Swahili, 19, 151, 159–68; Translation
Committee of the UMCA, 10, 18, 46,
78–83, 113
Travers, Duncan, 55, 80

Uganda, 15, 67, 80–81, 93–96, 98, 106, 108,
110, 115, 116, 134, 152–56, 173, 177
uhuru (freedom), 58, 174–75, 177
Ujamaa (familyhood / African socialism),
175–76, 181
Ulumana, Swithun, 56, 59
UMCA. *See* Universities' Mission of Central Africa
Unguja, 25, 44, 60, 62, 64
Universities' Mission of Central Africa
(UCMA), 1, 21, 28, 49–50, 72, 111; educational system of, 26–27, 29, 51–53,
91, 216n123; lay and clerical organization of, 27–28; students of, 29, 39–46,
51–53; during WWI, 89–91
University of Dar es Salaam, 123, 131, 173,
178
Upelekwa, 17–18, 48–49, 53, 58–60, 64–66,
69–71, 83–84, 88

Urelia, Korale, 45

Vaughan, J. H., 106
Velten, Carl, 76
Vierke, Clarissa, 170, 172

Wainaina, Binyavanga, 177
wa Kai, Hamisi, 30, 31–33, 37
Washington, Booker T., 141
Watts, Rawson, 99, 109, 114, 218n26
Weekes, L. C. H., 93–94
Werner, Alice, 106, 170
Westermann, Diedrich, 76
Weston, Frank, 53, 88, 90
Whiteley, Wilfred, 5, 98, 123, 131, 139–40,
178
Woodward, Herbert, 52, 78
World War I, 18, 86, 89–91, 115
World War II, 19, 117, 128, 150
Wright, Marcia, 75, 197n105

Yao language, 22, 28, 42, 52, 59, 82, 88
Yongolo, Daudi, 127

Zanzibar, 1–2, 9, 13, 15–17, 22, 24–31, 38–39,
48–57, 65–67, 72, 81, 88, 94–96, 100,
108, 110, 142–43, 152–59, 169, 176; sultanate of, 1, 23, 25–26, 30, 73, 96
Zaramo language, 42
Zigua language, 28, 41–42, 61